MISSED CONCEPTIONS

Overcoming Infertility

Anne
Mullens

McGraw-Hill Ryerson
Toronto Montreal

MISSED CONCEPTIONS: *Overcoming Infertility*

First published in 1990 by
McGraw-Hill Ryerson Limited
330 Progress Avenue
Scarborough, Ontario
M1P 2Z5

ISBN 0-07-549885-5

1 2 3 4 5 6 7 8 9 0 AP 8 7 6 5 4 3 2 1 0

Printed and bound in Canada

Canadian Cataloguing in Publication Data

Mullens, Anne
Missed conceptions: overcoming infertility

ISBN 0-07-549885-5

1. Infertility. I. Title.

RC889.M84 1989 616.6′92 C89-090571-1

Cover Sculpture

MOORE, Henry, British 1898-1986
Family Group, 1974
Original plaster
H. 40.6 cm
ART GALLERY OF ONTARIO, TORONTO
Gift of Henry Moore, 1974

Family Group (1947) is reproduced with the kind permission of the Henry Moore Foundation.

CONTENTS

Dedication

To my parents, Ted and Elizabeth Mullens, and to my sisters,
Claire, Jean, and Mary, whose love and support all these years
have been the foundation for anything I have done, this book included.

Acknowledgments

This book could not have been written without the support and assistance of many people.

First, thanks go to my agent, Denise Bukowski, who convinced me to write the book, and at McGraw-Hill Ryerson to editorial directors Denise Schon and Don Loney. My researcher, the meticulous, quick and thorough Sheila Hill, was a godsend and a pleasure to work with.

The research and production of this book would not have been possible without the imput of numerous people. Those interviewed are referenced in the chapter sources, and I thank them all for the time they spent with me. Two deserve special mention: Dr. Patrick Taylor, recently of Bourn Hall, England, and now at University of Manitoba, who not only welcomed me to his clinic and home at Bourn during the research but also read and commented diligently on the entire 1000-page manuscript; and Dr. Timothy Rowe, of the University of British Columbia, who gave encouragement, advice, comments and his valuable time during every stage of the book.

The following doctors and health professionals were invaluable in their criticisms and corrections of various chapters: Judith Bernstein, Weston, Massachusets; Dr. David de Kretser, Melbourne; Dr. Gilbert Haas, Oklahoma City; Dr. Larry Lipshultz, Houston; Dr. Peter McComb, Vancouver; Dr. Jerilynn Prior, Vancouver. All deserve thanks for the work they did to ensure that the information in the book was as accurate and up to date as possible. Any errors that occur in the text are mine alone.

Valerie Casselton, Elizabeth Godley, Frances Bula and Shelley Fralic, colleagues and friends at the Vancouver *Sun*, also read various chapters with their critical eyes and their editing skill. City editor Scott Macrae and managing editor Gordon Fisher gave me leave from the medical beat for six months and then understandingly extended it to ten months to enable me to finish the book.

Good friends played an important role: Jane Frazee and Paul Buitenhuis gave me sanctuary, countless dinners and a frequent cold beer at 6 p.m., and their delightful son, Jason, kept me entertained; Nancy Baron was a sounding board and a soul mate throughout; Jennifer Hillman, of the Vancouver Infertility Peer Support Group, started out as an interview subject and became a friend through the course of the book; and my closest friend, Keith Baldrey, listened to my worries and then made me laugh about them. Other good friends, who know who they are, understood when the pressures of the book superseded our usual good fun.

And finally, to the couples in Canada, Australia and Britain who shared their medical histories and their emotions, making the pages come to life, I thank you all.

CHAPTER 1
How Can It Be So Difficult?

You probably hesitated before you picked up this book and turned to this page. Perhaps you are in a book store, standing in front of a wall of books on childcare, or babies' first months, or pregnancy. Your eyes looked over the other titles and rested, reluctantly, on this.

Or perhaps your doctor or a friend lent you this book because he or she thought that it might help. Again, you open the cover with the wish this were one book you didn't have to read.

But, for some reason, you have been having trouble becoming pregnant.

Maybe you have a suspicion that something is not right and you want to find out more before you seek medical help. Or maybe you've been told you need a full investigation by your doctor or have been given a definitive diagnosis. Or perhaps you have been trying for months or years to have a baby and know with certainty you have a problem, but still pick up each new book to see what it says about your condition.

Acknowledging infertility is difficult. The word seems to have a cold finality to it. You may mistake "infertility" to mean "sterility."

But infertility is not a definitive end or a label from which there is no escape. It simply means that you have tried, with frequent, unprotected intercourse, to become pregnant for more than 12 months. The term infertile is more an acknowledgment of effort and time than a life sentence.

It applies to almost one in every six couples of childbearing age in all Western nations including Canada, the United States, Australia, Great Britain, France, Germany, and Scandinavia. The numbers of people combined approach tens of millions. In the United States alone, according to a recent report for the U.S. Congress, at least 2.4 million couples each year seek medical help for infertility. Those numbers do not take into account the number of single people or couples who have not yet tried to get pregnant—the definition of infertility means that only those who are actively trying to get pregnant figure in the tally; the total number of people who could have a problem conceiving is probably a great deal higher.

And yet, despite the numbers that walk the same path, infertility is one of the most isolating and lonely experiences. For the individual, it is a crisis that forces a redefinition of who you are and what your life will be. For the couple, infertility changes the nature of your relationship and your future plans. Often infertility is the first crisis couples have had to face together. Their relationship may have been harmonius and they may have been planning happily for a family, but now it is interrupted with upset and uncertainty. Sometimes couples fling resentment, anger and accusations at each other like weapons, propelled by disbelief, hurt and sheer disappointment.

> *The word "unfair" is on my mind every day. It is all just so unfair. You see a couple with their children and you think unfair. You see a woman yelling at her kids or hitting them—I would never hit my child—and you think how can she have children and not I? You see women on the street who are drunk and pregnant, or people who continue to smoke while pregnant. You see all these things and I think this just isn't fair. My husband and I would be such great parents, we want children so badly.* Unfair *haunts me. It is the number one word in my vocabulary.*

Perhaps we, the children born and raised after the Second World War, have a great deal more difficulty accepting or dealing with infertility than people in our parents' or grandparents' generation. Infertility, for some couples, was a problem then, too, and it caused pain and life adjustment. But we are the first generations in the history of mankind who have been able to reliably prevent conception and time pregnancy. Because we have been able to determine when the time is right, we expect that when we make the decision to stop using contraception, pregnancy will result without trouble. We are shocked when our fertility does not fit our timing; this is not how we thought the system would work.

It is also ironic. If it did not hurt so much you might even laugh. Think of all the times you fussed and fiddled with contraception over the years. How you both worried for weeks after the condom broke. Or how so many times you stopped cold in the middle of passionate foreplay to rush to the bathroom to mess with your diaphragm.

"Everybody says it, but it's true. All the money and worry you've spent on contraception over the years. God, we must have spent hundreds!" said Gordon, 39, who found that his sperm count was well below normal after a year of trying to start a family with his wife.

The odd thing about infertility, too, is that it is completely based on a state of mind, a want. If you did not want to be pregnant, if you did not want to have children, it would not be a problem. Even if you both had the most intractable causes, the most desperate conditions, if you did not know about them, and freely made the choice to be childless, that would not be a medical problem. You might never know you are technically infertile. It simply would never make a difference. But the act of wanting children changes all of that. Infertility takes what could be a choice and turns it into no choice.

"You have no control over infertility," says Jennifer, 35, who has been trying for ten years to become pregnant and experienced a miscarriage and two ectopic pregnancies, a life-threatening condition in which the fetus is implanted in the fallopian tube. "People will say to you, 'Look, be thankful you have your freedom. Our life hasn't been the same since our kids came along.' But the fact is they had the choice. We've been denied that. We have no choice at all."

There is one choice, however, that couples who are having trouble conceiving can make: to learn as much about infertility as they can. That is the choice you have. You can learn about how reproduction really works; learn about the successes or failures of various medical treatments; and learn about ways to cope with the emotional stress of infertility. You can also learn about the more complicated and controversial methods to overcome infertility—in vitro fertilization, sperm micro-injection, surrogacy—understand their risks and society's concerns, and decide for yourself where the boundaries of the technologies should be. You can become fully informed of your choices; and that is where this book can help.

Informed Decisions

The aim of this book is to give you detailed information, to present the pros and cons of treatments, to highlight the issues and problems in overcoming infertility—in short, to give you the information you need to make informed decisions. This book can also help you cope with infertility, to help you cope with the emotional upheaval it causes and to help you try to keep some balance and perspective in your life while you pursue ways to overcome infertility.

According to Dr. Arnold Relman, editor of the *New England Journal of Medicine,* information is one of the best allies a person can have in any medical endeavor.

> *. . . I think the more people know about medicine and health the better care they can take of themselves, the more intelligent questions they can ask of their doctors and the more likely they will be to stay well. There is no question that one of the things that protects you is information.*

Your infertility will make you face many crucial decisions, if you have not faced some already. The decisions may be simply whether you try a certain drug for a few months or whether you seek an infertility specialist. The decisions can be slightly more complex such as deciding whether to undergo major surgery, to try an experimental therapy, or to try in vitro fertilization. Perhaps the most difficult decision of all at some point will be when to discontinue infertility treatment. That is usually the hardest decision for couples to make.

This book is organized to help you gain information at different times. You may never need certain sections, while others may be crucial for you. Chapters 1 to 4 and Chapter 12 contain universal information on infertility, useful for anyone interested in the topic. Each of the other chapters is about specific parts of the infertility picture.

Misconceptions of Infertility

Infertility is surrounded with a few myths, not only in general society but among infertile couples themselves. One of the most common is that infertility is the same as sterility, that if you are told you are infertile that means you will not be able to conceive, ever. In fact infertility simply means "not fertile," that fertility is impaired.

The following are some of the most common misconceptions that couples have about infertility.

1. Infertility is a punishment for some thought or action or fundamental "unworthiness." This feeling can be particularly strong for couples who have a religious background and who believe their God has brought the infertility on them as a judgment. But even atheists or agnostics may feel that they have done something to deserve their infertility. The truth is that no one "deserves" to be infertile. It just happens.
2. Infertility is a sign of an essential incompatibility between the couple. Even the most loving couples, when suddenly faced with obstacles to conception, can believe it indicates on a basic level that they are unsuitable. The infertility is taken as a symbol of their relationship, even if their relationship has been strong and supportive. Compatibility has nothing to do with infertility; divorce courts and child custody cases attest that many couples who have irreconcilable differences had no trouble having children. The myth of incompatibility can be damaging to the relationship at a time the couple most needs to pull together.
3. Infertility is nature's way of saying you were not cut out to be a mother or a father and you should do something else with your life. Those who believe this myth find themselves searching for a vocation or feeling lost because they can not find one. "Nature," however, has no say in who would make a good mother or father. Parents who abuse or neglect their children are all too common and most had no trouble becoming pregnant.
4. A woman is not a woman unless she has experienced pregnancy, birth, and motherhood. This misconception is held by many women who are struggling to conceive and contributes to their depression and anxiety. Men, in general, seem to have less of their self-concept wrapped up in being a father (although some men do define their masculinity by their ability to impregnate). Women are under the influence of powerful biological and societal factors. The cyclical body changes, the mood changes and the menstrual flow that most women experience month after month, year after year, are constant reminders of their potential for childbearing. No wonder the urge to have a child has been named the biological clock—while the menstrual cycle is an alarm that sounds each month. Society, throughout history, has magnified that biological urge, making it into a creed and relegating women to childbearing as their "role" in life. In truth, childbearing probably became a woman's role because for most of history she had no control over her fertility. Without contraception or safe abortion most women had no choice whether they became mothers. A woman could not prevent pregnancy and so was forced to bear and rear her offspring even if she did not want to. Now that women have reliable birth control, the notion that a woman is not a woman unless she bears a child has no validity. Many women still find it desirable to bear children, but no longer is a woman's value dependent on it.

Besides the misconceptions of couples, the general public has even more misunderstandings and imposes them on couples who are trying to overcome their infertility. Some of the notions are similar to the ones already stated.

1. A couple's infertility is God's will and they shouldn't try to overcome it with artificial means. The Catholic Church has led this attitude, denouncing infertility treatment, particularly donor insemination, in vitro fertilization and other advanced reproductive techniques. Others suggest that it is nature's laws that a couple cannot conceive or that somehow the couple deserves it, either because of a wayward life or by not trying to have children earlier. This leads many people to adopt the attitude that the infertile couple should accept their fate.
2. Infertility is a female problem. This attitude has been prevalent for centuries and dies hard. The truth is that men are almost as likely to be infertile as women. In about 40 percent of infertile couples the problem can be traced to the woman; in about 40 percent the problem can be traced to the man; and in about 20 percent the problem is probably one of combined subfertility—both have a small problem and put together a greater problem is created. Some doctors believe that combined subfertility plays even a greater role than we have yet realized. The persistent attitude that infertility is a female problem, however, has caused male infertility to be hidden and stigmatized and caused medical science largely to ignore the problem until recent years. The medical understanding of male infertility has suffered as a result.
3. The world has enough children, many who need love and attention, and therefore it is immoral and selfish for infertile couples to pursue having their own children. This is a common attitude and while it is true that unfortunately there are far too many neglected children in the world, those children will not be helped simply because an infertile couple decides not to pursue having their own child. Infertile couples should not be made to take personal responsibility for the needy children of the world while others reproduce freely. The needs of children in the world should be the concerns of all society. Effort should go towards making every child a wanted child. That means helping infertile couples conceive and helping others prevent pregnancy by good contraception when pregnancy is not wanted.
4. The couple's infertility is psychological. In the past most people, even the medical profession, believed that at least 50 percent of couples had a psychological basis for their infertility. Either one or both of the partners was inhibiting pregnancy by an innate fear of it, by ambivalence to childrearing or by anxiety and stress. This attitude has led to the myth that all a couple needs to do is adopt a child or relax and then pregnancy will follow. Although stress does play a part in some cases of infertility, there has been no scientific proof that either relaxing or adopting causes couples to conceive more easily. Infertility itself, and its treatment, causes inordinate stress and anxiety. There is no way to determine how much stress caused infertility, or whether infertility caused stress.

5. The couple's infertility underscores a sexual problem. In the late nineteenth and early twentieth centuries, doctors believed that some women were infertile because they were frigid or did not enjoy sex, which of course is not true. Many infertile men face a similar prejudice by society. Male infertility is often wrongly linked to sexual prowess, making men even more reluctant to be open about their infertility. Conversely, many people assume that attempting pregnancy is just one sexual thrill after another for infertile couples. Any couple who has experienced futile attempts at pregnancy knows how untrue that misconception is.
6. The advanced infertility technologies, such as in vitro fertilization (IVF) and extensions of the technique, will remove women's body autonomy and place all of the reproductive process in the hands of scientists. This last myth has emerged since 1978 when the world's first test-tube baby, Louise Brown, was born in England and has been largely supported by feminist groups. The most extreme form is the concern that women will become obsolete because of the technologies. The problem with this myth is that the exaggeration of the threats of IVF can distract attention from the real concerns. Advances in IVF will not remove the need for women as long as fertile women exist—science will never be able to rival the efficiency and mastery of natural conception and gestation. But the new reproductive technologies do present hard and troubling choices for society.

Should couples be allowed to pay a woman to carry their pregnancy? Should information on donors be made available to the offspring they create? Should IVF be covered by health insurance or supported by tax dollars? Should embryo research be restricted? These are but a few of the many questions raised. Society does need guidelines or legislation in place to direct the pace, scope and development of the techniques. But we must not forget that realistically it is only the infertile couple, the couple with medical problems, or the couple with concerns about passing on genetic defects who use the reproductive techniques. No sane couple would undergo the invasive, stressful, expensive and potentially harmful medical methods if they could have a child naturally. For that reason, infertile couples should take an active part in helping society cope with the technologies. The infertile couple must take a hard look at these technologies and must not be seduced by science into pursuing a baby at any cost.

Medicine and Miracles

One of the more pervasive misconceptions surrounding infertility is that modern day medicine has got it licked. News reports showing a happy couple holding their baby created by any of a number of modern-day medical miracles have fuelled the perception that there is little that medicine can not cure when it comes to infertility.

There is no question that in the last 30 years medicine has made great strides in treating infertility. Fertility drugs have made a world of difference to women who do not ovulate regularly. Pelvic microsurgery has repaired some women's scarred fallopian tubes and removed growths of endometriosis. Other surgeries have rebuilt deformed uteri or reproductive organs. IVF has given some couples who had no chance of pregnancy at all the joy of bearing and rearing their own child.

But the hard truth is that infertility medicine is imperfect and incomplete. While it can help some couples, it is powerless to help others because much of the complex, intricate reproductive process is still shrouded in mystery. In many disorders of infertility there are many more questions than there are answers. Getting the answers has been difficult because the human body does not give up its secrets without a great deal of research, time, money and intellectual endeavor.

In addition to commitment to do research, the research itself must be good. The studies must be unbiased and well-designed, and the researchers must interpret their findings correctly. Then others must duplicate the original findings before the new information is widely accepted as valid. Unfortunately, the understanding of many areas of infertility has suffered from the lack of good scientific research.

Many people unfamiliar with the scientific process assume that science is absolute, that either something is right or wrong. People assume that a scientific breakthrough is akin to someone discovering a dollar bill lying on the ground and saying, "Ah, there's a dollar"; that once the discovery is made the scientific community knows exactly what the discovery is worth and how it works.

However, the process of scientific understanding is more like a space alien finding a dollar on his first day on earth. He might walk right by it, even if he sees it. If he does stop, he would not say "Aha! a dollar." He would say, "What's this? Is it valuable or is it worthless? What makes it different from any other piece of paper lying on the ground?" The alien might watch all the earthlings to see what they did with this special piece of paper. Depending on what he sees he might come away with any number of interpretations of what a dollar is. He might see five or six people hand a bus driver a dollar. If he stopped his research there he might report back to his own planet that the dollar is used to ride the bus. But if he walked farther he might see someone use a dollar to get a newspaper or a chocolate bar. Gradually, if he watched closely enough, he would realize that the dollar was used as an exchange for something else. He would begin to understand the notion of currency and a dollar's value. And if he then found a $10 bill he might be better able to understand its value because of what he had already learned. Such is the process of scientific learning.

Science is all about collecting information through observation and comparison and then putting the information together to come to a correct conclusion. Unfortunately, infertility medicine, like other areas of science, has suffered from poor research, or incomplete or inconclusive studies. One of the principles of good scientific study for a medical treatment is the use of a control group, a separate group strictly for comparison. To determine whether a treatment works it must be compared to another treatment. You can not just say

Treatment A works if it is not compared to something else. You must say Treatment A works better than Treatment B or better than no treatment at all.

Many studies of infertility medicine lack control groups, so precise conclusions can not always be made. Sometimes the researchers do not include control groups because they require more work and more money. Other times the researchers can not get couples to participate in a study in which they might be assigned to a group that receives no treatment. A couple's reluctance to become a control is understandable—they want help to overcome their own infertility, and not to advance scientific understanding.

However, if a researcher can not be bothered to design good studies and couples are not willing to participate, the understanding of infertility suffers. The result is that some treatments used for years in the belief they work may be found eventually to be useless, or even harmful. Such was the case with the drug diethylstilbestrol, which was given to women from the late 1940s to the early 1970s in the mistaken belief it prevented recurrent miscarriage. As early as the 1950s when DES was studied properly it was found to have no better outcome than using nothing at all. This research was largely ignored by the large number of uncontrolled studies that said it worked. Not until DES was found to harm offspring did the majority see it critically. If the early controlled studies had been heeded, or if more critical research had been done, a large number of offspring would have been saved the defects it caused.

Sometimes controlled studies are not necessary and good scientific information can be gleaned without them. Sometimes controlled studies are impossible or unethical, such as in the case of comparing surgery to no treatment (although one method of surgery could be compared to another method of surgery). At other times, however, controlled studies are essential. Without them, science is unable to obtain conclusive, unambiguous findings. The treatment and understanding of a number of areas of infertility, particularly endometriosis, male infertility and recurrent miscarriage, have been impeded by the lack of good, controlled studies.

A Glass Half Full

Statistics show that for 50 percent of couples who seek medical help for infertility, treatment leads to the successful birth of a baby. That statistic can be looked at positively or negatively, like a glass that is half full or half empty. The optimist says, "Great, with medical help we have a one in two chance of having a baby." The pessimist says, "What! Only a 50 percent chance?"

Individually, a couple's odds may be much greater or much less than 50 percent, depending on the cause of their infertility. Some couples may be easily treated after the woman takes a few months of the fertility drug Clomid. Other couples may see months turn into years of medical attention. But over all, half of the couples who seek help for their infertility will be successful and half will not. That statistic can not be ignored, and it means that an infertile couple should begin to assimilate two outcomes: having a genetically related child; and not having a genetically related child.

The possibility that you and your partner may be unable to have a blood-related child may cause you enormous pain and you may resist imagining such a fate. However, if you accept the idea that medical treatment may not work, you will be better able to set limits on how much time, effort and money you will expend working towards pregnancy; you will know when you should stop the pursuit. If you allow for both the success and the failure of treatments, you can gradually accept the idea that although you want to bear your own children, your life can still be full if you are unable to do so.

If you allow yourself to accept only one possibility—a genetically related child—you risk getting caught in an endless cycle of treatments to achieve your goal. If that goal should continue to elude you, but you do not allow yourself to accept other options, you may feel compelled to keep pursuing more and more treatment. There are couples who continue undergoing medical investigations, who keep on charting their fertility or keep on trying new treatments for 10 or 15 years, or longer—they cannot stop because they have given themselves nothing else to replace having their own children. If it should turn out that you, too, have been unable to give birth to your own child, and you are forced by age or menopause or other circumstances to finally stop trying, you set yourself up to feel that you have failed because you have defined success with only one possible outcome.

When undergoing medical investigation and treatment for infertility, it can become the focus of your life. It is a demanding process, emotionally and physically, and it can make you feel you have no energy or passion for anything else. That approach is equivalent to putting all your eggs in one basket. Psychologists and other counsellors for couples struggling with infertility stress that it is important to make overcoming infertility a part of your life, but not the center.

In a 1985 article on the psychological component of infertility in the journal *Fertility and Sterility,* Texan psychologist Dr. Patricia Mahlstedt, who counsels infertile couples, discussed what can happen when they start medical treatment for infertility.

> *They become patients and their lives begin to revolve around conceiving by following a physician's game plan. They focus their attention on what they have failed to accomplish and soon start neglecting other goals and needs in their lives. In most cases, this type of focusing leads to losses of self-esteem, confidence, security, health, close relationships and even hope. Some patients lose sexual potency or interest in sexual intercourse, losses that interfere with treatment goals and put significant stress on marriages. There is no balance in their lives. There is, instead, hope one week, grief the next.*

The following case history is an example of a couple who maintained, with some effort, a healthy perspective while undergoing infertility treatment. Barb and Brad, who were in their late twenties, had been trying to conceive for two years. After a number of months of infertility investigation, Barb was found to have hostile cervical mucus, which was killing Brad's sperm. They had begun intrauterine inseminations (IUI) in which washed and separated preparations of Brad's sperm were placed in Barb's uterus each month around the time of ovulation to bypass the cervix. They had undergone two inseminations when they were interviewed.

"We really want children, there is no doubt about that. We've decided right now to go through treatments for the next six months and at the end of that time will look at it again," said Barb. "We DO want children. But it won't be the end of the world if it doesn't work."

"We don't have any illusions that life is greener on the other side," Brad said. "People who have children have troubles, too. In fact it could be worse. It could be cancer or a brain tumor or something that threatens the life of one of us. We can see both the positives and negatives of having children. It is easy to get caught up seeing only the negatives. We did that for a while. But that only makes you unhappy. We can now see the advantages we could have in our life if we didn't have children. We are going to give treatment a try and we'll just have to accept what comes."

Barb's and Brad's attitude does not mean that they do not feel sad or unhappy at times. It just means they are not going to let their infertility dominate their lives.

The Emotional Stress of Infertility

Even with the best intentions to avoid letting the struggle with infertility consume you, there is no way to completely escape the emotional stress. Infertility can affect all aspects of your life: your concept of self, your self-esteem and body image, your emotional and sexual relationship with your partner, your relationship with friends and family, even the path you choose for the future, the direction of your life. "Patients often report that no part of their lives is untouched by the disheartening experience of being infertile," said Mahlstedt.

Stress on the Individual

I'd be lying if I told you my infertility wasn't the priority of my life right now. I go to bed each night and wake up in the morning and it is there. I can't get away from it. We'll have company and we'll all be laughing, but the moment they are out the door, or if I go to the bathroom, and I'm with myself again, I am right back into it. It's the same thought over and over again: I don't want to, I will not, I just can't live my life without children.

Each individual reacts differently to the news that he or she is infertile. The intensity of emotions depends, in part, on how important children are to the individual, what the diagnosis is and what the prognosis for treatment is. Despite the individual differences, there are a number of common feelings that people share: shock, disbelief, denial, anger, rage, depression, sadness, jealousy, envy, anxiety, panic, powerlessness, and fear.

The feelings are similar to those of people who find out they have a life-threatening illness such as cancer, or whose life is altered by a disability, such as paralysis following a spinal cord accident. Infertility does not present the specter of premature death or severe disability, but it does present the death of a dream and the loss of body function that was often taken for granted. It presents a future that is radically different from what one had imagined. The grief over the altered future must be worked through to eventually come to a state of acceptance.

One of the most pervasive feelings is that your body has let you down, that you are defective and abnormal. This can lead women to feel that they are unfeminine and unattractive. It can lead men to feel they are less masculine or less potent. For both men and women, the medical investigation, the physical examinations, the possible surgery, drugs or high-technology treatments exacerbate the feeling of being ill, unhealthy or an invalid. If until the time of trying to become pregnant you have felt healthy and vigorous, the investigation of infertility, the diagnosis and subsequent medical treatment can change your perception of yourself. However, your health or attractiveness has not changed; your perception of those things has changed.

It is so hard on your womanhood. You feel androgynous, sexless, ugly, just so blahhhh. I guess that's the depression part. To make matters worse sometimes I don't even feel like making an effort to make myself look good. I went for a while without getting my hair cut. Then one day I took a look at myself and said this is ridiculous.

I find myself preoccupied with my age these days. I feel old. I notice all my new wrinkles. Up until now I've never been concerned about my age. Now it seems that everything depends on it. It is like I have aged overnight.

Men who are diagnosed as being infertile also suffer damage to their self-image. They often feel less masculine. It is common for men to try to build up a macho image. Some men turn to weight lifting or body building to compensate for their wounded ego.

Another common feeling shared by most people who are having trouble conceiving is: Why me? We all search for meaning in our lives, and when infertility occurs it is common to hunt for the greater meaning behind it. Why? This is the question most asked of one's self and of one's doctor. The fact that there usually is no rhyme or reason, that it just happened, is hard to accept. You may find that in becoming caught up in overcoming your infertility, you lose interest in other areas of your life.

Nothing has any salt these days. I know I should be doing other things, coming up with new ideas at work, doing different activities, but I just can't seem to muster the energy. Everything feels so flat. I can't seem to care about anything else except getting pregnant.

Close friendships with those who have young children can become strained or painful. Family celebrations, such as Christmas and birthdays, surrounded by nieces and nephews can be particularly difficult.

I have been really close to my sisters and it is really hard when they are having babies and you are not. Sometimes I just have to say to them this hurts too much, I just can't see you right now. One of my sisters got pregnant at the same time I did. She hadn't even been trying and I'd been trying for years. We talked about how great it would be to have the kids born at the same time. Then my pregnancy started getting into trouble and I lost it. I didn't know how I was going to take it with her still pregnant. When her son was born I had a really hard time. It was just a month before my due date. I could hardly get myself to the hospital. I didn't want to be on a maternity ward and see all those babies. When I held him it wasn't so bad, but you can never forget that they would have been born at the same time.

Being around children sometimes is not as hard as being around their parents or a culture that is baby-centered.

Sometimes I just can't listen to people talk about babies any more. "Gee, she's sleeping through the night" or "He got his first tooth and he's fussy." I just can't bear it and so I choose to stay away. I can find myself starting to cry when a diaper commercial comes on TV or when I see baby clothes in a store. I have to turn it off or get out of there.

I don't find the children hard to be around at all, it's the parents themselves I find difficult. You know when they treat their children badly, or when they just don't care or when they say something stupid like "we really wanted a girl" or "I wish he had curly hair" or "ever since my pregnancy I just can't lose these six pounds. I'm so fat." It kills me that people can be like that. I find I have to hold my tongue.

Individual Coping Strategies

To cope with infertility you must be able to separate your infertility from your feelings of self-worth and your feelings of happiness. You must try to not define yourself by your ability to have children. Although you can turn down the invitations to baby showers and birthday parties of friends' children, you cannot take yourself out of society. You cannot avoid seeing pregnant women in shopping centers or diaper commercials on television.

Here are some suggestions for coping with infertility, culled from interviews with psychologists, counsellors, couples who have resolved their infertility and from some popular self-help psychology books aimed at getting through any kind of pain.

1. Keep in touch with who you are and what makes you feel good. Before infertility happened to you, you probably had a number of things that you did that brought you pleasure or satisfaction. Whatever those are, do not put them aside. Keep doing them. Look for ways to keep satisfied.

I had always loved being out in nature, bird watching, walking in the woods, just stopping to take a look at a wildflower or a new bud on a tree. It gave me real pleasure. Somehow during all this infertility stuff I forgot how much I enjoyed doing that. I did not go out and spend time in nature for more than a year. When I finally did do it again, it just felt so good. I was sitting around a campfire with a couple of good friends and I thought, God, I love this. Why haven't I been doing this?

2. Learn specific relaxation techniques or autogenic therapies to cope with stress. One method is the progressive tensing and relaxing of muscle groups. When you feel anxiety or panic or a wave of tears starting to come over you, tense muscles in your feet for five seconds and then release the stress for 20 seconds, really focusing on the pleasurable feelings the relaxation brings. Gradually work through all the muscle groups in your body. Or, try mental imagery, picturing yourself on a sandy beach in the sun or in one of your favorite places. There are other simple methods of relaxing: focus on your breathing, being conscious of every breath, in and out, trying to make it deep and slow; concentrate on saying one word over and over again, such as the word "one." You can choose a word that is comforting to you, for example, the word "love" or "cool" or "warm" or "peace" or "calm." Experiment to find the word or method that brings you a sense of peace and reduces anxiety.
3. Find your own methods that work for you to reduce stress and make you feel good: a bubble bath with a magazine; taking your car out to a favorite winding road, turning the stereo volume high and singing at the top of your lungs; writing personal thoughts in a journal; focusing on why you are feeling a certain way and what you can do about. Sometimes there may be nothing you can do about what you feel, but by putting your anxiety or pent up feelings on paper you can fix them there so that they no longer churn inside you. Experiment with other stress reducing exercises. Find out what works for you.
4. Understand that you *do* have the ability to control your feelings. You are not a victim of your emotions, unless you choose to be. You can choose to feel happy or sad, you can feel anger or forgiveness, depression or acceptance. That is one of the themes of the book, *Out of Apples: Understanding Personal Relationships*, by Tucson mental health counsellor Lee Schnebly. A thin, chatty book about her own psychological enlightenment, it is full of nuggets of wisdom about how to build up your self-esteem and to take control of your own emotions. "Many of us assume that we can't help our feelings. They just overcome us," Schnebly wrote. "We might think to ourselves I am only a helpless victim of anger or sadness or anxiety and I must just put up with them until they go away." A common belief is that when anything bad happens—such as infertility or illness or divorce—that we can not help the way we feel because it is the situation itself, not our response, that causes our emotions, Schnebly said.

   New York psychologist and author Albert Ellis, who founded Rational Emotive Therapy, came up with one of the best ways to examine beliefs and change them to bring about a change in emotions. He called his method the ABC system. The letters stand for Action; Belief; Consequence. Here is how it works for a situation such as infertility.

   Action: The diagnosis of infertility. Suddenly you are faced with the discovery that having children will be difficult, if not impossible, for you.

   Belief: I must have children—my own children—or else I will have been a failure. I cannot envision my life without my own child.

Consequence: Depression, loss of self-esteem, a feeling that the future is blank and uncertain. A sense of desperation for children and lack of control of what lies ahead.

Ellis's theory is that the action always remains constant, but if you change the belief the consequence changes. If we slightly modify the belief, we see what happens to the consequence.

Action: The diagnosis of infertility, etc.

Belief: Although I want to have my own children, my life will not be ruined if I do not. I can choose a form of adoption or other methods to have children in my life or I can choose to remain childless.

Consequence: Decide to pursue medical treatment to a reasonable extent, evaluating each stage of investigation or suggested therapy to determine whether or not it is worthwhile to continue. When medical therapy has little chance of success, then pursue other options.

There is no question that the infertility will still cause anxiety, sadness and upheaval in your life. But you do have a choice as to how much you will let it command your emotions. Many people can get caught in what psychiatrist Dr. Harold Bloomfield calls the "I'll be happy when . . . ." syndrome, not trying or even expecting themselves to feel happy now. Abraham Lincoln said, "People are about as happy as they make up their minds to be."

5. Keep a healthy amount of exercise, sleep and good nutrition in your life. Feelings of stress can be exacerbated by sleepless nights, poor diet or inactivity. Moderate exercise is one of the best ways to reduce stress. Regular walks have been found to alleviate depression, and aerobic activity has been found to increase feelings of self-worth and optimism. A healthy diet, which includes daily portions from the four food groups, can also enhance energy and feelings of self-worth. Avoid drinking too much coffee or other caffeinated beverages, which contribute to feelings of stress and anxiety. Alcohol, a depressant, can also exacerbate the problem, fooling you into thinking you are feeling better when you are actually making the problem worse.

I have started to run again and for some reason I don't think about my infertility when I run. I don't know why. I guess I'm looking at all the things I am going by. I feel good about myself when I do it. I actually feel great. That's such a contrast to the times when I hole up in the apartment and start working my brain the wrong way. Running can give me two hours out of the day where I feel good.

Stress on the Couple

While infertility is a crisis for individuals, it is even more traumatic for a couple, particularly if they had no idea before marriage that either one might be infertile. Although you may be able to modify your individual response and emotions to infertility, you cannot control the response and emotions of your partner. Author Linda P. Salzer, who wrote *Infertility: How Couples Can Cope,* said it is highly unusual for couples not to feel significant stress when infertility enters into their relationship.

> *You want and need your relationship to be strong, but instead mutual strength and support often seem to dwindle. Each of you may become obsessed with your own pain and anger; rather than uniting, the two of you may attack or withdraw from each other. The effect of infertility on couples varies, but it is unlikely that the strain of infertility will be avoided altogether.*

Salzer's book, which deals with the emotional aspects of infertility rather than the medical and biological aspects, goes into great detail about the various emotional strains of infertility and gives coping suggestions.

The reason so many couples experience an increase in hostility and anger towards each other during the first few years of infertility is that each expects the other to react in the same way and to intrinsically understand how the other is feeling, psychologists say. "You want someone to understand the intensity of your pain and want someone to make the pain go away. What better person to place these responsibilities on than your spouse," Salzer says in her book.

But one person cannot remove the other partner's pain. Nor can he or she be expected to mirror the reactions and feelings of the other. Psychologists stress that couples must remember that they are two individuals and their reactions and feelings will differ. Couples often mistakenly interpret the different reaction as a sign that one cares more or less than the other about the infertility. The fights occur because each makes assumptions about the other's reactions, says Patricia Mahlstedt. The key is to accept each other's differences. Compounding the problem with the relationship is the fact that infertility often rests with one partner, which can then distort the balance of the relationship. The partner who is diagnosed with infertility must deal with his or her own pain as well as cope with the feelings of inadequacy or guilt in depriving the other of children. When the diagnosis is first made the one who has the problem is often afraid the other will no longer love him or her and will want a divorce. The infertile partner often offers the other a divorce, almost in anticipation of the partner's rejection.

> *When we found out that he had a sperm problem, he moved out saying since I wanted a child I should be free to go out and have one with someone else. I now know it was his reaction to his infertility and that he could not stand the thought of me rejecting him, so he rejected me. It took me a long time to convince him that it was the relationship I wanted and that I wanted to find a way to work through it with him.*

The partner who is apparently fertile may inwardly resent the other for the infertility and then may feel guilty for thinking any negative thoughts. Each partner must deal with the pain of infertility, but each may not be able to fully comprehend the depth of despair and the specific feelings of the partner.

In some instances, however, both partners have a fertility problem.

I can honestly say I was relieved when they also found that I had a bit of a sperm problem, too. Then it wasn't just my wife, it was both of us and it was something we could face together.

Couples who have survived infertility and look back on the first years after the diagnosis describe them as being the worst.

I never thought we'd make it. Everything hurt so much. Everything was in an upheaval, our plans, our ideas for the future, even whether we'd buy a house or move to a certain place. We had such a hard time talking to each other. I was always crying and he was always withdrawing because he couldn't take my constant unhappiness. It took about two years for our relationship to adjust. It took a lot of work and a lot of reevaluation but I now know that we are stronger for it.

Communication

Faulty communication is often at the heart of couples' problems during infertility. There is little debate among marital counsellors, psychologists, or anyone that deals with couples going through any crisis, that good communication skills are one of the best defenses that a couple can have to weather the storm. Mutual respect and commitment to the relationship are also essential elements, but it is the ability to listen to each other and truly communicate that keeps the respect and commitment in place.

I want to show her support but when she is really upset it doesn't matter what I say. I could bring her a dozen roses and she'll still scream at me to get out. So then I just leave her alone and she'll get mad at me for doing that.

He totally withdraws. I want to talk about what has happened to us, what we are going to do, how we can start feeling good again. He prefers to avoid it. When I need him he's off doing something for work.

Communication is not easy in times of crisis; you have to learn how to do it effectively, and that is why it is often called a skill. At the heart of communication is the ability to listen to each other. "Couples who come for counselling have almost always developed an inability to listen to each other," says Dr. Harold Bloomfield who with his wife Sirah Vettese, wrote *Lifemates.* This book teaches communication skills "to share feelings, desires, sexual needs, even difficult emotions such as fear and anger" in constructive ways.

There are a number of ways that psychologists and marriage counsellors recommend for couples to develop better communication and foster a stronger relationship, but they all share the same core: taking time to listen to each other non-judgmentally and in a manner that allows each to express feelings with the other's acknowledgment, whether or not the feelings are shared. "One of the most important skills for healing a love relationship is for you and your lover to learn to hear each other's hurt, anger or frustration without becoming defensive," Bloomfield and Vettese say.

An argument can take the form of two people trying to "win" or show that his or her individual position is right. Both end up feeling that the other does not appreciate or understand what the other is saying.

Most experts recommend that a couple establish a routine in which one listens to the other without interruption. When the first has had his or her say, the other then gets a chance to talk without the other jumping in. Some counsellors recommend that the listener paraphrase what the other has said and repeat it back so that both acknowledge the other's position.

Bloomfield and Vettese developed what they call the "Tell Me More Exercise." They go into their den, unplug the phone and hang a "do not disturb" sign on the door. They sit facing each other in two comfortable chairs, close enough to feel intimate but still leaving space so they do not feel crowded. The one who has the gripe begins to talk and while he or she is talking, the other may only respond with the phrase "Tell Me More." When the first is finished, it is the other's turn to talk and the first may only respond with "Tell me more." The exercise is not over until both partners feel they have spent their feelings and replaced them with good ones. The routine avoids the trap of arguments that go no where and statements that are constantly met with a closed response or the same recurring pattern.

Using "I" messages rather than accusations is also a long-standing recommendation by those who teach communication skills. Instead of criticizing the other with something like "You are so selfish, you don't care about how I feel." Rephrase it: "When you withdraw from me I feel angry and hurt because I feel it doesn't matter to you how I feel."

Working on communication skills takes time and effort, acceptance of the other's point of view and a commitment to the relationship. There are many good self-help books available with tips on how to develop communication skills. When those methods do not work to foster good communication, some couples benefit from seeking professional counselling.

Infertility and Sexual Relationships

Maintaining an interesting and fulfilling sexual life is a challenge for all couples, not just those who are struggling with infertility. When the initial, heady passion has passed in a relationship, effort and attention are required to keep sex lives mutually satisfying and stimulating, but those who have been trying without success to become pregnant face additional hurdles. The goal of conception begins to supersede sex as an expression of love or an act of spontaneous enjoyment.

Have you tried goal-oriented sex, month after month? Believe me it gets really tedious. There are times when you just aren't turned on and it is more like work. Sometimes I think I may not be able to ejaculate.

It makes me so sad. I know that sex is not going to make a baby for us anymore. There used to be the time where after sex I'd think maybe this was it and we'd both lie together and feel so content. When I lost both my tubes I thought why even bother. Now we've been able to get our sex life back, but it is not the same. There isn't that joy of thinking maybe you've made a baby.

Unfortunately sex can become associated with a negative event. The more you try unsuccessfully to become pregnant, the less you feel like trying.

Many studies report that couples who previously had a satisfying and stimulating sexual relationship encounter sexual problems during infertility. Many couples report that sex becomes mechanical, frustrating and unsatisfying. Sexual intercourse is initiated by ovulation, not desire.

> *You keep trying to do it at the time of ovulation, but it never works. So then you start thinking—well, maybe if I don't make such a big deal of it I won't get feeling let down again at the end of the month. So you don't pay so much attention to your chart and just sort of go with the flow and let sex happen. And then you feel really guilty that maybe you didn't have sex when you were ovulating.*

Women who have been accustomed to having orgasms can be distressed that they no longer can, intensifying their feeling of unhappiness. "Even those women who had previously described themselves as having a high level of desire find that they were now rarely or never excited by sex," said New York specialist Dr. Charles Debrovner in an article on infertility and sexuality. In many situations the woman becomes the initiator of sex because she is the one who charts her fertility. "She is making sexual overtures without feeling sexual desire and without the prospect of deriving pleasure from the act she seeks to encourage," Debrovner said.

The same problem befalls men. Studies report that almost 50 percent of men in infertile couples experience temporary loss of desire or even impotence during the infertility work-up. As many as 75 percent suffer from temporary impotence if they receive the diagnosis of infertility.

Restoring passion and satisfaction to sexual intercourse can be difficult. But here are some tips other infertile couples have used to avoid the pitfalls of sexual tedium.

1. Spend time being sensual with each other, not necessarily for sexual intercourse but just to enjoy being together. Give each other massages, have a bubble bath together. Buy some sensual lingerie. Try a little candlelight and wine. Try whatever you think you would enjoy doing together. Use your imagination.
2. Take holidays from the temperature graphs and the tyranny of sex only for conception. Stop trying to become pregnant for a few months and let desire for each other be what initiates sex. (Studies have found that a woman's desire for sex increases just before she ovulates.)
3. Communicate your fears and anxieties about your sexual relationship to each other. Pent up frustrations, resentment or fears are the first to interfere with sexuality. Verbal communication can often restore the desire for sex.
4. Try to vary your sexual routine. If you are accustomed to always having sex before you go to bed or when you first wake up in the morning, try a Sunday afternoon in bed or a weekend away at a special place. Try having sex in some place other than the bedroom.

Couples may find that self-help books on sexuality may be beneficial. *The Joy of Sex*, by Dr. Alex Comfort, or Masters and Johnson's books have been staples of sexual therapy for a number of years. If sexual problems continue to undermine the relationship, couples may benefit by going to a certified sex therapist.

Single and Infertile

Some men or women may learn they are infertile while they are not in a committed relationship. Others may have a committed relationship end after they have undergone an infertility work-up. Both may find themselves with a diagnosis of infertility while they are meeting and dating new people.

My infertility didn't cause my marriage to break up—it was probably destined to end anyway—but it certainly didn't help it. But being single again and knowing I was infertile was awful. My self-esteem was so low. I thought I'd never fall in love again and that no one would ever want me. I thought I was damaged goods.

Men and women who start a new relationship knowing that they are infertile may worry about how and when they should tell prospective partners. Should you bare all on the first date or wait until the relationship gets serious?

Like any important personal information, it is only fair that at some point you share it with a person whom you respect and to whom you are becoming close. But you are under no obligation to tell someone when both of you are still unsure how you feel about each other. When it becomes clear that you are both interested in a serious committment, that is when you should think about telling him or her about your infertility.

To be sure, there will be some who would reject you based on what they learn—but those people are not the ones you want to be with anyway. You need someone who will love you for who you are, not for your baby-making abilities. People are more than a function of their reproductive organs. If you feel confirmed in your worth as a person, others will love you for being you.

I never would have chosen somebody with whom having a child was the most important aspect of our relationship and therefore our relationship would fall apart based on that. Even if I'd felt that I was fertile, it still wouldn't have been my motivation for being with somebody—that is too dangerous. You never know what can happen.

Many men and women have voluntarily undergone sterilization in a first marriage only to divorce and find themselves dating again. Their sterilization rarely interferes with their ability to find a new partner. It is all in the way in which they present themselves. If they are happy and living a full life, others will be drawn to them. In fact, compared to couples who discover infertility in the midst of their marriage, there may be an advantage to starting out a relationship knowing that one partner is infertile. The relationship does not get thrown out of balance and the fertile partner knows the score from the beginning.

I didn't marry her for her reproductive organs. I married her for who she is. Perhaps it was easier knowing before hand because it didn't come as some big surprise. I liked kids but I knew she was who I wanted to be with. I felt quite willing to see what happens. We went through IVF with the attitude of "let's try." We were very fortunate that it worked for us. But it wouldn't have changed our relationship if it hadn't.

The Road Ahead

Overcoming infertility is a long, arduous journey. There is no way of knowing when you start out how long you will be travelling and what your experiences will be along the way. What you need to pack in your bag is a sense of perspective, a sense of humor, and a feeling that you travel this road because you want to. You also need to take courage—inner strength to get you through the emotionally trying times. Courage will not only help during the journey, it will also help you decide when you want to end the trip, when you will cease trying to become pregnant.

CHAPTER 2
Prayers and Piety, Romans and Royalty: Infertility Through the Ages

Dearest Mother of the Infant Jesus, by that most treasured privilege of Your divine Maternity, I entreat You! In the name of those holy joys You knew when, in an ecstasy of love, You pressed Your little Baby to your breast, I implore You to hear and bless my petition! . . . . . Prayer to Obtain a Child, Catholic Prayer Book

The words of the Catholic prayer for children were often on the lips of Queen Mary I, who ruled England from 1553 to 1558. When she died her prayer book, which had been her constant companion, was found tear-stained and worn at the page. Like her father King Henry VIII, the unfortunate queen desperately wanted an heir for the throne and she prayed long and hard for it and shed many tears. But Mary was infertile and when she died childless and heart-broken at the age of 42, her subjects deemed her a failure both as a woman and as a queen because her prayers were never answered.

Those struggling with the longing and pain of trying to conceive a child often feel all alone and unique in their anguish. Around them, they see ample evidence of others' successes: pregnant women; families with young children; sisters and brothers with babies; grandparents and great-grandparents surrounded by their progeny. Faced with these images, you can feel as if no one else suffers as you do; but history is full of tales of troubled conceptions. Understanding the historical pursuit of fertility can help couples grapple with their own troubling and powerful emotions.

Throughout all human civilization fertility, or the lack of it, has been a preoccupation, a primal force, prompting in its honor the creation of deities, rites, rituals and prayers. Kings and queens have fallen because of it; history has changed. Even the course of Western civilization has been altered because of infertility.

Take, for example, Henry VIII and his six wives. Their fates and the events surrounding them are well known from a strictly political perspective. The break with Rome, the Act of Succession and the Act of Supremacy are seen as turning points of English history. But the motivation behind the succession of wives and the events they precipitated was one thing: infertility. In fact, it was Tudor sterility more than any other single factor that was behind far-reaching changes in the sixteenth century. Henry wanted a male heir. He wanted one so badly that he was willing to forsake his religious beliefs, his wives and his respected advisers to obtain a son. It was an insatiable urge, a fundamental need and because it was largely thwarted, history changed.

If Henry had fathered a male child by his first wife, Catherine of Aragon, it is unlikely that he would have tried so relentlessly to divorce her. Although Catherine bore Henry six children, most were stillborn or sickly. Only Mary Tudor survived infancy. He had an illegitimate son, the Earl of Richmond, but Henry was a moral man and he wanted a legitimate heir.

Henry blamed Catherine, who had first been married to his brother, for the failure of her fertility. He is said to have searched the Bible for clues as to why God had not blessed their union. He found his answer in Leviticus 20:21. "And if a man shall take his brother's wife, it is an unclean thing . . . they shall be childless."

With God's displeasure in his marriage made evident, Henry sought to divorce 42-year-old Catherine in order to marry young Anne Boleyn to fulfill his burning need for a son. As the Pope would not sanction the divorce or annul the first marriage, Henry secretly wed Anne. When news of the marriage surfaced, he was forced to break with Rome and the Catholic Church. He established the Church of England and himself as its supreme head, opened the floodgates of the English Reformation and forever changed English history.

But poor Henry's reproductive luck proved no better with Anne. Although Anne became pregnant before their marriage was even official, the baby, to Henry's extreme disappointment (and to the embarrassment of astrologers and soothsayers) was a girl. No matter that Elizabeth I was a healthy child and Anne was young and capable of further births; Henry's ardor for Anne cooled and his eye turned to Jane Seymour. His displeasure with Anne was cemented when she miscarried a son in 1536. Not long after, she was tried for adultery, incest and treason, was found guilty and beheaded.

Historians say it is not known whether the charges against Anne had any substance or were simply a means to rid the throne of a queen who had lost favor with the king. But many believe Anne's only guilt was one of reproductive failure in the eyes of her husband.

The Virgin Queen

When Anne Boleyn's daughter, Elizabeth I, ascended the throne everyone assumed she would soon marry and begin her own quest for an heir. The woman's role in Tudor society, as it has been in other eras, was to bear and rear children. This was also expected of the queen and even before she had taken the throne the constant speculation began about whom she would wed.

Despite continued pressures from parliament and her advisers to marry and produce an heir, and despite numerous marriage proposals, Elizabeth could never decide on a suitable husband. She allowed herself to be courted by every eligible suitor in Europe. She used the lure of marriage like a diplomatic weapon to bring various countries to her side. But no man managed to fit the bill as her mate.

Historians have debated whether Elizabeth declined to marry because she knew she was infertile—it is still being argued. During her reign the question whether she could bear children was of even greater political interest. Ambassadors representing prospective husbands paid spies in her household to report on her health and habits. The Spanish ambassador is said to have paid a laundress to report whether Elizabeth had regular menstrual periods.

From all accounts it seems Elizabeth was healthy and robust, menstruated regularly and should indeed have been capable of bearing a child. Her celibate state seems to have been a conscious decision to keep power in her hands.

Although it is impossible to know what Elizabeth really thought and why she never chose a spouse from her many suitors, she was no fool. She was astute enough to realize that by remaining single and by not testing her fertility—whether it was there or not—she would not risk losing her throne to a husband or the loyalty of her subjects through any perceived failure of womanhood.

In historian Lacey Baldwin Smith's account of Elizabeth's reign, *This Realm of England,* he quotes the Scottish ambassador James Melville who pinpointed the crux of Elizabeth's wiley thinking: "Ye think that if ye were married, ye would be Queen of England, and now ye are King and Queen both. Ye will not suffer a commander."

She had good reason to be wary of trying to have a child, simply based on the fates of the women who had been closest to her: her mother, stepsister, and father's first wife Catherine of Aragon, not to mention Jane Seymour who died 12 days after giving birth to Prince Edward. She knew that those women, who each had been queen and the most powerful woman in England, had been brought to ruin or death by trying to have an heir. Surely she must have asked why she should risk her power, her crown, or her life in the pursuit a child.

Instead, she chose to use her childlessness and her virginity as a way to endear herself to her subjects. Fighting off criticism from those in parliament who said she would lead England to strife if she did not produce an heir, she said, "Do not upbraid me with miserable lack of children, for every one of you, and as many as are Englishmen, are children and kinsmen to me."

Fertility Rituals

Long before the Tudor struggle with fertility, other civilizations and cultures made fertility a central part of their life and religion.

It is little wonder that fertility preoccupied the human race and that the seemingly magical ability of reproduction was deemed to be under the control of a powerful deity. The mysterious and wondrous process of birth was naturally linked to higher power. Even today in our scientifically sophisticated society, anyone who is privileged to see the birth of a baby is awestruck at the process. For our early ancestors it was even more incomprehensible and, as always, when a culture has no explanation for the mysteries of life, gods and goddesses take over. There is evidence that fertility goddesses were invoked by the people to insure fertility in the land and in themselves from the earliest known human eras.

The goddess of fertility had different names and attributes among different societies and religions, but her role throughout the world was essentially the same. She represented the creative force in all nature, the mother of all things, and was responsible for the periodic renewal of all life.

She was Ishtar in Assyria and Babylonia; Isis in Egypt; Cybele in Phyrgia and Lydia; Astarte in Syria and Palestine. In Greece she was represented by Gaea, Rhea, Hera, Aphrodite and Demeter, all of whom were associated in part with fertility, regeneration or childbearing. In Rome her attributes were found in Maia, Ops, Tellus, Ceres and Juno. Although she was a dominant figure in Middle Eastern and Mediterranean religions, similar figures are found virtually in every part of the world. Freyja, the Norse goddess of love, marriage and fertility, shares similar characteristics with her Levantine counterparts. Friday is named for her and so it can loosely be called fertility day.

One of the earliest fertility symbols was a voluptuous statuette, commonly called a Venus. The feminine characteristics of the small figurine were enlarged or particularly emphasized: she was a rounded, full-breasted woman with a swollen belly. Venuses are considered one of the earliest known art forms, dating from the Upper Paleolithic period when our earliest ancestors lived in hunting tribes. One of the most famous figurines, Venus of Willendorf, was found in Austria and is nearly 30,000 years old.

Once a man's contribution of semen was recognized as essential to the reproductive process, phallic symbols emerged. Archeologists have found carvings, images or stylized representations of the erect penis in virtually every society. The symbols are generally interpreted as an expression of the desire to reproduce. The exaggerated erections impart, as if by some magical process, the power of image into the men who created it.

Along with the symbols came fertility rites—magical-religious ceremonies that included dance, prayer, incantations, pageants, rituals or sacred dramas as a means to control the uncontrollable and to ensure fertility. In India, virgins were deflowered by a stone phallus called a lingam to ensure a fertile marriage.

Many of the rituals in primitive societies persisted for many centuries, some even into the modern age so that their origins as a fertility rite have been largely forgotten. The dance around the Maypole on the first of May derives from a spring ritual dance glorifying the phallus. Rice is thrown at the bride and groom as they leave the church to symbolize a fertile union. The celebration of Easter with the fertility symbols of colored eggs and rabbits comes from a pagan fertility festival glorifying spring. In fact, even modern dramatic comedy has its origins in the boisterous choruses and dialogues of the fertility rites of the feasts of the Greek god Dionysus.

In primitive societies when the invocation of gods and goddesses, the wearing of amulets or the performance of a dance or ritual did not bring about a baby for a couple, it was taken to mean one thing: the couple was out of favor with the gods.

Sarah, Hagar and Abraham

Accounts of infertile couples, who through the grace of God were finally granted children, abound in the Bible. The best-known biblical story is that of Sarah, Hagar and Abraham (Genesis 16) and the story itself has in it the legendary origins of both the Arabs and the Jews.

The story goes like this. Sarah and Abraham were an aged couple who had tried unsuccessfully for decades to have children. Sarah told her husband, "See now, the Lord has restrained me from bearing children, please go unto my maid, perhaps I shall obtain children from her." Hagar was her Egyptian maid and when Abraham lay with her she conceived. But instead of bringing the women closer, it enraged rivalries between them. The pregnant Hagar felt superior to her mistress and so despised her. In retaliation, Sarah treated Hagar harshly and beat her, causing Hagar to flee. She returned to the household after an angel assured her that she would bear a son, Ishmael, who would become the father of a great nation of wanderers.

Then God appeared to Abraham and told him he would make a covenant with him. The deal? Sarah, who had already entered menopause, would bear Abraham a son who would also be the father of many nations. In return, the couple would change their name (their original names were Sarai and Abram); all the male offspring would be circumcised and they must worship Him as their sole God, founding Judaism. Abraham agreed. When Sarah learned of the covenant she laughed. But God was true to his bargain and Sarah, at the age of 90, according to the Bible, bore a son Isaac by her husband who was then 100 years old.

Similar stories are repeated throughout the Bible: a woman of advanced years who has been infertile finally conceives through the blessing of God who "opens" her barren womb. In the Bible, and for many centuries following it, soil was the metaphor for the woman's womb and man's semen the seed to be sown in it. Just as the land that couldn't grow a crop was called barren, a woman in whose womb a man's seed could not grow also was called barren. As it is with many modern women who find themselves infertile, the women in the Bible who were barren grieved in torment, praying for the birth of a child. "Give me children or I die," pleaded Rachel, the eventual mother of Joseph.

In most cases a bargain was made with God in return for the blessing, usually devoting the child to His worship. Most of the children of these unusual births became prophets, kings or great leaders. Besides Isaac, the sons of infertile women include Joseph (of the coat of many colors), Samuel, Samson and John the Baptist, all of whom play prominent roles in the Bible.

Although the Bible has had decreasing significance for modern couples, its descriptions of the emotions and the pain surrounding infertility could apply today. Elkanah, the husband of "barren" Hannah, implored of his wife: "Why do you weep? Why do you not eat? And why is your heart grieved? Am I not better to you than ten sons?" (1 Samuel 1:8) Hannah "was in bitterness in soul and prayed to the Lord and wept in anguish." She vowed to God that if he granted her a son, the child would serve him all the days of his life. She bore Samuel.

Unfortunately the Judeao-Christian message that God grants fertility to those of his followers who are deemed worthy has done much to contribute to the angst and crumbling self-esteem so common to infertile couples in the ages that followed. Because the message has been reinforced so many times, couples faced with infertility search their souls and their conscience for what they may have done to put them in God's disfavor. Countless numbers of infertile Christian men and women have asked, "Why me? What have I done that has caused this affliction?" praying to God to grant them a child.

But in non-Christian cultures infertility is also seen as one of the worst curses that can befall a couple. Often it was the grounds for divorce and, unfairly, most often it was the woman who was seen to be at fault. In Babylonia, Persia, Egypt, and China the wife of a childless couple had to grant her husband a divorce if he wanted one.

Children were of paramount importance in Chinese society, so much so that the ancient Chinese way of writing the word "good" is a character depicting a mother and her children. Part of children's importance comes from the Chinese practice of ancestor worship, based on the belief that the spirits of dead relatives continue to dwell in the natural world and have power to influence the fate and fortune of the living. Without children the line could not be continued and ancestor worship could not take place.

The greatest curse for a Chinese woman was to be barren. If the man and woman decided to stay together, it was the wife's duty to find a concubine. Any children born to the man and concubine referred to the wife as mother, and the concubine as "concubine mother."

Infertility in the Roman Era

Sometimes whole societies, rather than individual couples, are plagued by infertility. That was true from the second century B.C. when the Roman Empire's birth rate began to drop. Although the Romans were at a loss to understand the factors that lowered their collective fertility, they knew that it was happening and a number of laws and policies were enacted in an attempt to boost the size of families and the number of babies—all to no avail.

To what extent population decline influenced the empire's eventual fall has been debated by a number of historians. Some believe the Romans' poor ability to replace their population with healthy offspring may have contributed as much to the society's demise as the marauding barbarians from the North.

Reay Tannahill, in her book *Sex in History*, identifies four significant factors that combined to lower the Romans' fertility, one of the most prominent of which was chronic lead poisoning. It has been well documented that lead poisoning, which can cause sterility in men and miscarriages and stillbirths in women, was rampant in Roman society. Lead was everywhere: the pipes carrying their water were lead; cups were lead; cooking pots were lead; pottery had lead glazes; white lead was used by women as a facial powder; the grape syrup for wine was thickened with lead and boiled down in lead pots.

Through modern science we now know that lead causes poisoning, infertility and significant neurological defects when it is inhaled or ingested over a long period of time. But the Romans were oblivious to the danger.

Other factors also contributed to the poor birth rate of the Roman people. They drank a great deal of alcohol and their wine was 17 percent proof. Excessive alcohol consumption has been shown to lower men's sperm count as well as interfere with the ability to have an erection. During banquets the Romans smoked marijuana, another intoxicant that adversely affects sperm counts and sperm motility.

The famous Roman baths—one of the elements that set them apart from other "uncivilized" nations—probably contributed to the problem. It was customary for men to attend the baths every day, but at temperatures of about 43 degrees Celsius (110 F) the caldarium, the hottest bath, was hot enough to impair the formation of sperm in the testicles. It was typical for a "self-respecting" Roman, says Tannahill, to first go from the tepidarium, or warm bath, to the caldarium, then into the frigidarium for a quick cold dip. The men spent most of the bathing hours, however, in the caldarium, often drinking wine at the same time.

Despite their poor fertility, the Romans also used contraception and abortion to prevent unwanted births. Their frequent sexual encounters and orgies also contributed to the incidence of sexually transmitted diseases such as gonorrhea and the occurrence of other organisms that scarred a woman's fallopian tubes or rendered a man sterile.

Although they did not know what was causing their birth rate to fall, the Romans knew that it was falling and leaders tried to correct the problem by either persuasion or legislation. Cicero tried to convince the population towards "less lust and larger families." But Augustus Caesar was the one who brought in legislation to promote population growth in 18 B.C. and then supplemented it in A.D.9. Called Lex Julia et Papia, the law was full of incentives for child rearing and deterrents for childlessness. Financial rewards were given to couples with three or more children. Bachelors were taxed and were unable to inherit property unless they married; it was almost impossible for unmarried men to hold office or to rise in rank, and widows had to remarry within two years and divorcees within 18 months. Class barriers were relaxed to allow intermarriage, including the marriage of slaves. Inheritance laws were changed so that couples without children could collect only half their inheritance. Freed men who had only one child had to bequeath half their possessions or property to their former owners, but if they had two children they gave one-third, three children, and they gave none.

The laws were not only unpopular, they did little to reverse the downward trend. Says Tannahill, "The Romans were trying to bring social pressure on a problem that was as much medical as social." Because the medical aspects of infertility were so poorly understood, there was little that could be done to solve the problem.

Discovery of the Reproductive Process

The Romans can't be blamed for their ignorance of the medical and biological aspects of reproduction. Scientists and medical researchers today are only beginning to understand the intricacy of the fusion of sperm and egg, the embryo's development, the growth of the fetus and the birth of the baby nine months later. Despite all that has been discovered—most of it in the last hundred years—there is much that remains unknown.

Some of the fundamental factors of reproduction, however, have been obvious from early on: a sexually mature man and woman must have sexual intercourse for a pregnancy to occur. The link between sexual intercourse and pregnancy was recognized by all but the earliest preliterate societies. For those earliest societies, sex was simply an enjoyable sideline, and gods, spirits or even bathing water impregnated the women. Eventually people concluded that sex was an essential prerequisite for pregnancy and birth, even if the gods still dictated the process and the outcome.

Just what was happening during sexual intercourse, however, was not understood, although there were a number of theories. The predominant thought was that man, with his clearly visible genitalia and his equally obvious emission of semen during intercourse, played the dominant role. His semen was thought to be the seed of life. The woman, whose reproductive organs were hidden and remained a mystery, provided the place for the seed to grow.

Granted, some cultures felt the woman probably contributed more, but just how much more no one was sure. Some Greeks and Egyptians believed that the semen contributed the bones to the fetus and the mother contributed the flesh. Hippocrates had the idea that the semen came from the spine of the man and the woman's menstrual periods collected over time to form the flesh of the baby. He also believed that since the child often resembled the mother, she must contribute a semen-like element. This idea was largely ridiculed by others at the time.

Although the Greeks and Romans had made strides in medical knowledge about reproduction, dissection of humans fell into disrepute and laws prohibiting it prevented full investigation of the reproductive organs. Human anatomy had to be observed from dead soldiers and gladiators, which meant few women were ever seen. For the next thousand years the Christian focus on theology and the afterlife rather than the here-and-now meant that no one even questioned how life began.

Renaissance

The journey toward understanding procreation had its first tentative steps in the Renaissance, when there was a resurgence of interest in human beings and their world rather than a total preoccupation with the Christian spiritual world. Along with the flourishing of art and architecture, interest in the principles of science and medicine grew, based on the flawed works of the Greeks and Romans. Working out the rudiments of the reproductive process took more than 500 years.

The first step was learning the basic anatomy of the reproductive organs. At the dawn of the Renaissance, schools of medicine were established and anatomy became one of the principle subjects. Mondino de' Luzzi of Bologna, Italy, who taught at the Bologna School of Medicine early in the fourteenth century, was one of the best early Renaissance anatomists. His book published in 1316 was the first in history to be devoted to anatomy and it was the best available for almost two centuries. Although his book contained many inaccuracies and mistakes, Mondino gave a general description of the human reproductive organs.

Two hundred years later Italian anatomist Gabriel Fallopius, a student of the famed Flemish anatomist Andreas Vesalius, described the slender, muscular tubes that came out of the uterus, with their ends "torn and ragged like the fringe of well-worn garments" each reaching out to the ovaries. He did not know their true function—he thought they were chimneys for the escape of "sooty humors" from the uterus—but the tubes are now called fallopian tubes in his honor. The picture did not begin to come together until the late seventeenth century.

In 1677 spermatozoa were seen for the first time by the human eye. Credit for the discovery goes to Dutch microscopist Anton Von Leeuwenhoek, who hand-ground lenses of such delicacy and perfection they were capable of magnifying up to 500 times. Some maintain it was actually his student, Stephen Hamm (his name also appears as Ludwig and Johann), who first saw the spermatozoa, and called his teacher to the microscope saying something like, "Take a look at these swimming things." Whoever it was that saw it first, the sighting was important. He thought the sperm looked like the microscopic "animacules" he had discovered in marsh water and had named protozoa, and so named the new discovery "spermatozoa," meaning seed animals. Leeuwenhoek nervously reported his observation of sperm to the Royal Society of London, fearing it might be considered obscene. "And if your Lordship should consider that these observations may disgust or scandalize the learned, I earnestly beg your Lordship to regard them as private and to publish or destroy them as you see fit," he wrote.

While Leeuwenhoek was peering under his lenses at everything from teeth scrapings to pond water, his compatriot Regnier de Graaf was busy studying the anatomy of the reproductive organs in minute detail. In 1668, Graaf described the fine structures of the testicle and in 1673 the ovary. His description of the ovary included the small sack-like structures on the ovarian surface, which a century later were called graafian follicles. Graaf mistakenly believed that the follicle was the beginning of life. Not until 150 years later in 1827 was the egg finally found when German embryologist Karl Ernst Von Baer opened the follicle in a dog's ovary.

Still, the actual process of fertilization was not understood. Ever since Leeuwenhoek had discovered sperm it was thought that the man had the leading role in the creation of life and that the woman was secondary. Some believed that sperm was tissue collected from every part of the body during orgasm. Others thought it represented a complete miniature man—cartoons of the time depicted a sperm as a tiny man in top hat and tails.

The true details of the intricate process began to come together in 1779 when Italian biologist Lazzaro Spallanzani devised an ingenious experiment to see whether sperm really was essential to reproduction. He made a special pair of "pants" for male frogs that collected the semen when they copulated with female frogs. Naturally, the unfertilized eggs failed to develop into tadpoles, but the ones he fertilized by hand with the sperm from the pants, did. Unfortunately, Spallanzani wrongly assumed that the sperm somehow nourished the egg, rather than fused with it. Nonetheless, he successfully artificially inseminated a dog in 1789, further proving that sperm was essential to the process.

In the nineteenth century, the outward mysteries of fertilization were gradually unveiled, starting with reports in the early 1840s of sightings of sperm in the outer shell of the egg. By 1875, just over 100 years ago, when German embryologist Wilhelm Hertwig demonstrated that the sperm penetrates the ovum and the male and female genetic material unites to form one cell, the fundamentals of the process were finally known.

Theories of Infertility

Since the reproductive process was shrouded in mystery for so long, when it didn't work and a couple did not produce a child there were even more outrageous theories surrounding it.

Even though the semen was designated as the crucial life force and the man had the dominant role, when infertility occurred, he was rarely considered to be part of the problem. The woman, almost without exception, was always held responsible for the failure to produce offspring.

"It may safely be said that amongst all nations, women who do not bear children are looked upon with either pity or contempt," said Dr. R.A. Gibbon as recently as 1923 in his book *Sterility in Woman, Its Causes and Treatment*. For centuries, infertility was considered to be the fate of women who were unfaithful, who had sex with evil spirits or who in some manner had invited God's displeasure.

By the nineteenth century, when society began to accept that infertility was not solely God's judgment on the couple, the medical theories still tended to blame the woman for some transgression or failing. The theories were as farfetched as they were varied. A predominant and enduring belief was that the woman had to experience orgasm, or at least enjoy sexual intercourse to conceive. The French gynecologist Chevalier Vincent Mondat described the prerequisites for conception in his 1844 book, *On Sterility in the Male and Female*:

> *Many females are sterile only because they co-operate coldly and passively in their conjugal duties; while the female who tastes the sweet delights of pleasure has already a presentiment that she will be a mother.*

Mondat goes on to say that the reason prostitutes rarely conceive is that the uterus has been stimulated by so many acts of intercourse that it becomes frigid and loses its sensitivity. Other gynecologists put forward the belief that women who enjoyed sex too much also tended to be infertile. A woman could not win.

Menstrual irregularities were attributed to numerous causes, some of which another French gynecologist, Marc Colombat de L'Isere, summed up in a treatise on uterine diseases of women, published in 1845. Colombat believed that both physical and moral factors contributed to so-called amenorrhea, meaning an absence of menstruation. James V. Ricci, M.D., reported in the medical text, *One Hundred Years of Gynecology,* that the moral factors Colombat de L'Isere attributed to a lack of menstruation included "vivid emotions of the soul, anger, disappointed love, celibacy, despair, jealousy, immoderate joy, profound depression, sudden reception of bad news, a sudden fright, extreme fear and sudden disappointments." The physical causes that stopped menstruation were:

> *sudden exposure to cold, immersion of hands and feet in cold water, cold ablutions (washing) of the sex organs, sitting on grass, ground or a stone bench, ingestion of ices, sherbets and cold drinks, action of strong odors and all circumstances capable of suddenly drawing in other directions than towards the uterus, the blood which ought to be exhaled by that organ.*

Education was also seen as interfering with the womanliness essential to bear children and to contribute to infertility. As recently as 1922 an American author, Charles Gardner Child, M.D., a professor of gynecology at New York's Polyclinic Medical School, said the mental strain of higher education was too much for the delicate constitution of women. In *Sterility and Conception* he says that "the higher education of women has marked inhibitory effects upon their reproductivity. Among college graduates, the highest percentage of sterility, 25 to 35 per cent, exists."

Child's book is a condemnation of the emancipated woman rather than a reasoned study of infertility. He calls athletic women "monstrous" and rails against any form of contraception, declaring it as subversive and that "the true woman, one deserving of the name, has always in all times, and in all lands, desired children."

Child theorizes that birth control leads to infertility, not because of the increased chance of sexually transmitted diseases that scar the fallopian tubes, but because birth control trains the uterus not to bear children: "When artificial means are used to prevent conception and are indulged in continually for any length of time they are quite likely to create the habit of sterility." As implausible as Child's views seem now, they were popular medical thought at the time and were echoed by his colleague R.A. Gibbon in *Sterility in Women, Its Causes and Treatment*:

> *Repeated coitus interruptus and other contraceptions lead to sterility because there is not the fulfillment of sexual pleasure. It is only right that women should be told the risk they run (by using contraceptives) when interfering with Nature's laws.*

Treatments for Infertility

Considering the knowledge available about infertility, it should come as no surprise that treatments were most often ill-founded and ineffective. They ranged from the benign to the barbaric, and often contained elements of mysticism or the invocation of magic. Some of the early magico-religious rites to ensure fertility have already been mentioned. But belief in good luck charms and talismans to bring about fertility has continued into the twentieth century. According to Alan Roy Dafoe, the pediatrician who delivered the famous Canadian Dionne Quintuplets, hundreds of infertile women travelled to the girls' home in 1934 after their birth to take back "magic pebbles" from the courtyard.

Throughout much of history and in all cultures, herbs, plants and animal extracts were used in a variety of concoctions and in a variety of ways to battle all types of reproductive problems. In ancient Egypt a raw onion bulb was placed in the woman's rectum "for a whole day and night" to cure infertility. In Persia, miscarriages were treated with cow's urine, both orally and as a douche.

The Cherokee and Tonkawa tribes of North American Indians made a weak tea of bull nettle root to drink for four days before breakfast and before bedtime to promote fertility in women. Those tribes also used fresh magnolia flowers steeped in boiling water as a cure for infertility. In Europe, the rue, a shrubby herb with a greenish-yellow flower, blue-green leaves, a strong odor and a bitter taste, was boiled with water for drinking every two hours to relieve congestion and cure amenorrhea.

The use of herbs and plants reached its zenith during the Middle Ages when it was believed that each plant had a signature given to it by God that would tell what it would cure. This belief, called the Doctrine of the Signatures, meant that all a person had to do was study the plants for their specific uses. Plants that had even the slightest resemblance to genitalia or reproductive organs were either used as aphrodisiacs or as cures for various causes of infertility.

The mandrake, with a forked, fleshy root roughly resembling the lower half of the human body, became most prized for treatment of infertility. A member of the nightshade family (to which the potato and tomato also belong), the mandrake was endowed with magical properties more than any other plant. From earliest times it had been associated with increasing passion and overcoming barreness. Its seeds, which contain a number of alkaloids, were used by the Romans as a mild narcotic to dull pain. It is mentioned in literature frequently. In the Bible in the book of Genesis Rachael asked her sister Leah to bring the yellow plum-like fruit of the mandrakes from the field to cure her infertility.

It was during the Middle Ages that the superstition and medicinal power attributed to the mandrake reached the highest point. People believed the plant was in the power of dark earth spirits, that it screamed when it was uprooted and that anyone who heard it would be driven mad, or worse, die instantly. For that reason it could be safely harvested only by a dog (some accounts stress a black dog) tied by a cord to the plant. By moonlight, after the proper prayers and rituals had been performed around the plant and when everyone was out of earshot, the dog would be commanded to pull up the plant. Its various parts would be used in brews and concoctions, and the highly prized forked root would be worn as a talisman around the neck to either attract a lover or ensure fertility.

While the herbal cures were often benign, causing little damage to the woman, other treatments were barbaric. It was all too common for women to be injured or even die from some treatments meant to help them conceive children. Some of the most intrusive interventions occurred during the nineteenth century. Among treatments recommended in medical texts of the time were numerous injections into the uterine cavity, including that of mercury, cocaine and turpentine. The injections often causes serious infection and pelvic inflammation.

In the case of amenorrhea, the application of leeches to the cervix or vulva was recommended as late as 1893. Physicians were warned to count the leeches at the end of treatment since incidences were on record of some crawling into the uterus "producing severe distress," according to A.K. Gardner in his translation of Italian physician Von Scanzoni's instructions on leeching in the 1861 text, *Diseases of Women.*

A procedure called cupping, which entailed creating suction by use of a glass cup to bring blood or "toxins" to the surface, was also recommended for the cervix. Cupping, although now out of use, was taught as recently as the late 1930s. At the turn of this century some physicians advocated "electric baths" and "galvanization" for the treatment of amenorrhea. "Rapidly interrupted galvanic currents yield excellent results," said Gibbons in his 1923 book, although he cautioned the physician must apply the current in such a way "to avoid shocks and burns" to the patient. The medical controversy of the day was whether galvanic or faradic currents were superior.

In light of such treatments, the recommendation by Colombat de L'Isere in the 1860s that women with amenorrhea be prescribed "dry fresh air, nourishing foods, particularly rich soups and roasts, wine and mineral waters," comes as blessed relief—and was by far the best advice.

"It is appalling to note the number of women in history who have been subjected to various examinations, treatments and even surgery with little success and often with no examination of the male partner," said Samuel L. Sielger, M.D., in his 1944 overview of infertility.

Fortunately, sexual intercourse, whenever possible, was also recommended by most physicians. That advice did more than most treatments combined to actually help couples conceive a baby.

CHAPTER 3
What's Going On

The human body can perform astonishing acts from determining the theory of relativity or scaling Mount Everest to digesting a good meal. But perhaps its most impressive feat is reproduction, the step-by-step process that unites the genetic material of a man and a woman to form a unique human being nine months later. The launching of a space shuttle is simple compared to the intricate interplay of body chemicals and coordination of key events needed to launch a baby.

Most people have some background in the basics of reproduction, even if it is only a hazy memory of a boring high school health class. You may be tempted to skip to parts of the book that deal directly with the treatment of infertility. But understanding the reproductive process when it works is helpful in understanding what happens when it does not work. You may learn something simple and effective that may eliminate the need to seek treatment.

Doctors tell stories of couples that came to them complaining of infertility when they had not been having intercourse—women who were still virgins after three or four years of "trying to get pregnant." While those situations are the exception, it is extremely common for couples to be confused about when to time intercourse or to be unaware of the ways they are lowering their fertility.

In the 1988 report to the United States Congress, the U.S. Office of Technology Assessment study of infertility showed that the majority of Americans know surprisingly little about fertility and reproduction. Only 10 percent of a sample of 802 people polled could describe that ovulation meant the release of an egg from the ovary. A significant number did not know that there are only 72 to 96 hours during a woman's menstrual cycle when she is fertile, nor did they know how to determine that fertile "window."

Ten Prerequisites

There are ten essential elements that must come into play for normal conception and pregnancy to take place.

1. The man must be making good quality, swimming sperm in sufficient numbers so that at least one has a chance to reach the egg.
2. The man must be able to deposit the sperm at the woman's cervix.

3. The sperm must be able to penetrate the cervical mucus and begin the journey up through the uterus.
4. The woman must have at least one open fallopian tube through which the sperm can travel to reach the egg.
5. In the weeks before the sperm begins its extraordinary voyage, the woman must mature an egg and release it at or about the time of sexual intercourse.
6. The newly liberated egg, as it falls through space, must be caught by the tentacle-like fingers called the fimbria and coaxed into the tube.
7. The egg and sperm must meet in the outer end of the slender tube. The sperm head must attach to the egg's outer layer and in a chemical reaction burrow into the egg, fertilizing it.
8. The newly created embryo must pass back down the tube, sending out hormonal messages that tell of its existence; at the same time it must elude detection by the woman's immune system.
9. The lining of the uterus must be spongy and thick and accept the embryo.
10. The embryo must settle into the lining, implanting itself and growing for the next nine months.

If any one of those steps fails, a baby will not be born. Given those stringent criteria, it is little surprise that conception often takes a year or more for normally fertile couples. The chance of pregnancy in any one cycle for normally fertile couples is only about 25 percent.

The pieces of the reproductive puzzle have gradually been put into place, particularly in the past 50 or 60 years. But what we have learned has often been like opening a door, only to find a dozen new doors. In some instances the scientific details of some of those requirements are still sketchy. For example, very little is known about what an embryo requires to implant successfully in the uterus, why one embryo will implant and another will not.

What follows is a general outline of human reproduction, simplified, and with some of the more esoteric details omitted.

Headquarters

The central clearing house of all reproductive activity in men and women, the command central as it were, is the hypothalamus, an almond-sized portion of the brain lying at its base right behind the eyes.

The hypothalamus is rich in nerve fibres and synaptic connections and it regulates most of the basic body functions: body temperature, blood pressure, heartbeat, sugar levels, metabolism of fats and carbohydrates and sexual reproduction. It processes nerve stimuli from the higher brain such as light, temperature, pain, emotional or physical stress, and prepares the body to adapt accordingly.

It is the interaction of the hypothalamus with the pituitary, a small oval gland that hangs by a stalk from the hypothalamus, that allows the hypothalamus's regulations to be carried out. Like a head office instructing its chief manufacturing plant, the hypothalamus sends out hormone pulses called *releasing factors* to the pituitary. The pituitary, the master endocrine gland of the body, then secretes more specific hormone instructions, which will be carried via the blood stream to designated organs. Beginning at puberty, the hypothalamus and pituitary, in concert, send and receive the hormone messages that tell the male and female sex organs what to do. They tell the man when to produce sperm and the woman when she should mature eggs, ovulate and start the cycle again.

Every 90 minutes in normally fertile adult men and women the hypothalamus sends out a pulse of a hormone called gonadotropin releasing hormone (GnRH). The word "gonad" comes from the Greek word for seed and "tropin" from the Greek word "to trigger." As such, gonadotropin means "seed-triggering" hormone. The hypothalamus, with its pulse of GnRH, is telling the pituitary to release hormones to stimulate the reproductive organs. GnRH is an acronym you will see often in the next chapters because it has a number of applications to infertility treatments.

In men and women, the pituitary responds to the hypothalamus pulse of GnRH by secreting two hormones, follicle stimulating hormone (FSH) and luteinizing hormone (LH). FSH and LH act on the male testes as well as on the female ovary but are named only for the action they have in the female because that is where they were discovered.

When the testes receive the FSH message they react by starting the production of sperm; the ovary by selecting and maturing an egg. The LH message

The Male Reproductive System

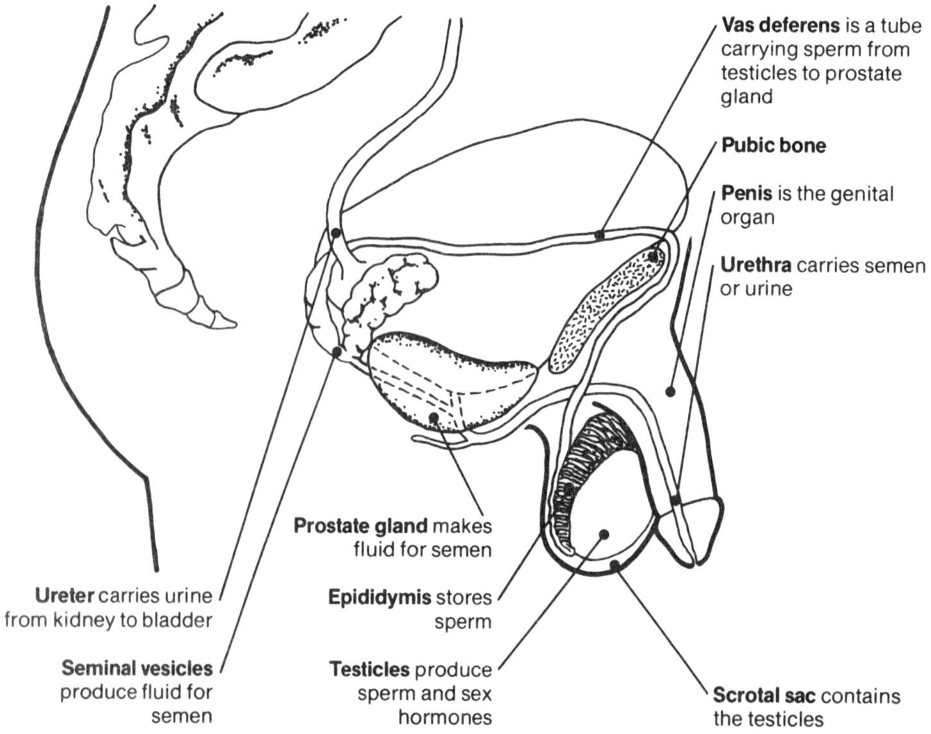

causes the testes to produce the sex hormone testosterone and the ovary, estrogen and progesterone.

The whole system of hormonal messages from the hypothalamus and the pituitary and feedback from the sex organs is called the reproductive hormonal axis or the HPO hormonal axis (Hypothalmic-Pituitary-Ovarian) and will be discussed in more detail in the section on the female menstrual cycle.

Of Sperm and Men

The sperm cell, or spermatozoon, the object of all the attention in the male, is one of the smallest cells of the human body. If the period of this sentence were a sphere, about 1000 sperm would fit around it.

Yet, despite sperm's diminutive size, they take about two-and-one-half months—72 days—from start to finish to be produced by the testes. Like a busy factory that works non-stop, the testes turn out millions of new sperm every day from their assembly line of tubules and ducts. The actual production of sperm is a complex series of cell divisions from a single "mother" cell called a stem cell. One line of cell-division descendants goes on to form the sperm, and the other line becomes companion cells that nurture and direct the maturation of its cousin sperm. There are millions of stem cells in the tubules of the testes.

It is beyond the scope of this book to describe in detail the process of cell division, called meiosis, which halves the regular 46 chromosomes found in all human cells to 23 chromosomes, enabling them to fuse with the 23 chromosomes from the woman to form a unique individual; or to detail the role of the nuturing Sertoli cells and the maturing process of spermatids to spermatozoa; nor is mastering the scientific data in this process necessary to understand fertility.

What you need to know is that sperm production is a fragile process. Interference during various critical times of sperm cell division can undermine the quality of sperm that is eventually ejaculated. "What is ejaculated today was actually starting to be formed three months ago," explains Dr. David deKretser, of Melbourne, Australia, a noted specialist in testicular function. "A fever or an illness that has happened in the last three months may lower the quality or the number of sperm ejaculated today."

Other factors that can lower sperm quality are high temperature, hot baths and drugs or toxic chemicals. Fortunately the effects are usually temporary and will only affect a certain batch of sperm. Certain chemicals or illnesses, however, can permanently damage the mother cells that initiate production, causing irreversible infertility.

The bulk of sperm-making action takes place in the seminiferous tubules, hundreds of fine, tightly coiled ducts, only one-fifth of a millimeter in diameter, arranged in compact strips in the testes. If stretched out, a coiled tubule would extend about 200 meters. After undergoing the cell division and formation from within the seminiferous tubules, the mature sperm, with a compact head and long whip-like tail, move out into another larger coiled duct called the epididymis. The epididymis lies on top of the testes and acts as a holding tank for the sperm. The name epididymis is derived from Greek meaning "upon the twins," the twins being the two testes. It is believed that sperm complete their maturation in the epididymis, taking 15 to 20 days, and new evidence is emerging that it is there that the sperm may be coated in a specific enzyme that helps them recognize and penetrate the egg. The sperm can stay in the epididymis holding tank for up to a month before they die.

At the same time the testicles are producing sperm, they are also producing the hormone testosterone, a powerful biological sex steroid that gives men their distinctive characteristics of facial and chest hair, larger bulk muscle, deeper voice and sexual drive. Well-functioning testes that are producing sperm and testosterone are about five centimetres in length and three centimetres in diameter—about the size of a small egg. Testicles much smaller than this may indicate a problem in sperm or testosterone production.

The whole testicular plant is housed in the leathery, muscular scrotum adapted to protect its charges and keep them at a constant temperature, a few degrees lower than body temperature. Formed inside the body during the growth of the fetus, the testes descend into the scrotum about two months before birth. It is common for the left testes to hang in the scrotum a bit lower than the right. Sperm production works best at a temperature of about 34 degrees Celsius and the scrotum maintains temperature control. In cold weather, it will pull the testicles in closer to the body to keep them warm. In hot weather it will relax, taking the testicles away from the body where they are more apt to be cooled. The scrotum's rich nerve supply makes it highly sensitive to pain or irritation, providing another way to protect the testes from harm.

Of course, the whole delivery of sperm to the proper site at the base of the woman's cervix depends on the man's ability to sustain an erection and achieve orgasm. Men who suffer from impotence or premature ejaculation as a result of psychological or physical factors will be effectively infertile even if their semen is teeming with good quality sperm. (Impotence and sexual dysfunction are discussed in more detail in Chapter 7.) A man may be unable to deposit sperm right at the cervix if the penis has an anatomical defect in which the opening of the urethra is not at the tip but somewhere along the shaft of the penis. The sperm instead will end up along the vaginal vault. This anomaly, called hypospadias, affects one in 600 to 1000 men to some degree and decreases the chance that a sperm will get to the egg even though sperm may be of excellent quality.

When the big moment arrives and sperm are launched on their journey to the egg, the sperm are released with force from the their holding tank in the epididymis. They are propelled by massive contractions along the long slender duct, the vas deferens, which goes up the back of testes. There the sperm are mixed with a milky white liquid, the seminal plasma, from the seminal vesicles. More lubricating fluid is expelled in contractions from the prostate gland and Cowper's gland adding to the semen's propulsive force. The mixture speeds down the urethra and out the penis, culminating in the ejaculation of between 40 million and 150 million madly swiming sperm.

All About Ova

In contrast to the tiny sperm, the human egg, or ovum, is the largest cell in the female body, about 30 times larger than the head of a sperm and almost visible to the naked eye. While men can make millions of new sperm each day from puberty until a ripe old age, women are born with a finite number of eggs, about 400,000.

The eggs lie quiescently in ovaries until puberty when they are kicked into production by hormones from the hypothalamus and the pituitary. From the time a woman first starts menstruating until she reaches menopause usually about four decades later, each month a group of eggs, called a chort, is selected to be stimulated. Under hormones pulsed by the pituitary, many eggs begin to grow but usually just one among them becomes dominant, ripens and is ovulated—many are called but one is chosen. The rest of the cohort die off, become "atretic" and the cycle starts again. A fertile woman ovulates between 350 to 450 eggs in the course of her reproductive lifetime.

The ovaries, like the testes, their biological equivalent, also manufacture the sex steroid that gives females their "female" characteristics. In the woman, that sex steroid is estrogen and it gives her softer, smoother skin, rounder physique and breasts. It also affects the quality and quantity of secretions from her cervix and the proliferation of the lining of the uterus. The ovary, as well, produces progesterone, which will be described in the discussion of the menstrual cycle.

The Female Reproductive System

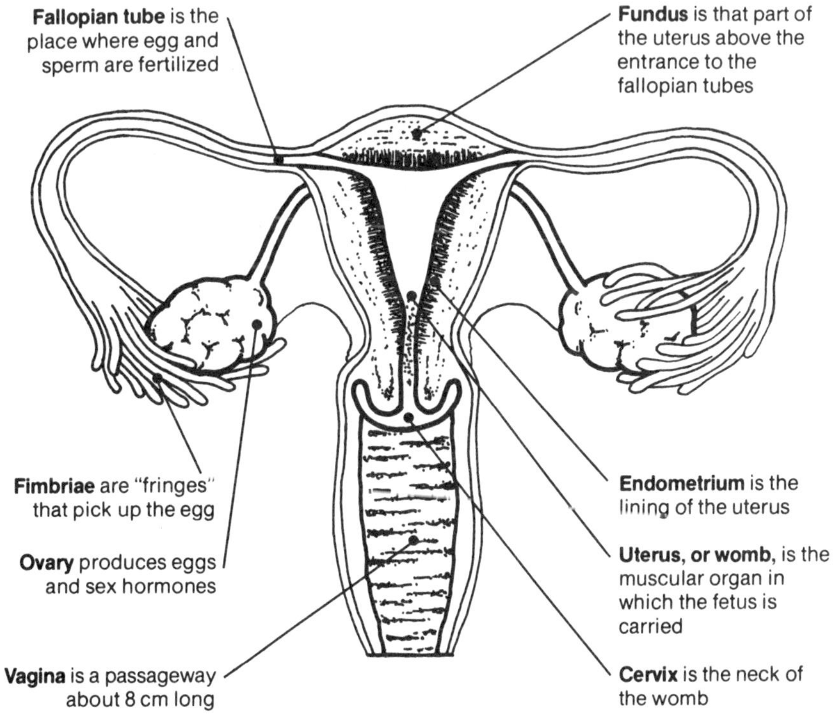

The Female Reproductive Organs

Many women, because their reproductive organs are hidden, have misconceptions or exaggerated images of their own reproductive anatomy, and so a brief description is warranted.

The vagina is the gateway from the woman's external genitalia to her internal reproductive organs. About 10 to 15 centimeters long, the vagina is muscular and ridged and produces a continuous flow of secretions to cleanse it and keep it slightly acidic to ward off infections.

At the top of the vagina is the cervix—like a fibrous donut with a tiny hole—the entrance into the womb. The cervix, which means neck, is really the bottom of the uterus. It is firm but flexible and will change positions in the vagina, moving higher or lower depending on the stage of the menstrual cycle. The small opening in the cervix is called the cervical os and leads to the cervical canal and then into the uterine cavity. The os is small and tight for most of the cycle, but during ovulation and then during menstruation it dilates slightly. During most of the monthly cycle, the os is impassable to sperm because of a thick, acidic, mucous plug. But when the egg is about to be released, the mucus becomes, wet, stringy, abundant and streams out of the os. This mucus around the cervix acts as a reservoir for sperm, which are able to live in it for a number of hours or even days, ascending in waves up to the tubes. The action of the sperm swimming through the streaming mucus is like salmon swimming upstream to spawn.

The uterus of a woman who has not had a child is surprisingly small, about the size and shape of a small pear lying upside down in the pelvis. It is firm and very muscular, pinky-red in color. During pregnancy it will grow 40 times in size, still retaining its thick muscular walls. Lining its inside is the endometrium, densely populated with tiny blood vessels that nourish and enrich the tissue. When the endometrium is ripe and full just before menstruation the walls touch each other.

Rising out of the top of the uterus are the two delicate but muscular fallopian tubes, sometimes called oviducts, about eight to 13 centimeters in length and the diameter of a pencil. The passageway inside the tube is very narrow, no larger than a thin pencil lead. Its thick walls have a velvety lining of regular ridges and hair-like cilia that beat the egg toward the uterus. At the outermost end of the fallopian tube are the flayed, trumpetlike fimbria, also covered in cilia, that sweep across the ovary.

The ovaries are white, about the size and shape of a walnut and are suspended on their own ligaments from the uterus. The ovaries look a bit like the inside of a pomegranate, its white outer jacket covering the follicles and eggs like the thin white pulp that covers the fruit's red, juicy seeds.

The Menstrual Cycle

For couples trying to conceive, the menstrual flow is the regular unhappy reminder that they have been unsuccessful again. The first spot of blood sends the woman spiralling into depression, taking her partner's hopes with her.

Despite what the menstrual cycle comes to signify over the months of trying, a couple will benefit from understanding its complex mechanisms to maximize their fertility or to comprehend just what might be wrong.

Typically, the length of a woman's cycle falls somewhere between 28 and 32 days. But a woman can have cycles longer and shorter than this, or cycle lengths that vary from month to month, and still be able to conceive. However, determining when she is fertile might be more difficult.

The menstrual cycle has two distinct phases, the follicular phase and the luteal phase in which four events take place: bleeding, egg maturation, ovulation, and corpus luteum formation. When the corpus luteum dies, the cycle starts over with bleeding. The first day of bleeding is always counted as day one of the cycle and the beginning of the follicular phase. It is marked by three to five days of bleeding, during which time the hormones secreted by the ovary (estrogen and progesterone) are at an all-time low. No longer supported by these nurturing hormones, the lining of the uterus is shed, aided by the fatty acid compounds prostaglandins. The prostaglandins are secreted from the uterine wall and cause contractions of the muscle and constriction of the tiny uterine blood vessels, inducing the endometrium to slough.

Near the end of the first five days of the cycle, the hypothalamus detects that estrogen and progesterone levels have been low in the blood. In regular pulses of gonadotropin releasing hormone (GnRH) it sends signals to the pituitary, commanding: "Get that ovary working!"

The pituitary responds to its "boss" by sending out follicle stimulating hormone (FSH) with a steady amount of LH to the ovaries. This is the start of egg selection and maturation and it starts at or about day six and lasts typically seven or eight days until ovulation. "Hey you guys, get production going we need an egg," the pituitary says to the ovaries with its continual FSH/LH message.

Many women wonder which ovary will mature and release an egg each month and whether there is a consistent pattern. Research shows that whether the right or the left ovary responds in any given natural cycle seems to be completely random, like flipping a coin and having the same chance of getting heads or tails each time. Some studies, however, suggest it may more often be the right ovary. But if there is only one functioning ovary it will be the one to ovulate each month.

The pituitary's FSH stimulates the group of follicles, or the cohort, in the ovary in which eggs begin to mature. The follicles begin to create estrogen, which sends a message on to the uterine lining, "Get ready, an embryo may be coming!" The rising level of estrogen in the blood gets back to the hypothalamus, which monitors it. "It's not enough," it tells the pituitary in its pulses of GnRH. The pituitary sends more FSH, which is absorbed by the follicles. As the estrogen level rises one follicle becomes dominant, the graafian follicle, and begins to absorb all the pituitary's FSH while the other cells die off. The rising estrogen continues to make the uterine lining thicken to accept any possible embryo, makes the cervical mucus increasingly wet and stringy and opens the cervical os. As the estrogen levels rise, the pituitary slows its release of FSH.

Ovulation

Ovulation occurs when the estrogen levels have sustained an all-time high for 48 hours. "Okay," says the hypothalamus in a pulse to the pituitary, "that's good enough. We're ready!" The pituitary, which has been sending out constant levels of LH, sends a sudden surge of LH ten times greater than before to the ovary to form the message, "Ovulate it!" The LH surge causes the wall of the follicle to burst and release the egg. The tiny sphere, surrounded by a protective cluster of so-called cumulus cells, falls through space.

The beating red fringe of the fallopian tube, the fimbria, themselves covered with beating cilia, catch and coax the egg and other cells into the tiny opening of the tubes. The action is like the tentacles of a sea anemone filtering food from the water.

Also, in response to the surge of LH, the cells of the follicle begin to make progesterone and send out the first bit of progesterone into the blood. Dr. Richard Blandau, a noted reproductive physiologist from the University of Washington in Seattle, believes this pre-ovulatory rise in progesterone causes the fallopian tubes to make rhythmic contractions that help move the egg along the velvety lining of the tube, aided by the sweeping of cilia. The egg will live for 24 hours there, during which time it must be fertilized by a sperm or it will die.

Luteal Phase

The luteal phase, which is the second phase, begins after ovulation when the ruptured follicle stimulated by the LH surge begins to produce progesterone in increasing amounts. The remaining cells in the burst follicle change (luteinize, meaning turn yellow) and become the corpus luteum (yellow body). The corpus luteum begins to pump out progesterone in earnest, sending it as a message to the uterus which causes the lining, or endometrium, to become more plush and secrete nutrients. (This phase is sometimes called the secretory phase.) The increasing progesterone causes the breasts to swell in anticipation of pregnancy, the cervical opening to shrink and the cervical mucus to change back to a white opaque state.

The LH from the pituitary begins to fall off, leaving the corpus luteum producing projesterone on its own. "Do I keep this up, or what?" it says, waiting for a signal that the egg has met with sperm and been fertilized.

If fertilization has occurred and the zygote begins dividing into an multi-cell embryo, it sends word back to the corpus luteum by way of a continual pulse of hormone called human chorionic gonadotropin (HCG). The HCG says to the corpus luteum: "Yes, I'm here—keep supporting me with progesterone." (HCG is the chemical that is detected in a pregnancy test.) Reassured, the corpus luteum happily turns out progesterone, supporting the pregnancy until the placenta takes over at about five to ten weeks.

If the ovulated egg fails to meet sperm, if the sperm can not penetrate the egg, if the embryo dies, or if the HCG message stops coming, the corpus luteum will abandon its job and halt production of progesterone.

The falling levels of progesterone, for many women, make their breasts lumpy, induce cravings for salt and sugar, and give the general ache and body tension called pre-menstrual tension, signalling impending menstruation. The decreasing progesterone also tells the uterus its services will not be needed. In a few days the endometrium breaks down, prostaglandins kick in causing contractions, bleeding begins and the cycle starts over.

Good Timing

Timing is crucial for conception to take place. Although sperm have been shown to live up to three days in fertile mucus, the egg is viable for only 12 to 24 hours after it is ovulated. That means there are, at most, 72 to 96 hours each month when sexual intercourse will put sperm in the right place at the right time.

Learning to predict when the woman will ovulate is often the most important step couples can take to become pregnant. In fact, a study in the early 1970s found that the vast majority of couples whose infertility was caused by poorly timed or infrequent intercourse were able to conceive when they learned how to chart their fertility and time lovemaking to coincide with ovulation.

As detailed in the last section, ovulation occurs roughly 14 days before the onset of menstrual bleeding. A woman with a 28-day cycle, therefore, ovulates about day 14, right in the middle of her cycle. But women who do not have 28-day cycles often mistakenly presume that they ovulate mid-cycle, too. A woman with a 36-day cycle might believe she ovulates around day 18. In fact, she is likely to ovulate about 14 days before she expects her period, or about day 22. Those four days can mean the difference between conceiving or not.

Counting back from the expected time of menstruation is imprecise. Couples can predict better when ovulation will occur if they observe and record daily the woman's subtle body changes during her menstrual cycle. An increase in her body temperature and an increase in wet, clear cervical mucus are two events that occur around the time of ovulation.

Basal Body Temperature Charts

The tracking of ovulation can be helped if the couple keeps a graph of the woman's resting temperature, a basal body temperature chart (BBT). The BBT chart is the daily record of the woman's temperature before she gets out of bed each morning. ("Basal" means the body is at rest.) It is based on the biological fact that a woman's average temperature at rest rises after she has ovulated because of progesterone entering her system. Progesterone resets the hypothalamus, like changing a thermostat, so that the body furnace burns slightly hotter.

A normally ovulating woman will have two distinct temperature levels before and after ovulation. The temperature in the follicular phase will generally be below 37 degrees Celsius. After ovulation it jumps at least three-tenths to a full degree higher. Basal temperature will vary from one woman to another, and can vary in the individual woman from month to month. But if the woman is ovulating, the average temperature will increase in the second half of the cycle.

Infertility specialists usually want to look at two or three months of charts to help them decide on further investigation and treatment. It helps to already have two or three charts to show them.

Along with recording body temperature, you should also note the type and quantity of cervical mucus and its changes throughout your cycle. When the mucus becomes abundant and feels wet and slippery, that is the time you are most fertile.

Doctors are most interested in the temperature changes and mucus to help their diagnosis, but for your own interest and understanding it is a good idea to also record other relevant factors such as mood, energy, sexual desire, ovulation or abdominal pain, backache, fluid retention, breast tenderness, food cravings and gastro-intestinal upsets such as constipation or diarrhea. By keeping a record of these symptoms for a few months you can learn the patterns of your own cycle and understand your body better.

Making a Chart

The first thing you need is a basal body thermometer. Standard thermometers do not have precise enough readings for BBTs. Specific BBT thermometers can be found in most drug stores and range in price from $5 for the most basic to $40 for digital ones. The cheapest thermometers are those with mercury scales reading degrees in either Fahrenheit or Celsius and can be used orally, vaginally or rectally.

Many couples prefer the new digital thermometers. Although they are more expensive, digital thermometers have a number of advantages over mercury column thermometers. They are very easy to read because the numbers are given directly and do not have to be translated from a scale. The readings are usually obtained faster, in less than two minutes as opposed to at least three minutes by mercury thermometer. The thermometer times the reading itself, beeping when it is ready to be removed and read. The digital thermometer does not need to be shaken down before using, nor is it subject to shatter as glass thermometers are. The only disadvantage of the digital thermometer other than its cost, is that it needs batteries. Manufacturers say the batteries will last for about three years of normal use and are easy to replace. The thermometers can be easily cleaned by occasionally washing them with soap and water or isopropyl alcohol.

Make taking your temperature as easy as possible to help yourself be consistent. Keep a pencil and paper by your bed so that you can write down the numbers, and later in the day when you are more awake plot them on the chart. Graphs for recording BBTs usually come with thermometers and they can also be bought from a pharmacist, but a sheet of graph paper is all you really need. Making your own BBT chart is often preferable if your cycles are particularly long and if you want space to comment on other observations. To make your own chart, copy the layout in the accompanying figure or design another that fits your needs, then make the number of copies you want on a photocopy machine.

Basal Body Temperature Chart

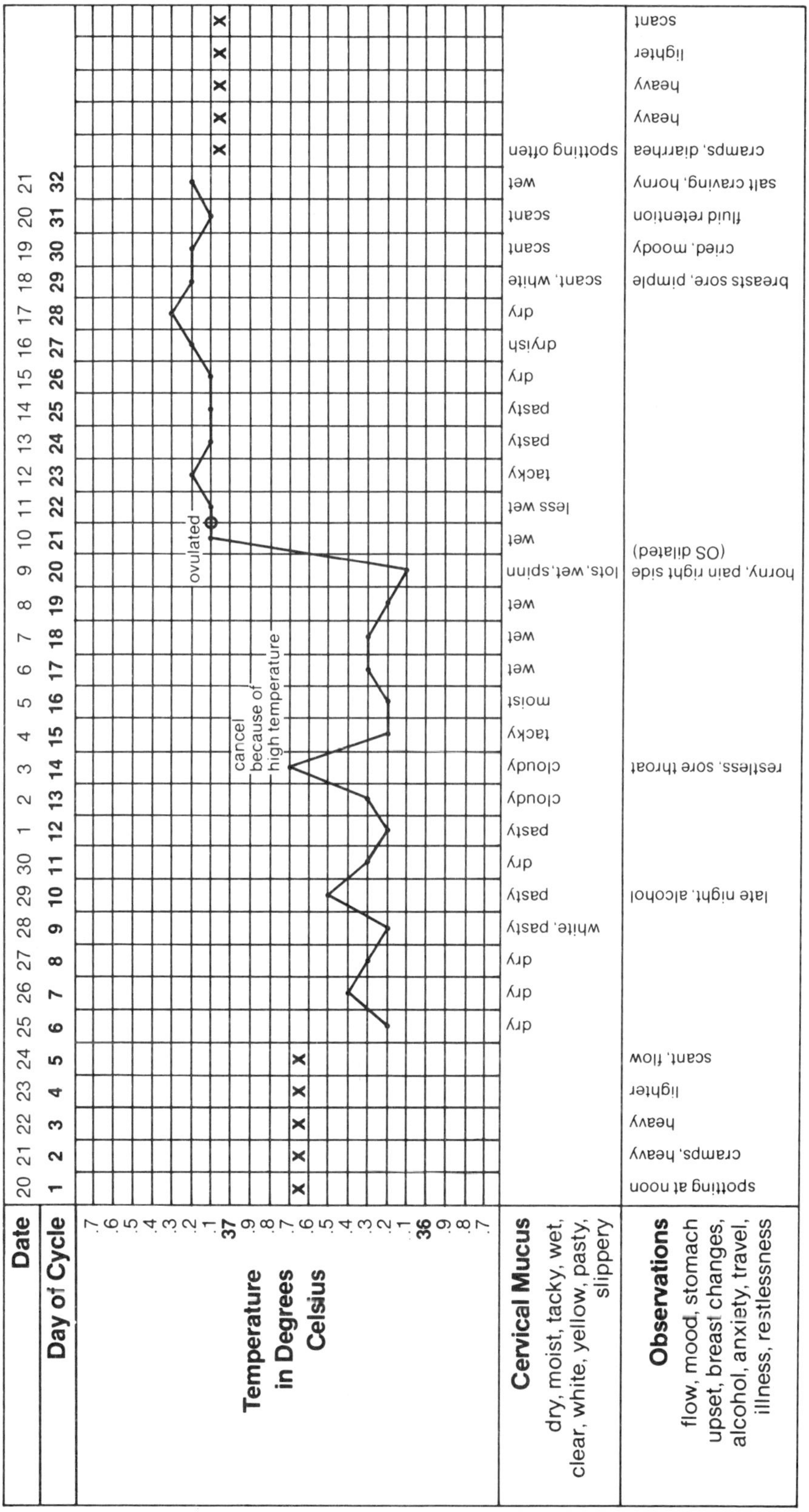

The basal temperature must be taken as close as possible to the same time each morning just before rising and after at least three hours of restful sleep. Also, be sure to take your temperature from the same part of the body each day as readings vary in different areas of the body. Any activity such as going to the bathroom, opening the curtains, answering the phone, or shaking down a thermometer is likely to raise your temperature. For this reason mercury column thermometers must be shaken down the night before, a requirement that some people find awkward, tedious or just plain bothersome.

Taking your temperature should be the first thing you do each morning while you are still lying in bed. When you roll over to turn off the alarm, grab the thermometer. If it is a weekend and you want to sleep in late, set your alarm for the time you usually get up, take your temperature then, and go back to sleep. If you do happen to sleep in and take your temperature later, note that on the graph.

Also note on the chart whether you had a late night, a restless sleep, a sore throat or any other illness or fever, whether you were travelling, drank alcohol, got up to let the cat out or to urinate in the middle of the night. All these things may affect your temperature reading, although not necessarily when you ovulate. Other things that can alter temperature are toothaches, sunburn, insomnia, alcohol or medications. Note those on the chart, too.

Mark the times that you have intercourse by circling the dot on the graph. To become pregnant it is important to make love just before and immediately after your have ovulated. Some women will find that their temperature dips slightly before it jumps up to the second level. That dip, if it occurs, is thought to indicate ovulation but most women do not see it. Where the temperature rises on your chart is likely evidence that you have ovulated. Try to bracket lovemaking around those times, about 24 to 36 hours before you expect your temperature to rise, and as soon as you know it is rising. Remember, when your temperature rises you have already ovulated so it is important to anticipate—based on the graphs of previous cycles—when ovulation will occur and act on it beforehand.

For the best sperm quality, doctors recommend that 36 to 48 hours pass between ejaculations, so intercourse need not be frequent when you think you may be ovulating. Pick your times, preferably the day before ovulation will occur and as soon as you know it is occurring.

The big problem with BBT charts is that they do not tell when you will ovulate, only that you already have. Some women take two or more days for their temperature to make the complete rise. By that time, 48 hours or more after ovulation, the egg is long gone. By keeping a few months of charts, however, you may begin to notice a pattern and can begin to anticipate when ovulation will occur, particularly if you note mucous changes along with temperature.

Cervical Mucus

Supplementing BBT charts with information about cervical mucus can also help you bracket the probable time of ovulation. The cervix has numerous glands that secrete fluid in varying amounts and consistencies according to the time of a woman's cycle. A woman can note the quantity and quality of the mucus as a discharge on her underwear or by inserting a finger in the vagina to take a sample. Following cervical mucous changes, often called the Billings method, has been championed by Australian doctors Evelyn and John Billings since the early 1970s. The Billings say noting cervical mucous changes alone, without taking body temperature, are enough to tell a woman when she is fertile.

For the first few days after menstruation has stopped some women may notice no discharge at all while others have a scant discharge of a whitish, or yellowish, color particularly when it has dried.

As ovulation approaches and estrogen levels are peaking, the discharge becomes more abundant, clear and wet. You may notice a slippery, wet feeling around the lips of your vagina, the vulva. You may also notice your vulva is fuller, plumper—this is also the effect of estrogen. About 12 to 24 hours before ovulation, mucus literally streams from the cervix. It is clear, elastic, slippery and will stretch between the thumb and index finger to a thin strand without breaking, a characteristic called "spinnbarkeit." Mucus with this property indicates the most fertile time in the cycle, the time to make love if you want to become pregnant. Some women may have wet mucus for three or more days, others for less than a day. It is the final day of wet mucus, what the Billings call "peak mucus," that is the most fertile.

After ovulation the mucus becomes creamier, white and less slippery. Some women have dry days after ovulation. By following your mucous patterns for a few cycles you will begin to understand your most fertile periods.

Cervical mucus changes should be noted throughout the day and added to the chart in the late afternoon and evening. Words you use to describe it are "dry, white, pasty, tacky, yellowish, clear, wet, abundant, 'spinn,' slippery." Also note if it has an unpleasant odor, a curdy texture or if it causes itching around your vulva or if you experience burning on urination as these are symptoms of a vaginal infection that should be treated. In noting your mucus, be careful not to confuse sperm and semen discharged from your vagina after lovemaking as a sign of a change in mucus. Do not note mucus when you are sexually aroused or just before making love as it will tend to be wetter and more abundant.

Women who have particularly long cycles may notice that they may have more than one time during the cycle when they have clear, wet and abundant mucus, but they may not be ovulating. Spinnbarkeit is triggered by estrogen achieving a certain level in the blood and women who have long follicular phases may have estrogen reach a peak more than once during the cycle. Note this wet mucus anyway, as it may help determine what is happening in your cycle.

The BBT Blues

I can never tell what's happening in my cycle. I take my temperature every morning, just like they tell me. But one day it's up here, next day it's down there. I'll have lots of mucus and I'll think: This is it! as I try to get it to stretch between my fingers. Then a week later I'll have lots of mucus again and I'll think, NO, maybe this is it! I dutifully chart it all down and make my husband make love on every little rise. I tell you, a couple of months of this and you're just ready to throw the whole damn thing against the wall!

It is very reassuring to have beautiful biphasic charts with clear jumps in mid-cycle and corresponding changes in the mucus. Ah, perfection! But unfortunately many women, particularly those who have long, irregular or frequently nonovulatory cycles, will find the BBTs an exercise in frustration that tells them little. And unfortunately that may happen to a significant number of women reading this book, particularly those with ovulation problems.

Women who tend to be restless sleepers or who get up a few times each night, women who are prone to anxiety or stress or whose job means they must travel often, particularly across time zones, will find it hard to get good-looking, biphasic BBT graphs. The frustration of not getting a comprehensible graph can add to any stress or anxiety you may already feel in trying to become pregnant.

Weird BBT graphs do not always mean you are not ovulating—they may mean that you just can't tell. But if you appear not to be ovulating, and the graph stays at one temperature without shifting higher, do not be dejected. You need to graph only two or three months to establish that ovulation, indeed, is not happening. After that, put the thermometer away. There is no need to do it month after month. The first graphs will help infertility specialists design your next course of treatment, usually fertility drugs.

The "BBT blues," or succumbing to the tyranny of daily temperature taking is extremely common. Some women take their temperature for years, unable to put the thermometer away on a vacation or simply to take a break. It becomes a ritual, a pious act each morning like the fertility rituals of old, that must be performed to conceive.

Charting BBTs can also become a sore point between couples. Since the job of taking BBTs often falls to the woman, the man can feel left out or at least unknowing about why his wife has a thermometer sticking out of her mouth every morning. Over the months, the woman can begin to resent that the BBT task is left to her. Both can feel uncomfortable that the woman, because she is keeping the graph, initiates lovemaking around the time the temperature is supposed to rise, regardless of how aroused each partner might feel.

I can always tell when it's time—she comes slinking over to me with this look: Honey? whether I am in the mood or not. Sometimes I think, gee, I wish I could get a stand-in.

Both men and women experience the difficulty of "sex on demand," the lack of romance. Both note the circled dots on the graph as a test of their sex life graded by the doctor. If ovulation passes without making love, you may even be tempted to add a few circled dots to the graph to make it look good to the medical staff—then you know you have the BBT blues.

There are a few things you can do to keep the blues at bay. First and foremost, try to make it a task you share together. Even something as simple as the man handing the woman the thermometer each morning can be an act of solidarity. What can work even better is the husband plotting the temperatures on the graph. That way he can share in the exercise, see the trend, anticipate lovemaking and learn more about his partner's fertility. Both the digital thermometer and mercury thermometer store the temperature until the next temperature is taken so that if you do not record the numbers in the morning, he can both read and plot them later in the day. The woman can add her comments and mucus observations to the chart numbers later, too.

Take regular vacations from BBTs, particularly when the blues start creeping in. When you always feel compelled to take your temperature and feel anxious if you miss a day, do yourself a favor and put the thermometer away—if just for a cycle. Remember that BBT charts are simply a tool to help you become pregnant. If the tool becomes the master and you its slave, and the stress it creates is greater than the stress it relieves, it is no longer helping. Get rid of it.

Ovulation Detection Kits

As a break from graphs and thermometers, or to supplement them, you can buy an ovulation detection kit from your local drugstore. The kits identify LH in a woman's urine and can be used to pinpoint the sharp increase in LH (the LH surge) that triggers ovulation about 24 hours later. In recent years, an increasing number of home ovulation detection kits have been coming on the market. The packaging and the set-up of the tests vary from brand to brand, but the principle is the same—a test of urine taken between 10:00 A.M. and 8:00 P.M. that identifies the LH surge by a color change. Some brand names that have been available longest are First Response by Tambrands, OvuSTICK by Monoclonal Antibodies, Inc. and OvuGen, by BioGenex Laboratories.

The actual procedure is complex biochemistry using principles of the immune system and antibodies. Antibodies are the body's warriors that identify an invader and hone in on it, attaching themselves to it so it can be destroyed. Usually the invader is a bacterium or virus, but in the early 1970s scientists learned how to custom-make antibodies, designed to specifically hunt for a single chemical, hormone, cell-line or compound and attach to it. They called these specialized antibodies monoclonal antibodies. A monoclonal antibody simply means a single, man-made antibody derived from one cell-line that identifies a single entity.

The ovulation detection kits use monoclonal antibodies that have been developed to seek out parts of the LH molecule excreted in the urine. Attached to one of the man-made antibodies for LH is a color-sensitive enzyme that can be made to turn blue to indicate the extent of LH in the urine. For example, the OvuSTICK, one of the first LH detection kits on the market, works this way: Picture the luteinizing hormone as a long molecule with a head and a tail. OvuSTICK's manufacturers have made two antibodies, one that attaches to the head and one to the tail of the LH molecule. The manufacturer coats the head antibody on the stick. The tail antibody is left floating free and attached to it is the color-sensitive enzyme. If the woman's urine contains LH its head will become stuck to the antibody on the stick, and its tail will pick up the tail antibody. Picture the result like a bristle brush, the individual bristles being the

LH molecule with an antibody on either end stuck on the stick. The more LH, the more bristles on the stick, and stuck to the end of the tail antibody, waving in the wind on the very end of the bristle is the color-sensitive enzyme.

The stick with the antibodies, enzyme and LH molecule attached is pulled out of solution, rinsed off and placed in a second solution that causes the enzyme to turn blue. The intensity of the blue on the stick correlates with the number of bristles on the stick, or the amount of LH in the original urine. So, if the woman is experiencing an LH surge and has lots of LH in her urine, more bristles appear on the stick and the blue on the stick will be more intense.

Whether the test kit involves reading blue liquid, blue on a stick, or blue on blotter paper, it always requires that you compare it to a standard or a reference color supplied by the company. The first tests required up to an hour before the results could be read, but now second generation tests, such as OvuQUICK, provide results within five minutes.

Despite the very complex theory behind them, the tests are actually quite easy to use, like following a recipe. Consumer studies have found that most people can perform the tests without difficulty, although concentration and careful timing are required.

The biggest problem with ovulation detection kits, however, is their expense. They cost between $40 to $60 each month. For women with unusually long or irregular cycles, the expense can be even greater. Women usually start testing three or four days before they are expected to ovulate and continue for three days after ovulation to confirm the surge. If the surge does not come before the test kit runs out, however, another kit will have to be purchased, doubling the expense for the month.

Some couples find it difficult to distinguish between the intensities of blue. In the case of Tambrand's First Response, in which the blue is liquid in a vial, the company recommends that if couples are having difficulty reading the color instead of throwing the day's test down the drain they should cap the vial and freeze it overnight. During the next day's test, the vial can be taken out of the freezer to warm up for a few minutes and can be compared with the current test to see if the intensity is increasing. The frozen vial should not be left at room temperature for more than 30 minutes, and the vials can be frozen for up to six days. Tambrands stresses, however, that a woman should always compare the color in the vials to the color chart to determine if she is having an LH surge.

Maximizing Fertility

Before seeking medical help and undergoing a barrage of medical tests, it makes sense to look at factors that may be undermining your fertility without your knowledge. A number of lifestyle factors and environmental conditions are known to decrease fertility, and by changing those you may improve your chances of conceiving without drug treatment or surgery.

Some of the suggestions below have not been scientifically proven in the strictest sense—controlled studies have not conclusively found that changing the habit automatically improves fertility. But all these have a theoretical basis and are strongly suspected of impairing fertility. If changing the factors does not improve your fertility, the changes certainly will not harm it and may improve your general health. Some of the factors such as smoking, drug use and excess weight apply equally to men and women, but their effects on each sex are different.

Improving Sperm Quality and Male Fertility

Here is a short list of suggestions that may help men improve fertility:
Avoid overheating the testicles.
Ejaculate at least once a month.
Keep body weight in a healthy range of normal.
Decrease alcohol intake.
Avoid marijuana.
Quit smoking.
Do not take anabolic steroids.
Avoid long-term exposure to pesticides and toxic chemicals.
Keep a healthy balance of stress and exercise.

Don't Overheat the Testicles

The delicate process of making sperm needs a cool environment—at least two or three degrees cooler than body temperature. When the temperature goes up, sperm are killed. Some doctors have gone as far as to suggest ice-cold baths for men with low sperm counts. Another doctor, New York urologist Adrian Zogniotti, has designed a special cotton jock strap called a testicular hypothermia device. The cotton jock cup is kept damp by a continuous drip of water carried in a reservoir at the waist. The damp cotton cools the testicles by evaporation. Zogniotti has reported that of 64 men who wore the device, 65 percent improved their sperm counts. The pregnancy rate for the group was 25 percent. In a more select group of patients with better sperm counts, a pregnancy rate of 53 percent resulted. No one has reported on the comfort of the device.

Most doctors, however, do not prescribe ice baths or water-cooled briefs but all would agree it is a good idea to avoid overheating the testicles. Frequent long hot baths, leisurely stints in a Jacuzzi, sauna, or steam bath, tight jeans or briefs that hold the testicles close to the body, working in a smelting plant or a place with raised temperatures—all have been shown to increase the temperature of the testes above 34 degrees Celsius and interfere with sperm production.

If you are concerned about testicle temperature you can try wearing boxer shorts or loose-fitting briefs, forego tight pants for a baggier fashion, and shower rather than soak in a hot bath. If you have a penchant for adversity, you can try regular cool baths. A study from Kansas in the mid-1970s found that some men were able to improve the number and motility of sperm in their semen by bathing regularly in cool water.

Ejaculate Monthly (At Least)

Sperm that stay in the epididymis longer than a month die and when mixed with new batches of sperm being produced will decrease the overall number of live, motile sperm in any given ejaculation. Looking under the microscope one can see the old, dead sperm in among the live ones. Since the chance of fertilizing an egg improves with the more live, swimming sperm there are to greet the egg, getting rid of dead sperm improves the odds.

This does not mean that men who are not having regular sexual relations risk lowering their fertility permanently. It simply means that couples who want a pregnancy should have sex more often than once a month to increase the number of live, motile sperm in the semen and improve the chances of fertilizing the egg. More frequent intercourse also means you are more apt to have sperm in the female reproductive tract around the window of ovulation. Doctors recommend that couples have sexual intercourse every other day during the middle portion of the cycle (from about day 10 to 18 for a woman with a 28-day cycle.)

Lose Weight

Excesses of anything are not good for fertility, and excess weight is no exception. Overweight men tend to have more problems with fertility than those of average weight. Body fat interferes with the hormonal axis between the hypothalamus, pituitary and testes because fat stores sex hormones, influencing the amount and potency of hormones circulating in the blood. Fat also converts the male hormones, called androgens (of which testosterone is one), into the female hormone estrogen, interfering with the message exchange between the testes and the pituitary. Fat's role in converting androgens into estrogens accounts for feminization of some obese men, such as the development of breast-like tissue, the softening of skin and lessening of facial hair growth. In the case of extremely fat men, girth can impede the full penetration of the penis into the woman's vagina.

Being underweight also appears to affect men's fertility by lowering libido (sexual desire) first. When body weight falls below 25 percent of normal weight, sperm production decreases. Eating a nutritious, healthy diet with daily intake from the four food groups is the best course to follow.

Drink Less Alcohol

Like excess weight, excess alcohol has been shown to decrease sperm quality. The problem with alcohol, however, is that no one knows how much is too much for an individual or what the minimum alcohol intake should be. However, men with severe alcoholism, when their liver has been compromised, have very poor sperm counts. How much alcohol to drink has to be left to the discretion of the individual. Professor Robert Winston of London, England, one of the U.K.'s leading infertility experts, suggests the daily upper limit of alcohol for men concerned about fertility should be no more than two or three pints of beer (five litres), a half bottle of wine or three shots of spirits.

The good of those actual limits is uncertain, but more than one doctor can recount non-scientific anecdotes of patients with poor sperm counts and years of childlessness who gave up alcohol and had a dramatic improvement in sperm counts three or four months later and a pregnancy soon after. Alcohol, besides lowering sperm counts, can also lower fertility by interfering with a man's ability to sustain an erection.

Quit Smoking

Cigarette smoking, too, has been linked to poor sperm counts, poor motility and abnormal sperm shape, but this is as hard to measure as the effect of alcohol consumption. Researchers in Sydney, Australia found that smokers had, on average, half the sperm counts of non-smokers. A 1988 paper co-authored by Greek and American researchers reported that when an electron microscope was used to examine a cross-section of sperm's whip-like tails significant defects in the tails' structures were discovered among men who smoked more than 20 cigarettes a day. Other research has shown increased percentage of abnormal sperm shapes among smokers.

In seemingly contrary findings, others have claimed they can find no significant evidence that smoking affects sperm quality. No one, however, has found that smoking *improves* sperm counts. Professor Winston states that quitting smoking is "the most important line of treatment" a man with a low sperm count can take. British urologist Timothy Hargreave from Edinburgh, Scotland, a noted specialist in male infertility, has studied smoking and male fertility. He says the data is always difficult to analyze for clear results because the effects may be subtle or occur after the period of study passes. "But I have been impressed, time and time again, by heavy smokers who had long-term infertility, who heed our advice, give up smoking and a year or two later a pregnancy seems to come along. These are clinical impressions and not scientific studies, but it seems to happen with regularity."

Don't Smoke Marijuana

Add cannabis and hashish to the list of substances you should avoid if you are worried about fertility. Marijuana seems to create poor-swimming sperm and impair general sperm production, and there is no rule to tell you how much is too much. "I tell my patients to try to get off all these substances," says Dr. Larry Lipshultz, andrologist at the Scott Department of Urology, at Baylor College in Houston, Texas, one of the leading U.S. centers for the study and treatment of male infertility.

Some prescription drugs, such as asulfadine for treatment of ulcerative colitis, may impair sperm production while the drug is being taken. Cancer drugs can render a man sterile. Ask your doctor if any medication you are taking interferes with your fertility.

Don't Take Anabolic Steroids

In recent years an increasing number of male athletes and weightlifters have been taking anabolic steroids. The steroids, which are derivatives of the male sex hormone testosterone, build muscle, but they also artificially cause testosterone levels in the blood to soar. The hypothalamus and pituitary mistakenly interpret the high testosterone to mean the testes are working too hard and slow down production. As a result, testes shrink in men who take steroids and their natural testosterone production falls. The number of men who have taken steroids who consult infertility clinics is increasing. Though doctors thought that once an athlete stopped taking steroids testes function would return, they are finding that some patients continue to have significant impairment of their hormonal axis and infertility long after they stop taking the drugs.

Avoid Long-Term Exposure to Chemicals and Pesticides

In 1977, a group of male workers in a pesticide plant in California casually noted that few of them had fathered children. That off-hand observation led to a medical investigation that showed those men who had worked at the plant longer than three years had significant impairment of their fertility—fewer than one million sperm per milliliter. Some of the men who had worked there the longest had no sperm at all. Only those who had worked at the plant for less than three months showed normal sperm counts of greater than 40 million per milliliter. The agricultural pesticide these men made was dibromochloropropane, or DBCP, a simple chemical compound made up of three carbon atoms, two bromines and a chlorine. Its effect was devastating and apparently permanent. Soon after that discovery other workers in other plants were found to be affected by the pesticide. Although it has now been banned from use, traces of it are still being found leaching into water in agricultural areas.

The greater lesson of DBCP was how silently and effectively chemicals can impair sperm production and reproductive health. What other chemicals impair fertility? Are we, like the Romans, poisoning ourselves? The answer is we do not know, but many people presume we must be. The difficulty in finding the answer comes because most individuals, unlike the workers in the DBCP plant, are exposed to a wide variety of chemicals and not a single agent. Farmers use numerous pesticides and herbicides; laboratory and industrial workers handle a range of compounds. Each one of us, day to day, may be exposed to some unknown toxin, so picking out cause and effect becomes practically impossible.

But some things we *do* know. Lead, much of it expelled into the air by cars burning leaded gasoline, is a proven reproductive hazard and there are significantly high levels of lead in urban areas and around some smelting industries. Ionizing radiation used in X rays and radiation treatment kills sperm-producing cells. Mercury poisoning can cause crippling neurological impairments, birth defects and reproductive problems, as we learned in the early 1970s from the sad legacies of the villagers of Minamata and Niigata in Japan. Another pesticide, chlordecone, has also been linked to sperm impairment. People who worked with vinyl chloride, the base of many hard plastic products, can suffer impotency, loss of libido and impaired sperm function. There is some evidence that exposure to paints, solvents, stains and varnishes can impair fertility. Men who work with manganese in steel manufacturing and other industries using alloys such as manufacturers of glass, ink, ceramics, paints, welding rods and rubber and wood preservatives may also have testicular impairment. In general, people working in agriculture, laboratories, oil, chemical and atomic industries, pulp and paper and textile work may be at an increased risk of reproductive problems because of the chemicals used in those jobs.

What can the individual do? Apart from working to improve the environment—using unleaded gasoline and lobbying for a crackdown on polluters, for example—there is little a man can do to protect himself or to even find out whether he has been affected. To find out if particular chemicals you are working with may have a detrimental effect on your fertility, consult the book *Reproductive Hazards of Industrial Chemicals*, by S.M. Barlow and F.M. Sullivan (1982, Academic Press), which lists all known data and studies on 48 industrial compounds suspected of impairing some aspect of reproduction.

Learn Coping Strategies for Stress; Don't Overdo Exercise

These two suggestions have been linked because both excess stress and excessive exercise appear to act on the hypothalamus, and the hypothalamus reacts by suppressing the hormonal axis. Under physically or emotionally stressful conditions the hypothalamus decreases its pulses to the pituitary, and the pituitary in turn stimulates the gonads less.

Studies of animals show that in cramped, confined or captive situations, such as a zoo, many animals stop reproducing. However, the effect of stress is difficult to prove by scientific experiment. Stress is defined as mental or physical tension, but stress to one man might be an elixir to another. Men in high-powered, stressful jobs often experience impotence and loss of libido. Studies of male runners or those who exercise compulsively, whose stress is physical, have also shown a suppressed hormonal axis and lessened libido, even with surprisingly little exercise. Dr. David Cumming, a University of Alberta gynecologist who specializes in exercise and reproduction, studied 15 previously sedentary men who started running 40 kilometers a week. After six months Cummings found that the men's blood levels of testosterone had fallen by 25 to 30 percent.

Each individual must assess his own life to determine whether stress may be a factor in his infertility. If you are running or exercising excessively it might be wise to cut down for a while. If you find work or life situations often make you tense, worried or preoccupied, bringing on a "fight or flight" response, try some of the relaxation techniques suggested in Chapter 1. Autogenics, a type of self-hypnosis, or creative visualization have helped people lower blood pressure and decrease feelings of stress. Regular, moderate exercise, such as walking or swimming, various forms of meditation, and relaxing breaks from routine are also effective in relieving stress.

Female Fertility

Many of the suggestions for helping men apply to women, with some variation. Here are some ways women can try to improve their fertility.
Learn coping strategies for stress.
Avoid excessive or compulsive exercise.
Maintain a healthy body weight, and a healthy diet.
Quit smoking.

Learn to Cope with Stress

There is much more evidence in women than in men that stress has an undermining effect on reproduction. But the topic is still controversial and no one has undisputed research that proves stress causes infertility.

Women have a reproductive barometer of stress—their menstrual periods. It is extremely common for women during a stressful time of their lives—a move, a job change, some type of upheaval—to stop menstruating for a few months, or to have irregular cycles. Wartime reports show the most convincing evidence of a link between menstrual irregularity and intense stress. Many women stopped getting their periods when their husbands left for war, and many nurses working in London during the Blitz also stopped menstruating. Up to 50 percent of women in concentration camps or internment camps stopped menstruating within two months of incarceration. As months went by, 90 percent of women in the camps stopped menstruating, probably because of malnutrition, but doctors say the initial disruptions in women's menstrual cycles were probably from emotional stress.

Sometimes the effects of stress are not outwardly apparent—a woman might menstruate regularly without ovulating. Hormone levels may decline, inhibiting implantation, and physical illness can also disrupt menstruation.

As in men, the root seems to be the hypothalamus that monitors the various stimuli and conditions affecting a person and adapts the body to meet them. Numerous experiments show that when the hypothalamus perceives that the body is under assault, it responds by shutting down or diminishing the activity of the hormonal axis. It is not known how the hypothalamus perceives the stress or what the mechanism is.

The decrease of fertility during times of psychological stress, even if it cannot be proved, is assumed to be to an evolutionary adaptation: the body naturally becomes less fertile when it perceives conditions for reproduction as being less than ideal. In one of many animal experiments for stress and fertility, mice were placed in an attractive outdoor enclosure, were given lots of food and allowed to breed freely. The population grew to a certain level and then grew no further. The females had fewer babies—they had somehow become less fertile. Scientists do not know whether the females, the males or combined factors led to the lowered birth rate of the mice. How did the mice know that more babies in their small cage would be detrimental to the entire population? Did the hypothalamus do silent census taking? Did it clue in on increased noise and smell? Somehow the animals were able to sense that more births would be detrimental to themselves and their environment. Many such experiments have similar results.

How do animal experiments relate to human stress and infertility? What happens, for example, to a woman who tends to feel stressed? Anxiety is a vestige of the primitive "fight or flight" response. In response to some perceived threat, whether or not it is real, the pulse quickens, breathing becomes shallow, the gut tightens. As a result, feelings of fear grow stronger, and in turn, the response becomes more pronounced. Why this cycle starts is anyone's guess and why some people tend to be more anxious is also difficult to answer. Chemical reactions in the body may be a factor. The hypothalamus, monitoring the anxiety, assumes danger is near and turns down the systems that are not needed immediately to concentrate on what it perceives as the immediate threat. Reproduction is one of the first systems to be put on hold until the danger has passed. But in the case of a person who is chronically anxious, the threat is continual and release never comes.

A few decades ago doctors assumed about 40 to 50 percent of infertility was caused by emotional or psychological reasons. Now it is generally felt that perhaps five to 10 percent of infertility may be stress-related. The lack of hard evidence of how stress undermines reproduction has given rise to a variety of theories—that a woman does not conceive because unconsciously she does not want a child, or that all she has to do is relax. Any theory put forward can be backed up with anecdotes—a couple conceiving after adopting a child is a favorite—but these stories are not conclusive. Studies have not found that couples who adopt conceive with any greater frequency than other infertile couples. The truth is we do not know how much stress causes infertility or how much the infertility causes the stress. Friends and family wanting to be helpful will tell infertile couples time and again "just relax and you'll get pregnant." While there may be a kernel of truth in that advice, trying to relax can increase tension. The idea conjures up the ridiculous image of someone lying awake at night fretting, "I must relax, I must relax."

However, the idea of learning how to handle stress should not be rejected. Try to look at your situation in a different light. Explore your own feelings and your own perception of stress in your life and see what you can learn. What do you think happens to those few celebrated couples who gave up trying or adopted a baby and soon became pregnant? Imagine how you would feel if, after years of trying to have a baby, you finally said "Okay, I've had it. No more trying!" What would your chief feelings be? Relief? Peace at last? Resolution? Lifting of depression?

What would you feel if you finally adopted a baby? Joy of being a parent? Validation of your role as mother and a woman? Meaning to your life?

If you think stress might be a factor in your infertility, examine how the release of that stress would make you feel. Then look for ways to bring those feelings into your life, now, without waiting until you give up or adopt. If you imagine yourself feeling peace, then look for ways to feel peace now—is it walking in the park, painting, meditating, accepting your limitations? If you think having a baby would give meaning to your life, look for things to do now that are meaningful. The answers are different for each individual. Only you know what is right for you. Explore it and try it.

One woman described her conflicting feelings this way.

> *There can be a tendency to feel that this childless period of life is nothing more than a painful waiting time and each month a cruel endurance test. Finding value in your life* as it is *is essential to your physical and mental health. This may seem obvious, but an unhealthy idea can creep in: perhaps if I'm unhappy enough, I will complete this penance and be rewarded with a pregnancy!*

Many health and psychology books are available that offer suggestions for coping strategies, relaxation techniques and the emotional aspects of illness. Books by Norman Cousins and Dr. Bernie Siegel detail their work with cancer patients and others with terminal illnesses. I am not suggesting that psychological techniques can cure your infertility, but you may gain insight into how to relieve stress from writers with some expertise.

One final suggestion—try to cut down on coffee and other stimulants such as caffeine-rich soft drinks, diet products or chocolates, particularly if you tend to be high-strung to begin with. Studies have shown that caffeine exaggerates feelings of anxiety and tension, quickens heartbeat and may contribute to the perpetuation of the fight or flight responses.

Avoid Excessive Exercise

Strenuous amounts of exercise are a physical, rather than an emotional, stress, but the result seems to be the same. The hypothalamus, perhaps assuming that the situation is not conducive to a successful pregnancy, suppresses the hormonal axis. The hypothalamus probably reduces the frequency of the pulses of GnRH it sends to the pituitary, and the pituitary in turn does not stimulate the ovaries to the same extent. The result can be irregular periods, anovulatory cycles (meaning no egg is released) and luteal phase deficiencies when the second half of the cycle is either too short or there is not sufficient development of the endometrium.

According to Dr. David Cummings, authority on exercise and reproduction from the University of Alberta in Edmonton, it is now generally accepted that vigorous exercise and endurance training are associated with menstrual problems and infertility and may delay the start of menstruation in adolescent girls. How common the problem is and how long its effects last are still being debated.

Some studies of serious runners show that as many as 10 to 20 percent have irregular periods and 4 to 6 percent may stop menstruating for longer than six months—a condition called athletic amenorrhea. Dr. Jerilynn Prior, an endocrinologist at the University of British Columbia, does not agree that exercise *alone* can halt menstrual periods for long periods of time in healthy women. In her studies of exercising women she found that only women who had other factors such as low body weight or stress in addition to strenuous exercise lost their menstrual periods.

However Prior did find that exercise caused subtle changes to the menstrual cycle that could interfere with a woman's fertility. In one of Prior's studies of the 48 basal temperature graphs of 14 women training for a marathon, two-thirds had abnormal cycles with no temperature rises, which indicate no ovulation, or else temperature rises lasting less than 10 days, indicating a short or inadequate luteal phase. Luteal phase abnormalities—which could interfere with the implantation of the embryo—appear to be the most common type of fertility problem induced by exercise. But Prior says she believes women who have long-term fertility problems associated with exercise also have another factor contributing to the problem, such as weight loss, stress or being under age 25. Prior says in healthy women of a healthy weight, increased exercise may produce a temporary disruption of the cycle but in a cycle or two the body will adapt to the increased level and begin to ovulate normally.

At the center of the debate over exercise and fertility is why it should occur. Some professionals speculate that exercise-induced infertility may be caused by an increase in endorphins and beta-endorphins circulating in the blood during exercise. Others believe excessive exercise and abnormal body weights may interfere with the menstrual cycle because the person's ratio of body fat is reduced. Women who exercise vigorously tend to have a leaner body composition, often with less than 20 percent body fat and this has the potential to interfere with reproduction.

Studies trying to determine how and why exercise decreases fertility are conflicting. A study of non-menstruating ballernias shows that those who stopped dancing because of injury had their menstrual periods return without any weight gain, suggesting that it was the strenuous activity itself that caused the cessation of periods. Other studies have confirmed that premise: when exercise is reduced, normal menstrual cycles return.

However, other studies, particularly by Dr. Rose Frisch, have shown that the body must have a minimum threshold of body fat in order for the menstrual cycle to start and if, through exercise or diet, the body fat falls below the threshold reproductive capability is compromised.

In all probability, it is a combination of exercise, body fat and psychological aspects that undermines fertility. "Exercise and weight are interrelated," Cummings said. "You can't take one component away from the other."

Whatever is happening, the advice still stands that if you are trying to get pregnant and you attend aerobics class every day or run more than 40 kilometers a week, experiment with less exercise. Go for a long walk in the time you would usually run.

Maintain a Healthy Diet

It is estimated that 50,000 to 80,000 calories are required for a woman's body to nurture a tiny embryo to become an infant. A further 500 to 1000 calories a day are needed to breast feed after the baby is born. Rose Frisch and others have speculated that in ancient times when there were frequent periods of famine and a variable food supply, a woman who became pregnant without having enough body fat as fuel to support the pregnancy risked her own life and that of her infant. As a result, evolution favored those women whose reproductive systems turned off when their body weight fell and reproduction became unsafe.

Today it is generally accepted that women need a minimum of 22 percent body fat to have normal menstrual cycles. Frisch found the average body fat for normal menstruating women in the United States was 28 percent.

Experts presume the hypothalamus suppresses the system when body weight falls, but they do not know what message registers to instruct the system to turn down. Frisch and others speculate that the signal to the hypothalamus might be changes in the body's temperature control or metabolic rate as well as the changes in estrogen that result when body fat is lost. As was mentioned in the section on male body weight, body fat stores the sex hormones and converts male hormones to estrogen. Women with less body fat will have less estrogen being converted.

Women who are consistently underweight or who diet frequently can have menstrual problems and decreased fertility. Usually when they regain the weight, regular menstruation returns.

Eating disorders cannot be ignored in relation to fertility, especially since anorexia nervosa and bulimia are at all-time highs in Western countries. An estimated 25 percent of college women have bulimic tendencies—binging on food and then purging themselves either by diet, laxatives or vomiting. Anorexia, the loss of appetite or rigid control of the intake of food, typically strikes younger women, but there is increasing evidence that excessive exercise is analogous to anorexia and that both are driven by a distorted body image and a fear of being fat.

In bulimia, the woman is usually driven to be in control. Even if her body weight does not fall below normal, the abnormal nutritional intake and the effects of purging can be enough to affect ovulation and fertility. Purging can disrupt the balance of electrolytes such as potassium in the body and can lead to malnutrition, even if the body weight is about normal.

If you are trying to become pregnant and you know that you have an eating disorder, seek help and try to eat a balanced, nutritious diet every day. Eat a selection of foods from the four food groups: meats and fish, dairy products, fruits and vegetables, grains and cereals. The eating disorders and the weight loss should be addressed before you go on any fertility treatments such as ovulation induction.

Obesity

Women who are obese often have problems with fertility and it is assumed this has to do with abnormal estrogen levels caused by the excess fat. Just like women who are underweight, women who are overweight can have more difficult pregnancies, making both the mother and the fetus at risk for complications or death.

Grossly overweight women trying to get pregnant should endeavor to lose weight, however difficult this might be. Some doctors will not treat obese women with fertility drugs or operate on them unless they lose weight because of the danger to the health of the woman and the fetus should a pregnancy result.

Quit Smoking

Studies have shown that smoking undermines egg production, disrupts the menstrual cycle and compromises the ability of the fallopian tube to move the egg from the ovary to the uterus. Not only that, but women who do get pregnant and continue to smoke have a much greater likelihood of miscarriage, premature birth, fetal injury or babies of low birth weight.

There is no good reason to smoke, and women who want to get pregnant can add decreased fertility to their list of convincing reasons to stop.

Coffee and caffeinated beverages, too, have been shown in studies to decrease women's fertility, so you are wise to drink less of them. Other drugs such as sleeping pills, tranquillizers or anti-depressants can interfere with ovulation, conception and pregnancy.

Protecting Your Fertility for the Future

Precautions should be taken to ensure that your fertility does not become worse in the years ahead. Nothing can be done about aging, which naturally decreases fertility, but you can protect yourself from sexually transmitted diseases and infection, leading causes of infertility.

Beware of STDs

Sexually transmitted diseases (STDs), particularly chlamydia and gonorrhea, can cause havoc with the reproductive organs of both men and women. Often the infections are silent. Men may notice a discharge from their penis or a pain on urination, but women can have no symptoms at all. Chlamydia, a microscopic organism, is the worst cause of silent infections that badly scar fallopian tubes in women and block ducts in the genital tract of men.

To avoid STDs you should limit your sex partners, be monogamous and use condoms whenever you are with a new partner or are unsure whether your partner is being monogamous. Men and women alike should learn the signs and symptoms of infections in their genital tracts and get immediate treatment.

Men who notice any inflammation of ducts in their genital tract, a drip, pain or burning on urination should go to the doctor.

Women should watch out for unusual vaginal discharges, odors or pain on urination. If you do not have a monogamous relationship you should periodically be tested for chlamydia and gonorrhea.

Women should also learn the signs of pelvic inflammatory disease (PID). PID is caused when germs and STD organisms spread into the uterus, tubes and even into the pelvic cavity. PID can follow an STD infection, childbirth, IUD use, abortion or other operations that introduce organisms into the pelvic cavity. It can be mild or severe, chronic or acute. Symptoms include all or any of the following: abdominal pain or tenderness, fever, chills, low back pain, pain during intercourse, abnormal discharge, bleeding between periods or after intercourse, urinary frequency or urgency, pain with urination or bowel movements, fatigue or weakness, cramping or rigidity of the abdomen muscles, swelling of the lymph nodes, nausea, vomiting or rapid pulse.

Do Not Ingest Sperm

Men and women who practice oral sex should not swallow semen. The evidence is not yet firm, but an increasing number of doctors working in immunologic infertility are concerned that women taking semen into their digestive tract may form antibodies to their partners' sperm. The antibodies may later attack and kill sperm when they are in the cervical canal. The effect may be like being vaccinated or inoculated. Indeed, animal experiments have shown that if mice are injected with sperm, as one would inject a vaccine, the animal will create antibodies to the sperm. Women should also not take semen into their rectum as the cells along its passage are also capable of mounting an antibody response.

Dr. Richard Bronson of New York, a leading expert in immunological infertility says, "We don't know yet whether this is a real concern, but to be prudent it is wise to say avoid ingesting sperm."

It is assumed that the amount of antibody response is dose dependent, meaning the more frequently the female is innoculated, the more antibodies she will create.

Men, too, should avoid ingesting their own sperm, as through oral-genital sex following intercourse. The man can make antibodies to his own sperm if he is exposed to them, causing his antibodies to coat his sperm or even kill them before they leave his body.

CHAPTER 4
Seeking Medical Help

When a couple has been trying to conceive for 12 months without contraception and without success, they should turn to specialized medical help.

In fact, many doctors have used that "year of trying" as a strict gatepost, telling couples who have not done their year's "time" to go away and come back when they have. The reason: perfectly fertile couples, having regular but untimed intercourse, can take at least a year to conceive naturally. Busy professionals may take even longer, simply by failing to have sex during ovulation, perhaps because of an out-of-town assignment or a late night of work.

The problem is not entirely bad timing, of course. Over the years the medical profession has learned that a couple's chances of pregnancy generally fall along a curve. In the first month of trying, pregnancy results for only 20 percent of couples; after six months, 60 percent; at the end of a year 80 to 85 percent will be successful. The remaining 15 to 20 percent of couples are those who may have a fertility problem.

Being told to return in a year can be extremely frustrating for couples eager to conceive immediately. Each month that goes by without a pregnancy leaves one less month to be successful. For couples whose reproductive life is winding down, those remaining months are like the last grains of sand dripping through an hour glass. There is the urgent feeling: "We haven't got time to waste."

Proving at least one year's duration of infertility is important. There is no point in undergoing a barrage of tests and investigations, some of which may be painful, awkward, embarrassing or stressful, when a couple is fertile but has had bad luck and bad timing.

All that said, however, many specialists are less rigid about couples proving at least a year's infertility. Some believe that if a couple is truly concerned about their fertility, particularly if they are over 30, that is reason enough to seek help. Less than a year is also warranted if the couple has been timing intercourse to ovulation for six months or if one of the partners' medical history suggests a problem, such as the woman having chronically infrequent or irregular menstruation or pelvic inflammatory disease.

Some doctors feel that if a man is worried about his fertility, and requests semen analysis, no matter how much time has passed, he should be given it because the test is non-invasive, inexpensive and effective. "We shouldn't turn a man away if he has finally got up his nerve to be tested," Dr. Larry Lipschultz, urologist at the noted Baylor College of Medicine in Houston, said at a 1988 American Fertility Society seminar on male infertility. "When a male patient comes in, regardless of how long the duration of infertility, he should be evaluated and given an answer."

Besides, it is extremely common these days, particularly in Canada, Australia and Britain, for couples to have to wait a number of months for a consultation with an infertility specialist. By the time they are sitting in the specialist's office, the recommended year of infertility may have long passed even if the couple's concern started a number of months earlier. Couples in this situation should come to the specialist's office with a few months of BBT graphs and menstrual patterns already logged so they can immediately start into further investigation and possible treatment.

Some couples, however, let two or three years of infertility pass without seeking help, either because they are afraid they may find out something is wrong or because they are optimistic that eventually pregnancy will occur. These couples would benefit from seeking help earlier.

Most infertility investigations start with the woman's family doctor or personal gynecologist. Even if the man is eventually the one found to have a fertility problem, it is usually the woman who becomes concerned first and introduces the subject in discussion with her own doctor. Studies have shown that men in their reproductive years seldom, if ever, consult a doctor. But women have usually established a long-term relationship with a doctor they trust. That age-old pattern is the reason the majority of infertility specialists have been trained in obstetrics and gynecology, even though close to 40 percent of infertility is diagnosed in the male partner.

No matter whether you start with your family doctor or your gynecologist, as soon as you bring up the concern of infertility, you should then be treated as a couple. Infertility is not just a woman's problem, it is a couple's problem. It is not acceptable for the woman to go through months of investigation and treatment without the man first having a semen analysis and being assessed by a doctor.

The doctor must have information on both of you so that you can be properly treated. If the man has a slightly low sperm count but the woman is completely normal, the treatment will be different than if the same man had a partner with a mild ovulation problem. The couple must been seen as a whole.

Most doctors now know that when a woman begins talking about infertility, a semen test should be ordered for the man along with recording the woman's relevant history. The doctor, if she is a family physician, will also ask to examine the man and record his medical history. A gynecologist will usually refer the man to a urologist or andrologist for evaluation and history.

Finding an Infertility Specialist

When should you look beyond your family doctor or personal gynecologist for medical help for your infertility? The 1988 study of infertility by the United States Office of Technology Assessment reported that almost 80 percent of all couples get their basic infertility evaluation and treatment from their family doctor or general gynecologist. Those doctors assess whether the woman is ovulating and her tubes are open, help couples time intercourse and perhaps try a short course of the fertility drug clomiphene citrate.

However, couples should seek an infertility specialist when their infertility proves to be more complex, of longer duration than two years, or when the first line of treatment has not worked after six to nine months of trying.

An infertility specialist is a doctor who devotes the majority of practice to problems of fertility and the reproductive process, and has trained beyond the usual four-year residency for obstetrics and gynecology to specialize in an area of infertility. Reproductive endocrinology, the study of the hormone control of reproduction, has been a certified subspecialty of obstetrics and gynecology in the United States since 1974. Doctors who wish to specialize in this area can take a two-year fellowship following the regular four years of their ob/gyn training and then pass a "board" or examination. Reproductive surgeons must also be extensively trained beyond regular obstetrics and gynecology in the delicate techniques needed to operate on the fallopian tubes, ovaries and uterus—usually by training under a specialized surgeon. In the last decade a new subspecialty has emerged—the field of andrology, which is devoted to the study of male hormones, sperm production and function.

In general, doctors and infertility advocates agree couples should be referred to an infertility specialist when:

1. Six to nine months of fertility drug therapy for ovulation is not effective.
2. More advanced drug therapy, such as injections of fertility drugs, are required.
3. Reproductive surgery is required for any or all of the fallopian tubes, ovaries, or uterus or when surgery for endometriosis is required.
4. The infertility points to a problem of antibodies, immunological interactions between the man and woman, poor cervical mucus or endometriosis.
5. The woman has had two or more miscarriages.
6. The man has a sperm abnormality.

Obstetrics and Infertility

Some infertility specialists continue to practice obstetrics, managing and delivering pregnant patients while they are treating infertile patients. While this arrangement can make medical sense, patients who are having difficulty conceiving will attest that it makes an unpleasant combination from the patient's point of view.

> *I used to hate sitting in his waiting room, surrounded by pregnant women after I had lost one pregnancy and had been trying for three years. Once, after I'd been waiting for about two months to see him, I arrived at his office only to be told my appointment was cancelled because of a delivery. You don't know how awful that is, when every month*

seems so important, to know that you might not get your chance this month because another woman is having a baby. It just intensified my feelings of life being unfair. I could hardly drive myself home I was crying so hard.

Some doctors who do continue to practice obstetrics have different office hours for their fertile and infertile patients to minimize the discomfort the infertile patients feel. However, deliveries can still cause appointments to be postponed.

Seek the Best

It is important to seek out the best available medical help to deal with your problem. Countless numbers of couples have spent years with well-meaning doctors who unfortunately did not have the required skills to help difficult cases of infertility.

When we first knew we must have a problem we went to my gynecologist—who was also my mother's gynecologist and had even delivered me. I had always really liked him. He did the regular work up. I had a really difficult ovulation problem. For five years he tried first one thing and then another and nothing happened. My husband and I became increasingly agitated but we felt uncomfortable asking for a referral. We kept hoping something would work. I think the doctor, too, felt he really wanted to help us and didn't want to disappoint us or the family by passing us on to someone else. We might have gone on like that, if the doctor hadn't retired, giving us both a way out. When we finally got to see an infertility specialist in the city, I could see him look at my pages of charts and failed treatments, biting his lip. He didn't say anything, but I was sure he was thinking, "oh, dear." In a couple of months of treatment by the infertility specialist, I got pregnant.

Asking for a referral to another doctor, or for charts and tests to be sent to a new doctor, can be awkward or uncomfortable. Patients often feel they owe allegiance to their original doctor. The doctor-patient relationship can be very personal, with patients divulging a great deal of intimate information into the doctor's trust. Breaking that arrangement can be hard.

Remember, however, that it is a contractual arrangement; the doctor is being paid for services. You do not need to feel disloyal if you choose to seek specialized help or if you are not getting the best treatment possible. There is no need to be hostile or accusing of the doctor, but it is perfectly legitimate to say: "I feel my infertility may benefit from seeing an infertility specialist. Would you be able to refer me to one with knowledge of my type of problem?" You might want to continue consulting your family doctor for other medical needs.

Most good doctors are happy to fulfil this kind of request or may even be first to suggest you see one of their colleagues when the problem is beyond their expertise. If you have been referred to a specialist by your family physician but are not happy with the specialist's manner, knowledge or treatment, return to your family doctor for another referral and request your charts from the original specialist so that repetition of tests can be avoided.

Finding a doctor whose reputation is good, whom you trust and to whom you relate well is important. There is a distinction, however, between finding a good specialist and compulsive "doctor shopping." Do not jump doctors every time you hear of someone new or when your present doctor's suggested treatment fails. A lack of success does not mean the care is bad, and frequent changing of doctors hurts your treatment and continuity of care. Patients can often be their own worst enemies when they change doctors on the slightest provocation and do not allow a relationship to develop or a treatment enough time to succeed. If the relationship is good, if the doctor is recommended, stick with it at least until you have definite evidence you would be better off elsewhere.

Help in finding a good infertility specialist can also come from infertility support groups in your area. You can benefit from other group members' experiences with doctors and find the names of good specialists who can treat your problem. In the United States the nationwide infertility support group, Resolve, has lists of infertility specialists by region.

A Team Approach

Increasingly, a team approach to investigate and treat infertility is being adopted by the medical profession, particularly in large cities and at university-linked medical centers. A team offers the advantage of having a broad range of experts in infertility for both women and men in the same spot, as well as having support staff such as counsellors, specialized nurses and technicians.

An infertility team usually consists of: gynecologist(s) specializing in reproductive endocrinology, the hormone control of the reproductive process; gynecologist(s) specializing in reproductive surgery (in many infertility practices one gynecologist might do both hormone work and surgery); and urologist(s) and/or andrologist(s) specializing in male reproductive tract surgery and male reproductive hormones.

Larger infertility clinics and programs might also have, along with the above, some or all of the following: medical personnel to offer assisted reproductive technologies including artificial insemination, in vitro fertilization (IVF) and gamete intrafallopian tube transfer (GIFT) or variations of IVF and GIFT (some centres freeze embryos and operate a donor egg program); psychiatrist(s), or psychologist(s) to help with the stress of infertility; genetic counsellor(s) to examine family histories and screen early pregnancies to avoid genetic abnormalities in offspring; and Ph.D. scientists doing research to support and advance the clinical infertility treatment being offered.

Small Town Blues

If you live in a small town or rural area at a distance from major centers with infertility services, you might feel exceedingly frustrated that where you live contributes to the continuation of your infertility. Treatment can be costly and time consuming, entailing a long car trip, full days off work and hotel bills in the city.

The lack of anonymity in a small town can also be difficult for couples if much of their infertility work-up is being carried on there.

> *You take the sperm sample into the lab and you know the girl at the front desk and you know the technician and they say "Oh, what's this?" And you went to school with the X-ray technician who is doing your hysterosalpingogram. The whole thing can be hard to handle.*

Even couples who live in major cities might feel that they are in the wrong place at the wrong time when they hear about treatments being tried in distant cities or other countries.

> *I hate reading about infertility breakthroughs in the newspaper when it's across the ocean or miles away. Instead of being excited I find myself thinking, well, there's another one we can't do or by the time it finally comes here I'll be too old to do it. Sometimes I get so angry when I think that maybe if I didn't live here and I lived somewhere else, I might be able to have a child.*

Living in a small town does not need to be all bleak. Most infertility specialists recognize the special problems that face couples who live at a distance from the clinics. They understand the strains of traveling to the clinic for appointments or treatments. Clinics often schedule appointments in blocks so that everything can be done at one time. They may make arrangements with your home-town doctors and have them conduct some of your care and follow-up under instruction from the clinic. Many couples decide to save holiday time for periodic trips to the city for their infertility treatment.

Let the Buyer Beware

The majority of infertility care available is of good quality and delivered by well-meaning, responsible physicians. Nevertheless, couples should still be judicious in seeking infertility help. *Caveat emptor*—buyer beware—applies. In fact, Dr. Howard Jones, a leading American infertility specialist who pioneered in vitro fertilization in North America, likened seeking medical help for some infertility problems, particularly in vitro fertilization, to buying a used car, and suggested that patients should be prepared to walk away.

Healthy patient skepticism is more necessary in the United States, where doctors and medical facilities can advertise and promote their services, often having profit motives. In Canada, Britain and Australia the government or medical groups themselves prohibit self-promotion. Infertility patients in those countries will find shopping around difficult, even if they want to or if it is necessary, as infertility specialists can have months-long waiting lists.

Good infertility specialists share the concern that some unscrupulous doctors may take advantage of infertile couples. In the November 1987 issues of *Fertility and Sterility*, the medical journal of the American Fertility Association, 11 leading American infertility specialists outlined concerns about the possible abuse of infertile couples. The article, "Are We Exploiting the Infertile Couple?" identified three areas of possible exploitation or misrepresentation.

1. Doctors inappropriately using credentials, such as memberships and

training course certificates, to appear to be more qualified than they really are.

2. Doctors misusing or overusing the new reproductive technologies, such as in vitro fertilization or microsurgery, without trying less invasive tests and treatments first.
3. Doctors using false or misleading advertising of success rates of treatments when the individual couple in the particular treatment or clinic cannot hope to have the same chance of success.

Misuse of Credentials

Know your doctor's training. During the four years of training to become a specialist in obstetrics and gynecology, a doctor is taught the basics of infertility management and treatment. To become knowledgeable in reproductive microsurgery, advanced ovulation induction, in vitro fertilization and gamete intrafallopian tube transfer, a doctor must take specialized training beyond residency.

As mentioned earlier, some doctors complete what is called a fellowship in reproductive endocrinology. In the United States these doctors can be certified and can call themselves reproductive endocrinologists. There is no certification process as yet in Canada, Britain or Australia, although the infertility specialists there generally have had post-graduate fellowships. Australia has plans to put a certification process in place. None of these countries has certification for reproductive surgeons or in vitro fertilization specialists. It is left to the doctor's discretion to attend an adequate number of training courses, to work as a subordinate under a skilled surgeon to learn his techniques, or to spend time learning at an established IVF clinic.

To help doctors develop their skills, the American Fertility Society frequently offers two-, three- and four-day workshops, or longer, in techniques such as laser surgery, microsurgery and IVF. In 1989, for example, 25 two-day carbon dioxide laser microsurgery courses, sponsored by the AFS, Baylor College of Medicine and the Houston Laser Institute, were planned to take place in locations around the United States. Other two-day courses were also planned for other types of lasers such as argon, KTP/532, and Nd:YAG lasers. The cost for a practicing doctor is about $1000 for two days. Course descriptions guarantee "hands-on" laser use with "at least six hours of laboratory time."

No one—not the teaching faculty, not the sponsors, nor the participants—suggests, at any time, that two days of teaching and six hours of laser use qualifies a doctor to be a good laser surgeon. These courses are offered as a service to keep doctors current on new techniques. The courses emphasize that participants should have further tutoring before they operate independently.

However, no one can stop a doctor from coming out of one session and saying he has been "trained" in that particular therapy. Some of the courses even offer certificates of attendance. The doctor is free to frame his certificate for the wall and try out what he has learned. Patients may erroneously presume from the certificate that he is proficient in the technique.

Writing in *Fertility and Sterility* in 1987, the concerned specialists said: "It must be emphasized that the courses are not designed to certify individuals for a mode of therapy. Those of us skilled in a particular technique must be careful about unintentionally exploiting practitioners by offering these courses with the pretense of adequately training them in a particular procedure."

A patient should be aware that a framed certificate on the wall does not guarantee expertise. The safest situation is to be referred by a doctor you trust, who herself knows first hand the reputation and ability of the surgeon to whom she is referring you. Usually, consulting a surgeon who is connected to a university medical school is good practice.

Do not assume that if the doctor is a member of the American Fertility Society or other fertility organizations, such as the Canadian Fertility and Andrology Society, the British Fertility Society and the Fertility Society of Australia, he or she is an expert in infertility. Membership in most medical societies is purely voluntary and open. The organizations promote research and dissemination of fertility knowledge and a doctor's membership simply indicates an interest in infertility diagnosis and treatment, not expertise.

Membership in the AFS, which was formed in 1944 as The American Society for the Study of Sterility, is open to any doctor who pays the membership fee. In 1988 the AFS had more than 10,000 members from North America. The organization tries to promote responsibility among its members, but it, too, is grappling with the issue of how to maintain quality control.

"The difficulty now is helping patients distinguish membership in the AFS from credentials," said Dr. Edward Wallach in a plenary session on the AFS's educational responsibilities to physicians and society at its 1988 annual meeting. Wallach, a past president of the AFS and an infertility specialist at Johns Hopkins in Baltimore, said the AFS can not police its members. "To date there has been no way to do this. The membership is open to anyone, who can then hang a certificate on the wall and practice infertility medicine. There must be voluntary, individual policing."

Inappropriate or Unnecessary Tests and Treatment

Do not be seduced by doctors who appear to offer the latest high-tech, razzle-dazzle, expensive treatment. Patients are often willing participants in this type of exploitation. You want the brand-new therapy you have read about in magazines and newspapers and so you seek out doctors who will give it to you—whether or not it is appropriate treatment for you.

The doctors writing in *Fertility and Sterility* expressed concern over doctors who take advantage of this: "The evaluations are at times inappropriate and often incomplete and frequently no time is allowed for pregnancy to occur after individual therapeutic steps."

There is general agreement among infertility practitioners that couples should have the least expensive, least invasive tests and treatments first, moving on to surgery and high technology treatments such as IVF at the end of the evaluation.

Do not demand that a doctor give you therapy and threaten to take your business elsewhere if he does not oblige. Patient pressure is often what fuels inappropriate tests or treatment and it is the patient who is harmed by it.

Dr. John Collins, of McMaster University in Hamilton, Ontario believes that patients are often given too many tests, unnecessary treatments, or treatments that have not been proven to help fertility. "The rationale of what we do must be based on outcome—meaning, if we do this test, if we give this treatment, does the couple have a significantly better chance of getting pregnant? If the answer is no, we shouldn't be doing it." Collins believes it is common for individual couples to go through a host of tests and therapies that have no bearing on whether they become pregnant in the end.

In a landmark study reported in 1983 in the preeminent *New England Journal of Medicine*, Collins and Canadian colleagues followed 1145 couples for as long as seven years after they had sought infertility treatment. Half the couples at the time of seeking help decided not to undergo treatment, the other half continued with medical therapy or tubal surgery. The surprising result was that of the two groups there was very little difference between the final outcomes. Of the treated couples, 41 percent became pregnant. But of the untreated couples, a full 35 percent eventually became pregnant, too.

A further surprise was that of the treated couples who became pregnant, 31 percent did so more than three months after medical treatment had stopped or more than 12 months after surgery. Collins concluded that those pregnancies should be considered as being independent from treatment. Of all the pregnancies in both groups, he concluded that 61 percent were unrelated to treatment, while only 39 percent could be said to be the result of treatment. The worst showing for treatment was unexplained infertility: a full 96 percent of those patients who became pregnant did so without medical help.

Collins's study has been criticized by others in the profession, partly because it is becoming out of date as infertility treatments are being refined each year. The study also does not take into account pregnancies from in vitro fertilization in which many patients without treatment stand no chance of pregnancy. Some doctors also maintain that in those patients who became pregnant after treatment had stopped or a year after surgery, their treatment could easily have played a role by resetting some hormonal button or allowing a tube to slowly heal over time.

Other studies however have also shown instances in which there was no difference between the treated pregnancy rate or the untreated pregnancy rate. Collins said those studies, and his, reflect what happens in normal infertility practices, and might not hold true for the very difficult cases of infertility.

Therefore, do not pursue treatment under the mistaken belief that anything is better than nothing. Nothing *can* be better. A wrongly used or inappropriate drug can further impair fertility, such as in the case of some fertility drug treatments for male sperm problems or unexplained infertility.

Some couples push for in vitro fertilization or variations of the technique, thinking that because it receives the most media attention and has the highest profile it must be the best. That is erroneous thinking. IVF has no advantage if a simpler technique works just as well, and IVF has an extremely poor success rate. An IVF attempt also gives a couple just one chance at pregnancy during the month it is tried, whereas a treatment such as surgery gives a couple a chance in each successive month after it has been performed.

False Claims and Raised Expectations

False or misleading advertising, particularly in the false reporting of success rates, was the third and final concern of the doctors' *Fertility and Sterility* article on preventing exploitation of the infertile couple. "Infertile patients often develop unrealistically high expectations regarding specific therapies. The medical community is partly responsible for the inflated expectations when practitioners claim pregnancy rates that far exceed those found in the current literature," they said.

The doctors also took to task the claims by some doctors that laser microsurgery is superior to other types of microsurgery. In the past few years many surgeons have been promoting the use of laser microsurgery as the answer for women with blocked or damaged tubes. But the truth is that in good surgeons' hands laser is no better or no worse than electrosurgery or scissors dissection. In unskilled hands, laser can do more damage and cause longer operations.

Of the greatest concern is the reporting of IVF statistics. Although in vitro fertilization is a proven treatment and for some couples the only hope of pregnancy, at the best clinics it has had only a 10 percent to 20 percent success rate in achieving a pregnancy for a given couple. If the couple is older or has other factors besides blocked tubes causing infertility, the success rates can be even lower than 10 percent.

In 1987 half of the 150 IVF clinics operating in the United States had yet to achieve a pregnancy. Yet, most of those programs were still claiming other clinics' success rates of about 20 percent or higher. Some clinics had totally inflated statistics, flagrantly claiming pregnancy rates upwards of 50 percent!

New drug methods of stimulating the ovaries to obtain eggs and further refinements of the procedure promise to gradually improve pregnancy rates. But, in general, the history of IVF has been marred by false advertising.

"The truth with regard to the expected pregnancy rate after IVF procedures has been widely abused (primarily by practitioners) and has tainted an otherwise meritorious record of scientific and clinical achievement," said Dr. Michael Soules, University of Washington infertility specialist, in an 1985 editorial in *Fertility and Sterility*, "IVF Success Rates: Let's Be Honest With Each Other." "One distortion has lead to other distortions.... sundry claims of 'success rates' in IVF are now viewed with either skepticism or disbelief." The exaggeration of IVF pregnancy rate appears to be a ploy to lure prospective infertile couples into becoming active IVF patients, Soules said.

The problem of the reporting of IVF success rates, and pointers on how couples can elicit meaningful statistics is discussed further in Chapter 10.

Good Treatment Checklist

In summary, the following are ways that couples can ensure they are getting good quality medical care for their infertility:

1. Use specialists referred by your family doctor or gynecologist who knows the specialist's reputation.
2. Attend local infertility support groups and learn from other couples' experiences. How did the doctor interact with them? How were they

treated both medically and professionally? What was the outcome? Would they return to or recommend that particular doctor?

3. Where possible, choose infertility specialists or clinics associated with reputable university medical schools or teaching hospitals. Doctors who have teaching appointments at medical schools are aware of advances in knowledge through research and refinement of techniques. The university medical schools are usually committed to fostering and maintaining a standard of excellence. Staff and faculty must meet the institution's standards. A doctor's ability is under constant scrutiny by peers and students.
4. Do not push for treatment if the therapy has no proven value to help you achieve pregnancy. Do not urge the doctor to "do something!" when no treatment is known to be effective or is inappropriate for your condition. In most cases, decline if the doctor says "we don't know if this works, but you can try it." The exception to this is if the doctor is doing a well-designed, controlled research experiment on the drug or therapy. In that case, you should be given a clear explanation of what the experiment hopes to determine, how the experiment is designed and how long you will be involved. You should understand the chance that it will not work or that you may be given what is called a placebo—meaning you do not get active therapy to compare the results to those patients who do. You should be able to decline or accept participation in the study with no pressure from the doctor and be able to drop out at any time without harming your treatment or relationship with the doctor.
5. Never undergo major surgery without knowing something of the doctor's medical reputation, background and training, either from your referring doctor, hospital contacts or infertility support organizations. Do not make your decision to undergo surgery with a certain doctor based on advertisements, framed certificates on the doctor's wall, or the upscale location of the office. Where possible, undergo surgery at a university-affiliated hospital or teaching hospital under a surgeon who has a university appointment.

Your Relationship with Your Doctor

A good working relationship with your doctor depends partly on you. To get the best help for infertility, learn to be a good partner in your treatment and to interact in an effective manner.

Many infertility doctors lament the growing hostility they feel from patients. Generally, these doctors are in the business because they want to help patients become pregnant. When you conceive, they share your joy. When you do not, they share your disappointment.

The hard fact of life is that many people do not become pregnant or they take a number of years to be successful despite their effort and the doctor's hard work. Patients whose desire for a child is thwarted tend to take out their anger and disappointment on the doctor. Instead of feeling that the doctor is doing his best, some patients feel he is failing them—he must not be trying hard enough.

One specialist who has been practicing infertility medicine for over a decade said, "It used to be that patients were always happy for anything you might be able to do to help. I really enjoyed working with them. But now I find patients increasingly hostile and angry. It is as if I am the reason for their unhappiness and that I am standing in the way of them becoming pregnant, rather than helping them. It gets very hard to work with after a while."

Just as in marriage or a love relationship, a good doctor-patient relationship is based on trust and mutual respect. When you have found a doctor to whom you can relate, whose credentials are sound and whose bedside manner is professional and caring, then give him or her the opportunity to help you. You may be angry and disappointed about your infertility, but do not take out that anger on the doctor. Do not be antagonistic unless there is a good reason.

If you needed a lawyer to defend you in court, you would get the best one you could find and then you would trust the person to build your case. If you did not like the way the lawyer was representing you, or if you thought you were being conned, you would change lawyers. It would do no good to vent anger, hostility or abuse. Treat your doctor the same way when you find one you like. You are in a partnership with the goal of pregnancy. Any distraction or negative undercurrents in your relationship could undermine that goal.

That does not mean that you should leave your brain, your opinions and your critical judgment waiting in the car when you enter the doctor's office. Ask questions and expect clear, courteous and informed answers. Seek explanations and ask the doctor to repeat or further explain anything you do not understand. Be as informed about your condition as you can be and discuss your options with the doctor. Be in charge of your own treatment. For example if the doctor suggests trying a certain drug for six months, find out all you can about it and remind him or her when that six months is up (it is common for doctors to forget) and say "now what?" The better informed you are, the better you can take care of yourself and get the health care you need.

Dos and Don'ts for a Good Relationship

1. Do be informed about your problem and your treatment. Read up as much as you can at your local library. Many libraries, particularly those at universities with medical schools, carry a wide selection of medical journals, books and texts. If you find an interesting article that relates to your treatment either copy or note it and discuss it with your doctor. Do not be discouraged or feel inadequate, however, if you can not understand the journals—they are written in scientific languge. Do not use an article as a way of scolding or reprimanding your doctor: "So-and-so is doing this, why aren't you?" Rather, use it as a way to open up more discussion: "I noticed this study and wondered if it might have application to my situation. What do you think?" That approach will be much more effective. Keep in mind, however, that many articles—even scientific ones—present only one side of an issue or are based on flawed

science. Do not assume that if the doctor disagrees with an article that he is wrong and the article right; it could easily be the other way around.

2. Do write down the names of tests and procedures you are undergoing, along with the doctor's explanations. Studies have shown that patients forget, or never hear, up to 50 percent of what they are told in the doctor's office. By taking notes you can refresh your memory outside the office and look up more information in your local library.
3. Do make a list of questions you want to ask when you visit your doctor. Many people forget the key questions they wanted answered.
4. Do ask why you are undergoing each test and what the doctor hopes to learn from it. For suggested treatments, find out what they will do and what your specific chances of success are. Find out any possible side effects and how long you will be kept on the treatment. Remind the doctor if this time period elapses and you are still on the treatment.
5. Do not try to discuss your case with the doctor when she does not have your files or charts. Do not stop your doctor on the street or in the halls to ask questions, nor phone at night, except in real emergencies. Without your file the doctor cannot be expected to remember details of your diagnosis and treatment. Book an appointment to discuss concerns and questions.

Doctor Idolatry

Many patients find themselves idolizing their doctor. He becomes the savior who will grant them a child, who figures out the workings of their bodies. The relationship can be very personal and intimate and the emotions strong. Some women even express feelings similar to falling in love when they first start seeing a specialist.

> *After my first visit I came home totally infatuated with my doctor. I couldn't stop thinking about him; I couldn't believe I was feeling that way and I didn't understand it. It was like I was 16 and had fallen madly in love. I felt really embarrassed and it didn't seem right. I had to talk it over with my husband. Then it started to make sense. Here was a person who I believed was going to finally make me pregnant. Why shouldn't I feel good about him? I think I just transferred those feelings—the euphoria of finally feeling this person is right and I know I'm going to get pregnant—I transferred that on to him.*

Those feelings are common. In fact the medical profession in the past has been accused of capitalizing on the natural tendency of patients to deify their doctors. Feelings of infatuation are usually temporary and the doctor soon becomes a human being again.

Stress of the Infertility Work-Up

At first seeking medical help usually brings about a temporary relief from the stress of infertility—no longer are you all alone. But, unfortunately, that respite is fleeting. Most couples describe the medical investigations and treatment of infertility as a highly stressful and difficult time. Depression, disappointment, anger and anxiety are all common. If you are fortunate and conceive quickly, the stress may be minimal. But if, like many couples, you take a number of months or maybe even years to resolve your infertility, the stress can become a dominant and pervasive force in your life.

Your feelings will fluctuate. At some stages you will feel fine, at others you will feel rotten. Studies have shown that the first year is very trying for a couple's relationship. This is the time of investigation and tests to determine the extent and nature of the infertility. The tests can be painful, embarrassing and time-consuming. The results can be devastating. Often psychological counselling is needed for couples to work out the confusion, disappointment, grief, hurt or even blame between them and to get their relationship back on track.

> *The first year of tests was awful—I look back and I'm amazed we made it. Everything was an emotional minefield, we had so much to talk about, but real talk was sometimes impossible, there was so much emotion in the way. Sometimes I thought we'd never get back to normal.*

Dr. Barbara Berg, a doctor of psychology at Western Illinois University, studied the emotional stress of the 104 couples at various times during the infertility work-up. Reporting her findings at the 1988 American Fertility Society meeting in Atlanta, Berg found that most couples start out the infertility work-up feeling depressed and with some disturbance in their relationship. In the first year the stress intensifies.

The second year, most couples report a stabilization of the stress and of their relationship. The medical investigation becomes more routine and familiar, the issues more easy to talk about. By the third year stress has returned to a high as initial therapies have not worked and more investigation or new therapies are required. The stress fluctuates until you resolve your infertility either by having a child or adopting or by deciding that you will discontinue treatment.

When you embark on the infertility work-up it is important to maintain your self-esteem, to enter into activities that make you feel good, to be with friends and family you enjoy. Do not define yourself by the success or failure of the investigation or treatment.

The Medical Investigation

The first and one of the most crucial steps of the infertility work-up is your medical history. On your first visit the doctor asks questions about significant events in your life, both medical and personal. The whole aim of the history is to find clues to the cause of your infertility by pinpointing specific factors that might have affected it in your past. The doctor also tries to determine whether you, in fact, might be fertile and if the problem lies with your partner. What is learned in the history will shape the logical sequence of tests to follow.

The history of both partners is equally important. Although earlier it was stated that infertility investigations are undertaken as a couple, the personal history taking is usually done in private with the doctor to encourage open discussion of pertinent information such as past abortions or a pregnancy with a previous partner. In infertility clinics that use the team approach, often the woman will consult with the reproductive endocrinologist or gynecologist at the same time the man sees the urologist or andrologist. When the histories and physicals have been completed privately, the doctors usually discuss the findings with the two together.

Female Medical History

The menstrual history, sexual history, lifestyle and general health are all of interest to the doctor to shed light on fertility problems. The questions the doctor might ask include those in the following paragraphs.

Menstrual Pattern

When did you first start menstruating? How regular are your menstrual periods? How many days long is your regular cycle? If your periods are irregular, how many do you get in a year and what is the variation in length? How many days do you bleed during your period? What is the pattern of bleeding—heavy? light? Do you get menstrual cramps, and if so, are they mild, moderate or severe? In the days before you start to bleed do you get premenstrual symptoms such as breast tenderness, bloating, or lower back pain? Do you bleed or spot in the middle of your cycle? Do you get ovulation pain, or mittelschmerz, in the middle of your cycle?

Information about your menstruation will establish the likelihood that you are ovulating and menstruating normally. A late start of menarche (first menstrual period), after age 16, can indicate a possible problem of the hormonal axis. Irregular or infrequent periods (oligomenorrhea or amenorrhea) can suggest a lack of ovulation and hormonal axis disturbances. Very light periods or very long heavy periods can also indicate hormonal disturbance. An absence of any menstrual cramps or discomfort can suggest anovulatory cycles, while severe cramping could mean endometriosis. Premenstrual symptoms, particularly breast tenderness and mid-cycle bleeding or pain tends to suggest that ovulation is taking place.

Previous Pregnancies

Have you had any previous pregnancies, including abortions, miscarriages and ectopic pregnancies? If so, how long did it take you to conceive? Did you require infertility therapy? Did any pregnancies occur with your current partner?

Establishing that pregnancy has occurred in the past indicates that at one time, at least, you were ovulating and so you can probably ovulate again. If a pregnancy was established with your present partner, that, too, establishes that at one time you were both fertile. If the pregnancy was ectopic, tubal problems are indicated. If just one pregnancy was lost in miscarriage it may have been bad luck or an infection; if two or more ended in miscarriage other factors such as genetics, immune problems or anatomical problems may be playing a part. Infertility after an established pregnancy, called secondary infertility, could indicate an infection followed the birth or abortion, leading to scarring that is preventing another conception. Secondary infertility can also be caused by a hormone imbalance.

The doctor might ask whether any other family members—your mother, sisters or aunts—have menstrual irregularities or had difficulty becoming pregnant. You will likely be asked if your mother took diethylstilbestrol (DES), a synthetic hormone erroneously thought to prevent miscarriages, during her pregnancy with you. DES caused the reproductive organs of the developing fetus to be malformed, which might be the root of your fertility problems. (See Chapter 6.)

Sexual History

The answers to the questions on sexual history help determine your coital habits and whether your contraception or sexual history might have put you at risk. What type of contraception did you use before trying to become pregnant—pill, IUD, condom, diaphragm, spermicides or other? If you used the pill, were your periods normal after stopping it? If you used the IUD, when did you have it removed? Through how many cycles without contraception have you tried to conceive? Do you and your partner know how to time intercourse to ovulation? How often do you and your partner have sexual intercourse? Do you use any lubricants?

It is common for women to have irregular cycles after stopping the pill, but within a few months most women revert to normal. Those who had irregular cycles before starting the pill, however, often continue to have irregular cycles after. Women who use the IUD have a greater incidence of pelvic infection and scarring than women who use other types of contraception. Some women mistakenly believe they have had their IUD removed when it is actually still in place and is the only thing preventing pregnancy. As detailed in Chapter 3, infrequent or improperly timed intercourse can often be the main reason for a couple's infertility. Lubricants can dilute or kill sperm.

Have you had more or fewer than 10 sexual partners in the past? Do you have pain or discomfort during deep intercourse? Have you ever been treated for a sexually transmitted disease (STDs) such as chlamydia, gonorrhea, or venereal warts?

The more partners a woman has had, the greater her chance of unknowingly picking up an STD that can scar reproductive organs. Pain during deep intercourse hints at pelvic infections or scar tissue. Treatment for chlamydia or gonorrhea could also indicate that the fallopian tubes have been scarred.

Associated Medical History

Questions will be asked about other factors that might have affected your fertility: Have you had previous pelvic surgery such as an appendectomy, dilation and curretage (D&C), or removal of an ovarian cyst?

Previous surgery can cause adhesions and scar tissue to form in and around the reproductive organs. A ruptured appendix is particularly worrisome as it can spread infection to the fallopian tubes.

Have you been treated for pelvic inflammatory disease (PID)? Do you get recurrent bouts of PID? PID also suggests scarred tubes.

Have you at any time had a milky discharge from your breast (galactorrhea)? This indicates high levels of the hormone prolactin. Have you noticed an increase in body hair (hirsutism) around your nipples or breasts, around your chin or upper lip, in a line extending from your pubic hair to your navel? Hirsutism indicates an increase in male hormones, androgens. Have you lost or gained more than 20 pounds recently? Weight changes could cause a temporary hormonal disturbance or indicate a more serious disease.

Your doctor will ask questions related to your lifestyle. Do you smoke cigarettes? How much alcohol do you drink each week? Do you do frequent vigorous exercise such as running or aerobic classes? Are you dieting? Do you eat a specific diet such as a vegetarian diet? Are you concerned with gaining weight and has this concern caused you to restrict your intake of food? Do you have an eating disorder such as anorexia, bulimia or overeating? Smoking and alcohol decrease fertility. Nutrition and eating habits can alter menstruation. Dieting can temporarily stop ovulation.

Do you have other health problems such as allergies, frequent vaginitis, headaches, dizzyness, or pelvic pain? Are you taking any prescribed or over-the-counter medications? If so, what types? Tranquillizers or antidepressants can affect sex drive and ovulation. Over-the-counter antihistimines or decongestants can alter cervical mucus.

The doctor will also want to know if you have had any major illnesses in the past such as cancer, hepatitis, kidney disease, tuberculosis, thyroid disease, or whether you still have any illnesses such as heart disease, arthritis, high blood pressure, epilepsy, diabetes.

The doctor will be interested in your intuitive feelings about your fertility and what might have affected it. For example, you may recall a bout of high fever, severe stomach cramps and nausea that you thought was flu; or instances when your menstrual periods changed during stress or upheaval. Feel free to bring up anything that might be related to your condition, even if the doctor does not ask about it. Often patients have good clues to their own problems.

Male Medical History

As in the female history, doctors want to know events or situations in the past that may have affected your sperm production, particularly injury, hints of hormone imbalances, possible STDs or exposure to reproductive toxins. The questions the doctor might ask include those in the following paragraphs.

Sexual and Developmental Background

Were both your testicles descended into your scrotum when you were born? Did you have an operation to move them into your scrotum? At what age did you go through puberty? When did you start shaving regularly or growing a beard? Is your beard heavy or light now? Undescended testicles (cryptorchidism) can cause impairment of sperm function, particularly if they are not operated on before puberty. A very late puberty could indicate a hormonal problem. Facial hair is an indicator of secondary sexual characteristics and testosterone, but it is also considered a "soft" sign because heredity is a factor—many men with scant beards are extremely fertile. However, if through heredity you would be expected to have a full beard but do not, that might suggest testicular impairment.

How many partners have you had? Do you have trouble getting or maintaining an erection? Do you have trouble with ejaculations? If so, are they premature? Is the volume of your ejaculate low or high. (If it is low volume, it might suggest that you have retrograde ejaculation, some of it going into your bladder.) Have you ever fathered a child with another partner? How often do you have intercourse with your present partner? Do you know the time of the month when your partner is ovulating and most fertile? Have you noticed a change in your sex drive recently? These questions are to determine whether sexual dysfunction or timing may be causing your infertility.

Have you ever been treated for any sexually transmitted disease such as chlamydia, gonorrhea, or venereal warts? Do you ever have any discharge from your penis, or pain or burning on urination? Have you had a swelling or pain around one or both testes or been diagnosed with an inflammation called epididymitis? These questions are to determine whether you might have had an STD that could compromise your fertility.

Lifestyle

Do you smoke cigarettes or marijuana? Do you use recreational drugs such as cocaine? Do you take frequent saunas or hot tubs? Do you usually shower or do you take a hot bath? What is your occupation? Are you frequently exposed to heat, chemicals, fumes, nuclear radiation or other factors such as vibrations? How much vigorous exercise do you get each week? Have you gained or lost more than 20 pounds recently? Do you eat a specific diet? All these factors may be toxic to sperm or impair hormone functions.

General Health

Have you been sick or had a fever in the last three months? Did you have mumps after puberty that resulted in inflammed testes? Have you ever had surgery in the pelvic area—hernia repair, appendectomy, or bladder surgery? Have you had a vasectomy reversed? Have you ever had an injury or been hit in one or both testes? Have you had torsion (twisting) of one or both testicles? Have you ever had a milky discharge from your nipples?

A recent fever could undermine the quality of sperm ejaculated and could cause your semen analysis to be misinterpreted. Mumps, particularly if the infection involves the testes, can permanently impair testicular function. Pelvic surgery can unknowingly compromise the reproductive tract. A vasectomy can be associated with raised sperm antibody levels. An injury to even one testicle can cause the other to stop working in sympathy. Nipple secretions indicate a raised level of the hormone prolactin, which can interfere with the hormonal axis.

Do you have other health problems such as allergies, arthritis, high blood pressure, headaches, diabetes, chronic bronchitis, epilepsy, heart disease, kidney disease, irritable bowel syndrome or ulcerative colitis? Have you had any serious illnesses in the past such as cancer, tuberculosis, hepatitis, seizures or others? Are you taking any prescribed or over-the-counter medications? Have you ever had an X ray of your pelvic area for therapy or diagnosis?

Like women, men's fertility can be impaired by medication, systemic disease or illness. Diabetes can cause retrograde ejaculation. Drugs for high blood pressure may lower sex drive or interfere with erection and ejaculation. (See Chapter 7.)

Physical Examinations

The Female Physical

After investigating your medical history, your specialist will conduct a physical examination. For women who have have had internal examinations the routine of the infertility physical is familiar.

The doctor notes your general health and physical appearance. Urinalysis, height, weight and blood pressure are usually recorded and a stethoscope is used to listen to your heart and lungs. The doctor notes secondary sexual characteristics such as breast development, fat distribution and hair growth around your nipples, on your face and on your abdomen. If you control unwanted hair by waxing, shaving, depilatories or tweezing, it is a good idea to either let the hair grow before the visit or tell the doctor so the extent of hair growth can be assessed.

The doctor feels your thyroid gland on your neck just below your larynx to see if it is enlarged or of abnormal consistency. An abnormal thyroid could indicate a hormone disturbance. She examines your breasts and squeezes your nipples to see if a milky discharge is extruded.

The doctor examines your abdomen by applying pressure and feeling the different areas to check for lumps and painful spots. In the pelvic examination, as you lie on the examination table with your feet in stirrups, the doctor first examines your vagina and outer genital organs for unusual anatomy or signs of sores or infection. She then inserts a speculum into your vagina and examines your cervix and vaginal walls. She looks for signs of infection, sores, growths, abnormal narrowing or erosion of the cervix, and takes scrapings of cells from the cervix for a Pap smear for cancer and cultures for STDs.

Removing the speculum, she carries out a manual pelvic examination by putting two fingers of one gloved hand inside your vagina and the other hand on the outside of your abdomen. By using both hands to exert pressure, the doctor can manipulate your reproductive organs between both hands, and feel the size, shape and texture of your uterus, your uterine ligaments, and your ovaries. She tries to feel any abnormal lumps, bumps or enlargements in your reproductive organs. The fallopian tubes usually can not be felt. The ovaries should be compact, not enlarged, and neither tubes nor ovaries should be painful when touched. The doctor notices if your uterus, ovaries and tubes move relatively freely, or whether they are held in place by scar tissue. Your uterus should be small and firm without any detectable bumps, abnormal shapes or muscular knots—fibroids. With the pelvic examination over, the doctor finishes the physical with an examination of your rectum by inserting a finger to feel for unusual growths, bulges or pocketing.

The Male Physical

A urologist, andrologist or a family doctor is usually the one who conducts the male physical examination. While women become quite accustomed over the years to having their bodies poked and prodded by doctors, the experience might be new to men, some of whom will not have visited a doctor for a long time. Being probed, particularly around the genitals, can be disconcerting.

As in the female examination, the doctor looks for signs that everything is working. He first notes your general appearance, paying attention to your secondary sexual characteristics of facial, chest and pubic hair, deepness of voice and physical build. He records your height and body proportions, including arm span and muscle/fat ratio. He notes whether you have fat distribution around your breasts (gynecomastia). All of these items tell him whether you have experienced the normal male pubertal development. The doctor also carries out a general physical including blood pressure, chest sound, urinalysis and neurological evaluation by reflexes. He examines your head and neck and feels your thyroid below your larynx for enlargement.

The examination of your genitals begins with the penis. The doctor notes the location of the opening, or orifice, of your urethra, whether it emerges at the head of the penis or opens somewhere along the underside of the shaft. The doctor notes any discharge, which will be cultured to see if it contains microorganisms. Any tenderness, unusual firmness or hardness along the urethra indicating a possible narrowing or inflammation is also noted.

Next, the doctor examines both testes, gently palpating them with his thumb and fingers, noting their size and firmness. He also feels along the epididymis that lies on top of both testes to check for tenderness or swelling, which could indicate an infection. He tries to follow the vas deferens duct as it leaves the epididymis and travels through the scrotum into the lower abdomen. Although some infertile men are born without a vas deferens, this condition cannot be confirmed without further tests or surgery.

The doctor also searches for a varicocele, an enlarged blood vessel in your testes similar to a varicose vein. He examines you lying on your back and standing up, asks you to do a Valsalva maneuver—you hold your mouth and nose closed while blowing out, as if you were clearing your ears while scuba diving, or bear down as though having a bowel movement. The abdominal pressure created by this maneuver can cause the varicocele to bulge and become visible. A varicocele is thought to raise the temperature of the testes, impairing sperm function. Just how much varicoceles impair fertility is controversial.

Finally, the doctor palpates your prostate and seminal vesicles while you are in a lateral position. With a gloved finger he feels through your rectum for the size and texture of your prostate gland. It should be a small round knob, firm and elastic. By massaging the prostate the doctor notes whether it is inflammed or enlarged, possibly causing a narrowing of the urethra preventing passage of sperm. Any emmission will be examined under a microscope and cultured for microorganisms. Your seminal vesicles, when they are normal size, are difficult for the doctor to distinguish or feel, but if they are inflammed, they may be palpable.

Neurological evaluation includes a test of the sensations you feel on your perineum, the area extending between the anus and the testes, as well as the tone of your rectal sphincter, the muscular closing of the anus.

When the male and female physicals have been completed, further tests will be conducted to determine reproductive function.

Infertility Tests

Semen Analysis

The semen analysis, or sperm count, is the single most important test in assessing a man's fertility. By evaluating characteristic elements of a man's semen and sperm, a great deal can be learned about the likelihood that he can father a child. The number of sperm, their ability to swim and their various shapes give clues to the source of a fertility problem. Other so-called parameters or characteristics tell of the health and function of a man's reproductive tract.

Despite the importance of the semen analysis, there is a great deal of medical debate over its fine interpretation. The most controversial aspect is determining what constitutes a truly normal sample and where, if at all, the line between fertile and infertile semen should be drawn. The problem is that semen analysis is an imprecise science. There are accepted concepts: there must be an adequate number of live, swimming, normally shaped sperm in order for one sperm to fertilize an egg. When there is absolutely no sperm now and no hope of sperm in the future, it is clear the man will not father a child. But when even a few sperm enter the picture the situation becomes more fuzzy. How many sperm does a man need? No one really knows. All that is known is that the more sperm a man has, the greater the chance he will naturally father a child, but even men whose sperm count is rated "poor" still manage to father children.

Semen analysis gives a couple a probability that one of the man's sperm will fertilize an egg. If the woman has subtle fertility problems, the probability goes down. The semen analysis can pinpoint possible problems and highlight areas of further investigation. If the first semen analysis is considered to be poor, two or three samples should be analyzed over a few months because of natural fluctuation.

Giving a Sample

Usually you receive written or verbal instructions from your doctor or infertility clinic about where and when to produce a sample. In general, most clinics ask that you abstain from ejaculating for two to three days before giving the sample to maximize sample quality. You are told to either masturbate at home and bring the sample in a clean glass container to a designated lab within an hour, or to masturbate in a special room provided at the clinic or lab. Make sure you know your particular instructions as it can be bothersome, or even amusing, if signals get crossed.

> *The first time I gave a sample I thought the lab where I was to take my specimen had a room where I could masturbate. But, in fact, I was supposed to bring the sample with me. I had taken my lunch hour and driven across town and when I arrived they said, "Where is it?" Well, there was no way I could drive all the way home, do it, and come back in time. So I got a bag and a container from the lab and went across the street to the MacDonalds. I can't believe I actually sat in the MacDonalds' washroom cubicle and did it. It's pretty funny now. But I kept thinking then: I could be arrested for this!*

If you produce a sample at home and bring it in, try to keep it at body temperature, neither too hot nor too cold, until it gets to the lab. Keeping it in an inside coat pocket is usually good enough, but if the day is particularly warm or if the sun is shining through the car window on the pocket the temperature could rise too high. Clean glass containers should be used because some plastic containers can kill sperm.

Some men have difficulty masturbating at the clinic or even at home. Others may be reluctant because it is prohibited by their religion. If that is the case, you can have sexual intercourse using a special non-spermicidal, non-lubricated condom and transfer the semen into a container. You may have to ask your doctor or pharmacist for the name of a specific brand as most condoms are spermicidal. Be sure to tell the lab technician that some of the semen volume was probably lost in the transfer. Coitus interruptus, pulling out just before orgasm, is a last resort as it is very difficult to avoid losing a few droplets before ejaculating into the container. Every drop, particularly the first, is important in the semen analysis. The technician will want to know how it was collected and whether there was any spillage as this could affect the results. The technician may also ask whether you had any fever or illness in the last three months or whether you are on any medication.

Semen and Sperm Parameters

An explanation of the different parts of the analysis of your sample follows.

Coagulation and Liquification When semen is first ejaculated it coagulates or thickens, and stays in this rather gooey state for about 30 minutes. It is thought that this thickening action helps the sperm stay up around the mouth of the cervix, giving them opportunity to swim through the cervical os and up to the tubes. After 30 minutes the semen reverts back to a liquid. The advantage of producing a semen sample right at the lab is that the technician can watch the transitions from liquid to gel and back to liquid. Semen that does not coagulate may lack the necessary factors contributed by the seminal vesicles. Semen that coagulates but does not reliquify may indicate a problem with the prostate.

Color and Appearance Fresh semen is usually whitish-grey and as it reliquifies it becomes somewhat transluscent in appearance. A slight yellowish tinge can be normal, but a yellow hue may indicate infection and the presence of white blood cells. A reddish or brown tinge may indicate blood in the semen.

Odor As semen oxidizes (interacts with air), it creates a pungent, almost sweet, but not unpleasant, odor. A foul odor may indicate infection. A total absence of odor can indicate a prostate problem.

Volume Between two and five milliliters of semen volume is considered normal. Volumes above or below that can cause infertility by interfering with sperm function. If the volume is less than one milliliter you may not have put all the semen in the container and this can greatly affect the sperm count and the ability of the semen to reliquify. Be sure to tell the technician if some has been lost. If all the sample was collected, the low volume could indicate retrograde ejaculation into your bladder, absence of the seminal vesicles, an obstruction in a duct, a deficiency in sperm production or too frequent ejaculation. Volumes greater than six milliliters can occur after a long period of sexual abstinence. High volumes can also be caused by overactivity of seminal or prostate glands. If volumes are too great, sperm may be diluted or unable to swim properly.

pH The pH or relative acidity or alkalinity of the sample is measured soon after the sample has liquified. Normal semen is just slightly alkaline, ranging between 7.2 and 7.8 (a neutral solution has a pH of 7). If the pH is either strongly acidic or strongly basic, an infection or inflammation of the prostate or seminal vesicles is suspected. Prostatic fluid is usually acidic, while seminal vesicle fluid is basic and when the fluids mix to comprise semen they neutralize each other. If either gland is out of line, the total pH will be disturbed.

Viscosity In a determination different from liquifaction, the technician evaluates the viscosity of the sample by drawing up a small sample into a pipette and letting it drip out. If the sample is too viscous and it streams out in a long strand, an infection or a natural condition of viscosity is suspected. If the viscosity is caused by an infection, antibiotics may be prescribed.

Sperm Concentration The technician mixes the semen well to obtain a representative sample, then draws out a few drops and places them on a slide. The actual sperm "count" can be done in a variety of ways. Some labs count a representative live sample of sperm, using a grid on the slide as a standard reference, and are able to come up with an estimate that takes into account sperm that are living, dead, motile and non-motile, normally and abnormally shaped all at once. Other labs fix the sperm so they can not move and then count them. Still others now use computers to scan a sample to analyze the density of sperm.

An average sperm count for fertile men is thought to be anywhere between 40 million to 120 million per milliliter. But there is a big difference between what is average and what is necessary for conception. The threshold between what the medical profession considers fertile and subfertile has ranged from a low of five million to a high of 60 million per millileter. The World Health Organization has set out that 20 million per milliliter is the lower edge of normal, and this figure is generally accepted. But pregnancies can, and do, occur when sperm counts are well below that, especially if other parameters such as shape and motility are normal and the woman's fertility is normal.

Motility Some doctors say that sperm motility rather than count is the single most important parameter that indicates whether a couple is able to conceive. Sperm must be able to swim to the egg and, so the reasoning goes, no matter how many sperm are in a sample, if they can't swim well they may as well not be there. By estimating the number of moving sperm in a sample and by grading their movement on a scale of one to four, the lab will come up with a percentage and average grade of motile sperm. Ways to estimate sperm motility vary from lab to lab. Many simply put a drop of semen on a gridded microscope slide, put on a coverslip, and count and grade the number of straight-moving sperm in several fields of vision. Under this form of analysis, 50 to 60 percent or more motile sperm is considered normal, with the majority being in grade two on the motility scale, or higher.

Dr. John Collins, of McMaster University in Hamilton, Ontario, has suggested that doctors use what he calls "Total Motile Sperm Count" to assess a man's fertility. The TMSC is sperm count multiplied by motility, multipled by volume. Collins's studies suggest that this number correlates well to a couple's chances of pregnancy.

Computer analysis with a videocamera and a microscope, or time lapse photography, are now used in some labs to measure motility. The system, called videomicrography, allows more objective analysis of motile sperm and also allows researchers to look at such esoteric measurements as lateral head displacement and individual sperm velocity. The computer systems may give unreliable results if the number of sperm in the sample is low or if there is debris in the sample. Some researchers find that the human eye can estimate motility as fast or faster than the computer. The computer systems, however, hold promise in developing standardized, objective measures of motility, count and even shape. Many researchers are working on perfecting the computer analysis now. By the mid-1990s computerized semen analysis should be the standard method.

Morphology The morphology, or shape, of the sperm is also estimated by the technician, but this is the least understood parameter for evaluating fertility. Sperm, like people, can have slightly different shapes and appearances. But in general, normal-shaped, mature, fertile sperm have oval heads, a cylindrical mid-piece and a long tapering tale. Abnormally shaped sperm may have two heads, oversized heads, two tails, curled tails, misshapen middles and other characteristics. An abundance of sperm with thin narrow "tapered" heads or tiny "micro" heads may indicate a varicocele. All semen samples contain some abnormal or immature sperm cells. To determine morphology a minimum of 200 sperm cells are examined under the microscope. If a sample shows that more than 50 percent of the forms are abnormal there may be a fertility problem.

Sperm Antibodies The technician notices whether the sperm clump together, either head to head, tail to tail or in other configurations. Sperm clumping, called agglutination, indicates either an infection or the presence of antibodies coating the sperm, probably from an earlier infection or injury. Antibodies prevent the sperm from swimming because of clumping, or slow down individual sperm like an anchor dragging behind a boat. If antibodies appear to be present in your sperm, further antibody tests will be conducted, such as an immunobead binding test. Antibodies, and specific antibody tests, are discussed in greater detail in Chapters 7 and 8.

Cultures The technician routinely cultures the semen, looking for bacteria and sexually transmitted diseases such as chlamydia, gonorrhea and ureaplasma (mycoplasma.)

Mucus Penetration Some labs do a screening test during the initial semen analysis to find out if the sperm can penetrate cow mucus. Cow mucus has similar biochemical qualities to human mucus; therefore, how well sperm swim or penetrate in cow mucus may indicate how sperm would perform in the real stuff. The test works in a fashion similar to a barometer. A thin glass column of cow mucus is placed with the open end down in a reservoir of sperm. The sperm swim up the column of mucus. After a period of time the column is examined under a microscope to see how far the sperm swam. This test might not be performed during an initial semen analysis because if mucus penetration appears to be a problem from the results of later tests, such as a poor postcoital test, a more definitive test using your sperm against your partner's mucus and donor mucus will have to be performed anyway.

Female Tests

The tenet of infertility investigation is to do the simplest, least invasive tests first. For a woman, three essential factors must be determined: whether ovulation is taking place; whether hormones are properly priming the endometrium and cervical mucus; and whether the reproductive tract is free of scar tissue or anatomical defects that might prevent the transport of egg, sperm and resulting embryo or its implanation.

All the tests given a woman will be to establish these factors. Often the tests do not yield definite answers; instead, the tests confirm by deduction and inference—if one thing happens therefore something else, the event we are really interested in, must have happened, too. Because of the difficulty of getting inside the female reproductive tract and watching, unobtrusively, all that happens in the natural system, tests that use deductive reasoning are the most common types of infertility investigation.

Depending on the information from your medical history and physical examination, the doctor schedules the logical sequence of tests. If, for example, you told him you have menstrual periods like clock-work every month but your history includes a ruptured appendix, pelvic infection or an STD, he might immediately order an X ray called a hysterosalpingogram or an operation called a laparoscopy to view your fallopian tubes. Some women have both an ovulatory and a tubal problem and their work-up involves confirming ovulation and tubal patency. Therefore the tests you undergo might take place in a different order than what follows below.

Confirmation of Ovulation

In a woman who menstruates regularly, there is no sure way of knowing that every month a plump, mature, healthy egg pops out of the ovary and goes along its merry way. More than nine times out of 10, however, if a woman has regular menstrual cycles with symptoms of breast tenderness and premenstrual tension, she is ovulating. By evaluating other factors surrounding ovulation, doctors can deduce with confidence that it is, indeed, really happening.

The first clue is your basal body temperature graph, the daily, early morning temperature readings you have plotted on graph paper. If you have not already started taking your temperature before you see the specialist as was suggested in Chapter 3, he may want you to start now. Chapter 3 outlines specific instructions for BBT graphs.

If the temperature graphs are biphasic, having two distinct temperature levels with the second phase at least half a degree higher than the first, you can assume that you are ovulating. After the egg is ovulated the increase of progesterone coursing through your body causes your average temperature to rise. The doctor scans through a few months of your charts, checking for the characteristic rise, but because some women who ovulate have monophasic charts, this is considered a "soft" determination of ovulation. If you have been using home LH monitoring kits to help you and your partner pinpoint ovulation, mention this to the doctor, too. This will also help confirm ovulation.

Serum Progesterone

The gold standard to confirm ovulation is to check for increased progesterone circulating in your blood in the second half, or luteal phase, of your cycle. If your cycles are regular, blood will be drawn for a blood test in the middle of your luteal phase. Blood will usually be drawn on day 21 of a 28-day cycle. In 95 percent of regular menstruating women, if a single mid-luteal phase blood test shows that progesterone is raised, that is enough to assume ovulation is taking place. The progesterone level should be greater than five nanograms per milliliter. (In rare cases blood samples can show progesterone increase but an egg still might not have been released, called lutenized unruptured follicle syndrome. This can happen in random cycles but is not a chronic problem.)

Evaluating serum progesterone levels is more difficult in women who have irregular cycles. Since it is not known when you will ovulate, the doctor may want to take a sample of your blood once a week starting at day 20 until you menstruate. If you are ovulating, at least one, and probably two, of the blood samples will show an increase in progesterone. This type of sampling, however, may not be practical nor meaningful for you or the doctor, particularly if the intervals between your periods are several weeks long. The doctor may examine your BBT graphs instead and knowing that you menstruate rarely, he will know you ovulate rarely. For that reason he might move straight to a full blood test to examine all of your reproductive hormone levels.

Endometrial Biopsy

The endometrial biopsy, the EB, is the final confirmation of ovulation and a confirmation at the same time that your endometrium is being properly primed by hormones. In the endometrial biopsy a small scraping of endometrial tissue is taken from your uterus. The tissue is then read under a microscope for characteristic changes. The EB usually takes place in your doctor's office one or two days before you are expected to menstruate, on day 26 or 27 of a 28-day cycle. While you lie on the examining table with your legs in stirrups, the doctor inserts a speculum in your vagina, cleanses your cervix and then dilates the cervical os. A metal currette is introduced into your uterus and gently scraped on the front wall. The resulting tissue sample is fixed and stained on a slide and sent to the pathology lab where it is read.

To confirm ovulation, the pathologist looks for evidence that progesterone has caused the lining to change and become secretory. If it has, ovulation will be assumed to be taking place.

The EB is also used to test the readiness of the endometrium. In this capacity the test is somewhat more controversial. As was detailed in the last chapter, the endometrium goes through marked changes every few days of the menstrual cycle. The pathologists examine your endometrial tissue for these characteristic changes and then give it an arbitrary, physiological date based on the developments they see. For example, in the second week of the luteal phase specific tissue changes occur in the underlying framework of the endometrium, called the stroma. The pathologists compare your sample to what they would expect to see, saying in effect, "This tissue looks like day such-and-such" and give it that date. Later, counting back from the date when you do menstruate, the physiological date of your sample will be compared with the real date of your cycle. Suppose you have a 28-day cycle and the EB is done on your day 26, but when the pathologist looks at the tissue she says it likely came from endometrium that is at day 23 rather than day 26. If you menstruate as usual on day 28, your EB will be determined to be three days out of phase with your cycle. An EB is considered abnormal if it is more than two days out of phase. Suppose instead of menstruating on day 28, as you usually do, in this cycle you menstruate three days later, on day 31. When the doctor counts back, your EB is not out of phase, but rather it is in phase, properly reflecting that your endometrium still has about five days to go before you can be expected to menstruate.

In this capacity the EB is used to determine luteal phase adequacy or the readiness of the endometrium to accept and nurture an embryo. If the endometrium is found to be inadequate, the diagnosis of luteal phase deficiency (LPD) may be given. LPD is discussed in greater detail in Chapter 5.

There are problems with endometrial biopsy dating, and its use is controversial and varied, particularly between countries. Infertility clinics in the United States use it frequently. In Australia and Britain it may be used for confirmation of ovulation but rarely to date and judge endometrial readiness. In Canada it is used less frequently than in the United States but not as rarely as in the other Commonwealth countries.

The criteria for dating the EB was refined by a team led by Dr. Robert Noyes and published in a landmark paper in the very first issue of *Fertility and Sterility* in 1950. The paper, "Dating the Endometrial Biopsy," is cited more often by other researchers than any other piece of infertility research. But that in itself creates some of the controversy. Noyes's work, although considered excellent, is almost 40 years old and was done before most of the finer points of ovulation were understood. Recent studies show a great deal of variability in how samples are dated by those who read them. In one study, five readers given exactly the same slide differed in their assessments by a range of plus or minus four days. Individual readers did not even rate the same slide the same way twice, fuelling medical arguments that EB results are unreliable and meaningless. As many as 30 percent of women who have an abnormal reading on the first test are apt to have a normal reading on the second. Many doctors recommend three EBs before the diagnosis of luteal phase defect is made.

Those who advocate endometrial biopsies, such as the noted and well-respected American infertility specialist Dr. Georgeanna Jones, stress that tissue samples must be read by qualified personnel. If the samples are taken well and read well, the information can be crucial to a diagnosis and treatment, she says.

If you must undergo an EB, or more than one, much of the medical debate will be immaterial. Whether or not you undergo one will depend on how your doctor stands on this issue. Some doctors recommend that women first be screened by serum progesterone tests and only those who show insufficient progesterone go on to have the EB.

Endometrial biopsies can be unpleasant or painful for some women during the procedure, like a bad menstrual cramp. It is over quickly, but some women complain of significant cramping or bleeding afterwards.

> *The endometrial biopsy—now there's a nasty piece of business. I was told by the doctor, the nurse, everybody, that it was just a little twinge. Not for me. It hurt like the dickens. But that wasn't the worst of it. They gave me a little panty liner "for the spotting" and sent me home. Halfway down the block I started to bleed profusely, just a gush. Fortunately I was about five doors away from a friend's apartment and I practically crawled there and begged her to let me in. I don't know what I would have done if she hadn't been home.*

Pain, of course, is subjective and, fortunately, most women do not have such a bad experience as the one above. Some women find an EB no worse than a pap test. If you are to have an EB, it is a good idea to pack a sanitary napkin in your purse, just in case, although most doctors give one at the end of the procedure. As some women say driving home after the procedure is difficult, you might want to arrange to be picked up, perhaps more for emotional support than for discomfort.

Some women undergoing an EB worry that if they are pregnant and do not know it the EB will cause a miscarriage. Studies have shown, however, that miscarriage rates are no higher following an EB. If you were pregnant an EB would probably not be enough to cause you to abort. (You may miscarry, but it will not be the EB that causes it, doctors say.) Still, if you are worried about that possibility, doctors suggest you use barrier contraception during the month of the EB.

Hormone Tests

Most doctors take separate blood samples at the same time they are taking serum progesterone to determine your prolactin levels and thyroid function, two other hormones that can influence ovulation and fertility.

Prolactin Prolactin is secreted by the pituitary and primes the glands in the breasts to secrete milk at the same time it inhibits ovulation. If prolactin is high, a condition called hyperprolactinemia, it can indicate a benign pituitary tumor. Often the cause of high prolactin is unknown. If your prolactin level is over 100 nanograms per millileter you may be scheduled for a brain scan to check for a tumor. For more about hyperprolactinemia see Chapter 5.

Thyroid Hormone Thyroid hormone regulates the body's metabolic rate, the rate of chemical change, and is secreted by the thyroid gland at the base of the neck. The gland, in turn, is regulated by the pituitary. Abnormal amounts of thyroid hormone, either too high or too low, can indicate a problem with the hormonal axis or diseases of the thyroid.

Reproductive Hormones If your menstrual history makes it obvious that you are not ovulating regularly—months without menstruating or radically irregular periods—a full blood test is recommended to assess all your reproductive hormones. If you do menstruate regularly but the initial tests (BBT, serum progesterone or EB) show you are not ovulating, a more in-depth hormone study may also be ordered.

Some doctors order blood tests three separate times during one menstrual cycle: early follicular phase, suspected time of ovulation and mid-luteal phase. Others feel three blood tests are unnecessary and too costly and take only one near the end of the cycle. In both approaches, the aim is to get a rough estimate of the ratio of the reproductive hormones FSH, LH, estrogen and progesterone, and to note whether there are any excess male hormones present. The levels and ratios of the hormones can tell the doctor what is the likely cause of your lack of menstruation or irregular menstruation. If all the hormone levels are low, you probably have a down-regulation of your hormonal axis, called hypothalamic amenorrhea. If your LH:FSH ratio is high and you also have elevated male hormones, you probably have polycystic ovaries, PCO. Both hypothalamic amenorrhea and PCO are discussed further in Chapter 5.

Ultrasound

Ultrasound is a valuable tool in infertility investigations, particularly for monitoring the ovaries. The high-pitched sound waves act like depth soundings at sea and are echoed back by the organ or structure that is being scanned. The machine picks up the variations in the returning signal and translates them into the bumps and dips that outline the organ it is scanning to produce detailed pictures. With this technique the doctor monitors the growth of the follicles on the ovary either in a natural cycle or a fertility drug-induced cycle. After the supposed time of ovulation, ultrasound can be used to check whether the follicle has actually collapsed and released an egg.

The ultrasound signal can be sent either transabdominally or transvaginally—through the lower belly or through a probe in the vagina. In both situations, conducting jelly will be applied to the probe to help transmit the signal. Transabdominal ultrasound requires that you drink at least a liter of water in the few hours before the procedure so that you have a full bladder. Water transmits the sound waves rather than echoing them back, and the full bladder, therefore, can be used as a watery window for viewing the ovaries. Transvaginal ultrasound does not require viewing through the bladder and is less uncomfortable for most women. An increasing number of infertility clinics are using transvaginal ultrasound, particularly for the monitoring of drug stimulated cycles and retrieval of eggs for in vitro fertilization and other assisted reproductive techniques. (See Chapter 10.)

Tests for Tubal Patency

If during your medical history or pelvic examination evidence emerges that you have been at risk for pelvic infection, adhesions or scarring of your reproductive organs, one of your first tests will be to determine if your fallopian tubes are open.

Hysterosalpingogram (HSG)

The HSG has been the standard screening test for tubal patency for about 20 years. The name is unwieldy, but it really just describes in Greek what it does—uterus (hystero) fallopian tube (salpingo) recording (gram)—it makes a record, or a picture, of your uterus and fallopian tubes.

The picture is taken with an X ray. But because X rays can not make images of soft tissue, the inside of the reproductive tract is defined by a radio-opaque contrast medium, making, in artist's terms, a negative space picture; that way the outline of the uterus as well as the flow of the dye can be seen. The HSG will often be performed by a radiologist, a doctor who is skilled in conducting and diagnosing X-ray studies. Your infertility specialist may refer you to a separate radiology clinic or a hospital radiology clinic to have the HSG taken. To be sure of the quality of the study, an HSG should be carried out by an expert.

If you have a previous history of pelvic infection, pelvic surgery, secondary infertility (following a first child) or pelvic tenderness on your physical examination, your doctor may decide to give you a course of antibiotics before the HSG to prevent a possible flare-up of infection after the procedure.

The study is done in your follicular phase, usually between day five and day 12 to avoid the hormone changes later in the cycle that can alter the way the tract looks. (There can be a false appearance of blockage in the fallopian tubes after ovulation during the progesterone phase.) Doing the HSG in the follicular phase also prevents interference with an early pregnancy.

For this test you wear an examining gown and you are asked to lie on the X-ray table. Usually no stirrups are used because they interfere with your freedom of movement; you are asked to change positions and your bare heels grip the table. The doctor inserts a plastic speculum into your vagina to expose your cervix (some doctors use a metal speculum but that can obscure the cervix and lower part of the uterus on the X-ray film, experienced radiologists say) and cleanses your cervix with an anti-microbial antiseptic.

A long metal instrument called a tenaculum, with two tiny teeth, is clamped onto your cervix to hold the cervix in place. A flexible, narrow nylon cannula or tube goes on the end of another tube that, in turn, is attached to a syringe full of the colorless contrast medium. The narrow tube is guided into the cervical os and passed through the entire cervical canal so that its tip pokes into the opening of your uterus. If your cervical opening is very tight a metal probe will first be introduced to persuade the os to dilate slightly. With all the hardware in place, you are positioned on the table for the X ray. Three tablespoons of the watery dye is injected into your uterine cavity by depressing the syringe.

Four to six images are taken from various angles. You are asked to move so that you are on both right and left sides. The various positions enable the doctor to see the way the dye flows and outlines the tract. The doctor pays particular attention to whether the dye flows out the ends of both tubes to confirm that your tubes are open. This does not confirm that the tubes are normal, but it does confirm that they are open. If either one or both tubes is closed the dye will outline where the obstruction lies, as well as any possible scarring or growths such as fibroids in your uterus that might interfere with embryo implantation.

When the doctor has verfied that the pictures are adequate, the instruments are removed. When you stand up you will pass a clear, sticky fluid, which you can wash up in the washroom. You will be given a sanitary napkin to wear for any bleeding or left-over dye coming from your cervix.

For some women the HSG is very painful, particularly for those who have blocked tubes, because of the pressure caused by injecting the dye. For many, the injection will trigger a hard cramping of the uterus. "You have to hold these positions on the table, first this way and then that, with all this stuff sticking out of your vagina. I had a monster killer cramp. I thought it was just awful."

Other women have very little pain or discomfort. "I had a bit of cramping, just a little bit painful—like a mild period cramp. The whole thing took 25 minutes at the most. I'd expected it to be much worse, but I didn't find it too bad at all."

No matter what you think your response will be, it is a good idea to arrange to have someone pick you up after the procedure. Many women feel shaken and do not feel capable of driving home, even if the procedure is not painful for them. One woman described her experience this way. "Mine went well, very little pain, but I was unprepared for how emotional I felt afterwards. It wasn't that the test result upset me—my tubes were fine. But I felt really shaken. Halfway home I pulled over to the side of the road and had a good long cry. I still don't understand why I felt that way."

There is some debate among doctors about which women can best benefit from an HSG. The technique gives a picture, but omits a lot of details doctors need. Should all women undergoing an infertility work-up routinely have it? Should only those who have had an obvious risk of pelvic infection or scarring in their past have the test, or should it be used for women who do not seem to have a tubal risk factor at all?

In Australia many doctors no longer use the HSG and begin tubal patency tests with a laparoscopy, a surgical procedure under general anesthetic to view the reproductive organs. In the United States some clinics combine the HSG with the laparoscopy, conducting the X ray while the woman is under general anesthetic.

Many doctors feel, however, that the HSG is a very good screening test for women who do not appear to be at risk for tubal problems. The HSG can outline problems in the uterus that cannot be seen during a laparoscopy. In Vancouver, two women who believed their IUDs had been removed, were each given an HSG, which showed the IUDs still in place. As soon as the IUDs were removed the women became pregnant. One woman had undergone 18 months of an infertility work-up in another city, complete with laparoscopy, but an HSG had not been done. These cases support the benefit of the HSG. Some doctors have suggested that the HSG can be therapeutic and the dye can remove a small block in the tubes, allowing the woman to get pregnant.

If an HSG shows no pelvic risk factors and shows open tubes, no more tubal investigation is carried out and there is no need for immediate surgery. If in six months to a year after the HSG you still have not conceived despite normal ovulation, you might then be given a laparoscopy. If a blockage is found on the initial HSG, you might be given a laparoscopy for a more definitive examination.

Laparoscopy

If in your past you have had pelvic inflammatory disease, wore an IUD, contracted an STD or had pelvic surgery, you will most likely be scheduled for a laparoscopy, which is a more costly and invasive test than the HSG and requires you to undergo general anesthetic in an operating room. But the information from a single laparoscopy is superior to what can be ascertained from the HSG.

In the past if doctors wanted to view the reproductive organs with their own eyes they had to open a woman's abdomen wide. There was no way to simply peer in at the functioning without a highly invasive operation. In the 1950s French and German doctors first began experimenting with a device that could peer into the abdomen, but getting a light source that would not get too hot but would still allow them to see the structures was a problem.

That was solved with the 1960s breakthrough in fiber optics, which enabled the bending and manipulating of light and image. Sophisticated medical "scopes" resulted, allowing the doctor's eye to travel like a camera lens or a fantastic voyager through the body's orfices and cavities. The laparoscope, meaning in Greek "view the loins," is a metal tube about half a meter long and a few centimeters in diameter that encases a bundle of optical glass fibers. It has an eyepiece and a powerful light source and is inserted into the abdomen by a tiny incision right by the navel. It can view all the organs of the abdomen, including the reproductive organs. When it was first used in the late 1960s by a handful of gynecologists, many thought it was merely a fad without useful application to their practice. But the laparoscope has become a powerful, indispensable instrument in infertility medicine for diagnosis and treatment.

A laparoscopy is usually conducted under day surgery—you check into and out of the hospital on the same day without staying over night. The procedure usually takes no more than an hour from start to finish. But even though the procedure is quick, you may need two or three days of convalescing at home. "After my laparoscopy I felt like I'd been run over by a truck. I ached all over and just slept solidly the whole next day," one woman said.

The doctor gives detailed instructions to prepare you for the operation. You are asked not to eat or drink anything for at least the 12 preceding hours—not even a glass of water—as any fluid or food in your stomach may be vomited under general anesthetic.

The anesthetist gives you a light anesthetic to put you to sleep and block pain. Your gynecologist swabs your abdomen and vagina with an antiseptic and then makes a one-centimeter incision at your navel. Using a Veres needle, he pushes through the layers of fat and muscle until he enters the peritoneal cavity where your reproductive organs are suspended. Then carbon dioxide is pumped into the space, like inflating a volleyball with air, to create more room around the organs for better viewing. He introduces the laparoscope and the operating table is tipped to lower your head so that your intestines and stomach slide away from the reproductive organs. In that position the doctor can get the best view of your ovaries, fallopian tubes, uterus and the ligaments that support them.

He may make one or two other small incisions by your pubic hair so he can insert other instruments to grasp and manipulate the reproductive organs. He examines the reproductive anatomy, noting any abnormalities in size or shape and looks for the extent and severity of any adhesions, fibrous bands of scar tissue that grow between the organs. Sometimes adhesions are so extensive that all the organs are stuck together by a dense web of tissue.

The doctor notes other scarring, particularly whether the fallopian tubes are swollen or distorted, or whether their tentacle-like ends, the fimbria, are closed or clubbed. While examining the fallopian tubes and fimbria, he asks an assistant to inject blue dye through the uterus while he watches the dye flow through the tubes, noting if it spills out the end.

The surfaces of the ovary, uterus and tubes are examined for endometriosis, abnormal patches of menstrual tissue that have migrated outside of the uterus and implanted on other surfaces. Endometriosis can look like dark red or even black or blue spots on the organs or tissues. The patches can be small, or larger than four or five centimeters in diameter, superficial or burrowed deep into the host tissue. The doctor also notes whether endometriosis appears on the lining of the abdominal cavity, the peritoneum, or on other organs such as the bowel or bladder. Ovarian cysts—unruptured follicles—are also noted.

The doctor examines you for any evidence of ovulation by looking for the corpus luteum—it looks like an inflamed open sore on the ovary. When all the reproductive organs and surrounding tissue have been thoroughly examined, the doctor lets out as much of the carbon dioxide gas as possible and removes the laparoscope and other instruments. He sews the tiny incision with a single stitch or simply covers it with a bandaid. Then the anesthetist brings you around.

Some doctors do a routine dilation and curretage, a scraping of the uterus, during a laparoscopy, but there is medical controversy whether women should routinely have a D&C, particularly if there is no indication of any uterine abnormalities or abnormal bleeding. Many doctors feel that there is often little reason to give a D&C to women under the age of 35 who have regular periods and who have not had children. "Given the attendant time, the lack of useful information, the cost and potential risk to the patient, the routine D&C in otherwise asymptomatic women in this study did not produce sufficient information to justify its performance," doctors John H. Mattox and Sherrie Bernat concluded in their study of 480 women undergoing laparoscopy at hospitals in Rochester and Buffalo, New York. Their findings were presented at the 1988 American Fertility Society annual meeting. These sentiments have been echoed by other doctors.

Before you undergo your laparoscopy you should ask your doctor whether she feels it will be necessary for you to have a D&C. There may be a good reason for you to have one, but it certainly is not always necessary, particularly if you have no indication of abnormal bleeding, uterine growths or endometrial hyperplasia (overgrowth).

During recovery you may be surprised to feel, along with aching and muscle soreness in your abdomen, aching and soreness in your shoulders. That common after-effect of laparoscopy is caused by the carbon dioxide gas, which irritates the phrenic nerve underneath the diaphragm in the chest wall. That pain is referred to your shoulders.

Hysteroscopy

Many doctors use hysteroscopy, a procedure in which a fiberoptic scope is used to examine the inside of the uterus, combined with laparoscopy. The hysteroscope gives additional information that cannot be obtained by a laparoscopy about the condition of the uterus and its endometrium. If a hysteroscopy is given, it usually precedes the laparoscopy. (A hysteroscopy alone can be carried out in the doctor's office, too.)

In a hysteroscopy your cervix is opened slightly and the narrow, metal hysteroscope is passed through the opening into the uterine cavity. The inner walls of the uterus normally touch one another, so, as in a laparoscopy, the cavity must be inflated for the doctor to properly view them. Either carbon dioxide or a fluid solution (dextran or Hyskon) are pumped into the cavity. Like a navigator with a telescope scanning the horizon for landmarks, the doctor peers about the cavity looking for abnormal growths and anatomical defects.

Normal endometrium should look pink and healthy. The doctor looks for abnormal tissue growths, or polyps, which hang in the uterus like stalactites and act as a natural IUD by interfering with implantation. She will also note any overgrowth of endometrium, called endometrial hyperplasia, caused by too much stimulation with estrogen. Scar tissue and adhesions can also form inside the uterus like spiderwebs between the walls. Adhesions can result any time the endometrium is damaged or traumatized following a pregnancy, an abortion or a too vigorous dilation and currettage (D&C). The adhesions can also obscure the junction between the uterus and the fallopian tube, preventing the passage of sperm or the embryo.

The doctor looks for distortions of the uterus caused by fibroids, abnormal whorls of tissue that bulge and grow in the uterine muscle. In some women fibroids are numerous or larger than a grapefruit. Sometimes a woman is born with an anatomical defect in her uterus such as a septum, a wall dividing her uterus into two chambers. The septum can be thick or thin, partial or complete and it, too, can interfere with implantation and fetal growth.

During the hysteroscopy the doctor may perform minor operations such as taking an endometrial biopsy, removing polyps with a sharp curette, separating adhesions or reopening the junction between the tubes and the uterine cavity, or even removing a thin septum. These minor operations at the time of the diagnostic test can sometimes cure a woman's infertility.

Postcoital Test

The postcoital is used to check the quality of the woman's mucus, the natural interaction between sperm and mucus, and the sexual techniques of the couple. It has the distinction of being many couples' least favorite infertility test. It is painless, quick and effective, but it's disliked all the same because it can be an intrusion of privacy; a grading of a couple's sex life by the doctor.

For the postcoital test the doctor asks you to have sexual intercourse in your usual fashion immediately before the woman expects to ovulate, when the mucus should be wet, clear and abundant. Do not douche or use lubricants before or after sex. Two to 16 hours later you come into the doctor's office where your mucus is assessed. Using a syringe or pipette, the doctor extracts at least two samples of cervical mucus from the cervical canal, noting it's consistency and pH. Fertile mucus is slightly alkaline and dries on a slide in a characteristic "ferning" pattern, resembling the leaf of a fern.

Examining the cervical mucus under a microscope, the doctor looks to see how many sperm are still alive and swimming. When cervical mucus is at its most fertile, sperm can live in it for a number of days. The mucus acts as a reservoir and the sperm ascend from it in waves to the fallopian tubes. For the PCT to be normal, the doctor should see five to ten live sperm in each magnified field. If, when the mucus is examined, the majority of sperm are dead, or there are no sperm at all, the doctor knows you have a problem of cervical mucus or sperm that needs further investigation.

PCTs can reveal the presence of antibodies in either the man or the woman that may be interfering with sperm function or even killing sperm. It can show whether a woman's mucus is toxic to her partner's sperm. If the man's sperm count is very high but no evidence of sperm is found in the mucus, there may be a sexual dysfunction that is preventing the sperm from being deposited at the mouth of the cervix. Impotence, incomplete penetration or premature ejaculation may be the cause.

The procedure sounds simple and effective enough, but the following two women explain common feelings about PCTs.

The day of our first postcoital test we set the morning alarm half-an-hour earlier so we'd have time to make love. Mornings are always hectic for us and we have a hard enough time getting out the door to work without being late. The alarm went off, we rolled over, looked at each other and groaned. The last thing we felt like doing was making love. It was very difficult for both of us to get aroused. At one point I felt like saying "Let's forget it." But we didn't want to phone the doctor and say we couldn't do it. Somehow we made it—God knows how.

I'll never forget walking into the hospital for my postcoital. I live in a small town and I know a lot of the people who work there. I was sure that everyone knew what I was coming in for and I felt really embarrassed. Plus you have that sticky, wet feeling—yuck. I was worried that it would all drip out before I got there. What made it even worse was the doctor found all the sperm dead. You're lying there feeling really embarrassed to begin with and then you get that news: you've failed. I can't remember when I've felt so rotten.

Some doctors no longer use the postcoital test because some studies have shown that the test has a poor relationship to actual pregnancies: couples who fail the test can go on to become pregnant; couples who pass with flying colors can still remain unsuccessful. Instead, those doctors use laboratory methods to assess sperm-mucus interaction such as the cow mucus penetration test explained in the section on semen analysis.

Contributing to the distaste of the PCT is the fact that many doctors do not perform it properly. One woman recounted going through four PCTs with the same doctor after the first one showed that none of the sperm were still alive. She was told to "come in sooner" until finally just 15 minutes had elapsed between lovemaking and examination. That sort of intrusion is unnecessary and shows a lack of medical understanding of what the test should show and how it should be performed. If the test is performed when the mucus is at its peak, normal couples will still have viable sperm at least 18 hours after sex.

Dr. Richard Bronson, a New York specialist in antibody-caused infertility, acknowledges the PCT has its problems, but stresses that if performed properly it is indispensable. "It is a very powerful screening test, which can tell us a great deal—are the coital habits normal? are the sperm being killed? If sperm aren't populating the cervix we know there will be a problem. It is foolhardy not to do the test."

He says many of the test's detractors cite studies that looked at only one PCT that was roughly timed to the woman's mid-cycle and not specifically timed to basal body temperature charts, mucous changes and LH surges.

"The timing is critical," Bronson said. "I see cases where if the PCT is done two days before the optimal time, there are no sperm. Then two days later when the mucus is right, the test is super. It must be properly timed."

Couples may have problems "performing" for PCTs, particularly if they must have sex on the morning of the test. But Bronson and others believe sexual difficulties can be minimized if the couples are told to make love the night before, and come in first thing in the morning. If the mucus and sperm interaction is normal, the test will still be normal.

Sperm-Mucus Cross-Penetration Tests

An abnormal PCT or suspected sperm-mucus factor is followed with a more specific laboratory test to pinpoint the problem, a cross-penetration test. Donor sperm and donor mucus will be used to determine where the problem lies.

In three similar tests, a slender glass column filled with mucus will be placed with the open end down in a reservoir of sperm. The sperm will then be tracked to see how far they travel up the column. In one test the man's sperm and the woman's mucus will be tested. In another, the man's sperm will be pitted against donor mucus. In the final test donor sperm will be pitted against the woman's mucus.

If the man's sperm is able to penetrate the column of donor mucus but is dead or absent in the woman's mucus, something in the woman's mucus is killing the sperm. It might be antibodies, lack of sufficient estrogen to make the mucus fertile or improper pH. But if donor sperm climbs the woman's column but the man's sperm does not, the man's sperm is the problem. It could be sperm antibodies coating the sperm and slowing them down or another sperm motility problem.

The cross-penetration test helps doctors plan the next step of diagnosis or treatment.

More Specific Testing

Some people need one or two of the tests described in this chapter, and others may have all of the tests, and more. Some of these tests may be repeated numerous times, particularly if you change doctors. Or, perhaps, after you have undergone six to nine months of treatment without success, you may have some of these for the first time to determine if other factors are affecting your fertility.

The result of these tests, whether it is an ovulation defect, blocked tubes, sperm problem or any of those combined, will give the doctor a working plan, establishing either the need for further testing or a blueprint for treatment. Of the couples who go through the initial infertility tests, in 40 percent the problem is with the woman, in 40 percent the problem is with the man and in 20 percent it is a combined problem or an unknown factor.

The next four chapters describe in detail the possible diagnoses arising from these tests, what the conditions mean, the range of treatments and the treatment success rates. In those chapters, where applicable, more specific tests are detailed. In the chapter on male infertility, for example, more detail is given on testicular biopsy, male hormone tests, egg penetration tests and sperm antibody tests.

CHAPTER 5
Disorders of Ovulation and Menstruation

In 20 to 30 percent of the couples having trouble conceiving, the problem can be traced to an ovulatory disorder in the woman. The problem may be obvious and the woman, if not her partner, has usually been aware of it for a long time, primarily by the pattern of her menstrual cycle. For example, she may go three months or longer without a menstrual period, or she may have irregular menstrual periods—one cycle 30 days, the next 55, the next 38, and so on.

In rarer instances, the woman may seem to have normal, regular periods. She may have assumed that because her period occurs every 28 or 30 days she ovulates each month, too. These types of cycles, called anovulatory cycles, can be determined only after doctors have seen abnormal results from serum progesterone tests, BBT graphs or endometrial biopsies.

Whether subtle or more obvious, ovulation disorders are almost always treated with fertility drugs, a process called ovulation induction, and it is one of the true success stories in infertility treatment in the last 30 years. Before the 1960s there was little that could be done for women who did not release an egg each month. The medical advice to the couple was to "keep trying" in the hope that luck and timing would be on the couple's side in a month when an egg was released. In most cases, luck didn't come through.

Now there are four or five possible drug treatments available for women who are not ovulating. The drug a doctor uses for you depends on the underlying reason for your ovulation problem.

Now between 60 to 90 percent of women treated for ovulation problems eventually conceive and give birth. The numbers of women who conceive are fewer than those coaxed to ovulate because fertility drugs can interfere with the cervical mucus or the ability of the endometrium to accept the egg. The drugs are powerful and have their drawbacks and side effects. Most women, however, need to use them for only a few months.

Before taking fertility drugs, you should have the reason behind your ovulation disorder fully investigated. The success of fertility drugs has led some doctors to simply give the drugs without delving into the underlying cause, but it is important to find the reason behind the problem. Only by understanding the intricacies of the malfunction can doctors give the most effective treatment.

In some instances women may have one, two or even more factors combined to inhibit ovulation.

Polycystic Ovarian Disease

AKA: Stein-Leventhal syndrome, polycystic ovarian syndrome

Polycystic ovarian disease or, PCO, is one of the most common causes of anovulation and infertility. About half of all women who have ovulatory problems have PCO; close to two-thirds of these women have it in a mild to moderate form, the remaining third have severe PCO.

PCO is a syndrome, which means that a number of signs and symptoms occur together to define the disease. In PCO the common characteristics are irregular menstrual periods or months without menstruation, enlarged ovaries, hirsutism, obesity, and irregular hormone levels, particularly raised luteinizing hormone and elevated male hormones, androgens.

The syndrome was first described in the 1930s by two American doctors, Irving Stein and Michael Leventhal, who noticed the association of infertility and irregular menstrual cycles in a group of female patients who had the same typical characteristics. The women tended to have a peculiar distribution of fat, predominantly about the middle and less on the hips and legs, and they had dark, coarse, body hair in "male" patterns—extending up to the navel, around nipples or on the chin. In pelvic examinations of the women, the doctors felt enlarged, bumpy ovaries, sometimes three times larger than normal. That classic description in 1935 led the disorder to be often called Stein-Leventhal syndrome, even if the classic symptoms are not all present.

Indeed, it is almost more common in PCO that all the symptoms are *not* present. PCO women may be thin, not particularly hairy, or their ovaries may be of normal size. But in general there are two hallmarks of the disease: a long history of anovulatory or irregular menstrual cycles dating back to the first menstrual period and an excess of androgens circulating in the blood. Many infertility specialists prefer to call the syndrome "hyperandrogenic chronic anovulation" to reflect better what is going on.

What *is* going on is a very complex interplay of hormones that have gone slightly awry from the hormonal axis described in Chapter 3. Like a Victorian comedy of errors in which the identities of the actors are confused and perpetuate more confusion, the abnormal hormones circulating in PCO perpetuate the continuation of abnormal hormones, and it becomes a vicious cycle.

Characteristics of PCO

By the time a woman with PCO seeks help for infertility, her hormone profile from blood tests, compared to those of fertile women, tends to show the following characteristics.

High Levels of Pulsing Luteinizing Hormone The LH is released from the pituitary in the same pulse frequency as in fertile women, but in a greater amount on each pulse. The LH level does not cycle as in fertile women and no LH surge occurs.

Normal or Low-normal FSH In normally ovulating women the pituitary usually secretes FSH and LH in about equal amounts. But in PCO the level of LH may be two or three times higher than FSH. The ratio of LH to FSH is represented by a number from the blood test, such as 2.5:1 or 3:1.

Elevated Male Hormones In fertile women the ovary secretes testosterone and another male hormone, androstenedione, biologically weaker than testosterone. In PCO the levels of those hormones, particularly androstenedione, will be elevated. Testosterone levels may be normal or just slightly elevated but the ratio of how much of the testosterone is "bound," or inactive, compared to how much is circulating "free" is higher in PCO than in fertile women.

Constant Estrogen Levels The estrogen levels are constant at about the level characteristic of a normal cycle's early to mid-follicular phase. Unlike fertile women, however, that estrogen does not come primarily from the developing follicles. Rather, the estrogen has likely been converted in the fat tissue from the excess male hormones circulating in the blood. The estrogen level may be particularly high if the woman is obese.

Progesterone Progesterone levels are low.

Cysts An ultrasound of the ovaries shows them dotted with swollen cysts and with thick walls between the cysts.

The hormone levels and how they perpetuate the problem of PCO are better understood when they are examined together with the process of the menstrual cycle in PCO. (If you need a refresher on how the normal menstrual cycle works, refer to Chapter 3.) In a severe, established case of PCO, the hormonal confusion is assumed to go something like this. The hypothalamus, which is monitoring the levels of estrogen in the blood to determine how much the ovary needs to be stimulated, senses that estrogen is normal or a little high. It assumes that this estrogen is coming from the normal development of a plump, ripe egg in the follicle. But it is being fooled because the estrogen really is coming from the testosterone conversion in the woman's fat and peripheral tissue. The duped hypothalamus instructs the pituitary to slow the release of FSH and to release the egg by increasing LH.

The developing follicles, no longer being primed with FSH, stop maturing. The continual high level of LH, however, keeps priming the tissue around the follicles to make androgens, which further arrests the development of the follicles, turning them into cysts on the ovaries. The androgens from the stimulated ovary then circulate in the blood. In the fat under the skin the androgens are converted to more estrogen, which feeds back to the hypothalamus. The poor, confused hypothalamus, sensing more estrogen, continues to instruct the pituitary to release the egg with LH and stop sending FSH, exacerbating the problem. The eggs are not ovulated and the ovary becomes dotted with unruptured small follicles—cysts. If a piece of the ovary is taken for a biopsy the tissue shows distinct pathological evidence of the effect of androgens.

There is medical controversy over where in the system the actual defect lies and how PCO starts. Does it start with the malfunctioning ovary or does it start with a malfunctioning hypothalmus that causes the ovary to malfunction? Or perhaps there is an extraneous factor, such as excess androgens secreted from the adrenal glands on the kidneys, excess insulin, or thyroid problems, which distort the delicate hormonal axis. "We really don't know what the initiating event is," said Dr. David Baird, an Edinburgh, Scotland reproductive endocrinologist who is an expert in PCO. "Many of us suspect it may be caused from a range of conditions which lead to anovulation and then it becomes a self-perpetuating event." In that way a number of upsets of the hormonal system could start to unbalance the hormonal axis and lead to PCO.

It is known that PCO seems to run in families, with some sisters or aunts showing a tendency to menstrual irregularities even if they are not infertile. It tends to be more common among women of Mediterranean descent.

The following woman represents a typical case history for PCO:

> *I started menstruating later than most of my friends. I was almost 15. From the start I was always very irregular. I'd never know when my period would be coming—it would be six months, then four months, then seven months. When my periods did come they would be extremely long and heavy. Around the time I turned 20, I noticed I was getting hairier. I had dark, pubic-like hair on the inside and back of my legs and some hair growing around my nipples—that was very unusual for my family as we tended not to be hairy at all.*

The effects of excess androgens usually take a few years to build up so it is typical that a woman first starts noticing hair growth, problems with excess weight or acne three or four years after her first menstruation. Menstrual periods, when they come, can be long and heavy because estrogen has been stimulating the endometrium unopposed for a long time. New research shows that a resistance to insulin has also been found in women with PCO and there is some evidence that insulin, which binds on the ovary, is part of the drive to the ovary to make too much androgen. Women with PCO may ovulate from time to time and can occasionally become pregnant without medical treatment. Pregnancy itself sometimes corrects the defect and subsequent menstrual periods after birth can become normal, but there is a large individual variation of PCO from one woman to the next.

Treatment of PCO

If your initial history and blood work point to chronic anovulation with raised LH and androgen excess indicating probable PCO, the doctor's first task is to determine the origin of the androgens in your blood. The doctor can then rule out the possibility of a more serious source of androgens, such as an ovarian or adrenal tumor, particularly if there has been a rapid onset of hirsutism or a development of other male sexual characteristics such as breast reduction or a lowering of the voice.

Fertility Drugs

When tumors have been ruled out, the first line of treatment for women with PCO who want to conceive is induction of ovulation with the fertility drug clomiphene citrate (CC), known under the trade names Clomid or Serophene. (See the description of clomiphene in Appendix A.)

Clomiphene Citrate

Clomiphene citrate is given in tablet form for five days, usually starting from about day five of the menstrual cycle until day 10. For women whose periods are extremely irregular, menstruation may first be induced by progesterone, given as an injection in the muscle or as a derivative in a pill. Because hormone levels in PCO are often constant, the CC may also be started any time, if there is confirmation that you are not pregnant.

It is common for women with PCO to be started on a dose of about 50 milligrams of CC a day, but recent experience causes some doctors to suggest starting with doses of about 25 milligrams or less. "The vast number of women with PCO will respond to ovulation induction, but the question is getting the right dose and the right time and monitoring the response properly," says David Baird. "I often get women referred to me who allegedly have been not responsive to clomiphene, but when you sit down with them and work out the dose, often decreasing it, you can get them to ovulate." In general, the lowest possible dose that can produce ovulation should be used, but some doctors have also found that increasing the duration of treatment to eight to 10 days works.

The drug Tamoxifen, another anti-estrogen with an action very similar to CC, may be substituted for CC. Patients with PCO are usually very responsive to either CC or Tamoxifen and between 70 to 90 percent ovulate. But only about 30 to 70 percent of those women actually conceive. Of the women that do become pregnant on the drug, more than 75 percent do so in the first four to six months. The rate of spontaneous abortion in women with PCO who do conceive on CC seems to be higher than in the fertile population and higher than in women with other ovulation problems who take CC. The chance of twins in women with PCO on CC seems to be even greater than for other women on CC.

CC Plus Human Chorionic Gonadotropins (HCG)

Women who have not ovulated on CC alone may be given an injection of the pregnancy hormone HCG approximately one week after the last dose of CC.

Human Menopausal Gonadotropins (Pergonal)

For the ten to 15 percent of women with PCO who can not be made to ovulate on CC and CC/HCG, the next step is generally the powerful fertility drug Pergonal, which contains both FSH and LH. (See Appendix B.) Patients must be carefully monitored while on the drug. Women with PCO should not use the drug until they have had a hysterosalpingogram or laparoscopy to check that their fallopian tubes are open and their reproductive organs are free of scar tissue. There is no point taking this powerful, expensive drug if other factors may be contributing to infertility.

Women with PCO tend to respond less well to Pergonal than women whose ovulatory problems are caused by other factors, research studies have found. Although about 70 to 80 percent of women with PCO will be made to ovulate on HMG, only about 21 to 40 percent will conceive, and they also have a greater tendency to hyperstimulation syndrome, particularly in the first cycle of treatment. About one in three will have multiple pregnancies.

Pure FSH

Since women with PCO tend to have raised LH to begin with, many doctors believe the combination of FSH/LH found in Pergonal is not needed and patients would do better with pure FSH stimulation alone. The drug Metrodin is now available, which has FSH with low or inactive LH. Like Pergonal, it is very expensive and may cause hyperstimulation of the ovary. It is administered in the same manner as Pergonal, with daily injections and daily blood tests to check estrogen levels. Ultrasound to assess the follicle growth may also be used. Initial studies show promising results with women who did not respond to clomiphene citrate. Multiple births are also more likely with pure FSH. Side effects, according to its manufacturer, Serono, can also include abdominal discomfort, pain, rash, swelling at the injection site, headache or gastrointestinal upset.

GnRH Analogues Plus GnRH Pump

A new treatment still being researched for PCO has excited researchers with its initial results. It uses GnRH analogues—look-alike molecules of the gonadotropin releasing hormone—to switch off the hormonal axis. The man-made GnRH analogues block the receptors in the pituitary, turn off the hormonal axis and essentially revert the woman to a temporary pre-pubertal or menopausal state. (The analogues are being used for a range of infertility treatments, including shrinking fibroids and endometriosis implants and for egg stimulation for in vitro fertilization. See more on GnRH analogues in Appendix D and Chapters 6 and 10.)

When the system has been turned off the doctors stimulate it again with a device called a GnRH pump that mimics the action of the normal hypothalamus. (See Appendix C.) The pump is the size of a cigarette pack that the woman wears on a halter or around her waist. A long plastic tube leads from the pump to the inside of the arm where it is placed under the skin with a needle. The pack delivers natural GnRH in 90-minute pulses just as the hypothalamus does. In effect, it is like a reset on the body's computer to wipe out the PCO bugs in the program and start afresh.

A GnRH pump alone is very successful for women who have other ovulatory problems, but the results for PCO have been less than satisfactory and it is not recommended on its own. Combined with the GnRH analogues, the pump appears to help the woman's system start up normally before the vicious cycle begins again. Dr. David Healy in Australia, who has been conducting studies out of Melbourne, says the initial results are very promising. The analogue-plus-pump is also more like the natural system and multiple pregnancies do not occur with this method. An added bonus of this technique may be an improved understanding of how PCO starts because the doctors are able to follow the progression of the disease to find out whether after the reset it slowly develops again.

Surgery

In Stein's and Leventhal's day the only treatment for PCO was an operation called an ovarian wedge resection. The doctor operated on both ovaries and removed a wedge of tissue, cutting out a triangular shape. The ovaries were stitched up, leaving them about the size of regular ovaries. No one was sure why it worked—perhaps it interfered with the ability of the ovaries to produce androgens—but about 80 percent of the women then ovulated. The problem was that, all the same, many did not become pregnant because the operation caused scars to form around the ovaries and the tubes, which prevented passage of the egg. The wedge resection is now largely out of favor, not only because it can cause significant adhesions, but also because it entails a major operation. It is used only when all other medical therapies have failed.

Some researchers are taking a renewed look, however, at operating on the ovary for PCO. A variation on the wedge resection is being tried in which the ovary is randomly cauterized or burned in eight or ten small spots. The procedure can be done under laparoscopy. Limited studies have shown that 80 to 90 percent of women ovulate after the operation and about 62 percent conceive without fertility drugs, said Dr. Gab Kovacs, a gynecologist from Melbourne, Australia who has been studying ovarian cautery. If drugs are used with the operation, the conception rate goes up to about 80 percent. The procedure, however, is still experimental and it is not known whether the same problems with adhesions will arise.

Variations of PCO

In some women further hormone interference from glands outside the hormonal axis can complicate the picture and confuse treatment. Abnormal thyroid function, elevated prolactin and excess androgen coming from the adrenal glands can also appear with PCO.

Androgen Excess from the Adrenal Glands

In a small, select group of PCO patients the androgen excess does not come solely from the ovary, but also from over-active adrenal glands on the kidney. Many of these women ovulate on clomiphene citrate alone, but those who are resistant to CC may ovulate and conceive when given a drug from the family of anti-inflammatory drugs called corticosteroids. The drugs used are a derivative of the synthetic drug cortisone and may also be called prednisone, prednisolone, dexamethasone or other designations in the family of corticosteriods. The dose of dexamethasone is small, about 0.5 milligram daily; prednisone is about 5 milligrams daily. It is given by itself or else in combination with clomiphene citrate.

The theory is that corticosteroid treatment suppresses the action of the adrenal glands, lowering the level of male hormones and enabling the ovary to be stimulated to ovulate. The drug is discontinued if you become pregnant. Reports of success with corticosteroids vary among studies. Some research groups have reported good success; others have reported poor success.

High Prolactin with PCO

In about 15 to 20 percent of women with PCO, the levels of the hormone prolactin are also elevated. Prolactin is the hormone responsible for the stimulation of breast tissue to create milk and as such inhibits ovulation. In PCO the levels are usually only slightly elevated (see the section on high prolactin) and is thought to be caused by estrogen stimulation of the part of the pituitary that is responsible for stimulating breast tissue. The high prolactin will usually be treated by the drug bromocriptine (See Appendix E.).

Special Problems of PCO

Above and beyond the problem of infertility, women with PCO can have other problems that warrant medical attention.

Overstimulation of the Endometrium

The constant high levels of circulating estrogen can cause the lining of the uterus to build and build. Without regular menstruation to break down the tissue, women with PCO run the risk of developing overgrowth of the endometrium, called endometrial hyperplasia, or even endometrial cancer. At least four menstrual periods a year are recommended to shed endometrial tissue. Your doctor may want to induce menstruations with progesterone every six to eight weeks. Even if you have more than four periods a year, you may be disturbed by the extreme heaviness of your periods. In that case, regular courses of progesterone help the bleeding pattern. If you are temporarily trying not to conceive, birth control pills may be prescribed to induce regular bleeding.

Hirsutism

The amount of hair growth in PCO is largely dependent on two factors: the type of hair growth pattern common in the men of one's family and, to a lesser degree, the amount of androgen circulating in the blood. As long as androgens are stimulating the hair follicles to grow, women with PCO recruit new hair follicles and have a problem with excess hair growth. Some women become very good at controlling the growth through depilatories or waxing, but the hair keeps coming back and permanent methods such as electrolysis may not be able to control the growth unless the androgen levels are brought down. The excess androgen must be eliminated to stop the velus (soft, uncolored) hair follicles from being converted to terminal (dark, coarse) hair. For women trying to become pregnant, this usually means taking the anti-androgen drugs cyproterone acetate or spironolactone.

These drugs are given in tablet form in the follicular phase of the cycle, and they should *not* be taken in the second half of the cycle or in early pregnancy as animal studies have shown masculinizing effects on the fetus. Four to five months of use are usually required before there is any change in hair growth. Cream application of both drugs to the hairy areas has also shown some success. The creams, too, should not be used in the second half of the cycle because of the potential effect on the fetus.

Cardiovascular Disease
It is not proved, but it is suspected, that women with life-long PCO may be at a greater risk of heart attack and stroke because of the increase in androgens circulating in the blood. Women with PCO can reduce any potential risk of cardiovascular disease by not smoking and by reducing the amount of red meat, dairy products and animal fats in their diet.

Hypothalamic Amenorrhea

AKA: hypogondotrophic hypogonadism, hypothalamic hypogonadism, exerciser's amenorrhea, weight-loss induced amenorrhea, stress-inducer amenorrhea, psychological amenorrhea

In recent years there has been an increase in the number of women with infertility caused by hypothalamic amenorrhea or hypothalamic hypogonadism. In this condition the hormonal axis between the hypothalamus, pituitary and ovaries has been turned down low, like the volume switch on a radio. It is a state of hibernation, as it were, induced by the hypothalamus, and it can be caused by a range of conditions, most commonly weight-loss, exercise and stress. The steady increase in cases of anorexia and bulimia have contributed to an increase in hypothalamic amenorrhea but the condition can also be caused by biological reasons such as an underactive hypothalamus or delayed puberty.

Symptoms

Women with hypothalamic amenorrhea tend to have very light or no menstrual periods. If periods are regular, no ovulation is taking place, as indicated by flat temperature graphs and lack of fertile mucus.

If you have hypothalamic amenorrhea your infertility work-up will show that all hormone levels are low. There will be little estrogen in your hormone profile, showing that your ovaries are quiescent. FSH and LH will also be low. Serum progesterone tests will show low progesterone with no ovulation.

Treatment

If your condition is caused by weight loss, stress or exercise, the doctor will first suggest that you gain weight or alter behavior to bring back your menstrual periods. A gain as small as 10 pounds or a small reduction in exercise can bring back menstruation.

Many doctors are reluctant to treat patients with intensive, potentially harmful fertility drugs, such as pergonal or GNRH-pump therapy, unless they have tried to gain weight or reduce exercise. Such a change in behavior, or change in the concept of how you should look, can be difficult. It can take a number of months to gain weight back. Many women who have a daily exercise routine find it hard to discontinue it. However, these changes may be necessary for a successful pregnancy.

If weight gain and exercise reduction do not turn your hormonal axis back on, or if biological problems are such that behavior modification is not an option, two therapies may be suggested, GNRH-pump and Pergonal. (See Appendix B on Pergonal and Appendix C on GNRH pumps.)

Women who have constant low levels of estrogen (as is the case in hypothalamic amenorrhea), are at risk of bone loss that may result in osteoporosis, a disease in which calcium is leached from the bone leaving it fragile, porous and susceptible to breakage. It usually affects women after menopause, but young women who do not ovulate and have a low level of estrogen risk developing the disease prematurely. Stress fractures are one of the earliest signs, particularly in athletes. The precise role of estrogen and ovulation in the maintainance of bone is not completely understood, although it is believed estrogen carries calcium to the constantly regenerating bone. The loss is reversible if normal menstrual cycles and hormone environments return, giving another reason besides infertility for these women to seek treatment.

High Prolactin

AKA: hyperprolactinemia; prolactinemia

About 15 to 25 percent of women with ovulation disorders suffer from high prolactin levels that inhibit the development and release of an egg. Prolactin is the hormone released from the pituitary and primes the breasts to develop milk for nursing. When prolactin increases, it disrupts the pulsing of GnRH to the pituitary, interferes with the feedback of estrogen to the hypothalamus, and interferes with functioning of the corpus luteum. In short, prolactin is like static interrupting the normal hormonal signals of the menstrual cycle. As a result, ovulation does not take place, or if it does, implantation does not occur.

The hypothalamus controls prolactin release from the pituitary by a process called active inhibition. The hypothalamus sends a chemical to block the release of prolactin. The inhibiting factor is thought to be the neurotransmitter, dopamine, although another as-yet-unknown chemical may also be involved. If the inhibition is overridden with a pregnancy or by the stimulus of suckling, prolactin levels rise.

When a woman is neither pregnant nor nursing, raised prolactin levels can be caused by a number of situations or conditions. Emotional or physical stress, exercise, sexual intercourse, nipple stimulation, or even a meal heavy in protein can temporarily raise prolactin levels, but usually not enough to chronically inhibit ovulation. The viral infection, shingles, or surgery around the rib cage can temporarily raise prolactin. A wide range of drugs including amphetamines, tranquilizers, anti-depressants and hallucinogens can also raise prolactin, as can beer. An underactive thyroid and polycystic ovarian disease may also result in high prolactin levels.

When prolactin levels are consistently raised and chronic infertility results, a benign pituitary tumor is one of the more common reasons behind it. The tumor can be less than one centimeter in diameter, called a microadenoma, or greater than one centimeter, called a macroadenoma. The larger tumor has usually been growing for a long time; it is not cancerous and does not spread to other parts of the body, but it can slowly grow larger and press on important nerves, such as the optic nerve.

A woman whose prolactin is high enough to inhibit ovulation and cause infertility usually has very light, irregular or no menstrual periods, or she may have short periods. In many cases, during the physical examination the doctor is able to extrude milk from the breasts by squeezing behind the nipple, a condition called galactorrhea. The doctor may test the grey-white discharge to find out whether it is really milk by examining it for fat globules.

At least two, perhaps three, blood tests will be taken to determine prolactin levels to rule out temporary rises in prolactin caused by stress or food. If the first blood test shows raised levels, you are asked to fast over night for the next one and have your blood drawn between 8:00 A.M. and 10:00 A.M. the next day. A third test will confirm the findings. Prolactin is considered to be high if blood levels are above 20 nanograms per milliliter. A level greater than 100 nanograms per milliliter indicates a probable pituitary tumor. Some women will have prolactin levels of 300 nanograms per milliliter or higher.

The first step will be to rule out causes of high prolactin other than a pituitary tumor, such as thyroid problems or stress. Tests may be done to check the functioning of your thyroid. A skull X ray or Computerized Axial Tomography (CAT scan) may be ordered to look for a pituitary tumor. Some doctors reserve the more expensive CAT scan for patients in which a tumor is all but certain. In the United States the CAT scan is often used to screen all women with high prolactin. If a tumor is seen on the scan, it will be classed as a microadenoma or macroadenoma, depending on its size. If a tumor is not seen on a scan and all other reasons for high prolactin have been ruled out, the diagnosis will be either a microadenoma, as yet too small to be seen, or idiopathic hyperprolactinemia, meaning the cause is unknown.

Treatment

Drugs

The drug bromocriptine is standard treatment for microadenomas and unknown causes of high prolactin. It may also be given when high prolactin is associated with other disorders such as underactive thryoid or polycystic ovarian disease. (See appendix E.)

Surgery

In cases where bromocriptine has been unsuccessful, particularly if a tumor is large and pressing on the optic nerve or on the hypothalamus, surgery is often recommended. The surgery is usually done through the nasal passage to remove the tumor. Although surgery can relieve the pressure caused by a large tumor, it does not always bring prolactin levels back to normal and may not help your infertility. Radiation of the tumor is also sometimes recommended for large tumors, but total loss of fertility may result.

Special Concerns of High Prolactin

Like women with hypothalamic amenorrhea, women with high prolactin who have gone months without a menstrual period or ovulation can sometimes have low estrogen levels leading to bone loss. The weakening of bone can lead to stress fractures. The return of normal menstrual periods corrects this problem. Even if fertility is not desired, for example after bromocriptine results in the successful birth of a child, women who have a microadenoma or macroadenoma, or are suspected of having an unseen microadenoma that may grow, should be examined at least every two years to check the growth of the tumor.

Luteal Phase Defect

AKA: luteal phase deficiency, corpus luteum deficiency, inadequate corpus luteum, luteal phase inadequacy

To understand luteal phase defects, and the controversy surrounding it, review the description of a normal menstrual cycle in Chapter 3.

The luteal phase is the second half of the menstrual cycle after ovulation when progesterone comes into play. The most important occurrence in the luteal phase is the formation of the corpus luteum from the follicle that liberated the egg. The ruptured follicle, under the influence of LH from the pituitary, luteinizes and starts to pump out progesterone to make the endometrium hospitable to accept an embryo.

The theory behind the luteal phase defect is that something happens to prematurely stop the corpus luteum working and/or prevents the endometrium from being receptive. The successfully fertilized egg is either never able to implant or else its HCG message is not enough to stop the corpus luteum from dying and hence removing the progesterone support for the endometrium. The endometrium sheds, taking the embryo with it. This happens usually before the woman even knows she was pregnant. In the most severe cases the cycle may be short, with the luteal phase less than 10 days, indicating the corpus luteum has failed. Other women may appear to have a very long luteal phase followed by a heavier than normal period. The menstrual period is believed to be, in fact, a spontaneous abortion of the developing embryo. This is sometimes called an occult pregnancy.

It is known that all women, at various times in their lives, can have a temporary disruption in the second half of their cycles. The defect often occurs around the first menstrual periods of puberty, the resumption of menstrual cycles after giving birth and breastfeeding, and the beginning of menopause—essentially any time the menstrual cycle is starting or stopping. These temporary glitches usually do not alter the woman's overall fertility. It is also believed that emotional and physical stress can subtly alter the luteal phase. Cigarette smoking, too, can disrupt it in the same manner, but the defect will correct itself when the causal factor is corrected.

The History of LPD and Its Controversy

Luteal phase deficiency was first described in 1949 by the Norfolk, Virginia specialist, Dr. Georgeanna Jones, in a study of 98 infertile women over a number of months of their menstrual cycles. She has remained one of its champions ever since. Her study found that about 13 percent of the women had abnormal basal body temperature graphs in which the temperature in the second half of their cycles stayed raised for only a short period of time or did not rise to expected levels. The endometrial biopsies, although they were unsophisticated at the time, showed 50 percent had what was thought to be abnormal progesterone influence. In the 1960s, through more sophisticated tests for hormones and biopsies, researchers found that in a small group of women progesterone inexplicably fell during the luteal phase, but LPD was not generally accepted by the medical profession as a significant problem. In the 1970s, the development of even better techniques to follow the intricacies of the menstrual cycle advanced the knowledge surrounding the disorder, but at the same time made the diagnosis more controversial.

In North America it is now common for about two to five percent of women in an infertility practice to be diagnosed with a luteal phase defect. However, it is highly uncommon in Australia or Britain for that diagnosis ever to be made. It is not that LPD is a strange disorder that affects only North American women and not those in other places. It is simply a medical disagreement over what is happening and what the disorder should be called.

British and Australian doctors believe that a problem *can* occur in the luteal phase to make the endometrium inhospitable. But, they say, instead of being a true "luteal phase defect" it is, in fact, a "follicular phase defect." Simply stated: if the ovary produced a good egg in the follicular phase, then there would not be a problem in the luteal phase. The corpus luteum is inadequate, and the endometrium inadequate, only because the development of the egg was inadequate. Therefore, doctors should be focusing on developing good eggs in the follicular phase, which usually means using fertility drugs to promote egg development.

The North Americans believe that, to an extent, the Brits and Aussies are right: good egg development produces a good corpus luteum and good endometrium. In some cases fertility drugs may be warranted, but luteal phase deficiency does not begin and end there, the Americans say. It can have subtle variations. In women whose hypothalamus and pituitary properly stimulate the ovary, developing and ovulating an egg, the corpus luteum can still fail and result in falling progesterone levels and an unreceptive endometrium. Their cycles can be short, truncated in the second half, despite ovulation. American studies have indicated that LH from the pituitary may fail to support the corpus luteum and so it dies. Fertility drugs for women who are already ovulating are not necessary, American doctors say. Instead, support shuld be given to the endometrium in the form of natural progesterone supplements in the luteal phase. They also point to new research that suggests that natural progesterone not only turns on receptors in the endometrium to enable it to accept the egg, but also lowers the immune response to prevent the mother from rejecting the embryo.

Obstacles to Resolving the Debate

The difficulty in studying and diagnosing LPD contributes to the continuation of the controversy. A number of endometrial biopsies are required from each woman to check the development of the endometrium. (See the information on endometrial biopsies in Chapter 4.) Endometrial biopsies can be painful for some women and so doctors are reluctant to do them repeatedly unless there is irrefutable scientific evidence of their merit. To be useful, the EB must be performed correctly by well-trained staff and properly read, which is more difficult than it sounds. The Brit-and-Aussie camp say that although they agree endometrium may be "in" or "out" of phase, they question its importance for the acceptance of the embryo.

The alternative method of taking blood samples to check progesterone in the luteal phase also has its problems. Progesterone levels can vary by as much as 600 percent from one hour to the next because it is released in pulses from the corpus luteum. Blood tests would be required daily in the luteal phase, even twice daily, to get an average level. Such blood tests are impractical. Although research is looking at other methods such as daily urine tests to check progesterone, the problem is a long way from being solved.

Studying LPD is difficult because researchers can not adequately access the inside of a woman's functioning uterus to see what is going on at the critical time when the embryo is being accepted or rejected. The process is like looking into a room through a keyhole or listening with an ear to the wall to figure out what is going on inside. Two or three weeks later when a positive or negative pregnancy test comes back researchers learn the outcome, and even then they do not know with 100 percent confidence all the factors that may have influenced that outcome. The studies of treatments of the disorder, particularly those giving progesterone to support the pregnancy, have had conflicting results. Some studies show that progesterone prevents early pregnancy loss, but numerous studies that have compared the outcomes of pregnancies in women given progesterone to those of women given nothing at all, can find no difference between the two.

Scottish specialist David Baird summarizes the ongoing scientific debate over LPD. "This sort of debate always happens in medicine when all the evidence isn't in yet. If a disorder and its treatment have been proven, then you will get nine out of ten of us all agreeing what should be done. But something like LPD, the reason it is so controversial, is that there is not undisputed evidence one way or the other. And it is so difficult to study."

The debate is expected to continue for a number of years because of those difficulties. Nevertheless, one day the debate will cease, particularly because American scientists such as Jones and Dr. Michael Soules, of the University of Washington in Seattle, are committed to understanding better LPD and proving it to its detractors. "At the end of my career I will be happy if the Brits finally say, 'Yes, it is a hard diagnosis, but it does exist and we now have a better way of diagnosing it,'" says Soules.

Indications of Luteal Phase Defect

All that said, a significant number of women each year will be diagnosed with luteal phase deficiency, and treated for it, and it is fitting to discuss their situation. LPD is most severe in cases of short luteal phases indicated on a basal body temperature graph. The woman's chart may show the jump from a lower temperature to a higher temperature, indicating ovulation, but after a few days the temperature may start to trail down and menses begin. A luteal phase is considered short when there are fewer than 10 or 11 days between the time of temperature rise and the start of menstruation. Another indication of an abnormal luteal phase, on the basis of the BBT graph, is a particularly long phase followed by heavy menstruation. The temperature graph shows the rise at ovulation and 20 days or longer of elevated temperature before heavy bleeding begins. This is suspected to be what is called a clinical or occult pregnancy that has aborted very early. It can happen to all women at some stages in their life, but if it is a consistent occurrence, LPD may be suspected.

Further Investigation

The investigation for LPD can be long and painful, requiring a great deal of follow-up. Along with looking at BBT graphs, a doctor performs endometrial biopsies, as described in Chapter 4. Because of the potential variation between one EB and the next, at least two EBs will be done to date them for endometrial development. A lag in development by more than two days is considered abnormal. If the results of the two EBs conflict, for example one being in phase and the other out of phase, a third EB will be done.

Your doctor may also recommend an ultrasound of your ovaries during the follicular phase to check for adequate growth (a size of at least 17 millimeters before ovulation is considered normal), and blood tests may be taken during the luteal phase to check the level of progesterone. So far, medical literature disagrees on what the normal level of progesterone is.

Treatment

According to Dr. Georgeanna Jones, some forms of LPD are very easy to treat. "The easiest luteal phase defect to cure is [that caused by] running. We stopped the women running and they are pregnant in four months." Quitting smoking or gaining weight are two ways women with LPD may also solve their problem.

If behavioral techniques do not work, progesterone supplementation is usually the first line of treatment, particularly if the BBT graphs show a too-short cycle or evidence of occult pregnancy. Natural progesterone is given in the form of vaginal suppositories. Jones and Soules recommend that progesterone be given as soon after ovulation as possible, usually three or four days after the LH surge. The suppositories are put high in the vagina close to the cervix. Doctors who use this technique say some women require just one 25-milligram suppository a day, while others may require two or three. The suppositories can be messy; some women prefer to insert them in the rectum. During treatment with progesterone, the doctor may perform endometrial biopsies to check that the proper dose is being given. Usually four or five months of treatment with progesterone are required for a woman to become pregnant. If pregnancy results, many doctors continue with progesterone support until about 12 weeks of pregnancy, although this has not yet been proved to be necessary.

If progesterone fails, clomiphene citrate may be tried to improve the follicular phase. But clomiphene is also known to induce luteal phase defects and alter cervical mucus in ovulating women who have adequate estrogen levels. If prolactin is thought to be abnormal, bromocriptine may also be given.

Some doctors have recommended that shots of human chorionic gonadotropin be given every three or four days in the luteal phase to mimic the message of HCG sent by the embryo to the corpus luteum. This treatment has not yet been proved.

Other Causes of Ovulation Defects

Oligo-Ovulation

In some women who ovulate irregularly no specific cause or defect can be found, called oligo-ovulation or non-specific anovulation. The hormones look normal, but menstrual cycles are sporadic and ovulation occurs only a few times a year. No one knows why. Even though no disease, no syndrome, nor anomaly can be found, because the women have fewer than 12 ovulations a year they have a decreased chance of conceiving. In these cases clomiphene citrate is usually given with good results.

Post Pill Syndrome

Between one and five percent of women who stop the birth control pill after using it for a number of years fail to resume normal cycles for six months or longer. It is assumed that the pill has somehow disrupted the hormonal axis. Usually it happens to a woman who did not have regular or normal cycles before starting the pill. With time the defect usually corrects itself although irregular ovulation can persist for up to 30 months, or longer, making pregnancy difficult. After other causes of ovulation defects are ruled out, clomiphene citrate can be given to increase the number of ovulations a year and hence increase the chance of conception. Bromocriptine also may be prescribed if after stopping the pill prolactin levels have increased enough to inhibit ovulation. (See appendix E.)

Premature Ovarian Failure

In a small number of women the ovaries stop working, which brings on early or premature menopause when they are still in their thirties. The cause can be natural or induced by drugs, disease, surgery, trauma or cancer.

It is not known why some women suffer from natural ovarian failure years before others. There is a theory that it might be hereditary and that the woman has fewer eggs to ovulate and so uses up her quota before other women. In generations past, when women had children in their early 20s, such a familial trait may never have been noticed or critical. But when childbearing is left until later in life the problem can be devastating. Other causes of natural premature ovarian failure are speculated, such as overstimulation of the ovaries by the pituitary, but the real reasons are not yet known.

Sometimes premature menopause is brought on as a consequence of disease or medical intervention. Fertility drugs, particularly human menopausal gonadotropin, cause early menopause only if hyperstimulation occurs and the ovaries are damaged and have to be removed. (See Appendix B.) Surgical removal of the ovaries will bring on immediate menopause. Severe pelvic infection can lead doctors to control the spread of the infection by removing all the pelvic organs, including the ovaries. In rare instances pelvic surgery cuts off blood supply to the ovaries, killing them. Radiation therapy can cause the ovaries to fail, as can drugs to fight various cancers. Ovarian cancer itself requires removal of the ovaries.

Natural ovarian failure will be diagnosed by extremely high levels of follicle stimulating hormones (FSH) and luteinizing hormone (LH) in the blood or in the urine, as the pituitary pumps out the hormones to try to bolster the flagging ovaries. Estrogen levels will be low.

For women who experience early menopause or premature ovarian failure, there is no accepted drug therapy that can be given to bring back fertility. Some doctors have experimented with giving fertility drugs in case a few viable eggs remain in the ovary, but this is not widely practiced. If, however, the uterus is still functional, doctors in some infertility centers use donor eggs and in vitro fertilization to help women with premature ovarian failure become pregnant and deliver a child. The donated egg is fertilized with the husband's sperm and implanted in the infertile woman's womb, allowing the couple to have a baby that is at least genetically related to the husband. A number of donor-egg babies have now been born around the world.

Appendix A Clomiphene Citrate

For the past 25 years the drug clomiphene citrate, known by the trade names Clomid or, recently, Serophene, has been the mainstay of infertility treatment. It has been used by tens of thousands of women around the world to coax them to ovulate and, with hope, conceive. The majority of women diagnosed with ovulation problems get a course of CC at some point in their infertility treatment.

Ironically, this most favored of fertility drugs, was actually first considered as a possible contraceptive. In the 1950s researchers trying to develop birth control pills turned to an anti-estrogen compound, triphenyl ethylene, which had been discovered in the late 1930s. With a few chemical modifications it was synthesized in 1956 as clomiphene citrate by researchers at drug manufacturer William S. Merrell Company. But instead of the intended anti-fertility effect it had the opposite result—it stimulated the ovaries, and it gave medicine the first drug therapy for infertility caused by ovulation disorders. In 1960 the first clinic trials of the new drug were started for women who were infertile because of anovulatory cycles or lack of menstruation. By 1961 a number of research groups reported in medical journals the first successful results of the drug. By 1968 it had been approved for ovulation induction for infertility by the United States Food and Drug Administration (FDA). Until recently Merrell held an exclusive patent on the medication and for years Clomid has been synonymous with clomiphene citrate. That patent has now expired and Serono, which developed the other cornerstone of ovulation induction, Pergonal, is now manufacturing the drug, too.

How It Works

The difficulty of precisely charting the human body at work means the precise mechanism of CC is not completely understood. Many experimental models, however, have led researchers to assume the following: CC competes with estrogen for the receptor sites on the hypothalamus. The concept is like a look-alike key fitting into a lock, occupying it so that the real key can not fit in. By blocking the estrogen receptors in the hypothalamus, CC encourages the pituitary to continue to pump out FSH and LH to stimulate the ovaries to develop eggs despite the feedback of estrogen. When CC is stopped, the hypothalamus suddenly is able to detect the estrogen and it triggers the pituitary to send an LH surge to release the egg.

Women Who Should Be Given CC

The drug is used only when pregnancy is wanted and may be effective when infertility is the result of the following problems: highly irregular, non-ovulatory cycles such as those with polycystic ovaries; regular cycles in which no ovulation takes place;

infrequent ovulatory cycles. Although some women with hypothalamic amenorrhea respond to CC, the manufacturers and studies have shown that these women who have a low level of estrogen as well as other hormones in general do not respond well.

Women who should not be given CC Women with certain conditions are not candidates for CC therapy.

A woman who has a cyst on her ovary should not be given CC as the drug can cause the cyst to grow and even rupture, causing hemorrhage, twisting or even loss of the ovary or reproductive organs.

The drug should not be taken during pregnancy. This may seem obvious, but because women who do not menstruate regularly are candidates for CC, it could happen that the next course of the drug is started before the menstrual period begins. A lack of a period may be mistakenly interpreted as a failure of that cycle when in fact the woman is pregnant. In animal studies CC has been shown to cause birth defects if taken during pregnancy. As a rule, the drug should not be taken until after menstruation occurs. If your temperature chart has shown a rise but menstruation does not occur, pregnancy or an ovarian cyst should be ruled out by a pelvic examination and pregnancy test before the drug is started again.

CC is cleared from the body through the liver so women whose liver function is compromised by liver-disease should not take the drug.

Before taking the drug, women with extremely heavy bleeding or unusual bleeding should be fully checked to rule out the possibility of early cancer.

Studies have shown that CC may be of no help to women who ovulate but who remain infertile for unknown reasons. In fact, the use of CC may make the problem worse by distorting the cervical mucus or creating a luteal phase defect. Only women with proven ovulatory problems should get the drug.

Before going on CC therapy you should have a complete infertility work-up.

Method of Use

Most women start at a dose of 50 milligrams taken from day five to day nine of the menstrual cycle. The pill, which is the size and color of an Aspirin and comes in 50-milligram tablets, should be taken at the same time each day. If you forget to take a pill, take it as soon as you remember. If you forget until the next day's dose, double the amount. If you miss two days, call your doctor. If the starting dose does not result in ovulation it may be increased to 100 milligrams (two pills) daily for five days. Some doctors continue to increase the dose to a limit of 250 milligrams daily (five pills) until ovulation is achieved. Some will also prescribe the drug for more days during the cycle. Patients on higher doses should be monitored carefully. Some women who have polycystic ovarian disease or who tend to develop ovarian cysts may be very sensitive to stimulation. They may do better on doses of 25 milligrams or less, studies have shown. If clomiphene is going to work, studies show it will usually do so within six to nine months. If after nine months you are still unsuccessful on the drug, discuss with your doctor the merits of modifying the dose or discontinuing treatment. Most women who will conceive do so in the first three months of starting the correct dose.

About 75 percent of women who take CC ovulate, but according to reports, only about 35 to 40 precent become pregnant and deliver a term baby. This number may be artificially low as many women on CC are lost to follow-up, presumably those women who become pregnant and do not return to their infertility specialist. However, the lower conception rates are believed to be in part because CC can interfere with the luteal phase of the cycle and inhibit implantation or make the cervical mucus inhospitable to sperm.

To monitor ovulation you will be required to keep a BBT graph (see Chapter 3) to note the rise in your resting body temperature after ovulation. Your temperature should rise at least a half a degree Celsius six to ten days after stopping the drug. The rise signals ovulation and your temperature should stay up for at least 11 days. The doctor may do serum progesterone measurements in your luteal phase to confirm ovulation. You and your partner should make love every other day for about a week, starting three or four days after your last tablet.

The manufacturers recommend a monthly pelvic examination while taking the drug to monitor any ovary enlargement. However, some doctors with years of experience in using the drug believe pelvic examinations are necessary only for women complaining of pelvic pain or who do not menstruate after a course of CC therapy. The doctor should check the quality of the cervical mucus on CC as it can be adversely effected by the drug. Sometimes estrogen tablets are given with the CC to improve mucus. An endometrial biopsy may also be done to check the quality of the endometrium after a patient starts CC therapy.

Side Effects

The most common side effect women experience while taking CC is hot flushing, similar to the hot flushes described by women during menopause. Many women experience a feeling of bloating, an increase of mid-cycle pain or other abdominal discomfort and tenderness, usually from the stimulation of the ovaries. Breast tenderness may occur and some women feel nauseated or vomit on the medication. Dizzyness, lightheadedness and headaches may also occur. Doctors may tend to underplay the emotional effects, but many women report feelings of depression, moodiness, increased anxiety, insomnia and tiredness while taking CC. Some women have reported weight gain and temporary hair loss.

The most serious but relatively uncommon side effect is overstimulation of the ovary. This usually occurs several days after the medication is stopped. If you experience pelvic pain after stopping the medication, see your doctor for a pelvic examination.

A few women taking CC experience blurred vision or other unusual visual symptoms such as spots before the eyes or flashes, particularly when the light is variable or bright. This can be dangerous if you are driving a car or using heavy equipment. If visual symptoms occur, stop taking the drug and contact your doctor.

Multiple Pregnancies

Women who take CC are seven times more likely than the fertile population to conceive twins, triplets and quintuplets. More than 90 percent of reported births on CC, however, are single births, but about 10 percent of the births are twins. (Twins occur naturally in fewer than 1 percent of the population). Triplets occur in about one in 3000 CC births, about ten times the rate of the normal population. You and your partner should discuss with your doctor the chance of multiple births before going on the drug.

Effect on the Fetus

Under normal doses taken during the follicular phase, no adverse affect has been shown to date on the human fetus or subsequent growth and development of the child. However, a great deal of concern has been expressed by some women about possible unseen effects. Some women's advocacy groups are concerned that CC is similar to the drug diethylstilbestrol (DES). DES was given to pregnant women from the 1950s to early 1970s in a mistaken belief that it prevented miscarriage. It caused the abnormal formation of reproductive organs in offspring and a peculiar type of cervical cancer in the female children. Although CC is similar to DES, in that both are estrogen-like synthetic steroids, they are used differently. DES was given continuously during pregnancy while the embryo was developing, and CC is not to be taken during pregnancy. Clomiphene usually is given for only five days during the follicular phase. It is known that clomiphene is excreted from the body slowly and traces of it can still be found a number of weeks after it has been given. There has been concern that this lingering effect might be detrimental to the developing tissue as was DES. Studies to date, however, have not been able to find DES-like changes in mice given clomiphene. It is believed, and all evidence to date suggests, that taken at this time it is not detrimental. However, spontaneous abortions are more common with CC therapy and genetic analysis of the aborted fetuses have shown a greater incidence of genetic abnormalities. Of the babies born, the stillbirths and congenital defects have been of the same rate as the general population and are not thought to be related to treatment.

Thousands of children have been born around the world as a result of CC therapy and now some of those children are reaching their late twenties. Some doctors say that if CC were to cause abnormalities, the effects would have begun to appear by now. The prudent thing to say, however, is that no evidence, *yet*, has been found that CC is unsafe or detrimental to children. Except for the cases of ovarian hyperstimulation during treatment, no long-term persistent adverse effects have been found on the mother. Animal studies have shown the development of cataracts on long-term high doses. Two women treated with clomiphene have been reported to develop breast cancer in both breasts, but it is not known if the drug caused or accelerated the condition. Like most medical therapies, CC has its risks and benefits. While it may help you become pregnant, CC may in the future be found to have a previously harmful effect. You must discuss the risks and benefits of CC therapy with your doctor, and make your decision accordingly.

CC Plus Human Chorionic Gonadotropins (HCG)

Women who have not ovulated on CC alone may be given an injection of the pregnancy hormone HCG approximately one week after the last dose of CC. When used with CC the HCG is like an LH surge and acts as a "kick-in-the-pants" to the egg in the follicle, spurring it to be released from the ovary.

Appendix B Human Menopausal Gonadotropin

AKA: Pergonal, menotropins

The other cornerstone of infertility therapy, which has been in use almost as long as clomiphene citrate, is human menopausal gonadotropin. It is a powerful fertility drug used after clomiphene has failed. In the 1950s while scientists were perfecting clomiphene citrate, others were looking for ways to extract and refine follicle stimulating hormone (FSH) and luteinizing hormone (LH) from the pituitary. The idea was to give it to anovulatory women, whose pituitary might not be secreting enough of the hormones, to stimulate them to ovulate. In 1958 Swedish scientist Carl-Alex Gemzell, of the University of Lund, reported the first success in getting anovulatory women to ovulate with FSH/LH extracted from the pituitaries of human cadavers. Although human pituitary gonadotropins (HPG) were successful, they were impractical in most countries because too many pituitaries were needed—an awkward and prohibitively expensive situation. Only in Australia, where there was a national system to collect pituitaries from cadavers primarily for extracting growth hormone, was HPG use for infertility practical.

Fortunately, about the same time Gemzell was working on hs pituitary extract, Italian scientist P. Donini was refining a method of using the FSH/LH naturally excreted in the urine of menopausal women. At menopause, when a woman's ovaries start to decline, the hypothalamus/pituitary senses estrogen levels are falling. In efforts to keep the ovary working, the pituitary begins to pump out excessively high amounts of FSH/LH. It is of no use to the ovary and the FSH/LH is excreted in the woman's urine. Donini collected urine from menopausal Italian nuns to purify for FSH/LH. His success built the Serono Pharmaceutical Company, a leader in infertility therapy. Serono's drug Pergonal has been synonymous with HMG ever since. The process of purification is complex, making the drug expensive; a cycle of treatment can cost between $500 to $1500 depending on how many ampules are used. Between 10 and 20 ampules might be required for one cycle of ovulation induction.

Not only is Pergonal expensive, it also is extremely powerful. It carries with it a significant risk of overstimulating the ovaries or producing multiple births. It must be administered by a trained infertility specialist who has considerable experience with HMG. The therapy is complex and requires that the patient go to the hospital or clinic once or even twice every day for as long as 10 or 12 days at a time.

Unlike CC, which acts on the hypothalamus and the hypothalamus then in turn stimulates the ovaries, HMG stimulates the ovaries directly to produce eggs. The doctor must act as the hypothalamus, determining how much to stimulate the ovaries.

The procedure requires careful monitoring of the feedback of estrogen from the developing follicles and the growth of the follicles by ultrasound.

Women Who Should Be Given HMG

Infertile women with hypothalamic amenorrhea, women with polycystic ovarian syndrome who have failed on properly monitored clomiphene citrate (CC) and CC/HCG therapy; and women with irregular ovulation who have failed on properly monitored CC may benefit from HMG therapy.

Women Who Should Not Be Given HMG

Women who have a high level of urinary FSH/LH, indicating primary ovarian failure or early menopause; women with levels of prolactin that indicate a pituitary tumor; and women with thyroid or adrenal problems should not be given HMG.

Method of Use

If you have a menstrual cycle, the drug will be given by injections starting about day five of your cycle. If you have not been menstruating you may be given progesterone to induce bleeding or you may be started on the drug at any time. Before administering the drug, the doctor usually takes an initial blood test to measure your starting level of estrogen and administers a baseline ultrasound to view your unstimulated ovaries to use as a comparison during treatment. A physical and pelvic examination is also carried out before the drug is started. The injections, usually 150 IUs a day into a muscle in your leg or buttock, will be given in late afternoon. Some clinics teach the partner to give the injection so that it can be given at the same time each evening, at about 7:00 P.M. or 8:00 P.M. A blood test is taken each morning at about 8:00 A.M., sometimes followed by ultrasound of the ovaries to monitor the developing follicles. Some doctors do not start monitoring estrogen or the ovaries until after a few days of Pergonal shots. The response from the developing follicles and the amount of estrogen being produced determines the number of vials to be injected and how long the treatment will go on; 10 days is typical.

When estrogen levels in your blood show mature follicles (between 600 to 1500 pg/ml of estrogen) and ultrasound shows a "main" or leading follicle of 16 millimeters to 25 millimeters in diameter, a shot of HCG (human chorionic gonadotropin) is given to spur ovulation. HCG, which mimics the LH surge, causes the egg to be released about 36 hours later. Some doctors also instruct partners to give the HCG shot. You and your partner should have sexual intercourse on the day of the HCG shot and every day thereafter until ovulation has been confirmed. (Some doctors recommend sex every 12 hours if the man's sperm count is good and recycles fast, or every other day if the sperm count is low or low-normal and does not recycle fast.) You will notice an increase in cervical mucus and discharge caused by the increasing estrogen in your system.

If too many follicles are present on ultrasound or if estrogen levels are too high, you and your doctor will discuss whether you should go ahead with the HCG shot because of the risk of multiple pregnancies. (See Chapter 11.)

Risks and Side Effects

Human menopausal gonadotropins are extremely potent and potentially dangerous. The most serious side effects are multiple pregnancies and hyperstimulation of the ovaries, meaning the drugs have stimulated the follicles too much. In some cases a series of events, arising from the overstimulation of the ovaries, may take place. This is called hyperstimulation syndrome.

Many women experience pain, rash or swelling at the site of the injections. Because of bruising and soreness in the muscle from the injection, new injection sites often have to be found. Some women develop a fever from the shots.

In recent years, partly because of confidence gained through Pergonal use in in vitro fertilization, doctors have been aggressive with its use. Sometimes the line between not enough stimulation and too much stimulation is thin. Studies show higher pregnancy rates in cycles where mild to moderate hyperstimulation has taken place, and pregnancy, itself, makes the ovaries more susceptible to hyperstimulation. About 50 percent of all women show symptoms of mild to moderate hyperstimulation; abdominal pain and swelling occur about a week after the HCG shot has been given. The majority of cases are mild and will usually subside in about two or three weeks.

In about 6 to 7 percent of cases hyperstimulation is moderate, marked by weight gain, pain and nausea. The ovaries enlarge by five to 10 centimeters. If you develop moderate hyperstimulation you must be observed carefully by your doctor and must avoid intercourse until your ovaries return to normal size because of the potential danger of rupture and bleeding.

About 2 percent of women on Pergonal develop severe, sometimes life-threatening hyperstimulation in which the ovaries swell by greater than 10 centimeters, sometimes fill with fluid and start a cascade of dire problems, called hyperstimulation syndrome.

Severe hyperstimulation syndrome develops suddenly about three to seven days after the HCG shot. Severe pain and weight gain usually occur and may be accompanied by nausea and vomiting. At this stage the woman must be hospitalized. Over the next week to 10 days the condition usually runs its course. Fluid collects in the abdomen and chest; blood clots are apt to form more easily. Sometimes fluid must be removed from the abdominal cavity. The grossly swollen ovaries are at risk of rupturing or bleeding and extreme care must be taken not to disturb them. If rupture or bleeding of the ovary occurs, surgery is required to repair them, and often they must be removed. Blood clots that blocked important arteries have been reported in four patients on Pergonal who developed hyperstimulation syndrome. Two of the patients died.

Multiple pregnancies are a considerable risk with HMG. Although 80 percent of all reported births with the drug result in a single pregnancy, 20 percent are multiple births. Of those, about 15 percent are twins and 5 percent triplets, or more. Even with extensive monitoring of follicles by ultrasound and blood estrogen levels, multiple pregnancies still occur. Cases have been reported in which only two follicles were seen on ultrasound and yet three or more conceptions took place. In one case, ultrasound detected four follicles in a woman but at six weeks of pregnancy seven gestational sacs were seen on ultrasound. In the last 20 years the celebrated reported cases of quadruplets, quintuplets and even septuplets have almost all been caused by HMG. Multiple pregnancies can lead to premature birth and death of the babies and can be dangerous to the mother. Some centers do a procedure called selective reduction, in which multiple pregnancies are reduced to two or three fetuses by selectively killing the fetuses easiest to reach. The risks and the controversy of selective reduction is described in more detail in Chapter 11.

Effect on the Fetus

No data are available on its effects on the developing baby. Reported birth defects have occurred in about 1.7 percent of births from Pergonal, which is at the same rate as the general population.

Success Rates

Pregnancy rates range between 20 and 60 percent, depending on the cause of anovulation. Women with hypothalamic amenorrhea fare best on HMG therapy with as many as 60 percent becoming pregnant within the first three to six cycles of treatment. Spontaneous abortions occur in about 25 percent of pregnancies, a rate that may or may not be higher than the general population. A lack of certainty results over comparisons of spontaneous abortions because in the general population the loss of early pregnancies may go unnoticed or unreported while the outcomes of all Pergonal pregnancies are reported.

Appendix C
GnRH
Pump

In the early 1970s Dr. Andrew Schally, of Tulane University, broke the code of gonadotropin-releasing hormone, the peptide released by the hypothalamus as its messenger to stimulate the pituitary. Piece by piece he was able to put together the long-chain molecule, giving him the ability to bypass the hypothalamus and stimulate the pituitary to make the ovaries ovulate. His work earned him the Nobel Prize. Unfortunately, for the first eight years no one was sure how GnRH should be given.

Researchers tried daily injections, continuous injections, injections every six hours, but the results were always less than expected—fewer than 40 percent of the women could be made to ovulate. Separate researchers in 1970 had determined that luteinizing hormone (LH) was released in a pulse-pattern every 90 minutes in monkeys but it wasn't until 1978 that that information was applied to GnRH. Sure enough, given about every 90 minutes, GnRH mimicked the action of the hypothalamus. A pump was made that could deliver the rhythmic dose. In 1980 the first births by GnRH-pump infusion for anovulatory women were reported. The pump is expensive, about $1000 (U.S.) but it is available in some cities for monthly rental.

Who Should Use the GnRH-Pump

Infertile women whose hormonal axis is turned down so that all hormone levels are low are the most responsive to pump therapy, as are women with delayed puberty. Other indications for its use are still being researched.

Who Should Not Use the GnRH-Pump

Women with premature menopause or ovarian failure should not use this type of drug therapy. It appears that women with polycystic ovarian syndrome also do not do well on pump therapy although some studies have claimed the contrary. Research that adjusts the dose or pulse frequency may make PCO women more successful.

Method of Use

Slightly larger than a cigarette pack, the battery-run pump can be worn around the waist or hung on a halter around the neck, concealed under loose-fitting clothing, and it can also be carried in a pocket. A long plastic tube leads from the pump and at the other end is a small needle, which is placed under the skin, usually in the fleshy part of your upper arm or in the skin of the abdomen. It is held in place with tape or a large bandage. The site may have to be changed during treatment. If you are resistant to the initial therapy, the needle may be placed in a vein in a subsequent trial. The pump will be programmed to deliver GnRH in a pulse every 60 to every 120 minutes night and day. The reservoir for the hormone in the pump will have to be refilled every two to three days.

Side Effects

Women complain of soreness at the site of injection and awkwardness in wearing the device, particularly in airports or in other locations where they must go through security scanning.

> *It was really embarrassing. We were flying back east and there was a huge line of people to go through the security clearance. My pump, of course, set off the alarm and I had to explain to the guard why I had this thing strapped to my waist. They took me into another room and I had to lift up my shirt and show them what it was. I was just dying, it was so embarrassing.*

Despite the pump's awkwardness, because the GnRH is a naturally occurring hormone, there are few reported side effects. Multiple births are rare. Mild ovarian hyperstimulation, resulting in abdominal discomfort, is possible, but uncommon.

Success Rates

Women with hypothalamic amenorrhea have the best results with an estimated 90 percent ovulating and 50 percent or more becoming pregnant.

Appendix D GnRH Analogues

The discovery in the early 1970s of the molecular structure of gonadotropin releasing hormone paved the way for researchers to try creating other long-chain molecules similar to GnRH but not the same. The result was GnRH analogues, man-made peptide almost identical to natural GnRH except that a few amino acids in key locations have been switched. The analogue is similar enough to occupy the receptor sites on the pituitary meant for natural GnRH, but not similar enough to allow it to work properly. It is often described as a "key jamming a lock." The result is that the pituitary does not stimulate the ovaries with follicle stimulating hormone and luteinizing hormone, the ovary does not produce estrogen and progesterone and the woman goes into temporary menopause.

GnRH analogues (GnRHa) are being used to treat fibroids, endometriosis, and polycystic ovaries, and to improve the outcome and control of ovarian stimulation regimens in in vitro fertilization. Their use is essentially the same in all instances: a temporary shut-down in the woman's reproductive system to allow a correction of a defect or manipulation by the doctor. Doctors often call the action of GnRHa "down-regulation."

Agonist and Antagonists

There are two basic types of GnRH analogues, agonists and antagonists, and they have slightly different actions. Both bind to the GnRH receptor on the pituitary for a long time, but the antagonist immediately turns the pituitary off. Within minutes of the antagonist's administration the woman's system has been shut down. In contrast, the agonist, to which the drugs Buserelin, Leupron and Leuprolide belong, first turns the receptor on. Scientists call this initial stimulating reaction the "flare up." When the agonist is first given it works like natural GnRH and stimulates the pituitary, but then unlike the natural molecule the agonist keeps blocking the receptor site. The pituitary, which is used to receiving pulsed signals, does not like having its receptor sites continually occupied. It soon ignores the signal and shuts down.

To date the fast-acting antagonists developed have had too many side-effects—mostly an allergy-like response—to be used in treatment. Scientists have been working on creating a safe and effective antagonist and it is expected one will be available soon. For now, however, the agonists are the ones that are used.

Method of Use

GnRH analogues are given either for a short time with fertility drugs for IVF stimulation and ovulation induction or for a number of months for the treatment of fibroids and endometriosis. They can be injected, put under the skin in a pellet, or inhaled as a nasal spray. Some IVF practioners use the "flare up" as part of the stimulation of the ovaries while others wait until the reproductive system has shut down. The use of GnRHa for IVF has been described in more detail in Chapter 10.

Side Effects

The common side effects of GnRH analogues are the side effects of menopause: hot flashes, dizziness, dry vagina, and in some cases vaginal itching, insomnia and emotional upset. The side effects are usually more intense and bothersome when the woman takes the drug for a number of months. Few side effects are reported during short term use for IVF.

When GnRHa are taken for an extended period for the treatment of fibroids and endometriosis, the most serious side effect is bone loss, which may predispose women to osteoporosis. For that reason it is not recommended that GnRHa be taken for longer than six to nine months. The long-term effect on the woman's health after the drug has been stopped is not known.

Appendix E
Bromocriptine

The drug bromocriptine is the standard treatment in women and occasionally men whose prolactin levels are too high, causing an interference in the functioning of the hypothalamus. First introduced in the late 1970s, bromocriptine goes by the trade names Parlodel, by Sandoz, or in some countries, Serocryptin, by Serono. Bromocriptine, a so-called dopamine agonist, acts like dopamine by blocking the prolactin-secreting cells in the pituitary and inhibiting them from releasing prolactin. It does not cure high prolactin, but while bromocriptine is being taken prolactin levels fall. Once it is stopped, prolactin levels usually rise again. In cases of large tumors, macroadenomas, bromocriptine can be given to shrink the tumor to allow for an easier operation or to postpone the need for an operation.

Dose for Women

To help patients tolerate the drug, the dose starts out low and gradually increases. For the first four or five days either one-half or a whole pill (1.25 milligrams to 2.5 milligrams) will be taken at bedtime with a bit of food. By the second week the dose will be increased, usually to about one 2.5-milligram tablet twice a day with meals. Some women may have it increased to three tablets daily. The pill should always be taken with food to help prevent nausea. You should avoid drinking any alcohol while on the drug as the alcohol's effects will be magnified and the side effects of bromocriptine possibly intensified. The drug is continued every day, for up to six months, but the course will be less if you become pregnant. You should keep a BBT graph to chart your ovulation. If you miss a menstrual period, if your temperature rises and does not come back down, or if menstrual periods never resume, you should have recurrent pregnancy tests.

Side Effects

Many men and women feel nauseated or ill when first starting bromocriptine. The drug can lower blood pressure and so it is common to feel dizzy or even faint, particularly when standing up quickly. In the first week you may have to be careful while driving a car or using equipment until you are certain you will not suffer fainting spells. Headaches occur in about 20 percent of women taking the drug. Less common is vomiting, abdominal pain, constipation or diarrhea, but lightheadedness and nasal congestion are also reported. Usually these symptoms go away after the first week. If a severe, constant and unrelenting headache develops, you should contact your doctor and the drug will probably be discontinued.

Effects on the Fetus

When bromocriptine was first used, it was felt that the drug should not be taken in early pregnancy. Now a substantial number of pregnancies in which bromocriptine was taken have been reported. Of 1410 pregnancies reported to Sandoz in which Parlodel was taken during the first weeks of pregnancy, there was a 3.6 percent incidence of congenital abnormalities, both minor and major, which is slightly higher than the general population. The spontaneous abortion rate, of about 11 percent, is considered normal. Pituitary tumors can grow much larger during pregnancy; sometimes the doctor decides to continue bromocriptine therapy throughout the pregnancy, weighing the danger of the growing tumor to the mother against the potential, as yet unsubstantiated, harm of the drug to the fetus. Animal studies have shown no adverse effects on the fetus if the drug is continued through pregnancy. In most cases, however, bromocriptine therapy is not continued during pregnancy.

Success Rates

In close to 70 percent of women, ovulation and normal menstrual cycles return within the six months of treatment. Of those about 70 percent become pregnant.

CHAPTER 6
Tubal Disease and Anatomical Problems

Blocked or scarred fallopian tubes rank as one of the most common causes of infertility. At least 30 to 40 percent of infertile women, maybe even more, have damage somewhere along the delicate conduit leading from the ovary to the uterus. When the numbers of women whose fertility is impaired by tubal damage are combined with those suffering other possible impediments to pregnancy, such as abnormalities in the shape of the uterus, uterine growths and adhesions (scar tissue), the category of physical barriers to pregnancy becomes even larger and accounts for some 30 to 40 percent of all infertile couples.

For the most part, surgery to remove the barrier in the tube or uterus is the first approach to the problem. If surgery of tubal problems fails to achieve pregnancy, the couple is usually referred to in vitro fertilization to attempt to bypass the obstacle all together. Unsuccessful surgery for uterine problems leaves few subsequent options.

The causes and treatment of tubal obstructions and other tube-ovary problems that impair fertility are discussed first. Uterine abnormalities, such as unusually shaped uteri, polyps, adhesions and fibroids, and their treatments follow. Endometriosis, which is believed to cause infertility by creating obstructions and by altering the hormonal environment, is discussed at the end of the chapter.

Tubal Obstruction

AKA: blocked tubes, inflammatory tubal disease, tubal occlusion

Each fallopian tube is just a bit longer than the length of a woman's index finger and less than a third as thick. The tubes extend from either side of the uterus like outstretched arms to the ovaries. Each tube is divided into four distinct parts: first, the delicate flared and fringed ends, the fimbria, that cradle and sweep over the ovary; next, the widest portion of the tube, the ampulla, which narrows to become the isthmus; the final section is where the tube joins the uterus in a muscular passage, called, interchangeably, the intramural, intramuscular or interstitial segment, or the uterotubal junction.

The function of the fallopian tube may seem simple—transport of the egg, sperm and embryo—but it is not. It transports the sperm and eggs in opposite directions, is the site of fertilization, nurtures the embryo over its first three days and delivers it to the womb. The role of the fallopian tubes, in fact, is so complex as to be, so far, incapable of replication. Attempts to make artificial tubes have all failed, as have tubal transplants.

As described in Chapter 3, the fimbria catch the ovulated egg and coax it into the narrow velvety tube. The cilia beat the egg from the fimbria toward the middle of the tube, directed by ridge-like folds, the rugulae. The sperm must meet and fertilize the egg in the fimbria or ampulla. But from there the resulting embryo does not simply pass into the uterus, but it is shuffled back and forth by muscular contractions along the tube, up to a centimeter in one direction, back a few millimeters, then forward a little farther, then back again, until it finally enters the uterus, about three days after fertilization. New research suggests that the cells of the tube may secrete a chemical that helps the development of the embryo.

Pelvic Inflammatory Disease

The problem with the magnificent fallopian tubes is their vulnerability. They are the Achilles heel of the reproductive system. Sperm ascending into the woman's reproductive tract can carry microorganisms that can inflame and irritate the delicate lining. Damaging microorganisms can also be introduced into the tubes by the string of an intrauterine device, a ruptured appendix, an abortion, a miscarriage or infection following a birth. Infection can spread through all the reproductive organs and the pelvic cavity.

The general term for a pelvic infection is Pelvic Inflammatory Disease, or PID. PID can be acute, causing severe pain and fever and usually requiring hospitalization, or it can be more subtle, sometimes barely noticeable to the woman.

PID can hit all the structures of the reproductive organs or just some of them. In medical terms, if the infection is in the fallopian tubes it is called salpingitis (*salpinx* is the Greek word for the fallopian tube). If one or both ovaries are infected, the term oophoritis may be used. If the lining of the uterus is inflamed then it is called endometritis. If all or part of the lining of the pelvic cavity, the peritoneum, becomes inflamed then it is called peritonitis. The suffix "itis" simply means inflammation. Any or all of these inflammations can result in damage to reproductive tissue that can block or compromise the fallopian tubes or other reproductive organs.

The term, inflammation, describes the chain of reactions, or the physical process, that body tissue goes through as a result of infection or injury. It is a multi-step process that includes the reaction of the tissues to the attacking agent, the immune response that involves the destruction and removal of the injurious material, and the healing response that repairs the damage. Inflammation usually has the hallmarks of redness, warmth and swelling, pain, and disruption of the function of the affected tissue, either temporarily or permanently. The redness, warmth and swelling is caused by increased blood flow to the area. The pain usually comes from pressure or stretching of the nerve endings caused by the congestion of the area, and the disturbance of the injured or infected tissue's regular function results from destruction of the tissue.

It is this involved inflammation process that causes the left-over damage in PID resulting in infertility. When an infecting agent, such as a sexually transmitted disease or bowel organism, enters the woman's genital tract, the body tries to defend itself from the infection and to stop its spread. It sends special infection-fighting white blood cells called phagocytes to the area to engulf the invaders in a process called phagocytosis. As a result of the battle between the body and the infection, a great deal of pus can form, filling the fallopian tubes. Pus is like a littered battlefield, made up of microorganisms that caused the infection, dead white blood cells that succumbed in the fight, and decomposed tissue.

Tissue surrounding the infection also tries to contain the spread by building fibrous scar tissue like a wall. As a result, the tubes can block at either end to stop the infection from going through the rest of the body. The infecting organism can inflame the lining of the tube, sticking the lining together. An abscess of sealed-off pus and infection can form along the tube or between the tube and ovary. Watery fluid and pus can fill the closed-off tube, making it into a distended sac of fluid, called a hydrosalpinx. If the infection spreads into the pelvic cavity, bands of fibrous scar tissue may grow like a dense web sticking the uterus to the ovary, the ovary to the intestines, the intestines to the fallopian tube and so on. A pelvic abscess of sealed off pus in scar tissue can also form, and any of the abscesses can rupture, sending the infectious agents farther afield.

Whether or not a woman becomes infertile after PID depends on a number of factors, such as how soon the infection is treated, how bad the infection is, how well the woman's body, in general, is able to fight and heal after an infection and whether she has a tendency to scar heavily. The more recurrences of PID, the greater likelihood of infertility.

Incidence of Infections

Each year in the United States more than one million women are diagnosed as having tubal infections. The incidence is also high in Canada, Britain, Australia, and Europe. Women in many developing nations have an even greater problem with tubal infection, although it may go undiagnosed and untreated. In her book *Sex and Destiny*, Germaine Greer reported that in some African tribes as many as 40 to 50 percent of all women may be sterile as a consequence of PID.

One indicator of the prevalance of tubal damage is the rate of occurrence of ectopic pregnancies—pregnancies that occur outside the uterus. When disease or infection has damaged the delicate tube, the embryo can become stuck on its way to the uterus. Since the 1970s the rate of ectopic pregnancies has tripled in the United States. Researchers have estimated that the risk of ectopic pregnancy increases seven times after a single bout of PID. Ectopic pregnancies, and how to recognize them, are discussed in more detail later in this chapter.

Causes of PID

STDs

The most common cause of PID is sexually transmitted disease, predominantly gonorrhea and chlamydia. Recent reports say that as many as one in five sexually active women under the age of 25 have a sexually transmitted disease. Doctors who studied women attending a university health clinic in Ottawa, Canada, found that one in every 10 women had chlamydia. Based on their findings, the doctors predicted that as many as one in every 10 women by the year 2000 will be infertile because of an STD. In 1988, about four in every 100 women were infertile by an STD.

The biggest problem with gonorrhea and chlamydia is that many infected women have few or no initial symptoms. Gonorrhea, caused by *Neisseria gonorrhoeae* bacterium, may cause burning on urination, an increased vaginal discharge, and/or redness and swelling around the vulva. For at least 70 to 80 percent of women the symptoms are so mild they go unnoticed. All but 10 percent of men with gonorrhea have symptoms, usually a discharge from the urethra, so women must rely on their symptomatic male partners to inform them if they have an STD so they can both get treatment.

Chlamydia, caused by the virus-like bacteria *Chlamydia trachomatis*, has the same mild symptoms as gonorrhea, if any symptoms at all. Only since the early 1980s has the medical profession realized how potentially damaging to fallopian tubes the tiny chlamydia organism is. Even more women have silent chlamydia infections than those who contract gonorrhea. Both organisms can lead to PID, but in many women even the PID is slient. Sometimes the only clue that an organism has wreaked havoc with a woman's fertility is when the infertility surgeon peers into the woman's pelvic cavity for the first time, investigating the reason behind her infertility.

"It can look like someone has dumped a pot of crazy glue in the pelvic cavity and stuck everything together," said noted tubal microsurgeon, Dr. Victor Gomel of Vancouver. "In my experience, more than 60 percent of the women who [have] bilateral hydrosalpinx will give you no history of pelvic inflammatory disease. Absolutely no recollection of infection. Usually it has been chlamydia."

Other sexually transmitted microorganisms, called ureaplasma, have been found in the reproductive tracts of women with PID and tubal damage. Mycoplasma is a strain of the nonmotile bacteria, which, like chlamydia, also has some characteristics of viruses. It can be cultured along with chlamydia in genital tract infections in both men and women, but at the time of writing researchers are not sure whether the organism actually causes tubal damage. It is very difficult to culture and identify, so the understanding of these organisms' role has been limited.

Dalkon Shield and Other IUDs

In the early 1970s an intrauterine device called the Dalkon Shield was marketed as the best contraceptive device for young women who had not yet had children. Manufactured by the American pharmaceutical company, A.H. Robins, the small IUD, the size of a coin and shaped like a prickly shield, was inserted in more than 4.2 million women around the world. Many of those women developed complications, most commonly severe PID, although pregnancies and perforated uteruses were also reported. At least four women died as a result of uncontrollable infection; the death toll may be as high as 20. The IUD was removed from the United States market in 1974, and the manufacturer recommended that it be removed from any women still wearing it. Despite the recall, many women unknowingly continued to wear this IUD into the 1980s.

By 1987 more than 300,000 women, worldwide, had filed claims against A.H. Robins for damages allegedly caused by the IUD. The most common claims were for irreparable tubal damage or the necessity of complete or partial removal of reproductive organs to stop the spread of infection. A.H. Robins declared bankruptcy to protect itself from more lawsuits and at this writing the settlement is still being negotiated.

It is believed that the synthetic string of the Dalkon Shield was behind most of the problems. Braided like a candle wick, the string seems to have acted by capillary action like a ladder to bring organisms from the vagina into the uterus and tubes. A.H. Robins has based its defence on the fact that an infection of chlamydia or gonorrhea or another organism could have been just as much to blame for the women's infertility as the Dalkon Shield. Although that argument is ostensibly true, research has found the IUD greatly increased a woman's risk of getting PID, no matter what she was exposed to. Dr. Nancy Lee, of the United States Center for Disease Control conducted a study that showed that women who wore a Dalkon Shield were seven times more likely to develop PID than women who did not use an IUD, and five times more likely to get PID than women who used another brand.

Abortion and D&C

Infection can occasionally be introduced to the tubes by an abortion or by a dilation and currettage, an operation in which the uterus is scraped to remove the endometrium. During these procedures, organisms that would usually be stopped at the cervix by the mucous plug make their way into the uterus because the cervix has been dilated.

Appendicitis

Inflammation of the vermiform appendix, a small blind tube of tissue leading off the large intestine, can sometimes cause infection and scarring of the pelvic cavity. The inflammation is usually caused by bacteria trapped in the baby-finger-sized appendage. The appendix is in close proximity to the reproductive organs so if it becomes inflamed it can cause scar tissue to build around the ovary and fimbria of the fallopian tube, particularly on the right side. If the appendix ruptures and releases bacteria into the pelvic cavity, causing peritonitis, the damage and resulting scar tissue can be very extensive.

Other non-sexual infections, including tuberculosis of the genital tract, can leave scar tissue. This infection is very rare in Western countries, but much more common in developing nations.

Surgery

Any surgery in the pelvic cavity can cause scar tissue to form around the ovaries and fallopian tubes, which may later impair the organs' functions and cause infertility. An appendectomy to remove an inflamed appendix can result occasionally in a band of scar tissue between the appendix and the ovary. An operation to remove an ovarian cyst, endometriosis, an ectopic pregnancy or a benign tumor all can cause adhesions to form. Even surgery to correct infertility—such as an ovarian wedge resection for polycystic ovaries—or to repair damaged fallopian tubes can cause scar tissue to form around the ovaries and fallopian tubes.

"Anybody who has a history of any operative procedure, you must think of adhesions," said Dr. Robert Franklin, a reproductive microsurgeon at Baylor College of Medicine in Houston, Texas. "Especially if the operation has taken place during or before puberty. The young girl who is operated on for an ovarian cyst or other causes—you have to think of adhesions."

Like an infection, surgery can injure tissue and cause bleeding, resulting in the body mounting a healing response. If two damaged surfaces come in contact with each other they can, in effect, weld together with scar tissue built by the surrounding cells.

Sterilization

Tubal sterlization is the most popular form of contraception in North America but at least one percent of all women who undergo the operation subsequently change their minds and want it reversed. Marriage to a new partner is the most common reason women give for their change of heart. Reversal of sterilization now accounts for almost 30 percent of all tubal repair, doctors say. The success of the operation depends on how much of the length of the tubes remains and whether the original operation damaged surrounding tissue.

The Feeling of Guilt

The guilt can eat you up inside.

More than any other type of infertility, tubal disease, adhesions and uterine damage caused by infections inflict not only physical damage but a tremendous amount of guilt as well. A previous abortion, a sexually transmitted disease, an IUD, a vague pelvic pain you ignored—everything and anything in your past can grind the wheel of guilt inside you. It does little good for others to say "You shouldn't feel guilty" "How were you to know?" "Times were different then."

You *do* feel guilty. You go over and over past actions and curse yourself. "If only I hadn't done that!" or "If only I'd known!" If only . . . .

Oscar Wilde said: "Not even the richest man can buy back his past." Still, some women torment themselves with the thought that at some point in their lives they must have been fertile.

> *With the Dalkon Shield I felt I should have been smarter. I felt it was my fault for not asking more questions. I felt: 'Me of all people! I should have prevented it because I don't let things just happen to me!' I couldn't get over the stupidity. I was angry at the medical profession for letting something like the Dalkon Shield on the market. But I was just as angry at myself for taking it. For stupidity.*
>
> *I now resent the attitude of the 1960s and the 70s, the sexual freedom part, you know, sex as a sport. I bought into that. I thought then: I've got no hang ups about sex, no big deal. Now I think about all the people I slept with and I cringe over some of them. One of them probably gave me an infection. When I read risk factors for infertility and see* MULTIPLE PARTNERS *in big letters I just kind of die inside.*
>
> *I don't know what happened, the doctors think I must have had a silent chlamydia infection somewhere in my past. Chlamydia? I only heard about it for the first time three years ago. I can't figure it out. I just keep thinking that somehow I'm being punished for something—I don't even know what. Enjoying sex? Not settling down and having babies at 24? Who knows? But I feel guilty all the same.*

Guilt can be very hard to put behind you. One woman described it as "a black hole" that captures you and won't let go. To make matters worse, you may feel that others are intensifying your feeling of guilt. You may feel that your partner blames you for your inability to have a child. You may feel, whether right or wrong, that you are being judged and categorized by others—your family, his family, even your doctor—when the diagnosis is made. The guilt and remorse can bring your self-esteem lower and lower, and the lower your self-esteem falls the more susceptible you are to blaming yourself and feeling guilty. The black hole.

Overcoming guilt and putting it behind you requires two things: forgiveness and acceptance. First, forgive yourself. Do not blame yourself, whether or not there is something to blame yourself for. All women are susceptible to tubal infections. Countless numbers of women have abortions and do not become infertile. Countless women have multiple partners, or PID, or any number of events that might cause damage of the tube and yet their tubes are not damaged. Likewise, a woman may have no predisposing factors, nothing that she can put her finger on, and she may still be infertile because of tubal damage. It makes no difference if a woman has one partner or 50, if that one partner unknowingly gives her an STD that damages her tubes. There is nothing fair about it, but neither are you being punished. Do not blame yourself.

When you stop blaming yourself and feeling guilty you will probably then feel angry at the unfairness of it all. "If I have nothing to feel guilty about, then why did this happen to me? Why me and not other women?" Your anger, instead of being directed at yourself, as it is in guilt, may then be directed at the rest of the world, or individuals in it—a doctor, a past lover, a pregnant woman in the street, even your partner.

Anger, too, can be very hard to leave behind; but it, too, can consume you. It is important to recognize that you are angry. Then, at a certain point you must choose to leave it behind. The world may seem wretchedly unfair, but no amount of cursing will change it. Whatever happened to your fallopian tubes, happened. You cannot change what has happened to you; you can only change how you feel about it. You can choose to continue feeling angry or bitter; or you can accept what has happened to you. You can allow the cycle of guilt and resentment to pull you down; or you can surrender those feelings and move on. Just give them up. Take a deep breath, and move on.

Repairing Tubal Disease

Microsurgical Tubal Reconstruction

Until the mid-1970s, most women who had tubal damage and adhesions had one treatment option: traditional laparotomy surgery. A laparotomy is a procedure in which a woman's abdomen is opened with a surgical incision to expose the reproductive organs. The scar tissue is burned or cut away with conventional scissors, electrodes or scalpels, now called "macrosurgical techniques." The success of this type of operation was limited, with even the least difficult of procedures—the removal of adhesions—achieving less than a 50 percent pregnancy rate. The most difficult procedure, creating a new opening for the tube, had a success rate of less than 15 percent.

It was in the late 1960s that the idea of using magnification and operating microscopes, already in use in other types of surgery, was first tried for tubal surgery. In Sweden in 1967, Dr. Kurt Swolin did the first tubal repair under magnification. Soon after it was picked up and advanced by a number of international surgeons, notably Dr. Victor Gomel in Vancouver and Dr. Robert Winston in London and a handful of American surgeons in various centers including Dr. John Rock, Dr. Luigi Mastroianni and Dr. C.R. Garcia.

Like laparotomy macrosurgery, laparotomy microsurgery involves opening the pelvic cavity, usually with a "bikini line" incision that goes across the top of the pubic hair. Using an operating microscope, which magnifies the tissue up to 20 times so the smallest structures can be seen, the delicate reproductive organs can be repaired.

According to Gomel, microsurgery entails the following principles: careful handling of the tissue and using fine instruments that do the least amount of tissue damage to minimize new adhesions; keeping the tissue irrigated, or wet, to keep it from drying out (irrigation also exposes the smallest bleeding vessels); keeping bleeding to a minimum by visualizing and cauterizing any bleeding vessels; removing any or all dead and diseased tissue; precisely re-aligning the tissue when sewing it back together; and carefully avoiding damaging or cutting of the blood supply to any other tissues in the pelvic cavity. The use of magnification allows all these principles to be carried out better because small trauma or structures can be seen.

Types of Tubal Repair

A surgical procedure that restores function is often called a "plasty." For that reason tubal surgery is often given the overall designation of "tuboplasty." The name, however, has led some patients to mistakenly believe that plastics are used in the repair. The types of tubal damage that may be diagnosed and the types of tuboplasty that may be recommended are listed below. The conditions may occur individually or may occur together. Some adhesion removal and minor tubal repair may be done under laparoscopy. The more extensive the damage, however, the more need there will be for laparotomy microsurgery. If, however, the damage is too great, surgery may be of no use. A couple's option would then be to go to in vitro fertilization.

Adhesions

Tough fibrous bands of scar tissue can stretch between any or all the pelvic organs—ovary and tube, uterus and ovary, tube and intestine and so on—impairing or preventing their proper function. The most severe cases of adhesions are sometimes called frozen pelvis, when all the organs are welded together. Some women who have extensive adhesions report experiencing pain during activities such as exercising, stretching, twisting, having a bowel movement, or having sex. Other women, however, with just as extensive adhesions, report no unusual symptoms.

An operation to remove adhesions is called lysis of adhesions, from the Greek meaning to loosen. Ovariolysis is the removal of adhesions around the ovary. Salpingoovariolysis is the removal of adhesions around the fallopian tube and ovary. In the operation the surgeon puts tension on the adhesion by gently stretching the two joined structures apart and then carefully separating the structures by cutting the adhesion either by a microelectrode or laser. Adhesions are usually removed first to allow access to the reproductive organs for repair.

Ampullary, Isthmic or Cornual Occulusion

A blockage in a section of the tube, either in the ampulla, in the isthmus or at the junction of the uterus and tube, can prevent passage of sperm, egg or embryo. Tubal sterilization, which women have subsequently decided to reverse, is often the reason behind the occlusion, although mild tubal disease or an ectopic pregnancy can also cause a small portion of the tube to close. An operation, tubal anastomosis, to remove the section of damaged tube and rejoin the remaining normal sections will be suggested. Depending on where the obstruction and the rejoining take place, the name may be slightly different: tubocornual anastomosis is performed at the junction of the tube and uterus; tubotubal anastomosis is performed along the middle of the tube. If the damage to the tube is confined to just the one blocked spot in the middle of the tube, usually caused by sterilization, the success rate is very good. Up to 60 percent of women who undergo sterilization reversal by microsurgery subsequently become pregnant. The pregnancy rate following tubocornual anastomosis is reported at about 56 percent.

Fimbrial Phimosis

When infection enters a woman's genital tract, the delicate fimbria may attempt to stop its spread into the pelvic cavity by clumping together and reducing the opening of the tube, called fimbrial phimosis. The infection may cause the fimbria to become encased in scar tissue, but underneath the fimbria may remain relatively undamaged. An operation, called a repair of a fimbrial phimosis or a fimbrioplasty, is recommended to release the fimbria. It entails delicately removing the scar tissue while keeping the fimbria intact. The success of the operation depends on the amount of damage caused by the infection. Success rates of 30 to 50 percent have been reported.

Hydrosalpinx

Sometimes infection causes the fimbria to close completely and become like clubs or stumps. The tube may then distend with fluid, called a hydrosalpinx. A salpingostomy, an operation whose name literally means to make an opening in the fallopian tube, will be performed. If the fimbria have been destroyed the surgeon tries to recreate a fimbria-like end. Starting in the center point of the club, the surgeon makes careful dissections radiating out from the center point like spokes from a hub. A few sutures are placed around the outside to keep the new opening in place. Variations on this technique may be performed depending on the extent of damage. The tube may remain open, but the ultimate success of the technique, whether or not the woman becomes pregnant, depends on how much internal tubal damage has taken place. Hydrosalpinx can cause the destruction of the inside of the tube, killing the cilia, the hair cells that move the egg and embryo, and eliminating the rugae, or folds. For this reason only about 20 to 30 percent of women having this operation become pregnant, despite the surgical "success" that yields open tubes.

Obstruction Close to the Uterus

In 1987 the world press reported a novel approach used by doctors at Chicago's Mount Sinai Hospital. Borrowing the concept of angioplasty in heart surgery, in which a small balloon is inflated in a narrowed artery to open it up, the doctors tried using the balloon technique to open up blocked fallopian tubes. They called the technique balloon tuboplasty. In carefully selected patients who had a blocked tube close to the uterus, the doctors guided a modified cardiac catheter through the uterus to the fallopian tube. The balloon was inflated at the point where the tubes connect to the uterus; then dye was washed through the tubes to see if an opening had been made. In the initial report of 12 patients, seven had their tubes reopened. One subsequently had the tube reclosed, and two patients conceived.

Most surgeons, however, do not hold out a great deal of optimism for balloon tuboplasty because its application is small—it is possible only for patients who have an obstruction close to the uterus—and so far results have not been significantly successful. More experimentation is needed before this technique will be widely recommended. Critics of the procedure say it shows a lack of understanding of the functioning of the tube and that the successes could be attributed to the injection of the dye, which is also known to clear small blockages.

Laser or Electrocautery?

In recent years there has been a great deal of debate about which is better for tubal and reproductive surgery, laser microsurgery or electrocautery microsurgery. Laser uses a light source, reflected many times by mirrors, so that it emerges as a powerful uniform beam of light, all the same wavelength and all in phase. The effect of the laser beam on tissue is similar to the way light focused through a magnifying glass burns at a point. In contrast, electrocautery uses a fine wire filament heated by electric current. Both tools cut by burning, which at the same time cauterizes the cut blood vessels and stops bleeding. Many laser surgeons claim that laser microsurgery is superior to electrocautery microsurgery. Research does not support those claims. The truth is that both work equally well, providing either instrument is in the hands of a qualified surgeon who is an expert in that technique. Laser, used inexpertly, can damage surrounding tissue.

"The basic aspect in both, is technique," said Dr. Robert Franklin, who himself prefers to operate with a laser. "The real answer is how tenderly and gingerly you treat the tissue, destroying as little tissue as possible, no matter what instrument you use. If (the surgeon) is good with micro-cautery, he should use that. If he prefers laser, he should use that."

There is some evidence, however, that laser may be more effective for surgery of endometriosis in the pelvic cavity, particularly to vaporize the implants, Gomel said. Gomel, however, prefers using the electrocautery for tubal repair where tissue destruction must be avoided.

For women who are considering tubal surgery, then, the important aspect is not to seek a certain type of therapy, but to seek a good tubal surgeon with considerable experience in tubal repair. If the surgeon is good, accept the mode of treatment that he or she is best with.

Tubal Repair by Laparoscopy

Increasingly, doctors in leading infertility clinics are using laparoscopy rather than laparotomy when they perform tubal repair operations. The principles of microsurgery—moist tissue, gentle handling, minimal bleeding and minimal tissue destruction—are inherent in laparoscopy because the woman's pelvic cavity is not opened. Removal of adhesions, fimbrioplasty, salpingostomy and ectopic pregnancy removal are all now routinely performed at the more advanced centers by laparascopy. Less invasive and less expensive, laparoscopy means that the woman spends less than 24 hours in the hospital and is left with a tiny scar. However, special training is required for this type of surgery and not all doctors have the skills to perform it.

Undergoing Pelvic Surgery

For most women whose infertility is caused by tubal damage or pelvic abnormalities, the suggested treatment is pelvic surgery. For many women, but not all, it is the answer to their fertility problems. However, this treatment should not be taken lightly because it is major surgery with the potential for complications. It may entail three or four hours in the operating room under general anesthetic. The anesthetic itself has its inherent risks—one in every 30,000 operations has a severe or fatal complication. After the operation is over, most women require at least three or four weeks off work to convalesce, although occasionally a patient makes a very speedy recovery, getting back to normal routine within three weeks. Some women take six weeks or longer to regain their energy and stamina and a few women even report taking a number of months.

All that said, however, microsurgery for tubal infertility offers some couples their best chance—perhaps only chance—to some day conceive a child. Before deciding to undergo surgery, you should discuss the risks and benefits of the operation with your doctor and get an honest appraisal of your chance of successful surgery.

Preparing for the Operation

In the weeks and days before your surgery, use your time of good health for tasks that will make things easier for yourself when you return from hospital. Although some partners easily take on the role of cooking for and catering to a convalescing mate, others may have some difficulty in making sure things are done with the minimum of fuss and bother. Meals top the list. You can prepare some meals in advance and freeze them in small portions. Stock your shelves with crackers, soups, cans of favorite treats or any other easy-to-open, easy-to-eat food. You may not feel like producing meals or cleaning up while you recover. Laundry and housecleaning are also chores that you should not take on in the first few weeks back home. Arrange to have a friend or housekeeper come in to help, and arrange to have your partner or someone else do the shopping.

At your job, finish major projects before undergoing the operation, or assign them to someone else. You may imagine yourself doing work in the three or four weeks you are convalescing: "good time to read such-and-such" or "that's when I'll prepare that proposal." *Wrong*. Most people do not feel like working. The effect of general anesthetic makes concentrating difficult for all but the simplest activities. The healing of wounds after surgery requires a great deal of energy. Do not add to your stress and worry by expecting yourself to accomplish work-related chores while convalescing. Instead, think of the first weeks at home as a time to rest and heal. As the days go by you may feel more like reading the books you always wished you had time to read. Sit back and relax.

Packing for the Hospital

For pelvic surgery by laparotomy you spend two to four days in the hospital. What other women found helpful to take along may help you pack your bag.

Housecoat, comfortable slippers, favorite pyjamas, several pairs of underwear, warm socks For the first day or two you will be in a hospital gown, but after that you can wear your own clothes. A housecoat is a necessity, and you will need a pair of slippers that stay on your feet when you shuffle to the bathroom or down the hall. You may even want to splurge and buy yourself a nice pair of pyjamas—you will be spending a lot of time in them. Some women buy a luxurious pair of pyjamas before their operations.

Toiletries and cosmetics Pack all your regular toiletry articles: toothbrush, toothpaste, hairbrush, deodorant, perfume, blush, and lipstick. In the first day following your operation you might not be allowed to bathe or shower, although you can have sponge baths. Brushing your hair and applying a bit of makeup may make you feel more refreshed. Pack your favorite soap, shampoo and conditioner to use once you are able to bathe.

Special body and face creams, lip balm The general anesthetic and the hospital air tends to dry skin. You will appreciate having nice body cream to soothe your skin and lip protector to moisten cracked lips.

Portable "Walkman" tapeplayer with headphones Listening to your favorite music, books on tape, inspirational lectures, or the radio can pass the time without exhausting you. However, leave other valuables, such as jewelry, at home.

Earplugs and eyeshade Hospitals are brightly lit, noisy places and these devices may help you rest and sleep better.

Magazines and other light reading, telephone/address book, personal journal You will not feel like reading Dostoevsky or James Joyce's *Ulysses*. Instead, pack light reading you enjoy such as short story collections and magazines. Most rooms have a telephone. Writing in a journal may help you deal with powerful emotions. Some women pack a special picture that reminds them of home or happy times to put by their bedside. A small travel clock can also come in handy.

Loose-fitting outfit to wear when returning home Your incision will be sore and your abdomen swollen for a few weeks, so do not pack a pair of tight jeans or snug fitting skirt to wear to leave the hospital. A loose shift, a baggy pair of sweats or another outfit that does not constrict your incision will be more comfortable.

Pre-Operative Preparation

You are usually asked to check into the hospital the afternoon before your operation so that medical staff can do final blood and urine tests and ensure that you are prepared for the operation. You will likely be visited by your surgeon and anesthesiologist when you have settled in. The anesthesiologist discusses the anesthetic procedure for the next day. He or she will be interested in your general health, particularly if you have any heart or lung problems and if you or any of your family has ever had any difficulty with anesthetic. He or she will also look in your mouth to check for loose or false teeth and to look at the structure of your airway in case there may be problems in "intubation"—putting a tube into your airway.

If you have any questions about the anesthetic, this is the time to ask the doctor. Write down your questions so you do not forget them. The doctor will also discuss with you the importance of having an empty stomach while undergoing the operation—any food or fluid can be inhaled into your lungs during the procedure, causing serious complications. Do not drink water during the night or even suck lozenges and candies. If you do, the operation may have to be postponed.

An enema, which introduces a fluid into your rectum to stimulate a bowel movement, may also be given the night before to flush out fecal matter. An enema removes the necessity for a bowel movement until three or four days after the operation, saving strain on your incision, decreasing gas pains after the operation, and lessening the chance of infection being introduced from your colon during the operation. Not all doctors agree on the benefit of an enema, but if your doctor orders it, it will be given to you as you lie on your left side. However, you can request to do it yourself. After the enema you will be asked to shower with antiseptic soap. At this time you may want to wash your hair because it may be a few days before you will be able to wash it again.

You may also be asked to remove colored polish from your fingernails. The anesthesiologist and recovery room staff may want to notice the natural color of your fingernails, a sign of oxygenation of the blood, as you come out of the anesthetic.

Morning of the Operation

When you wake up on the morning of surgery you may be given pre-op medications, depending on whether your doctor feels you need them. A tranquilizer to help you relax and an antacid to settle your stomach are the usual medications. The medications may make you feel dizzy and disoriented. If you have a history of pelvic infection, antibiotics by intravenous drip may be given as a preventative measure to ward off infection following the operation.

Before the operation, your lower abdomen and pubic hair may be shaved around the site of the incision to lower the risk of infections. Recent studies have questioned the value of shaving and many doctors no longer request it.

About 30 minutes before your operation an orderly or nurse takes you on a gurney, or stretcher, to the operating room. Outside the operating theatre, the nurse checks your name and chart to make sure the right person is being taken in for the operation. You are wheeled into the operating room and transferred from the gurney to the operating table. The room feels cold, harsh and clinical. The temperature is kept cool so the medical personnel do not get too hot while they work. The sparse metal furnishings and tile floors make for easier disinfection and cleaning.

Anesthetic

The anesthesiologist starts an IV line into a vein in the back of your non-writing hand. Electrodes are placed on your chest to monitor your heart and an automatic blood-pressure cuff is placed on your arm. An oximeter, which measures the oxygenation of your blood and your pulse, is placed on your fingertip. (Some oximeters are placed on the earlobe.) Then you will be given a quick-acting drug through your IV line to induce sleep. The drug may be thiopentone, sodium pentathol or another of the pentathol family of induction agents. It usually takes less than 10 or 15 seconds from the time the drug enters your arm for you to lose consciousness. You may be asked to count backwards from 100, but you won't make it to 90. You may feel as though a cold heavy liquid is rising in your arm. By the time it reaches your shoulder, you will be out. Your next moment of awareness will be as you come to in the recovery room a few hours later when the operation is finished.

As soon as you are alseep the anesthesiologist inserts an endotracheal tube through your mouth into your trachea, or windpipe, and secures it in place either with tape or by tying it. This feeds oxygen and the anesthetic gases into your lungs. Your eyes may be taped closed to protect them from drying. Then you will be given a muscle relaxant. Earlier, the relaxant was curare, derived from a South American plant, which worked by blocking transmission of nerve impulses from the muscle to the brain. Now newer neuromuscular blocking agents based on curare, such as pancuronium or vecuronium, are used. Then the anesthetic gas, usually isoforane or halothane, will be given mixed with your oxygen through the endotracheal tube. The anesthetic gas makes up less than 2 percent of the oxygenated air you receive. Nitrous oxide may also be mixed with the anesthetic. The anesthesiologist monitors all your vital body signs throughout the operation.

Meanwhile, the surgical team prepares your abdomen for the opening. Antiseptic is painted on your belly. A sticky plastic wrap, like adhesive Saran Wrap, is placed over the incision site of the lower abdomen. Your legs are put in stirrups to allow instruments to be inserted, enabling the injection of dye, which will flow into the fallopian tubes later in the operation. Sterile operating cloths, called drapes, are placed so that they cover your entire body, leaving a small window-like square through which the surgeons operate.

The Operation

Using a scalpel, the surgeon makes a four- or five-inch (12 or 15 centimeters) incision, usually just above the pubic hairline. Using an electrocautery knife, which cuts and cauterizes (seals the bleeding vessels by lightly burning them) at the same time, the layers of tissue are dissected: first the skin, then the fat, then the fascia—the fibrous tissue that sheaths the muscles—then the muscle itself, then the peritoneum into the pelvic cavity.

Once the pelvic cavity is opened, a plastic sheet, called a wound protector, is placed around the pelvic cavity. A metal device, a retractor, pulls back the walls of the incision in four directions, leaving a square window through which the surgeons can work. The operating table is tilted slightly head-down, and the intestines gently positioned out of the way and held in place with a wet pad. Wet cotton cloths soaked in an anti-coagulating solution are placed into the cavity below the reproductive organs to elevate them gently to the top of the opening, enabling the surgeon to work on them with more ease. Any adhesions that restrict the movement of the uterus or access to the organs are carefully removed. The reproductive organs are kept wet, or irrigated, with a solution throughout the procedure. The operating overhead microscope is swung over the organs and adjusted to the surgeons' needs. Then the delicate process of freeing the reproductive organs from adhesions and reconstructing them to return their function will begin. After the repair, blue dye is injected through the tubes to ensure they are open.

At the end of the operation the instruments, cotton pads, plastic protector, and wound retractor are removed. Then comes the job of "closing"—the layer by layer suturing (stitching closed) of the incision. A dressing is put over the incision, and the anesthesiologist begins to bring you around by decreasing the amount of anesthetic gas and increasing the oxygen. A drug to reverse the affect of the muscle relaxant is usually given, as is a narcotic to diminish pain, and an anti-nauseant. The surgical drapes are removed and replaced by another sheet to cover you. Still in deep slumber and attached to machines that monitor your vital signs, you are transferred to a gurney and are wheeled to the recovery room.

Recovery

You feel groggy and disoriented for a number of hours following surgery. You may not even be aware of the two or three hours spent in the post-op recovery room (PAR for post-anesthesia recovery) while nurses watch you, turn you and get you to wiggle your fingers and toes. You are able to respond to the requests but very few people have memory of it when they finally regain full consciousness. You will probably be back in your room when you first become aware of where you are and realize that the operation is over.

Next, you start to feel your body. You may have a slight sore throat from the endotracheal tube. Your whole body feels stiff and sore and you do not feel like moving. Pain medications diminish the pain coming from your incision, but you may be aware of it when you cough or move. You should cough regularly and breathe deeply. This helps clear your lungs, which may have become congested during the anesthetic. When you do cough or move, put pressure on your incision, either by placing a pillow, a towel or your hand over it. This will help support it. Most of all, you feel like sleeping. And that is what you should and will do, off and on, for most of the next few days.

The first day after the operation you are encouraged to get up and walk, though you may not feel like doing so. "I thought they seemed awfully cruel to make me walk so soon," one woman said. Walking, however, is good for you and speeds your recovery. Your first shuffling, slow, walking trips are to the bathroom and back.

Gas pains are common during the recovery as gas moves through your intestines. These can be extremely painful and may start by the second or third day after the operation. Relieving the pain may be difficult, but try rolling on your side and elevating your buttocks to help the movement of air. To reduce the amount of gas, drink lots of water, but do not drink carbonated beverages;

do not use a straw as this may cause you to swallow air; try not to swallow air by eating too quickly or talking while eating; and walk as much as you can. Constipation may also be a problem. You can ask for a gentle laxative to relieve constipation and for simethicone tablets to chew to help reduce gas.

Any time from the first to the fourth day after the operation any stitches or staples used to close your wound are removed. You are now able to shower, and you can feel the hard healing ridge in your incision, which will thin and flatten over time.

Going Home

You will be discharged two to four days after the operation. When you go home take it easy. If you live in a multi-level house, you may want to get your partner to set up a daybed for you on the main floor so you do not have to climb stairs. Be careful not to lift anything heavy. Try to walk regularly but do not push yourself too far. Many doctors recommend no strenuous excercise for 10 days. Spend time sleeping.

Many women, particularly those who have had adhesions removed, become afraid that more debilitating adhesions may grow back after the surgery. Some find it helpful to use creative visualization to picture their reproductive organs healing cleanly and without scars. There is no scientific evidence yet that this sort of visualization works to reduce scarring, but it certainly reduces feelings of worry and fear. A number of books are available to teach you the technique, for example, *Creative Visualization* by Shakti Gawain.

You may resume sexual intercourse when you feel ready. Pregnancies can occur soon after the operation and a few patients conceive before their next menstrual period. Studies have shown the average is about five to 10 months for conception following surgery. Some women, however, may not become pregnant even though their tubes remain open.

Second-Look Laparoscopy

Some surgeons suggest that women have a laparoscopy 10 days to three months after the surgery. This allows the doctor to view the healing, check to see that the tubes are still open and remove any adhesions that may have formed around the operation site. These adhesions are usually still very fragile and easily removed.

Ectopic Pregnancy

AKA: extrauterine pregnancy

An ectopic pregnancy means a fertilized egg that implants outside the uterus. Normally the dividing embryo is propelled down the fallopian tube by cilia and muscular contractions and then implants in the plush lining of the uterus. In an ectopic pregnancy, something causes the embryo to implant on inappropriate tissue and try to continue growing there. In more than 95 percent of ectopic pregnancies, the embryo implants somewhere along the fallopian tube, usually in the ampulla. The embryo can also, more rarely, implant in the ovary, in the cervix, in the junction of the uterus and fallopian tube, and even in the abdomen wall. Any ectopic pregnancy, no matter where it is located, can be very dangerous to the health of the woman. Only the uterus has the ability to expand and grow with the developing fetus. Ectopic pregnancies can rupture, resulting in severe bleeding that can cause significant complications or even the woman's death.

The rate of ectopic pregnancies has tripled since the 1970s, predominantly, it is believed, because of the increase of sexually transmitted diseases that scar the fallopian tubes. The number of women who have had tubal surgery and previous ectopic pregnancies has also contributed to the climbing rate of subsequent ectopic pregnancies. In the 1970s ectopic pregnancies were responsible for less than 2 percent of all maternal deaths; by the mid-1980s they had become the leading cause of maternal death in the United States.

Any narrowing, growth, partial obstruction, loss of cilia or abnormality of internal anatomy of the tube, caused by disease or surgery, can trap the embryo or delay its passage. Unable to make it to the thick, nurturing endometrium of the uterus, the embryo tries to burrow into the muscular lining of the tube. Sometimes the embryo dies in the tube and is slowly reabsorbed by the body. The woman may not even know that this has taken place, although her tube may become scarred or blocked at the location of the ectopic. Other times a tubal abortion occurs—the tube expells the embryo into the uterus or out the fimbriated end into the abdomen. A tubal abortion can bleed a great deal, either externally or internally.

Sometimes it can be difficult to distinguish a tubal abortion from a uterine abortion. And at other times the embryo continues to grow, distending the tube more and more. In this case, one of two things may happen. Either it ruptures slowly, almost like a slow leak over weeks, or it ruptures suddenly, often causing massive bleeding. Any ectopic pregnancy that causes bleeding may be life-threatening to the woman and usually necessitates prompt surgery.

Symptoms of Ectopic Pregnancy

An ectopic pregnancy can be difficult to diagnose. Its symptoms often mimic other pelvic conditions such as an attack of PID, an ovarian cyst or a threatened abortion. But an aware woman and an astute doctor usually make the right diagnosis. Women who know or assume they have some tubal damage, or women who have had tubal surgery should be on the lookout for ectopic pregnancies. "Whenever a woman who has undergone salpingostomy (tubal surgery) is thought to be pregnant, the pregnancy should be considered to be ectopic until proved otherwise," says tubal surgeon Dr. Victor Gomel.

An ectopic can start becoming a problem two or three weeks after the egg is fertilized but it may also be eight or ten weeks before a rupture occurs. In the first weeks before an ectopic ruptures, you may experience vague discomfort in your abdomen, usually on one side, or pain in your rectum. Sometimes it is described as a "stitch in the side." You may have missed your menstrual period and may already assume that you are pregnant. But a urine pregnancy test for the pregnancy hormone HCG (human chorionic gonadotropin) may or may not be positive. The HCG message that the embryo sends out may be very weak and that is why ectopic pregnancies sometimes give a negative urine test result. The HCG signal can be so poor that it might not be strong enough to interfere with the stimulation of ovulation and so some women continue to menstruate. You may experience bleeding or spotting off and on for a number of weeks. Sharp intermittent pain may increase over the weeks. Any change in your normal menstrual period should be brought to the attention of your doctor, who may or may not be able to feel a bulge in the tube in a pelvic examination. If an ectopic is suspected, you will be given more tests: a blood test for HCG beta subunit, an ultrasound or laparoscopy.

A rupture may be brought on by straining—forcing a bowel movement, or by sexual intercourse. You may experience severe pain, sweats and chills, faintness, vomiting and nausea. If bleeding is severe, you may go into shock—your blood pressure falls, you become pale, cold and clammy and may have difficulty breathing. If you are bleeding excessively into your pelvic cavity you may experience pain in your shoulders. This means that blood is under the diaphragm and irritating your phrenic nerve, referring the pain to your shoulder tips. If any of these symptoms occur, go *immediately* to the hospital.

Diagnosis and Treatment of Ectopic Pregnancy

When it comes to diagnosing an ectopic pregnancy, doctors compare what they know about normal pregnancies to what is happening to you to see if it adds up to a good pregnancy or an ectopic. It is a process of deduction. A blood test for HCG beta subunit and an ultrasound assessment are the first steps to determine what is going on. If the blood test shows a pregnancy hormone, the doctor counts back with you to discover when your last normal menstrual period took place to determine the time of conception. If it was more than six weeks ago, the doctor uses ultrasound to find out whether a developing fetus can be seen. A normal intrauterine pregnancy can usually be seen in the endometrial cavity six weeks after the last normal menstrual period. If no evidence of a pregnancy can be found where it should be, it is likely an ectopic. It will be confirmed by laparoscopy.

In an emergency if the doctor suspects that an ectopic has already ruptured, culdocentesis may be suggested—a diagnostic test in which a needle is inserted through the top of your vagina into the pelvic cavity to see if it draws out blood. If unclotted blood is collected into the needle, you are bleeding into your pelvic cavity.

If ectopic pregnancy is confirmed, the approach taken to remove it depends on whether the tube has ruptured and whether your condition is stable. Laparoscopy is becoming the most common way of removing an ectopic pregnancy. In the operation, the fetal tissue is removed through a slit in the oviduct, or a portion of the tube is cut away with the ectopic pregnancy inside. If a portion is removed (called a segmental excision), at a later time microsurgery can be performed to rejoin the tube. Occasionally the entire fallopian tube may need to be removed. When the tube has been conserved it is mandatory that the doctor perform weekly HCG-beta subunit tests until they are negative to make sure no ectopic tissue has been retained in the tube.

In some cases an ectopic pregnancy requires a major operation and, if necessary, to control bleeding. A laparotomy with a "bikini" incision is usually the approach. In cases of extreme emergency, when speed is essential, a vertical incision may be made extending below the navel. Blood transfusions are sometimes necessary to replace lost blood in the case of rupture. Most doctors try to conserve the fallopian tube while removing the fetal tissue to try to maintain fertility, but if damage is severe, the fallopian tube may be removed. In the infrequent case of a ruptured interstitial pregnancy, at the junction of the uterus and tube, bleeding may be so severe as to require a hysterectomy to save the woman's life.

In some circumstances, particularly if the woman has been on fertility drugs, one pregnancy may implant in the tube, while another pregnancy implants normally in the uterus. All attempts are made in surgery to save the normal pregnancy while removing the ectopic pregnancy. This, however, is not always possible and the normal pregnancy may be lost.

Some studies explored treating an ectopic pregnancy chemically in the early stages before rupture. One drug used is methotrexate, an anti-cancer drug, that may be given to stop the division of cells, killing the embryo. Over time the fetal cells are reabsorbed by your body.

A common question women with ectopic pregnancies ask their doctors is whether the tiny fetus can be moved from its spot in the tube to the uterus. Unfortunately, due to the complex nature of the implantation, the answer is no.

Adding to the emotional and physical pain of ectopic pregnancy is that by having one, you are much more likely to have another one. Some studies have suggested that as many as 60 to 70 percent of pregnancies following an ectopic pregnancy are ectopic again. Now, because doctors try to save the tubes when removing ectopic pregnancies, some women who are trying to conceive experience three, four or even more ectopic pregnancies.

> *I'd gone to the hospital because of a suspected ectopic. I'd had three already and I knew the symptoms. I hoped so much that this time it was okay. I went in for laparoscopy for them to have a look around. When I woke up I felt the feeling, you know, coming out of major surgery. I put my hand down and felt the bandage on my incision—oh, God another one. I just started to cry. When the doctor came he told me he was sorry and I told him: "Take my fallopian tubes out, I can't go through it again!"*

Ectopic pregnancies are emotionally wrenching. There is no thrill of pregnancy, just hopes dashed again. It is enormously frustrating and frightening. The woman knows that she is fertile—the egg can be met by sperm and fertilized—if only the embryo could make it to the uterus. After wanting pregnancy so badly, she feels it has come so tantalizingly close, and yet is still so far away. The next pregnancy can not be anticipated because there is always the risk it will be ectopic again. Some doctors feel that because of the high incidence of recurrent ectopic pregnancies, IVF may be the best treatment for these otherwise fertile women, particularly if they have had three or more ectopic pregnancies.

(The woman quoted above did have her fallopian tubes tied off later. She and her husband went on to have successful in vitro fertilization. After enduring so much pain and disappointment with four ectopic pregnancies, they are now the parents of a little girl.)

Uterine Abnormalities

In a relatively small number of infertile women, the problem lies in the uterus. Growths, scar tissue or abnormal shapes can impair the implantation or development of an embryo. Some women are born with a congenital uterine abnormality. Other women, through disease or injury, develop uterine abnormalities later in life. In all types, the result is either a failure to implant, early spontaneous abortion or miscarriage.

Fibroids

AKA: leiomyoma, fibroid tumors, fibromyomata, myomata uteri

Fibroids are whorls of muscular tissue, like a knot in a tree trunk, that arise in the myometrium, the thick layer of smooth muscle in the uterus. Fibroids are very common, occurring in one of every five women over age 30, and they are even more common among black women. The fibroids can be single or multiple, microscopic or as large as a four-month pregnancy. They are often called fibroid "tumors" but they are not cancerous. Tumor is a Latin word simply meaning "swelling." The tumors are benign and do not spread to other organs in the body. Many women with fibroids complain of heavy and, occasionally, painful menstrual periods with the flow gushing or flooding. Some women become anemic because of the amount of blood lost. If menstrual problems plague a woman, and surgery to remove the fibroids is not an option, many doctors recommend a hysterectomy. This is a highly difficult decision to make for a woman still hoping to conceive, although it may be the best course if the fibroids are beyond treatment.

The cause of fibroids is not known, but several factors are often associated with their growth: high levels of estrogen, birth control pills and pregnancy.

The uterus is made up of three layers of tissue. The outermost layer, like the skin of the organ, is the serosa: the next is the myometrium, which is composed of three layers of smooth muscle fibers. Each muscle layer runs in an opposing direction, one horizontally, one vertically and one diagonally, giving the organ its tremendous strength. The innermost layer is the endometrium, the plush, internal lining where the embryo implants. Fibroids arise in the myometrium, as small dense whorls of fibrous muscle, usually grey-white and surrounded by a tissue capsule.

The fibroid may stay where it begins, called an interstitial (or intramural) fibroid, growing slowly, or it may bulge outwards or inwards. If it bulges to the outside serosa layer it is called a subserosal fibroid. If it protrudes towards the endometrium, it is called a submucosal fibroid. Subserosal or submucosal fibroids may migrate so much that they separate from the body of the uterus and become suspended on a stalk, a pedicle, and they are called pedunculated fibroids. A submucosa pedunculated fibroid may dangle within the endometrial cavity like a chandelier. A subserosal pedunculated fibroid may perch on the uterus like a TV antenna. Women with fibroids rarely have just one tumor; more often the fibroids are multiple.

It is easy to understand why a large fibroid that obliterates the uterine cavity causes infertility; it may be so large that it occupies the entire uterine cavity, but the reason why some other fibroids impair a woman's fertility is not known. Many women with fibroids have no trouble conceiving, while others do. Research shows that 40 percent of women with fibroids have repeated miscarriages, premature labor and infertility.

Various suggestions have been made why fertility is compromised. The fibroid may interfere with blood flow to the endometrium, or, as stated, distort the shape of the uterine cavity. A pedunculated fibroid may act as an IUD in preventing an embryo from implanting in the womb. A fibroid may compress the junction of uterus and tube, preventing the passage of sperm or embryo. Fibroids can also exist in conjunction with endometriosis or tubal disease while not being the main cause of infertility. Sumucosal and interstitial fibroids are most likely to be associated with infertility. Subserosal fibroids do not seem to compromise fertility.

Diagnosis

A doctor can often feel fibroids during a pelvic examination. They feel like hard round knots, but touching them does not usually cause pain. During the infertility work-up, a hysterosalpingogram (dye X ray) shows any distortions or protrusions into the uterine cavity caused by fibroids. These are usually confirmed at hysteroscopy. Uterine fibroids may also show up on ultrasound or magnetic resonance imaging (MRI). During the laparoscopy, fibroids on the outside of the uterus can also be seen.

Treatment

There are basically three approaches to treatments for fibroids: drugs, surgery or doing nothing. Many doctors take the conservative approach, and watch and wait to see what happens with the fibroids. Sometimes no treatment is required.

Drugs

Since fibroids are estrogen dependent, drugs that interrupt the estrogen stimulation of the uterus can shrink fibroids. In essence, the drugs aim to put the woman into chemical menopause. Two treatments are the most popular: Danazol and GnRH analogues.

Danazol, which goes under the trade name Cyclomen or Danocrine (by Winthrop), is a testosterone derivative that inhibits the pituitary from stimulating the ovaries and has been used on fibroids with moderately good results. It is most commonly used for the treatment of minor endometriosis. (See the section on endometriosis later in this chapter.)

A promising drug treatment for fibroids is gonadotropin releasing hormone analogues (GnRH analogues). (See appendix D of Chapter 5 for more on the drugs and their side effects.) When the analogues are given to a woman with fibroids the pituitary does not send the FSH/LH to the ovary, and the ovary, in turn, does not produce estrogen. Starved of the estrogen they need to grow, the fibroids shrink.

The drug is usually given by nasal inhalation or in a pellet under the skin daily for about six months. Initial research using GnRH analogues for fibroids has been very promising, showing that the tumors can shrink by up to 40 percent or more. The big problem is that while on the therapy women can not conceive: it is physically impossible because no eggs are being produced. Unfortunately, as soon as the treatment is stopped, the fibroids start to grow again. However, sometimes the treatment allows conception before the fibroid grows too big.

Many doctors advocate drug treatment with analogues to shrink fibroids, followed by surgery to remove the shrunken remains. This use of analogues also appears very promising.

Research is being done on progesterone analogues that block progesterone receptors. The abortion pill RU486, which received a great deal of media attention, particularly in France where it was first released, is a progesterone antagonist. It competes with natural progesterone for the receptor sites in the uterus. RU486 also has anti-estrogen action and in this role is being studied for the treatment of fibroids. Dr. Gary Hogden, an American scientist who is working on progesterone antagonists for a wide variety of applications, such as endometriosis, labor induction and abortion, says progesterone antagonists theoretically could work well to shrink fibroids. He predicts, however, it will not be until the mid-1990s that a progesterone antagonist will be readily available for fibroids.

Surgery

Myomectomy, major surgery to remove the fibroids, has significant risks and requires a surgeon who has extensive experience in operating on uterine muscle. In the operation, the surgeon cuts out the accessible fibroids, taking care when sewing up the uterus to align the muscle tissue. Pediculated fibroids or subserosal and submucosal fibroids are the easiest to remove. Some submucosal fibroids can be removed by operative hysteroscopy, a special fiber optic scope put into the uterus through the cervix that is combined with operating instruments. It allows the doctor to both view the cavity and remove the growths, alleviating the need for pelvic surgery.

If multiple fibroids are buried deep in the tissue, the operation can be very difficult or even impossible. Often doctors are not sure whether the fibroids can be removed until the operation is taking place, and about 10 percent grow in again after surgery. The uterus has a rich blood supply; therefore, extensive bleeding can be the major complication of myomectomy, and often a number of blood transfusions must be given to replace blood loss. As in all pelvic surgery, there is a risk of adhesions forming after the operation, which may further impair fertility. Any other causes of infertility such as ovulation disorders or male sperm problems should be corrected before resorting to uterine surgery. Discuss the risks and benefits of surgery for your own particular case with your doctor.

Endometrial Polyps

A polyp is any tissue that bulges or projects out of the normal tissue, often on a stalk or pedicle. Endometrial polyps are soft outgrowths of the endometrium, almost like stalactites in a cave. They tend to occur more frequently in women near the end of their reproductive lives, but women of all ages can get polyps. Polyps can interfere with implantation by acting as a natural IUD.

Diagnosis

The most common symptom of endometrial polyps is abnormal menstrual bleeding, usually with spotting between periods. But many women have no symptoms at all until polyps are discovered in the infertility work-up. Polyps can sometimes be discovered by the dye X ray, the hysterosalpingogram, if they are distorting the uterine cavity; by a hysteroscopy to view the inside of the womb; or by a dilation and currettage (D&C).

Treatment

Endometrial polyps are soft and easily removed by a D&C. This is the standard course of treatment. Under general anesthetic, first the cervix is opened and a metal currette is put through the cervix and gently scraped along the lining of the uterus, removing the endometrium. The tissue removed by a D&C is sent to the lab to be examined. The removal of a polyp is sometimes all that is needed for a pregnancy to result.

Asherman's Syndrome

AKA: intrauterine adhesions

Joseph Asherman was a Czechoslovakian gynecologist who practiced in the early- to mid-twentieth century. He was the first to publicize the description of bands of scar tissue in a woman's uterus joining one part of endometrium to another, or in some cases totally sticking the walls together. In Asherman's time the culprit was usually tuberculosis or back-street abortion. Today, Asherman's Syndrome is most often caused by abortion, a too-vigorous D&C or the aftermath of pregnancy.

Any time there is significant trauma to the lining of the uterus, such as the scraping in a D&C, suction or scraping in an abortion, infection following an abortion, or separation of the placenta, scar tissue may form between the "hurt" tissue. The walls of the uterus are very close together and the adhesions may totally adhere one wall to another. Pregnancy then becomes impossible or aborts early in its development. Menstrual periods may also be very light or nonexistent because the basal layer of endometrium may be too scarred to build up additional endometrial tissue.

Diagnosis

If in your medical history you have had an abortion, D&C or pregnancy, your doctor may suspect intrauterine adhesions. The hysterosalpingogram may show "filling defects," meaning an unnatural shape of the uterine cavity. A hysteroscopy to view the inside of your uterus may also show the cavity crisscrossed with bands of scar tissue.

Treatment

The bands of scar tissue can sometimes be removed under operative hysteroscopy. (See the description of hysteroscopy for the septate uterus on page 157.) Afterward, an IUD or balloon-like device is put in place to keep the walls separated while they heal. High doses of estrogens may also be prescribed to help the endometrium regrow. The success of this procedure has been good, with 70 to 80 percent of women becoming pregnant following the procedure.

Congenital Abnormalities

The female reproductive tract begins developing when the tiny fetus is less than eight weeks old. Less than an inch long, the fetus at this stage is a mass of rapidly dividing, migrating and differentiating tissue. What eventually becomes the upper vagina, cervix, uterus and fallopian tubes starts at this stage as being two small tube-like ducts, called the Müllerian ducts. These ducts fuse just before eight weeks and begin forming to become the reproductive tract. Occasionally something occurs that throws off this intricate developmental process, resulting in a congenital abnormality: a double uterus, a misshaped uterus, only one horn or one fallopian tube and so on.

It is estimated that one or two of every 1000 baby girls may have a developmental abnormality in the reproductive tract. The drug diethylstilbestrol, DES, which some women took during pregnancy from the 1940s to 1970, increased the number of reproductive anomalies in the women's offspring. It is described in more detail below. Many women with abnormal reproductive tracts will never know because they have no trouble conceiving. Some women, however, learn that they have a congenital abnormality when they are investigated for infertility or recurrent miscarriage. The following are the types of congenital abnormalities that can occur.

Congenital Absence of the Uterus

If there are no Müllerian ducts, no uterus will be able to form, and usually the woman lacks an upper vagina. She may have functional ovaries, however, which would enable her and her partner to have a genetically related child through in vitro fertilization. Her egg is fertilized by her husband's sperm and the resulting embryo is transferred into the womb of a surrogate mother for nine months. (See Chapter 10 on IVF.)

Double Uterus

If the two Müllerian ducts do not fuse completely, a double uterus can result. The extent of the deformity varies. If no fusion takes place at all, a woman can have two upper vaginas, two cervixes and two uteruses (but only two fallopian tubes). This complete doubling of all the reproductive tract is called a didelphic uterus. The woman may tend to have very heavy menstrual periods because she has two endometriums that are shedding each month. If just the uterus is double but the vagina and cervix single, it is called a complete bicornuate uterus. Many women with a double uterus have no trouble conceiving. Each half of the double uterus will act as a single uterus. In fact, a case of twins, one in each of the wombs, has been reported. If there is only a single pregnancy in one uterus, the other uterus may continue to cycle and bleed during the pregnancy. A bicornuate uterus, however, can result in a difficult birth.

A partial bicornuate uterus is the name for a uterus that is partially fused and looks heart-shaped from the outside. An arcuate uterus is almost completely fused but has a little dip across the fundus, or top. A partial bicornuate uterus and an arcuate uterus can cause miscarriage, premature labor or a difficult birth. A metroplasty, an operation to fuse the uterus, can be performed by an expert in uterine surgery. An intense tailoring job of the uterus, the operation involves cutting through the uterine muscle, removing excess tissue and sewing the uterine walls back in a new configuration. This is a major operation, and it should be performed only after an infertility expert has ruled out any other cause of miscarriage, such as an incompetent cervix, chronic illness, luteal phase deficiency or genetic abnormalities. At least four to six months should pass after the operation before a couple attempts pregnancy.

Septate Uterus

From the outside, a septate uterus in the pelvic cavity looks like a normal uterus, but on the inside a tissue wall, or a septum, divides the uterine cavity in two. When the Müllerian ducts fuse, one of the last processes is the reabsorption of the vertical uterine septum that formerly separated the two. The septum can be complete, extending through the whole uterus, or partial. A septate uterus may cause recurrent miscarriage before three or six months of pregnancy. By hysterosalpingogram it is impossible for the doctor to distinguish between a bicornuate and a septate uterus, but at laparoscopy the septate uterus looks normal, while the bicornuate has two horns, or is heart-shaped.

Until a decade ago, removal of the septum required major pelvic surgery. Now most doctors recommend the septum be removed by operative hysteroscopy. The scope is introduced into the uterus and the uterus is inflated with a gas or fluid medium (a solution called Hyskon is recommended by some doctors) to keep the walls apart so the surgeon can view the cavity. Then either scissors or a resectoscope that allows the surgeon to use electrocautery will be used to cut away the septum. If bleeding occurs a medical balloon to stop bleeding may be placed in the cavity. About two or three months following the operation, the couple can attempt a pregnancy.

Communicating and Non-Communicating Rudimentary Horn

Uneven fusing of the ducts with one side more developed than the other can cause infertility. The result is a bulge, or horn, on the undeveloped side. Sometimes the fusing is almost complete and the uterine passages connect. This is called a communicating rudimentary horn. It is like a small "den" off the larger "living-room" uterus connected by a passage. An embryo that implants in the "den" can result in miscarriage because that portion of the uterus does not have the ability to expand as much as is needed for the growing fetus. The effect is like that of an ectopic pregnancy.

Sometimes the undeveloped side is completely separate from the more developed side, with no connecting passage. This is called a non-communicating rudimentary horn. To take the architectural analogy one step further, the non-communicating rudimentary horn is like a separate guest house connected to the uterus by only a band of connective tissue. The problem is that the non-communicating rudimentary horn is still lined with endometrium that every month menstruates. The menstrual blood, however, can not escape through the vagina because it does not connect. The blood has only one place to go—back out the tubes, which can lead to endometriosis in the woman's pelvic cavity. The blood can also fill the horn, which creates problems. Occasionally an embryo travels from the other side and implants in the non-connecting horn, resulting in an ectopic-like pregnancy. The treatment for both types of rudimentary horns is pelvic surgery to remove them.

The Legacy of DES

From the early 1940s until the early 1970s, the first man-made estrogen, diethylstilbestrol (DES), was given to women for a variety of complaints: threatened miscarriage, past history of miscarriage, early bleeding in pregnancy and even diabetes during pregnancy. It was thought that the synthetic estrogen would prevent miscarriage. Instead, DES has gone into the history books with thalidomide and the Dalkon Shield as medical inventions that women would have been better off without. DES did not prevent miscarriage, but it did cause problems in the formation of the reproductive tracts of the sons and daughters who were tiny fetuses when those women took DES. It is estimated that more than one million women, world-wide, between 1940 and 1970 took DES during pregnancy. The impact of DES on men is discussed in Chapter 7.

The impact of DES on the daughters was first noted in 1971 when Dr. Arthur Herbst and his colleagues reported in the *New England Journal of Medicine* that they had seen seven young women between the ages of 15 and 22 who had a very rare form of vaginal cancer, clear cell adenocarcinoma. A great deal of medical investigation showed the linking factor to be that all of the girls' mothers took DES during pregnancy. Since that time, DES has been linked to a number of reproductive abnormalities, including increased risk of vaginal cancer, increased risk of cancerous cell changes in the cervix and increased risk of unusual cells lining the vagina, called vaginal adenosis.

But the concern of most women reading this book who may have been exposed to DES is that the drug also has been linked to infertility. The drug in some women interfered with the normal fusing of the Müllerian ducts. As a result, DES daughters can have abnormally shaped uteruses—a T-shaped uterus is most often reported, but septate and double uteruses also occur. The usual result of uterine abnormalities in DES daughters is recurrent miscarriages. DES-exposed fallopian tubes may be narrower than normal, increasing the risk of ectopic pregnancies. The cervix of a DES daughter can also be abnormally shaped and may have fewer glands, interfering with the production of fertile cervical mucus. Some studies have also reported that DES daughters appear to ovulate less frequently than the average population and to be less fertile. (It is not fully established that this is caused by DES; the same ovulation defects may affect other women.) However, all that said, it seems that about 80 percent of DES-exposed women still are able to become pregnant.

Treatment

Reproductive surgery for a T-shaped uterus has not been shown to be necessary. A septate or double uterus can possibly be helped by reconstructive surgery. Clomid and other fertility drugs have been suggested for DES women who do not ovulate regularly although it is not known whether it would work in the same manner. Understandably, many women who have been affected by DES are reluctant to take fertility drugs or other hormones.

Emotional Aspects of DES

It is very difficult for both my mother and me. She feels terribly guilty that something she took more than thirty years ago may be denying me children and denying her grandchildren. It hurts us both. On top of that, being a child of DES has made me suspicious of the medical profession. My relationships with my doctors tend to break down. One doctor told me I was a very difficult and angry patient. I guess I am.

The lack of infertility treatment options for DES patients, the feeling of being victimized, and the increased chance of cancer can be particularly difficult for DES offspring. They feel helpless, and the best option for these people may be to join a DES support group. There are a number of chapters of DES Action throughout the United States and Canada. They print a newsletter called DES Action Voice, which keeps members informed of medical developments and also supplies contact names and phone numbers for medical help. In the early

1980s the organization printed a booklet *Fertility and Pregnancy Guide for DES Daughters and Sons,* available through libraries and the organization itself. (See the address list on page 375.)

Endometriosis

Endometriosis, menstrual endometrial tissue growing outside the uterus, is one of the most baffling causes of infertility. The disease was first described in 1860 by Carl Von Rokitansky, an Austrian pathologist, and was named in 1927 by American gynecologist John Sampson. Even though it has been recognized longer than many other causes of infertility, it continues to be one of the least understood.

Endometriosis occurs when fragments of the lush, blood-rich lining of the uterus implant and grow on other tissue: usually on the ovaries; on the ligaments that suspend the uterus; on the uterus itself and on the structures and tissues in the lower abdomen such as the large intestine and peritoneum. Under the influence of the cycling reproductive hormones, each month the implants proliferate, break down and bleed just as the endometrium of the uterus does. But the blood of endometriosis has nowhere to go. Instead, it bleeds into the pelvic cavity causing irritation, inflammation and the building of scar tissue. Scar tissue can surround the growths, causing a blood filled cyst that swells and regresses each month. The cyst can rupture and spread endometrial tissue farther. In more severe cases the wandering endometrial tissue has been found inside the bladder, rectum, intestines, and vagina and vulva. In very rare cases it has been found in distant locations, inside the lung, the hip and in the skin of the underarm, for example.

The incidence of endometriosis in the general population of women is not known. It is thought to affect perhaps 15 percent of all women, but likely only a portion of those complain of infertility or pain, or both. Of women who do seek help for infertility, between 15 and 30 percent are found by laparoscopy to have endometriosis. Doctors say the incidence of endometriosis appears to be increasing, but it is not known whether that means more women are getting the disease or simply that more women are seeking help for it.

In years past it was known as "the career woman's disease" because it tended to show up in women between the ages of 30 and 40 who had not had children. It was also seen as being a disease of white middle-class women rather than women of other racial groups. Now it is known that this supposition was false and based on societal and cultural factors more than scientific fact. Educated career women were more likely to seek help for pain and infertility and postpone pregnancy and to have good medical coverage. If women in other groups did seek help, studies have reported that because of medical bias their pelvic pain would be more likely diagnosed as pelvic inflammatory disease.

Endometriosis can affect all women. It is true, however, that endometriosis tends to become worse with reproductive age and many women seek help for it when they are in their thirties and forties. That many women are putting off childbearing until those years may account for the apparent increase in the disease. With menopause and the cessation of menstrual bleeding, it generally is cured. However, with more menopausal women using estrogen supplementation, cases of postmenopausal endometriosis have occurred. Doctors believe that pregnancy, because of the cessation of menstruation for nine months, may cure or at least lessen the severity of the disease. It is also believed that some women may have a genetic predisposition to the disease.

Theories of Origin

Why endometriosis starts in the first place is still unclear. The most widely accepted theory to date is that in the monthly bleeding some menstrual blood is shed through the fallopian tubes into the pelvic cavity, a process called retrograde menstruation. Menstrual blood is made up of blood, extracellular fluid and clusters of endometrial cells. It is believed that the free-floating endometrial cells implant on receptive tissue in the pelvic cavity. This theory is borne out by the fact that the majority of implants seem to be distributed on the organs and tissues in a logical, gravitational path as if it came from the fallopian tubes, though the tubes themselves are usually not the site of implants. This theory explains why the ovary, situated at the opening of the fallopian tube, is the most common site of endometriosis, followed by the ligaments, lower portion of the uterus and bottom of the pelvic cavity, the posterior cul de sac.

The theory of retrograde menstruation was first suggested in the 1920s and for a long time it was thought that it was abnormal, that only women with endometriosis would have retrograde menstruation. But recent research suggests that in 90 percent of all ovulating women some menstrual blood backs up out the tubes during menstruation, as can be seen by the presence of menstrual blood in their pelvic cavities at laparoscopy. But if retrograde menstruation is now considered normal, why do not all women get endometriosis? No one knows that answer. It has been suggested that women who get endometriosis may have an altered immune response or that their tissues may be more receptive to implants, but the reason is still unknown.

Other theories suggest that the disease has its origins in left-over embryonic tissue, or that women with endometriosis have pelvic tissue that retains the embryonic ability to differentiate into other tissue: to keep dividing, changing slightly, and dividing again. One of these theories based on differentiation, celomic metaplasia, states that all the cells in the pelvic cavity retain the potential under the appropriate stimulation to differentiate into other tissue. Endometriosis arises when the adult tissue has continued to differentiate, resulting in endometrial tissue in the wrong places. Some believe that the endometrial implants are left-over pockets of embryonic tissue that has differentiated into endometrium. Today these theories do not have a great deal of medical support.

A final theory is that endometrial cells could be transported through the circulatory system and lymphatic system to other locations. This theory explains why endometrial lesions have shown up in other parts of the body. This type of transmission is rare. Surgery, such as a hysterectomy or cesarean section, may also cause endometrial tissue to be transplanted inadvertently in the pelvic wall or other locations in the pelvic cavity.

Despite all the theories, most doctors believe that endometriosis is caused primarily by retrograde menstruation in susceptible women, and only sometimes by transport of cells by the blood or lymph to the abnormal locations.

Symptoms

The most common symptoms of endometriosis are pain and infertility. An estimated 30 to 40 percent of women with endometriosis have trouble conceiving. Pelvic pain, particularly around menstruation, and pain on deep intercourse is also extremely common. Unlike a cramping pain, pain caused by endometriosis is usually steady and dull, becoming worse with each menstrual period. Oddly, the amount of pain women experience seems to have no relationship to the severity of the endometriosis. Some women who report very few symptoms can be found to have extensive disease, while other women with mild endometriosis can experience a great deal of pain. Women with endometriosis on their intestines may experience constipation and pain when having bowel movements, particularly around the time of menstruation. In rare instances, bleeding can occur from the rectum or bladder at the time of menstruation.

Diagnosis

Occasionally during a woman's pelvic examination, the doctor feels tender bulges that suggest endometriosis on the uterosacral ligaments, uterus or pelvic cavity. The only accurate way, however, to diagnose the disease is for the doctor to use a diagnostic laparoscopy during which time the abnormal tissue can be seen.

What the doctor sees by laparoscopy varies from woman to woman. The lesions may be tiny bluish or dark brown dots on the ovary or ligaments, or there may be large patches four or more centimeters in diameter. They may be superficial, "powder-burn" lesions or they may have burrowed deep into the host tissue, in which case they are called endometriomas. If the ovary is affected, it may respond by covering over the endometrial tissue with fibrous scar tissue, enclosing the endometriosis in a cyst. Thus enclosed, the implant grows and bleeds in response to hormone stimulation, causing it to swell with bloody fluid. Over time the collected blood becomes thick and syrupy and turns dark brown or black, called a "chocolate cyst." At times the chocolate cyst can swell and rupture, causing the blood to be released and implant on other tissue. The swelling and occasional rupture can be the reason behind some women's severe pain with endometriosis.

The cyclical bleeding of the implants can cause irritation and inflammation in the pelvic cavity, resulting in the growth of adhesions. The adhesions are filmy and thin at first, becoming more dense and deep as the disease progresses. When endometriosis is most severe and long-term, the reproductive organs become covered with a mass of adhesions. The uterus may be entrapped in a web of fibrous scar tissue and fixed in a bent position back toward the spine. The fixed uterus or the entrapment of the ovary can be the reason behind the pain on deep intercourse.

Classifying the Severity of Endometriosis

Because of the variation in severity of endometriosis, in the 1970s doctors tried to devise a classification system for the disease, with common, accepted guidelines. A few clinicians came up with schemes to rate endometriosis, but each scheme had its flaws. In 1979 a committee of the American Fertility Society (AFS) drew up a system of classification based on giving points to what the doctor sees in the woman's pelvic cavity. For example, a superficial implant of less than one centimeter on the ovary was given one point, while a deep implant greater than three centimeters on the ovary was given 20 points. Filmy adhesions on the ovary were assigned four points, and dense adhesions, 16 points. The AFS classification suggested doctors systematically review the structures in the pelvic cavity and assign points to the type of endometriosis. The addition of all the points results in a patient's score, which is consistent with other doctors' findings.

The initial AFS scheme was revised in 1985 to remove some of the scoring problems. Despite some continuing debate over the fine points of classification and scores, the revised AFS system is largely accepted for rating endometriosis. North American doctors are being encouraged to use it to help foster consistency in research and treatment of endometriosis. The AFS classification now breaks endometriosis into four stages: minimal, mild, moderate and severe. A woman has minimal endometriosis, stage 1, when her score is less than five points; mild, when her score is six to 15 points; moderate, when it is 16 to 40 points; and severe, when it is greater than 40 points. There has been some criticism of the arbitrary basis of the scores, particularly because the scores do not always relate to a woman's chance of pregnancy. The classification method may be still further refined.

Endometriosis and Infertility

It is easy to understand why infertility might occur when endometriosis is severe and pelvic adhesions enmesh the ovary, uterus and fallopian tubes. The adhesions could distort the pickup or transport of the egg, prevent the sperm from reaching the egg, or impede the passage of the embryo back down the tube. The impact of severe endometriosis in these cases could be similar to adhesions caused by Pelvic Inflammatory Disease.

When endometriosis is mild or moderate, the reasons why it undermines fertility is not as clear-cut, but there are a number of theories. What role any or all of them play in preventing conception and pregnancy is not known. Research has shown that as many as 25 percent of women with endometriosis do not ovulate regularly, and again, the reason is not known. Researchers have suggested that the disorder, luteinized unruptured follicle syndrome (LUFS), in which the egg develops but is not released from the follicle, occurs more frequently in women with endometriosis. Others do not believe this is so. More research into LUFS is needed to resolve the debate.

The inflammation associated with endometriosis may also contribute to women's difficulty conceiving. One theory suggests that the implants irritate the pelvic cavity, starting an inflammatory response. Immune cells, or macrophages, collect in the cavity to fight the implants. Research shows that a woman with endometriosis has more macrophages in her pelvic cavity than a fertile woman, and that these macrophages attack sperm or secrete destructive enzymes toxic to the eggs, sperm or embryo. Some researchers have reported that during in vitro studies, fluid from the pelvic cavities of women with endometriosis stopped development of embryos in the early stages of cell division.

An increased amount of prostaglandins have also been linked to women who have endometriosis. Prostaglandins are fatty acids found throughout the body that perform a variety of jobs. A type of prostaglandin is found in the uterus and is involved in the shedding of menstrual tissue and contractions of the uterus. Endometrial implants are known to produce prostaglandins, and women with endometriosis seem to have higher levels of prostaglandins in their menstrual fluid. It is theorized that prostaglandins in endometriosis may impair ovulation or the ability of the tube to transport sperm or the embryo, and might also impair implantation of the embryo. The role of prostaglandins in normal menstruation and in endometriosis is still being studied.

Spontaneous abortion is reported to be higher in women with endometriosis than in normally fertile women. One-third of women with endometriosis lose their pregnancy in the first 12 weeks. The causes of the spontaneous abortion are likely the same factors that potentially cause infertility in endometriosis: altered immune response, toxic components secreted by macrophages, prostaglandins or a disrupted menstrual cycle.

Treatment

In general, there are three avenues of treatment for endometriosis if infertility is the main complaint: drugs, surgery or doing nothing. Each approach has its benefits and disadvantages. If endometriosis has led to extensive scarring, blocking the tubes or preventing pickup of the egg, surgery to attempt to free the reproductive organs is the only course. If endometriosis is milder, without scars, there is some suggestion that pregnancy rates following surgery are slightly higher than after the use of drugs, but this is not conclusive. To date no treatment cures endometriosis, but only decreases its symptoms and extent, perhaps allowing a pregnancy to take place. Endometriosis may return when therapy is discontinued. Medical understanding of the best endometriosis treatment has suffered from a lack of controlled studies and strict standardizations, making comparisons of treatments difficult.

The treatment of endometriosis, if pain is the chief complaint, can follow a slightly different course than for infertility. What follows is the medical rationale if pregnancy is the woman's main concern. Often both drugs and surgery are combined.

The Case for Doing Nothing

Many women, who through laparoscopy are diagnosed as having minimal or mild endometriosis, go on to become pregnant with no medical therapy. Either these women are essentially fertile or the diagnostic laparoscopy helped them become pregnant, perhaps by the injection of dye through their tubes. Some doctors think that immediate therapy for women with mild endometriosis may decrease their chances of becoming pregnant. Drugs to treat endometriosis stop ovulation while they are being taken. Therefore, if a woman must take a drug for three to six months, she loses the chances of conceiving during those months. A delay of six months can be significant to a woman who is in her mid-thirties. Surgery may cause subsequent adhesions, lowering fertility. Some doctors, therefore, advocate six to 12 months of observation before prescribing a drug or recommending surgery. Other doctors recommend quick action, such as a few months of drug therapy or laparoscopic surgery to remove spots of endometriosis to prevent the problem from intensifying and to improve, overall, the woman's chances of conceiving.

Whether or not your doctor recommends you wait for at least six months or go on to therapy depends on factors such as your age and how long you and your partner have been trying to conceive.

If you are under the age of 30, waiting may be suggested, whereas if you are 36, therapy may be the route. Similarly, if you have been attempting pregnancy for less than a year, further observation may be best. But if you have been trying for two years or more and all other reasons for infertility have been eliminated, therapy without delay may be suggested. Whether or not you experience pain as well as infertility also affects treatment decisions.

Drugs

It has long been known that pregnancy and menopause are two events in a woman's life that may improve or cure her endometriosis. Historically, hormone manipulation to disrupt the cycle of menstruation, stop ovulation and so disrupt the proliferation and bleeding of the implants, was first tried. Over the years high doses of estrogens, progesterones and male hormones have all been used to interrupt the cyclical process in endometriosis. The treatments were successful in that they stopped menstruation, but the side effects exacted a heavy price. Androgens (male hormones) caused a reduction of breasts, deepening of voice and hair growth. High doses of estrogens caused nausea, weight gain, overgrowth of endometrium and potentially serious complications such as blood clots or increased risk of cancer. High doses of progestins (a generic name for a natural or man-made substance that acts like progesterone) caused breakthrough bleeding and could stop menstrual periods for up to a year after the therapy was discontinued—unacceptable for women trying to conceive.

Two approaches are now generally being used to treat endometriosis: putting the woman into a temporary menopause or tricking her body into believing she is pregnant.

Danazol

Danazol, a derivative of the male hormone testosterone, is the most widely recommended drug treatment for endometriosis. It induces a menopause-like condition as well as interfering with other body functions that may augment its success. Danazol (Cyclomen or Danocrine, by Winthrop) has been the preferred method of treatment for endometriosis since the early 1980s. It stops ovulation by inhibiting the functioning of the pituitary, preventing the rise of FSH levels and the LH surge. This stops the development of the egg in the follicle and stops the production of estrogen and progesterone, the essential hormones that feed the growth of endometrium. As well as inhibiting the reproductive hormonal axis, danazol also directly interferes with the ovarian enzymes that are responsible for making estrogen and progesterone. Danazol also seems to inhibit the androgen and progesterone receptors on endometrial tissue, like the wrong key jamming a lock, stopping the endometrial cells from growing.

As a final benefit, recent research shows that danazol may alter the immune system of women with endometriosis. The immune system in women with endometriosis and some other diseases such as lupus, is "turned on" making it particularly sensitive and prone to attacking the body's own tissue as well as foreign invaders. There is a possibility that danazol decreases the number of so-called auto-antibodies circulating in a woman's blood. This theory is still unproved but may hold promise if part of the reason endometriosis causes infertility is the result of immune problems.

Method of Use Danazol is usually taken in a capsule form two or four times a day, usually at the highest daily dose of 800 milligrams. The treatment is started in the first days of menstrual bleeding. It is important not to take the drug if you are pregnant, so if you have not had a menstrual period, pregnancy must be firmly ruled out before starting the drug. Treatment continues for three to six months, and possibly as long as nine months. While you are taking the drug your menstrual periods may stop altogether or become irregular. The drug manufacturer, Winthrop Laboratories, recommends the use of a barrier or non-hormonal contraceptive, such as diaphragm or condom, to avoid pregnancy while taking the drug. The effects on the fetus are not known but it possibly causes masculinization of a female fetus. Danazol is expensive, about $6.50 a day for 800 milligrams. A six-month course of treatment can cost, in drugs alone, at least $1500. Recent research has supported the use of danazol combined with surgery. Using this approach, a three- to six-month treatment of danazol may be used to remove superficial endometriosis, followed by surgery to remove the remaining, more resistant endometriomas. Danazol treatment for a few months may also follow surgery to prevent regrowth.

Side effects Danazol's side effects are almost all caused because it is "androgenic," meaning it acts as a male hormone in the woman's body, or "anabolic," meaning it promotes tissue growth. Common side effects are weight gain, bloating, decrease in breast size, hair growth on the chin or breasts, acne, oily skin or hair, muscle cramps and deepening of the voice. The voice changes and hair growth can be permanent. Women may also experience an increase in moodiness and an increase in sexual desire. Other side effects, caused by the decrease of estrogen and similar to the symptoms of menopause, are hot flashes, sweating, vaginitis, vaginal drying, vaginal itching or bleeding as well as anxiousness or moodiness. In rare cases a woman may experience an enlargement of the clitoris as a result of the androgens.

GnRH Analogues

The onset of menopuase is the best known treatment of endometriosis. If a woman's ovaries are not functioning, either because of natural menopause or because of surgical removal, the problem of endometriosis is eliminated. Unfortunately, fertility is eliminated too. In recent years a new type of therapy that creates a temporary menopause is causing excitement. Gonadotropin-releasing hormone analogues (GnRHa) for treating ovulation disorders and fibroids have already been mentioned. (See appendix D of Chapter 5.) Their use is the same in endometriosis: a temporary shut down of the system to correct a defect. Initial research with GnRHa and endometriosis has been promising, showing a regression of symptoms and of implants for a number of months following therapy, but more research is required.

Progesterone Antagonists

Preliminary research of man-made compounds that compete with progesterone is exciting to scientists because of the potential application to endometriosis. There are more than 200 potential progesterone antagonists, compounds that are almost identical to progesterone except for an addition of a carbon or a hydrogen atom. RU486, the abortion pill released in France in 1988, is a progesterone antagonist. Other compounds are ZK 734 and ZK 299 being developed by Schering. Like GnRH analogues, the progesterone antagonists work by what scientists call "competitive inhibition." The man-made antagonist competes with the real progesterone for progesterone receptor sites anywhere they occur—the hypothalamus and pituitary, the breasts, the central nervous system, cervix, uterus myometrium and (most importantly for endometriosis) endometrial tissue. The progesterone antagonist blocks the receptor site and will not give the real progesterone access. Research is still preliminary and it may be a number of years before full results become available, but animal studies and initial clinical studies show that it shrinks endometrial implants and may, in some women, eliminate them. The compounds have not yet been found to be safe for long term use.

Surgery

Surgery to physically remove the implants or barriers to pregnancy has been used as a treatment for endometriosis since 1929. When endometriosis is extensive and lesions are large, or when pelvic adhesions are dense, surgery is usually the best course of action. In recent years, however, more doctors have been advocating surgery for mild and moderate forms of endometriosis, particularly if it can be done under laparoscopy. Some doctors believe women in their thirties who want to become pregnant should first be treated by surgery because it avoids the delay required by drug therapy. Surgery combined with drug therapy is also being advocated. Pregnancy rates for mild endometriosis treated by surgery have been reported at between 66 and 75 percent. For moderate endometriosis it drops down to 37 to 74 percent. Severe endometriosis treated by surgery has a reported pregnancy rate of between 29 to 48 percent.

Two surgical approaches can be used: laparoscopy, in which a fiber-optic scope is introduced into the belly through a bandaid-sized incision, or laparotomy, in which the abdomen is opened to direct view with an incision across the top of the pubic hair.

Laparoscopy Laparoscopy, which is the less invasive operation, is usually used for less extensive endometriosis. The endometrial lesions are most commonly destroyed by cautery, burning of the lesion with an electrode. Any lesion that the surgeon can view with the laparoscope can be cauterized. If the lesion is bigger than one centimeter, it may be first cauterized and then cut away. In recent years, the carbon dioxide laser has been advocated for use with the laparoscope. The laser "vaporizes" the implant by bringing the intracellular water in the tissue to a boil. The laser is more awkward for the surgeon to use but some believe it may reduce the risk of damage to other tissue and prevent adhesions from forming after surgery. Some doctors, however, are concerned that the smoke from the laser may be damaging or carcenogenic to other tissues. An apparatus similar to an exhaust pipe to remove the smoke plume is available. It is not yet known, however, whether laser is better than cautery, or vice versa.

Laparotomy In cases of extensive endometriosis and pelvic adhesions, laparotomy using microsurgical techniques is recommended. It is a major operation that entails at least four days in hospital and a number of weeks convalescing. Once the abdomen is opened, pelvic adhesions are removed first, either by cautery or laser. The same debate exists over whether laser or cautery is superior during laparotomy for endometriosis, and so far the issue has not been resolved. Some people believe vaporization of the lesions prevents less damage to other tissues. Still others believe it offers no advantage and that it may cause more damage, particularly if used on large cysts on the ovary. The procedure also takes longer. In cases of extensive endometriosis it may be impossible to remove all the implants, especially if by removing them other important organs might be damaged, such as the bowel or bladder.

Neurectomy Some doctors may suggest that while they remove endometrial implants and adhesions in laparotomy, they also cut the nerves that transmit pain signals from the lower abdomen to the brain. This procedure is called a presacral neurectomy. Its use in North America is becoming increasingly rare. If this procedure is suggested to you, seek a second opinion.

In Vitro Fertilization and Other Advanced Techniques

Women with endometriosis who have been unsuccessful with conventional treatments are being referred to IVF and other techniques such as gamete intrafallopian tube transfer (GIFT). The success rates seem to be the same or a bit lower for women with endometriosis compared to other women undergoing IVF, which means the success rates are about 10 percent or less. But it is an option when everything else has failed. (See Chapter 10.)

Emotional Consequences

I can honestly say that my endometriosis makes my life miserable. I have both emotional and physical pain. Not only am I infertile but every month I have to deal with almost crippling pain. I am often moody and unhappy. I am tempted to get a hysterectomy to stop it once and for all, but I am torn by our desire for a child. While I took danazol it worked and stopped the pain, but I gained 25 pounds and grew hair on my chin. Soon after I stopped the drug, pain came back and we still haven't got pregnant. I don't know what to do.

Endometriosis can be an agonizing disease that affects every aspect of a woman's life. It can take a great toll on her relationship with her partner and friends. It can interfere with her work or plans for a family. It can make sexual intercourse painful or uncomfortable. Even when the endometriosis has been successfully treated the woman can be consumed with fear that it will return.

I was diagnosed with endometriosis four years ago, after I'd had a lot of pain and we'd had no luck getting pregnant. I was treated with danazol and then surgery. But my husband and I divorced soon after—I believe my endometriosis had a big role in the break-up. But for that reason I didn't try to get pregnant then. I've been remarried for just over a year and we've been trying to get pregnant since we got married. I've been sure it was my endometriosis. I imagined it coating my organs like a cancer and each month I convinced myself my pain was getting worse. I've been preoccupied with it. Well, last month I had a laparoscopy and they found one small spot—one spot, that's all. I felt incredibly relieved. But I also realized how afraid I was of it coming back and how I'd convinced myself it HAD come back. It was like psychological torture.

The burden of endometriosis can be difficult for a woman to carry alone. That is why many women have been helped by support groups made up of other women with endometriosis. The Endometriosis Association, founded in 1980 in Milwaukee, Wisconsin, has a number of chapters throughout North America, Britain and Australia. The self-help group promotes research, the exchange of information about treatments and new findings, emotional support and sharing of experiences. Local chapters hold regular meetings. For more information about the association, see page 375.

CHAPTER 7
Male Infertility

In close to 40 percent of men who submit semen for analysis as a routine part of the couple's infertility work-up, the results will come back as a devastating blow. Flaws in the semen sample suggest it is unlikely, or impossible, that his partner's eggs will be fertilized by one of his sperm.

> *It was my wife who went to her doctor first. They said I needed a sperm test so I said, no problem. Then a few days later the doctor's office phoned and said I should come in for an appointment. I hadn't been in a doctor's office for years. I wondered a bit, why they wouldn't tell me anything over the phone—but I thought he must want to talk to me about my wife. It was a total shock when the doctor looked at me and said: "I'm sorry, but your test showed no sperm." I just sat there in absolute and total shock. Me?*

The news is hard to take because there is usually no forewarning, no hint that a man may be infertile. Unlike some women who question their fertility if their periods have been irregular or they have known they have had Pelvic Inflammatory Disease, most men take their fertility for granted. Many men assume the problem rests with their partner and undertake the semen analysis with little thought to what the results might bring. When they get the negative news their world is shaken.

The diagnosis of male infertility is intensified because of the misconception that has surrounded the extent and nature of infertility in the past. The predominant attitude has been that infertility is a female problem. The myth has been that few males are infertile and those who are are less masculine, maybe even impotent. Male infertility has wrongly been linked to male sexuality: verility is assumed to be the ability to get a woman pregnant. The unfortunate result of this pervasive but erroneous attitude is that the infertile man often feels isolated, inadequate and inferior, and he often feels he can discuss his infertility with no one. Male infertility can be one of the loneliest of the infertility diagnoses, even though thousands upon thousands of men each year are told they are infertile. Adding to the stress of the situation are the numerous trips to the doctor for more tests and poking and prodding. Most men dislike visiting a doctor; it intensifies the feelings of being out of control, inadequate and ill.

In this chapter the causes and treatment of male infertility are discussed, along with further tests that may be required to pinpoint the problem after the semen analysis. The unique emotional factors of male infertility are discussed at the end.

The Enigmatic Male

Male infertility is one of the least understood areas of infertility medicine. Historically, research efforts have focused on female infertility while male infertility was simply circumvented by using an anonymous donor to impregnate the woman. As a result, medical understanding of what is going wrong in the infertile male and then how to treat it has suffered. There are few universally accepted treatments that are known to work to cure male infertility.

In the last 20 years, andrology, the study of the male reproductive process, has emerged as a specialization. Andrologists and urologists have been trying to address the research imbalance. Strides have been made, particularly in the last 10 years, but there is still a long way to go. "In the male we are just scratching the surface," says Melbourne andrologist Prof. David de Kretser. "In 30 to 40 percent of cases of male infertility we have no idea of what the cause is. There is a tremendous need for basic information. And until we understand what is happening, we will be unlikely to find very effective treatments."

To date about 35 percent of male infertility is thought to be related to varicoceles (a varicose vein in the testicle); about 10 percent to blocked or absent ejaculatory ducts; about 5 percent to antisperm antibodies; about 2 percent to hormone imbalances; about 5 percent to anatomical defects; and a few percent here and there to genetic problems, congenital abnormalities, retrograde ejaculation and infections. The remaining 30 to 40 percent are men who have subfertile semen and the doctors are not able to figure out why.

This may be bleak news: it is not reassuring to learn that little is known about one's problem. But there is a point of optimism in all this because it is clear that in men there is no strict cutoff between fertility and infertility. Where there are sperm, couples still have hope of a pregnancy. This concept will become more clear in the following discussion about the semen analysis and what it means.

Tests for Male Infertility

The History and Limitations of Semen Analysis

It was in the 1940s when researchers first started to analyze men's semen in a systematic way, assessing the sample for the number of sperm it contained, the sperm's shape and ability to swim, as well as the sample's volume and pH. The results were then used to infer whether or not the sample was fertile. In 1950, Cornell University researchers John MacLeod and Ruth Gold compared the semen samples of 1000 men who had fathered children with 1000 men who had not. The study was limited to the sperm counts and the volume of ejaculate from the men, but the researchers were the first to objectively come up with a demarcation of what separated fertile semen from infertile semen. MacLeod's and Gold's infertile group of men tended to have sperm counts less than 20 million per milliliter, and the fertile men tended to be distributed above that line. The study was published in 1951 in the *Journal of Urology*. Guidelines for motility and morphology have been added and refined many times since that landmark paper, but the principle has remained the same.

As detailed in Chapter 4, not all specialists agree with each other on the definitive number for count, the sperm's ability to swim and the sperm's shape. The International Society of Andrology set 40 million sperm per milliliter as normal while the World Health Organization (WHO) and other groups use 20 million as the lower edge of normal. (See Chapter 4 on semen analysis.)

Here is a summary of the general guidelines, based on WHO figures on what is considered *infertile* semen.

- *Sperm Count* less than 20 million sperm per milliliter
- *Motility* more than 40 percent of sperm not moving or moving poorly
- *Morphology* more than 40 percent of the sperm abnormally shaped
- *Dead Sperm* more than 35 percent of the sperm dead
- *Semen Volume* less than 2 milliliters or greater than 6 milliliters of ejaculate

Sometimes only a single item, or parameter, is wrong, such as low sperm count while the motility and morphology are fine. More often samples show two infertile parameters, and sometimes three. A low sperm count is called oligospermia; poor sperm motility is called asthenospermia; abnormal shape is called teratospermia; when there is no sperm at all in the semen it is called azoospermia.

Probability, Chance and Outcome

The analytical reasoning that is the basis of the semen analysis has one main weakness: it is deductive, not conclusive. It tells the scientist or doctor all the things that are associated with a man being able to establish a pregnancy, but it does not say what actually determines the fertility of a particular sperm.

"It is very hard to know which sperm, and what characteristics about it, ultimately fertilizes the egg," de Kretser says. "Semen analysis is looking at the periphery rather than getting to the central matter." For that reason, men with semen that falls in normal fertile parameters may still be unable to establish a pregnancy, while men who fall under the infertile characteristics are actually quite fertile—they father babies.

Therefore, when talking about male infertility, couples must remember that everything is couched in terms of "probability" and "likelihood." A low sperm count makes fertilizing an egg less likely, but it does not remove the chance altogether. Unless there is absolutely no sperm in the man's semen, no possibility of sperm in the future, couples should not lose hope.

"One shouldn't get too strung out over a low sperm count or a particular number," cautions British urologist Timothy Hargreave. "The lower the sperm count, or the worse the quality of sperm, the worse the chance of pregnancy. But at what point it becomes critical, it is indefinite."

Throwing Peas at the Moon

Hargreave, who works out of Edinburgh, likens the action of trying to conceive to throwing peas at the moon. "What we are talking about is the mathematical chance of a sperm colliding with an egg. When sperm are released at the cervix, it is a bit like launching a handful of peas into the universe. The more peas you throw out the better chance you have of hitting the moon. If you throw out millions and millions of peas, you really have quite a good chance. It is all mathematical probability."

Studies of pregnancy rates have shown time and again that men whose sperm counts are well below the WHO guidelines still have a realistic chance of fathering a child, provided their wives do not also have a fertility problem.

Hargreave has conducted one such study of 600 couples, researching a couple's chance of conceiving in the first year after they had been investigated for male-factor infertility. The study shows that if the couples had been trying to get pregnant for a year before seeking help, and the man had a total of at least five million moving sperm per millilitre of ejaculate, the couple had a 45 percent chance of conceiving in the next year with no medical help except instruction on how to time intercourse to ovulation. Even men who had only 500,000 moving sperm per milliliter, well below what is considered fertile, had a 23 percent chance of fathering a pregnancy in the next year, provided their partners were normal and they had only a year's duration of infertility before seeking help. The longer the couple had been trying to become pregnant before seeking help, the lower their pregnancy rate in the following year. But even couples who had been trying, for eight years, when the male partner had a total motile sperm count of between six and 10 million per milliliter, had a 14 percent chance of pregnancy in the next year.

Hargreave's study of the 600 couples was originally published in 1983 in the British *Journal of Urology*, but now more than 2000 couples have been followed for 10 years. "The larger study has confirmed the original numbers. The numbers are still holding true," Hargreave said.

Other specialists agree. Australian andrologist de Kretser says that pregnancy frequently occurs at motile sperm counts of well below 20 million, provided the female partner is fertile. "The rates really don't drop off until five million," he said.

According to Dr. Amnon Makler of Haifa, Israel, writing about male infertility in the medical text *Reproductive Failure*, "In practical terms, there is no lower limit except in cases of irreversible azoospermia, where conception may not occur."

If, however, the female partner has a subtle ovulation problem combined with the man's semen problem, the couple's chance of pregnancy is greatly reduced. That is why it is extremely important that both the man and the woman get a complete infertility work-up so that any subtle factor in the wife will not be missed. Hargreave, de Krester and others believe that it is common these days for the man and women to both have "subfertility," that when combined magnifies their barrier to pregnancy. If either one had a highly fertile partner, there would be no problem of childlessness and therefore no need to seek help. But when the two "subfertile" partners get together, infertility results.

Sperm Fluctuations

Another problem with semen analysis is that an individual man's sperm count, sperm motility and morphology is subject to a wide range of fluctuation over time. The changes can be very dramatic, from a low of less than 10 million sperm per milliliter to a high of 180 million per milliliter in the same man over only a few months. Numerous reports have been made that followed an individual man over a number of months to a year to see how his semen parameters varied. A graph depicted in the *WHO Laboratory Manual for The Examination of Human Semen* shows the results of bi-weekly semen analysis for one man over 120 tests. The man took no medication and had no illness, but his sperm counts showed enormous variation from 20 million, up to 80 million, down to 10 million, back to 75 million, way down to five million, back up to 30 million, all in about 20 weeks. American male infertility specialist Dr. Richard Sherins has done similar sequential semen analysis on individual men and found that one man could have his counts vary from 20 million to 200 million in the period of sampling. If the sperm sample was collected without allowing 36 hours of abstinence, the variation was even greater.

All the factors that could cause this wide fluctuation are not known, but illness, fever, external temperature variation and, possibly, stress have been verified. "The values for a single semen analysis, even two, can be very misleading," Sherins concludes. Most infertility specialists recommend that at least three semen analyses be done on a man whose count is low or on the 20 million borderline so that a true value can be obtained.

Series of Tests

Many men start their infertility work-up through their partner's family doctor or gynecologist. When the semen analysis points to potential male infertility, however, the man should be referred to a urologist or andrologist who specializes in male reproductive problems. The greatest benefit comes from seeking the best help available.

In most cases, the specialist performs more tests. Which tests, and how many, varies depending on the semen analysis results, and the man's medical history and physical findings. The results of one test may either remove the need for one test or logically suggest the need for another.

General Laboratory Tests

Most men are given standard lab tests to assess general health and to rule out underlying disease that may contribute to infertility. A urine test is done to rule out diabetes, impaired kidney function or infection. Two or three vials of blood are taken and analyzed for blood count, electrolytes or for evidence of syphilis or underlying blood disorders such as anemia or leukemia. If semen contains little or no sperm, the urine should be tested for the presence of semen to rule out retrograde ejaculation.

Fructose Test

Fructose is a simple sugar found in normal ejaculates, (it also is the sugar found in honey and fruits and is often called fruit sugar) produced by the seminal vesicles. If you have few or no sperm in your ejaculate, a test to indicate whether fructose is present helps determine the location of the problem in your reproductive tubing and ducts.

For the test, a chemical reagent is mixed with the semen and heated. If the sample changes to an orange-red color, fructose is present. Fructose in a sample with no sperm suggests the seminal vesicles are working and the problem exists between the seminal vesicles and the testes. It might mean a blockage along the vas deferens or in the epididymis, or testicular failure. If no fructose is present and no color change occurs, the seminal vesicles may be malfunctioning or absent (the vas may be absent, too), or there may be a blockage in the ejaculatory ducts between the seminal vesicles and the outside. Such a blockage in the latter section of the duct could be caused by a cyst in the pouch of the prostate, called the prostatic utricle, or an inflammed prostate, both of which can pinch the duct closed. A lack of fructose could also signify retrograde ejaculation.

Hormonal Tests

Some specialists recommend routine hormone tests for all men with low or absent sperm counts. Other specialists, however, recommend hormone tests only for severe oligospermia (fewer than 5 million sperm per milliliter) or azoospermia (no sperm). The hormone tests assess the level of follicle stimulating hormone (FSH), luteinizing hormone (LH), prolactin and "bound" and "free" testosterone. The hormone tests determine whether the hormonal axis between the hypothalamus, pituitary and testes is functioning properly. If levels of FSH, LH and testosterone are high, this indicates testicular failure, for which their is no treatment. If, however, the hormones are all low, drugs may be able to stimulate more sperm production. High prolactin, as in women, can interfere with the hormone axis in men. In some cases of low sperm counts when no reason can be found to explain it, a more complete hormone work-up may be done to investigate not only FSH, LH and testosterone but also the levels of estrogens and other androgens, particularly one called dihydroepiandrosterone (DHEA). If the levels of these are raised the man may have a problem in the way his body makes hormones and other steroids.

Genetic Tests

Some doctors recommend a chromosome study (a karyotype), if the man has no sperm or if the sperm are severely abnormal in shape. A karyotype is a picture of the 23 paired human chromosomes arranged in descending size. It gives information about whether there is a genetic defect, such as Klinefelter's Syndrome, in which the man has an extra X chromosome.

Sperm-Antibody Tests

A test for sperm antibodies is done if the man's sperm has poor motility, a poor ability to swim through cervical mucus, or if the sperm tended to clump together in the semen sample. Men who have had vasectomy reversals are also tested for the presence of sperm antibodies because the original vasectomy can lead to sperm-antibody formation. Sperm antibodies are a result of the man's immune system reacting to itself. Somehow, through injury or infection, the immune system has "recognized" the sperm and sends out antibodies to coat them. The antibodies are sticky and can cause the sperm to clump together or act like anchors as the sperm try to swim through the channels of the mucus. Antibodies do not always cause infertility but they may contribute to lowering the couple's fertility. The antibodies can not be seen and so a test must be used to pinpoint them by tagging them with an enzyme or plastic bead or radioactive marker.

There are a number of tests to detect antibodies; some examine the blood and others examine the semen directly. One such direct test is the immunobead binding test. Tiny plastic beads, half the size of a red blood cell, are coated with an antibody that seeks out any antibodies on the sperm. The two antibodies fit together like interlocking puzzle pieces. The sperm are made to swim through a suspension of the beads. If the sperm are coated with antibodies the beads stick to the sperm. Under the microscope, the sperm with plastic beads stuck to them can be clearly seen. Sperm antibodies and their possible treatments are discussed in more detail later in the chapter.

Testicular Biopsy

If a man has little or no sperm in his semen but his testes size is normal and his FSH is normal a testicular biopsy may be performed. The biopsy determines if sperm are being made in the testes or if there is a block somewhere in sperm transport. The test is carried out in the operating room under local or general anesthetic. An incision is made in the scrotum and a small sample of tissue is taken from both testes. The tissue is fixed and then examined by a pathologist for various stages of cells in the production of sperm. If there is an absence of particular cells or an arrest of development, the testes are not functioning properly. While the surgeon has the scrotum opened, he examines the epididymis for any sign of obstruction caused by an infection or inflammation. The surgeon also follows the ductal system to make sure there is a vas deferens, rendering them sterile. While conducting the testicular biopsy, the surgeon may also do a vasography.

Vasography

Vasography is an X-ray examination of the sperm transport ducts using radio-opaque dye and is the male equivalent of a woman's hysterosalpingogram. Once the scrotum is open, the contrast dye is injected into the vas deferens and/or the ejaculatory ducts. The X-ray machine takes pictures at a variety of angles to visualize the dye flowing through the tubes. The vasogram allows the surgeon to pinpoint the location of any block. If a blockage is found, the man may be a candidate for microsurgery to remove the blockage and repair the duct.

Tests to Detect Varicocele

If a varicocele—a varicose vein in the testicle—is suspected of causing infertility but one has not been found during the physical examination (described in Chapter 4), further tests may be conducted to try to locate it. A varicocele is usually suspected if all three sperm characteristics—count, motility and morphology—are poor. Eighty percent of varicoceles are discovered during the physical, but venography is the standard method used to visualize occult varicoceles. It is similar to vasography except the contrast dye is injected into the renal vein, which then outlines the spermatic vein to view the blood flow around the testes. Other methods that have been less frequently used are ultrasound, in which sound waves are bounced off structures in the testes; Doppler ultrasound, which bounces sound waves off moving blood; and scrotal thermography, which uses infrared to detect temperature gradients in the testicles.

Hamster-Egg Penetration Test

The hamster-egg test is used in an attempt to answer the question that semen analysis alone can not answer: if this man's sperm met with an egg, could it fertilize it? If a man has mild oligospermia or normal semen characteristics, the test may be used to find out if the problem lies in the ability to fertilize the egg. In the test, one million of the man's washed and matured sperm that have been "capacitated" (the sperm head has undergone a complex membrane change necessary to penetrate the human egg) are incubated with 20 to 25 hamster eggs. The hamster eggs have had their protective outer shell, the zona pellucida, removed. This allows the sperm to penetrate the egg but also prevents any possible development. Pathologists count the number of sperm that have penetrated the egg and from that result come up with a ratio to measure the fertilizing potential of the sperm. Some infertility specialists have criticized this test for being unspecific and unreliable. (In Australia the test is not used because hamsters are not allowed into the country.) But now second generation tests, which are more specific, are being developed by infertility researchers.

A more specific test, a sperm penetration assay (SPA), has been developed at the Scott Department of Urology at the Baylor College School of Medicine in Houston. The SPA uses a different method to capacitate the sperm (egg yolk buffer) and also compares the penetration to a high and low standard. The second generation tests appear to be more sensitive and give fewer false positives. The SPA often is used in advance of IVF to predict whether or not the male partner's sperm will be able to fertilize the egg before the couple undertakes the expense and risk of the procedure.

Other Tests

The postcoital test and the sperm-mucus penetration test, which are sometimes used to pinpoint male infertility problems, are discussed in detail in Chapter 4.

Causes and Treatment of Male Infertility

One of the first problems of male infertility is defining what is going on. Unlike female infertility, male infertility does not have one categorization scheme unanimously accepted by the medical profession that neatly takes in all the possibilities of what can go wrong. Some specialists divide male infertility into treatable, potentially treatable, and untreatable conditions. Others make the distinction between sperm production problems, hormonal axis problems, or obstruction to outflow problems. And still others define the groups as primary testicular failure, secondary testicular failure and extratesticular failure. Dr. Gerald Bernstein in his chapter on male infertility in the medical text, *Infertility, Contraception and Reproductive Endocrinology,* suggests male problems be defined by six categories: anatomic, endocrine, genetic, inflammatory, exogenous (outside factors) and idiopathic (unknown). That scheme will be used here because it is detailed and at the same time straightforward.

Anatomical Problems

Male anatomical problems that can result in infertility include varicoceles, undescended testicles, congenital abnormalities and spermatoceles (sperm-containing cysts).

Varicocele

A varicocele is a swollen, pooling of blood in the spermatic veins leading from the testicles. It occurs when the valves in the spermatic veins fail and allow blood ascending to the heart to flow backwards, engorging the vein. Blood circulating the body is propelled through the arteries by the muscular contractions of the heart and muscular tension of the walls of the arteries. But when the blood is returning to the heart it must fight gravity. Most veins have one-way valves that prevent the blood from flowing backwards. When the valves weaken or fail, the backflow of blood can cause the vein to dilate, twist or lengthen. This is how varicose veins in the legs occur, too.

A varicocele seems to be more often found in the left testes, likely because the left spermatic veins enter the renal vein at a right angle—like a side street on to a busy street—causing more backwards pressure. The right spermatic veins enter the vena cava at an angle like a merge lane, allowing smoother flow. But varicoceles can be found in both testes or in the right testes only. They can be large enough that they can be seen; moderate so they can be felt during the physical examination; or so small they can not be detected.

It is not known why a varicocele impairs sperm production, but the most commonly held theory is that the pooling of blood raises the temperature of the testes above the optimal level for making sperm. Other theories are that a varicocele causes toxins in the blood—the by-products of the body that are usually removed by the kidneys—to remain around the testes or that the pressure from the collected blood distorts the flow of arterial blood through the testes. Whatever its mechanism for impairing fertility, a varicocele seems to cause a lower sperm count, poorer sperm motility and worse sperm shape.

Often the semen typically contains immature sperm or sperm with narrow, tapered heads.

A varicocele is one of the most common findings in men undergoing infertility work-up. Between 20 to 40 percent of infertile men are diagnosed with the condition. It has been treated since the early 1950s with surgery to tie off the engorged veins. Although it is one of the oldest and simplest treatments for male infertility, it is still quite controversial. There is debate over the true effectiveness of surgery.

Studies of the surgical treatment in the past did not compare the outcome to others who did not get surgery. There has been criticism that the operation has been performed too often in cases of minor varicoceles that do not need treatment. Adding to debate is the fact that up to 20 percent of all men are found to have a varicocele, but infertility is found to be a problem in only a portion of them. Some believe the reason one man with a varicocele is fertile while another man with a varicocele of the same size and extent may be infertile, lies with the female partners rather than in the varicocele itself. U.K. urologist Hargreave is one of the proponents of this theory. He says a varicocele probably lowers the man's fertility, but it may become a persistent problem of childlessness when the man tries to have a child with a woman whose fertility is also slightly compromised, perhaps by a subtle ovulation defect. The two problems compound each other and result in infertility. But if the man with a varicocele has a very fertile partner, the problem of childlessness may never emerge. If the sperm quality is poor the varicocele should be fixed, but the partner of a man with a varicocele should not be ignored, Hargreave said. Other factors in the man may contribute to his infertility, which the varicocele masks.

Treatment

Not every man with a varicocele needs surgery to repair it, according to urologist Dr. Larry Lipshultz, Baylor College of Medicine. However, if the varicocele causes pain, causes the testical to shrink, or if all other causes of poor semen quality have been ruled out, surgery is indicated. Some doctors advocate the operation be done in day surgery under local anesthetic; others recommend an overnight stay in hospital and general anesthestic. The surgeon makes an incision in the groin and locates the spermatic cord, which is made up of the spermatic vein, spermatic artery and the vas deferens. The vein is carefully spearated from the artery and vas deferens, and is tied off above the swelling with a silk or polypropalene suture.

> *My testicles and groin were really sore when I woke up and I had a hard time walking for about a day. I remained sore for four or five days, but after a week I felt like my old self again. My sperm count went up by almost eight million after the first three months.*

A day or two of convalescence is all that is usually required following the operation. After seven days the man may resume sexual intercourse. It takes at least three months for any improvement in semen quality to show up in the ejaculate because of the 72-day production time for sperm. The reports of improvements of sperm quality after the operation have varied widely. Some specialists say men can show a 60 to 70 percent improvement in all semen parameters; others report less than 20 percent improvement. Of the men who do show improved semen quality, only about 30 to 40 percent go on to establish a pregnancy in their partners. The pregnancy rates are highest in men whose sperm parameters were mildly infertile, such as sperm counts around or just below the 20 million per milliliter mark before the operation. The reason the pregnancy rate is well below the rate of sperm improvement is not known, although some feel that other compounding fertility problems, as stated above, may be the cause.

Undescended Testicles

When the male fetus is developing in his mother's womb, his reproductive tract is being formed by progressive cell division from two primitive duct systems. The development of the testes takes place high in the abdomen close to the kidneys. As the fetus nears the time of birth, the testes migrate into the scrotum and at birth the testes of the majority of male babies has already completed the journey and settled. But in close to 3 to 5 percent of male babies, one or both testes may still be somewhere in the abdomen. This anomaly is called cryptorchidism, meaning hidden testicles.

In the majority of babies the testes descend into the scrotum on their own within four months. But in the remaining 1 percent the testes stay where they are. In years past it was common to wait to see if the testicles descended by the time of puberty. Now the medical field suggests the earlier the problem is treated the better it will be for the boy's future fertility.

Treatment

The first line of treatment is to give shots of human chorionic gonadotropin hormone (HCG) to spur migration about six months after birth. But if after one year or so, the testicles are still hidden, an operation called an orchipexy is routinely done to surgically move them into place. The reason for the operation is two-fold: the testes do not perform their sperm-making function well in the warm abdomen so untreated cryptorchidism usually results in sterility; and the testicles are more prone to becoming cancerous in their abdominal spot.

Some men, however, have never had their undescended testicles treated, and by the time they come for infertility work-up it is usually too late to help them because the sperm making function has been destroyed. There have been some reports of successful operations, however, for teenage boys at puberty, or just after, that have resulted in reasonable sperm counts. If one testicle has descended and the other remains hidden, sperm production may be normal or low normal; however a man is at a greater risk of testicular cancer in the hidden testicle.

Even if orchiopexy has been performed in childhood, however, many men with this condition still have poor quality sperm as an adult. It is believed that the poor semen may be a part of an overall testicular abnormality that caused the testes not to descend in the first place. The best treatment for these men is unclear. The couples may be able to achieve pregnancy, however, by using intrauterine insemination (IUI) using the man's sperm.

Hypospadias and Epispadias

Another anatomical abnormality of the reproductive tract that arises during fetal development is if the opening of the urethra in the penis occurs somewhere along the shaft of the penis rather than at the tip. Most commonly the opening is on the underside of the penis, a condition called hypospadias. More rarely it occurs on the upper side, epispadias. The sperm quality of the man with such a defect may be fine; the couple will have trouble conceiving because the sperm are not being deposited directly at the woman's cervix. This defect can be treated by an operation to close the unnatural opening and create a new one at the tip of the penis.

Spermatocele

A spermatocele is a sperm-containing cyst in the epididymis or spermatic ducts that can partially or totally block the outflow of sperm. It can sometimes be corrected with surgery.

Congenital Abnormalities of the Vas Deferens

A small proportion of men are born without a vas deferens. Called congenital absence of the vas, this defect renders the man sterile even if the testes are producing millions of sperm. For an unknown reason, men with an absent vas have not had the narrow duct develop while the rest of their reproductive tract formed normally. The seminal vesicles are absent, too. Although his semen volume may be low, the man usually has no knowledge that anything is wrong until his semen analysis shows azoospermia. The defect has been essentially untreatable, but since the early 1980s researchers have been trying to take sperm directly out of the epididymis of these patients and use them to fertilize the partner's eggs in vitro, with very limited success. These advanced techniques are described at the end of the chapter.

The synthetic hormone diethylstilbestrol (DES), which was prescribed from the 1940s until the early 1970s to some women during pregnancy, has been linked to some congenital abnormalities in the male offspring who were fetuses at the time the drug was taken. Evidence is not firm but it appears the hormone may have damaged the formation of the seminiferous tubules, leading to poor sperm counts. Other developmental abnormalities of the ductal system include the failure of the vas to join with the epididymis or an absence of a portion of the epididymis. These defects can sometimes be corrected by surgery to join the disconnected ducts or to put in a reservoir to collect sperm in the epididymis (the reservoir may be called a spermatocele), which is then prepared for insemination of the female partner.

Endocrine Factors

As described in Chapter 3, the testes are stimulated to produce sperm by hormone messages from the hypothalamus and pituitary. The hypothalamus sends pulses of gonadotropin-releasing hormone (GnRH) to the pituitary, which in turn pulses FSH (follicle stimulating hormone) and LH (luteinizing hormone) to the testes. FSH stimulates Sertoli cells, which nurture the germ cells, which in turn divide to produce sperm. The LH stimulates Leydig cells to produce testosterone. The testosterone feeds back to the hypothalmus as a message that enough LH is being sent. A hormone called inhibin feeds back to say enough FSH is being sent. The process is similar to what occurs in women except it is constant, not cylical, and therefore much less likely to develop a defect.

In about 1 to 2 percent of infertile men, however, the problem can be traced to abnormal hormone control of the testes. The result will be azoospermia or severe oligospermia.

Hypogonadotrophic Hypogonadism

This unwieldy name simply means that a lack of hormone stimulation has resulted in a lack of testicular and sperm development. In the most severe cases, men with this condition have small testes and have not gone through puberty. They have no sperm in their semen. Their bodies still appear to be that of a young boy, and their hormone profile shows abnormally low levels of FSH and LH.

A severe form of this disorder is called Kallman's Syndrome and men suffering from it have low hormone levels, azoospermia, delayed development plus an inability to smell—part of the disordered development. Although the disorder is rare, it usually responds well to treatment with hormone shots of human menopausal gonadotropins (Pergonal or pure FSH). GnRH pumps, described in Appendix C of Chapter 5, which pulse the missing GnRH molecule to the pituitary have been used, but reports are still limited. If Pergonal is used it will usually be given in an injection three times a week for up to 180 days. An injection of HCG twice a week is combined with the Pergonal. The results of this treatment have been very good, with a large proportion of the men establishing a pregnancy with their partners.

Some men have less severe hormone deficiencies with hormone levels just below the normal range or with low levels of just one hormone. The reason is unknown. These men may respond to hormone therapy that stimulates testes production. Clomiphene citrate, Pergonal, HCG, testolactone and other hormones have been used over a number of months to spur sperm production. Reports of the success of these treatments have varied, primarly because these conditions are rare and the treatments have been given to men who do not have low hormones and so can not benefit from hormone stimulation. Some have reported improved sperm quality, but just as many or more report that it makes sperm quality worse. If the hormone levels are low, however, Pergonal or Clomiphene may be the best choice for treatment.

Other Hormonal Problems

Like women, some men can have high prolactin levels, perhaps from a benign tumor in the pituitary. It is not known to what extent high prolactin interferes with testes production. The drug bromocriptine, described in Appendix E of Chapter 5, is being tried on some of these men. It has not yet been determined whether this is effective. Men who have a large pituitary tumor interfering with their fertility may have it removed by surgery.

Abnormal thyroid hormones, either too high or too low, can also interfere with sperm production. Thyroid problems usually cause severe symptoms in other areas, and are treated before the man comes in for infertility work-up.

When the testes have been damaged and have slowed or stopped the production of sperm, hormonal tests show an increased level of FSH. The high level of FSH is not causing the sperm problem; rather it is a reflection that the Sertoli cells of the testes are damaged. Without the feedback of inhibin to tell the pituitary to stop sending FSH, the FSH remains high in attempts to stimulate the testes. This is called primary testicular failure and there is no treatment.

Genetic Abnormalities

Klinefelter's Syndrome

The most common genetic disorder that causes male infertility is Klinefelter's Syndrome, which occurs in about 1 to 2 percent of infertile men, or about one in every 400 men in general. Men with this disorder carry an extra X chromosome on their sexual chromosomes. The defect is believed to arise from the moment of conception when the sperm fertilizes the egg and the sex of the developing embryo is determined. The fertilizing sperm carries either a Y sex chromosome or an X sex chromosome; the female egg carries only the X chromosome. When the egg and sperm unite, the resulting embryo will develop into a boy if the sex chromosome reads XY. A girl will develop if the product of sperm and egg union is XX. But in Klinefelter's Syndrome the resulting embryo has an extra X chromosome, depicted as XXY or sometimes XXXY. No one is sure why it happens; perhaps the sperm carries an extra chromosome or the egg carries the extra chromosome.

A man with Klinefelter's Syndrome may have decreased development, may shave infrequently, his testicles may be small and hard; he may have fatty breasts or gynecomastica; and his pelvis may be wider. Except for these anomalies there is little evidence of his chromosomal abnormality. Some men with Klinefelter's Syndrome show no outward signs at all. They have normal sex lives, but some men may have a decreased sex drive. Usually a man learns he has Klinefelter's Syndrome when he goes through infertility work-up and finds he has no sperm in his ejaculate and his testes are not producing sperm. A man with Klinefelter's is sterile and there is no treatment for it. Some men have mosaic Klinefelter's, in which some cells have the normal XY complement and other cells have the extra chromosome. These men may have some sperm in their testicles, but will usually be infertile, too.

Klinefelter's Syndrome can be a very difficult diagnosis for men to accept. Some parents in the United States have been trying to start a support group for families and young children with the syndrome but there are no support groups for adults. Men can be shocked to learn they carry an extra female chromosome and feel isolated in their abnormality. However, many couples have found that donor insemination resolves many of the emotional issues of infertility caused by the syndrome.

Young's Syndrome

A lesser known abnormality, which is believed to be genetic in origin, is called Young's Syndrome. It is rarely diagnosed in North America but Australian infertility specialists report up to 30 or 40 new cases each year. This syndrome has also been reported by Japanese and Chinese researchers. It is not known if it is more common in those regions or if researchers there are simply more aware of the disorder and better able to diagnose it.

Young's Syndrome appears to be a disorder of the cilia in the body. A man with the syndrome typically has azoospermia and a history of respiratory problems. The epididymis is found to have a thick mucous plug, which prevents the passage of sperm. It is believed the epididymis is blocked because the cilia there do not properly clear out the mucus. The cilia in the lung likely do not do their job adequately. There is no known effective treatment for this disorder.

Another cilia defect, caused by a gene, is called Immotile Cilia Syndrome. A specific genetic defect results in a sperm tail that can not propel the sperm. The man may have a count of 100 million sperm per milliliter, but all will be stuck in one place, unable to move. There is no known treatment for this disorder, although experiments of micromanipulation of sperm are being tried to inject the sperm into the egg and naturally fertilize it.

Infection and Inflammation

Viruses, bacteria and other microorganisms can infect the reproductive tract and cause inflammation of the testes, the epididymis, the prostate or the seminal vesicles, impairing sperm production or the transport of sperm.

Mumps

An acute, contagious viral infection, mumps typically strikes children between the ages of five and 15. The virus incubates for 14 to 21 days in its human host and then breaks out in an acute stage for about three days. The acute stage is marked by fever, malaise and the telltale pain and swelling of the salivary glands, giving an egg-like lump along the jaw line. Mumps is never fun for a child, and in severe cases can lead to pneumonia. But it is even more serious when it hits an adult male. About 25 percent of adult men who get mumps have pain and swelling of one or both testicles, called orchitis. Mumps that attacks the testes can destroy or undermine their ability to make sperm. The amount of destruction of the testicles bears no relation to the amount of swelling or infection of the testicles. Some men recover fully after orchitis while others become sterile with no possibility of treatment. Blood tests during the infertility work-up show raised levels of FSH and LH, indicating the hypothalmus and pituitary are trying to stimulate sperm production, but the testicles have failed.

Other organisms and disease can cause the testicles to become inflamed and lead to sterility, including syphilis, tuberculosis and pancreatitis. Any time a man has swelling or pain in his testicles he should seek immediate medical help.

Epididymitis

Bacteria and microorganisms can also infect the epididymis, leading to scarring and possible blockage. The result can be oligospermia or azoospermia. The worst culprits are the sexually transmitted diseases gonorrhea and chlamydia. Usually men have symptoms indicating that they have an infection of the epididymis—swelling, pain, a discharge or pain and burning on urination. If the infection is discovered early enough, antibotics to kill the invader can stop its damage. If the infection has occurred in the past, microsurgery to remove the obstruction or scar tissue and rejoin the ducts may be possible. Earlier, surgery did not have a good success rate, but with new microsurgical techniques some doctors have reported good results in eliminating an obstruction and rejoining the epididymis to the vas. The success rates usually depend on the skill of the surgeon and the location and size of the block. Obstructions that are close to the vas deferens can usually be repaired so that the duct is open, and sperm are once more in the ejaculate. But the possibility of pregnancy depends on whether the function of the epididymis has been destroyed.

Sexually transmitted diseases and microorganisms can also inflame the prostate, seminal vesicles and urethra. While the infections are acute, fertility will be lowered. (The man also risks passing the infection to his partner, which could render her sterile without her knowledge.) The infections can be treated with high doses of antibiotics but may recur, particularly infections of the prostate.

The aftermath of the infections can cause blockages of the ejaculatory ducts, usually at the point where they join the urethra. An ejaculatory duct obstruction is usually suspected if semen volume is low; if the semen is azoospermic; and if there is no fructose in the ejaculate. It is a rare occurrence, but it usually can be treated with an operation. On the vasogram the blocked duct looks like a large swollen cyst inside the prostate: the duct comes to a blind end and fills with fluid. While the man is under general anesthetic, the doctor introduces a fiber optic operating scope (a resectoscope), into the urethra in the penis until it is positioned at the block. According to Dr. Sherman Silber in the text, *Reproductive Infertility Microsurgery in the Male and Female*, bites of tissue are then taken out of the "roof" of the obstruction, "like drilling for oil," until the dilated duct is reached. The operation is risky and may cause incontinence or retrograde ejaculation in the man if the valve to the bladder is harmed.

Immunological Factors

In recent years the immunological basis of infertility has been receiving more attention, aided by our growing understanding of the complex working of the immune system through other areas of medicine, such as organ transplants and AIDS. It is a burgeoning field of infertility research, and while some questions are being answered, a tremendous amount remains unknown.

Antisperm Antibodies

It is estimated that about 5 percent of infertile men have sperm coated with antibodies that interfere with sperm motility or prevent the recognition and fertilization of the egg. Antibodies are the warriors of the body's defence system. There are thousands of antibodies in the human body, each specific to a particular aspect of a particular foreign invader. The aspect of the invader that turns on the antibody is called the antigen. When antibodies detect the presence of their particular antigen they latch on to them. Then, in a diverse number of ways, the antibodies are able to get rid of the threat. Some neutralize toxic bacteria by binding with them; others remove substances from the body's circulation; still others coat the invaders, causing them to become sticky and to clump together, called agglutination. Antibodies attached to antigens can start a cascade response, called complement, which brings in other parts of the immune system fighting squad to break down and destroy the invader.

Usually antibodies are aimed at outside threats, but sometimes the antibodies attack cells or proteins produced by the body itself. This process is called an auto-immune response. In some men, antibodies have been produced that single out and attack their own sperm; no one knows why or how, but there are some theories. These theories arise because men who have vasectomies tend to have a high incidence of anti-sperm antibodies form in their semen. It seems that men who have had an infection, injury or a block preventing the sperm's exit also have a higher incidence of antisperm antibodies.

The original theory was that the testes are a special place, sequestered like a fortress from a man's immune system, and that there is a barrier preventing the immune system from normally coming in. The separation was deemed to be necessary because the sperm, which are produced at puberty, were not there when the immune surveillance system was being set up in childhood. Sperm are antigenic, meaning the body forms antibodies against them. Therefore, if the immune system could get into the testes, sperm would be seen as foreign and would be attacked. The antibodies occurred only when that barrier had been broached, such as in a vasectomy, an injury or during an infection when the immune system had to be called in. They would "see" the sperm for the first time, form antibodies, which would subsequently attack any sperm it saw in future.

That theory has had to be modified, because it has been learned in recent years that sperm, in fact, are not sequestered and the testes are not impermeable. Lymphocytes, the immune cells that make antibodies, line the epididymis, and antibodies can circulate in parts of the testes. Now the theory is, instead, that active immune suppression takes place in the testicles preventing the normal immune response from occurring. It is a protective mechanism that prevents antisperm antibodies from being formed. Researchers do not understand what that mechanism is. It is clear, however, that infection, injury or vasectomy can cause the mechanism to fail. It is estimated that 60 to 70 percent of men with vasectomy reversal have anti-sperm antibodies.

When antisperm antibodies are present, they can significantly interfere with the process of conception. Woman can also mount antibodies to sperm and that is discussed in Chapter 8. A few antibodies coating a few sperm are not enough to cause marked infertility. But the more antibodies present, the worse the fertility. Different antibodies can attach to different parts of the sperm and interfere in different ways. All antibodies can slow down the sperm, impairing their motility. Some can cause the sperm to clump together, either tail-to-tail or head-to-head. Others may cause the sperm to stick like flies on flypaper, to the woman's cervical mucus. Other antibodies may coat the sperm head and interfere with its binding to the shell of the egg, the zona pellucida, or fertilization of the egg.

Treatment

It is possible for men with antisperm antibodies to establish a pregnancy with no treatment at all. If fewer than half their sperm are bound, they have a 50 percent chance of success. If 90 percent are bound, the chance of pregnancy falls to 10 percent or less. Those spontaneous rates should be remembered when treatment is being considered, say infertility specialists, particularly because there is no treatment for antibodies without drawbacks or risks. The treatment options are corticosteriods, intrauterine insemination, in vitro fertilization and donor insemination.

Corticosteriods are anti-inflammatory agents that are used to suppress the man's immune system. The drugs methylprednisolone, prednisone or dexamethasone have been used. It is not known exactly how corticosteriods interfere with the process; they may eliminate the number of antibodies present or they may block some action of the antibody or the immune system's action against the sperm. Some doctors have recommended high doses of corticosteriods but this treatment has concerned other doctors because of the potential side effects. The most worrisome side effect is possible aseptic necrosis of the hip, destruction of the hip joints. Doctors can not predict what dosage on whom will produce this devastating side effect. Other side effects include skin rashes, intense irritability or depression, indigestion, weight gain or fluid retention. Some doctors recommend low or moderate doses given over an extended period of time, or high doses at intermittent intervals. The benefits of one method over the other have not yet been determined. Studies show a zero to 56 percent success rate for this therapy. The average success rate is about 30 percent.

Intrauterine insemination, in which the specially prepared sperm are placed via a catheter in the female partner's uterus at the time of ovulation, is another method being used to try to treat antisperm antibodies. It can be used, however, only when the antibodies prevent the passage of sperm through the cervical mucus, not when the antibodies prevent fertilization of the egg. The pregnancies with IUI seem to occur in the first six months of treatment, and doctors say there seems to be no advantage to carrying on IUI longer.

In vitro fertilization can be used in some cases of antisperm antibodies, if the antibodies do not prevent the penetration and fertilization of the egg. If the eggs fertilize, the couple has about the same chance of having a pregnancy as other couples undergoing IVF for other reasons. The success rate is between 10 to 30 percent.

Donor insemination sometimes holds the only possibility for pregnancy for severe cases of anti-sperm antibodies that have not responded to treatment.

Outside Factors

A number of outside factors that can impair sperm quality, testicular function, or reproductive ability have already been mentioned. Cigarette smoking, high alcohol consumption, recreational drug use, even excessive exercise have all been linked to poor sperm counts or undermined sexual performance. Some prescription drugs for ulcers, ulcerative colitis, inflammatory bowel disease, high blood pressure and depression have been linked to infertility. Radiation from X rays or other sources can also impair fertility. (See Chapter 3.)

Injury

A sports injury or accident that damages a testicle can impair future fertility. But even if only one testicle is damaged or destroyed, the other may become impaired in sympathy. Torsion, a condition of the testes twisting inside the scrotum, can also lead to testicular damage. Men with this condition usually receive immediate attention because of the pain. Surgery in the pelvic area, such as a hernia repair, has been known to occasionally injure the vas deferens or spermatic artery. Bladder operations have also, on occasion, damaged nerves or structures, which has lead to retrograde ejaculation.

Retrograde Ejaculation

Semen and urine must share the same corridor, the urethra, to exit the body. Urination and ejaculation are both controlled by the parasympathetic nervous system. When the corridor is being used for one function it cannot be used for the other. When ejaculation occurs, nerves in the spinal ganglia, a cluster of regional nerve cells, cause the vas deferens, the prostate and the seminal vesicles to contract. The contraction causes the bladder neck to partially close. Further nerve stimulus causes contractions of the muscles around the base of the penis, which completes the closure of the bladder neck and completes ejaculation.

If the bladder neck does not close completely, as can happen with nerve damage caused by diabetes or structural damage caused by surgery, all or part of the ejaculate can go into the bladder. The man will not be able to tell if this is happening, but on semen analysis there may be a low semen volume, with very low sperm counts or no sperm at all. By looking for the presence of sperm in the urine, the specialist can make the diagnosis of retrograde ejaculation.

Treatment

Retrograde ejaculation is treated by retrieving the sperm from the bladder and preparing it so it can be artifically inseminated into the female partner. The disorder had been treated with limited success until 1986 when researchers in the division of Urology at the Utah School of Medicine came up with the simplest, most successful treatment to date.

The procedure goes like this: the female partner's cycle is followed carefully and timed for ovulation by LH levels secreted in her urine. The man is instructed to abstain from intercourse for at least two days before the anticipated day of ovulation. On the day of ovulation the male patient is instructed to take two sodium bicarbonate tablets with water every two hours, starting about eight to 12 hours before the insemination is to take place. The sodium bicarbonate tablets make the man's urine more alkaline so the sperm can survive in it. About 30 minutes or an hour before insemination, the man urinates; then he either has sex with his partner or masturbates.

Immediately after sex he urinates again into a clean glass container and brings the sample immediately to the lab. The sperm is washed with a special nutritious solution, Hamm's F10, is gently spun so the sperm condenses to a pellet. The pellet is separated from the liquid and resuspended in a millimeter more of Hamm's F10. That solution, provided the sperm shows good motility, is inseminated into the female partner. Each couple goes through about six inseminations of good motile sperm.

The Utah researchers reported that of seven couples who tried the technique, six conceived (one couple twice). This technique is now being recommended by most centers.

Sexual Dysfunction

In as many as 5 percent of couples, sexual dysfunction may be the cause of their infertility. Premature ejaculation and impotence are the two most common occurrences and can prevent pregnancy even if the semen is teeming with healthy, swimming sperm. When the couple is being evaluated for infertility, they should be honest about sexual difficulties so they can receive the help they need. Impotence, the inability to sustain an erection, can be caused by disease, such as diabetes, or drugs such as anti-hypertensives. It can also be caused by psychological factors, such as fear, inhibition or loss of sexual desire. Sometimes impotence is temporary, caused by stress or illness. If the doctor knows the origin of the impotence, treatment can be given to help the couple have intercourse. If the impotence is caused by psychological factors, the couple can be referred to a qualified sexual therapist.

Premature ejaculation, which means the man's orgasm occurs outside the vagina or before full penetration can occur, also may prevent conception. Men with this problem can learn to control ejaculation with specific techniques. The techniques can be learned through sexual therapy or through books such as those by Masters and Johnson's, or Dr. Alex Comfort's *Joy of Sex.*

Infrequent intercourse, less than once or twice a month, or too frequent intercourse can also be the cause of a couple's inability to conceive. Without regular sexual intercourse, the couple lowers their chances of having sperm in the reproductive tract when the egg is ovulated. As well, the sperm can age and die in the epididymis if it is not ejaculated at least once a month. On the other hand, sperm may be depleted below fertile levels if ejaculation takes place too frequently. Studies have shown that for most men, sperm numbers return to fertile levels when at least 36 hours elapse between ejaculations.

Idiopathic Infertility

Unfortunately, for the majority of the men reading this book, the reason for their infertility will be unknown. The semen analysis may show that one of their parameters, such as their sperm count or motility, is below what is considered fertile, but with investigation no reason is found.

Other men have certain findings that explain their poor sperm counts, such as elevated FSH, which indicates the testes are failing, but likewise there is no explanation available.

Infertility specialists estimate that as many as 40 to 50 percent of men with low sperm counts or poor motility fall into the idiopathic category. If medical specialists do not know why something is going wrong, they are usually unable to fix it. "If you don't have a diagnosis, then it can't be treated," Hargreave says. "A low sperm count is not a diagnosis, it is a symptom of some form of testicular damage. If we don't know what the cause of the testicular damage is, there is probably not much we can do about it."

Male infertility specialists say the key is more research into the basic biology of the testicles and the male reproductive system to find more causes of oligospermia. For example, there is a recent finding that some men with low sperm counts may have fewer androgen receptors in their scrotal tissue than fertile men do. The significance of this finding is not yet known. Basic biological findings take a long time to translate into treatments for the man coming for help to a infertility clinic.

The Debate About Fertility Drugs

Should a man who has a low sperm count of unknown cause take fertility drugs to try to improve his sperm count? That question has been asked by many researchers. Numerous studies have been conducted using clomiphene citrate, human menopausal gonadotropin (HMG), human chorionic gonadotropin (HCG), low and high doses of testosterone and other compounds to try to boost sperm production.

When the studies have been done without comparing a group of men getting treatment to those not getting treatment, then there has been the impression that some of the hormones may work to improve sperm counts. But when studies have been conducted by rigorous scientific standards—so-called double-blind controlled studies—drug treatment has never been found to be better than no treatment at all.

Here is an example of a controlled trial: American researchers Dr. R.V. Clark and Dr. Richard Sherins did a study of the drug testolactone, which prevents the man's testosterone from being converted to estrogen in his peripheral tissues. The reasoning behind using testolactone for infertility was that some men may have an increased level of estrogen, which may inhibit sperm production. Testolactone might lower the level of estrogen being made. Sherins and

Clark conducted what is called a randomized, placebo-controlled, cross-over, double-blind study, the most unbiased type of scientific experiment, the gold standard.

In their drug trial, men with idiopathic oligospermia who came into their clinic were randomly assigned to one of two coded treatment groups. One group took a placebo, or fake pill, for four months, and then crossed over for the next four months and got the drug testolactone. The other group started out getting testolactone for four months and then had a cross-over to placebo. Neither the men nor the doctors treating them knew at any time who was getting what treatment—hence the name "double-blind." Regular semen analysis was conducted during the study. At the end of the eight months the code was broken and the results were compared.

But here is the sort of results they found: one man had started out with 8 million sperm per milliliter and in the first four months stayed at that level. Then in the second four months he jumped to 20 million per milliliter—a remarkable change, but, in fact, he got placebo in the second half. Another man had the same pattern, remaining at a low level of the first four months then having an improvement in the second; his improvement occurred on testolactone. The researchers found no consistent pattern in comparing one group with another. Each one cancelled the other out; no group had more pregnancies than the other. The researchers found no difference between giving treatment or not giving treatment.

Those types of results have happened in almost every double-blind controlled study of hormone treatment for idiopathic male infertility. Some individual men show sperm count improvements or establish a pregnancy on a drug. Others do not. Researchers have no way of knowing whether it was the drug that caused the pregnancy or just the natural fluctuation of sperm counts. Pregnancies as high as 50 percent occur in oligospermic men without treatment. Some studies have found that for some men, drugs like clomiphene or HCG make them even less fertile, dropping their sperm counts. One treatment that was tried in a number of studies, which involved giving high doses of testosterone for about four months in the hope that sperm numbers would rebound to higher levels, is now condemned. Some men never rebounded and their sperm levels remained much lower than when they started, long after the drug had been stopped.

It can be very difficult to make sense of all of this and decide what to do. Many men ask for some type of treatment because it feels better than doing nothing. Male infertility specialists say that if a man specifically asks for drug treatment, they give it, usually clomiphene, HCG or HMG. But the doctor stresses that no one treatment appears better than another and there is no criteria to determine who should get what treatment.

If you opt to try a drug, it is recommended that you do so for only about four or five months, enough time to determine if a treatment is working. Treatment protocols vary from one center to another, but in general, a drug is given consistently. For example, clomiphene may be given at 25 or 50 milligrams every other day for four or five months. Men may experience the same side effects as women on the drug, including headaches, visual problems, weight gain or loss, mood changes, decreased libido and skin rashes.

HCG and HMG are usually given in injections two or three times a week. No reports of side effects are available.

Treatment Options

Artificial Insemination by Partner

Insemination of the female partner using a specially prepared sample of the man's semen is frequently used in cases of male infertility. The use of the infertile male partner's sperm is called homologous insemination. Three types have been used: cup insemination, intracervical insemination, and intrauterine insemination.

Cup insemination involves placing a cup of the husband's semen, sometimes washed or separated through glass wool to improve motility, at the female partner's cervix at the time of ovulation. For intracervical insemination, semen is spun in a centrifuge to concentrate the sperm, the most motile sperm are removed and then deposited by a catheter in the woman's cervical canal. Couples must come to the clinic for at least an hour each month at the time of ovulation for sperm preparation and insemination, interfering with their schedules and normal sex lives.

Studies of the success rates of cup and intracervical insemination have been no better than spontaneous conceptions for oligospermic men. Many doctors feel that since the results are not significantly better than the natural way, the couple would probably be better off to stay at home and make love instead of using this technique.

Intrauterine insemination, however, has slightly better results, provided it is timed correctly. To use Hargreave's analogy of the peas and the moon, IUI takes the peas very close to the moon, increasing the chance that one pea will hit it. In IUI the semen sample is usually washed by spinning it with a sample of the partner's blood or with albumin, which results in a pellet of sperm washed of semen. Then the most motile sperm are separated from the dead or deformed sperm either by "sperm swim-up" or by Percoll separation. Both processes result in a sample of the most motile sperm. Some labs put antibiotics in the resulting sample to kill bacteria. The prepared sperm is then passed in a catheter through the cervix into the uterus and released. Some procedures also stimulate the woman with fertility drugs so that more than one egg is released. This is much more intense treatment, involving therapy of both partners. It is described in more detail in Chapter 8.

Donor Insemination

Using the semen of an anonymous donor to inseminate the infertile man's partner remains the most common method to overcome male infertility. Of course, it is not really a treatment of a man's problem; rather, it is a way to overcome childlessness. Some couples can easily choose this option, others have great difficulty.

Advanced Reproductive Techniques

Since the early to mid-1980s, when in vitro fertilization and related techniques became more widespread, male infertility has been treated with increasing frequency with these options. The technique of in vitro fertilization was developed to help women with blocked or damaged fallopian tubes conceive and in the first years of its existence, IVF was reserved for women who fitted that criteria. But as medical experience grew with the technique, doctors learned that men who were infertile because of low sperm counts would also be good candidates for IVF because fewer sperm were required to fertilize an egg in a Petri dish, outside the body, than in the natural habitat. At first researchers thought at least two to six million motile sperm should be placed with the egg. That number was adjusted downward until it was learned that about 50,000 motile sperm was the optimum number for fertilization.

Since that time other advance techniques such as gamete intrafallopian tube transfer (GIFT), zygote intrafallopian transfer (ZIFT), tubal embryo transfer (TET), pro-nucleus stage transfer (PROST) and techniques described by other acronymns have been used for a wide variety of causes of infertility, including male infertility. All involve the same principles and similar methods—their various names simply refer to the stage of development of the eggs, sperm or embryo and the location in the woman's reproductive tract where the tissue is placed. These techniques are discussed in Chapter 10.

If men with idiopathic infertility are interested in these techniques, they should keep in mind that IVF and other techniques are stressful, expensive, time-consuming, and often disappointing. Even with sperm counts of fewer than five million per milliliter, couples have about a 23 percent chance of conceiving spontaneously in the first year after diagnosis. IVF has a pregnancy rate of 10 to 30 percent at most centers.

Other experimental techniques are being tried, combined with IVF techniques, to overcome even more severe infertility such as azoospermia caused by obstruction, zero motility, or inability to fertilize.

Epididymal Bypass

The epidymal bypass is a process for men who produce sperm in the testes but cannot ejaculate because of a block, absence of the vas deferens or a vasectomy. In an operation, immature sperm are taken out of the epididymis and cultured in the laboratory. The female partner undergoes the hormone stimulation regime for IVF and her eggs are removed from her ovaries. The artificially matured semen and the eggs are placed in a Petri dish. Any resulting embryos are replaced in the partner's uterus or fallopian tubes. Success with this technique has been very limited. Researchers in Australia have been working on the technique since 1980 and by 1988 had tried it on 50 couples, reporting only one pregnancy. By 1988 American researchers had reported using this technique on 17 patients, from which three pregnancies resulted, and two births (one pregnancy miscarried). In early 1989 another birth by epididymal bypass was reported by American researchers.

Micromanipulation

For men whose sperm are not motile, low in number or incapable of fertilizing the eggs, a procedure called micromanipulation is being used experimentally in about a dozen centers internationally. Since the sperm can not penetrate the egg's outer shell, the zona pellucida, researchers are trying various ways to help the sperm get below the surface. The female partner's ovaries are stimulated with drugs, as if for IVF, to produce a number of eggs. The eggs are suctioned out of the ovaries. In the laboratory, under view of a microscope, the tiny, fragile egg is held with gentle suction on the end of a pipette and is fertilized artificially, either by injecting a single sperm or opening the egg to allow sperm to enter. The first pregnancies from this technique were reported in early 1989.

Micromanipulation is a controversial and experimental procedure that poses ethical questions for researchers and society. The biggest concern is that the selection of the sperm by a researcher for microinjection goes against the principles of natural selection. How is the researcher to know which sperm is the one that should fertilize the egg? Some fear that the resulting embryo may have chromosomal or congenital abnormalities. Many people also fear that it is one step closer to the frightening *Brave New World* scenario of Aldous Huxley and that it marks our increasing involvement in orchestrating the reproductive process.

Couples who consent to try these techniques must first understand that the techniques are very experimental. They should decide for themselves what they think the limits of the technology should be. They must feel completely at ease with their choice and remember that they are creating a potential child. It is the child, in the end, not the parents, who has to live with the knowledge and results of his or her origins. If the parents feel comfortable with it and proud of it, the child is more likely to, as well. As that potential child's parents, the couple must have no conflict about their choice, so they and the child can live happily with the decisions.

The following methods are used to put the sperm below the zona pellucida.

Microinjection

The healthiest, most normal-looking sperm is selected by microscope from a prepared semen sample. The chosen sperm is taken into a microscopic syringe with a needle thinner than the thinnest hair. The needle is used to pierce the zona and the sperm is injected into the perivitelline space between the zona and the egg. The sperm fuses with the egg on its own. This is the technique developed by Dr. Alan Trounson at the Centre for Early Human Development at Monash University in Australia. A number of other centers use his technique. Trounson has bred mice by microinjection and had some embryos cleave, or grow. By mid 1989, however, no pregnancies had been reported because the group halted experiments to wait for the state's ethics committee to approve the research. However, a pregnancy from the technique has been reported in Singapore.

Zona Opening

A small crack is put in the zona of the egg by using two tiny, microscopic glass hooks. Pulling with the hooks, the researchers make a tiny tear in the shell. The opened egg is placed with the sperm sample with the hope one sperm will make it through the hole, fertilizing the egg. This technique was developed by Australian researchers under Prof. Ian Johnstone and Dr. Alex Lopata at the Royal Women's Hospital, University of Melbourne. Like Trounson's group they have transferred resulting embryos to the female partners, but as of mid-1989 no women had become pregnant.

Zona Drilling

Like zona opening, zona drilling involves making a tiny hole in the zona through which a sperm cell can reach the egg. The holes are made by acid, like putting salt on a slab of ice. Then the egg is incubated with a low concentration of sperm. This technique was developed by New York infertility specialist Dr. Jon Gordon. Gordon reported his latest research at the 1988 American Fertility Society Meeting in Atlanta. Of a total of 12 couples who had all previously had no eggs fertilize under normal IVF technique, 23 of 49 eggs fertilized with zona drilling. Of those 23 only 12 were viable. The other 11 had more than one, and as many as seven, sperm fertilize them. This condition is called polyspermia. Gordon did not put any eggs back into the women. A related technique, zona stripping, used by IVF founder Robert Edwards in Cambridge, has had the same problem of polyspermia. Edwards removed the zona completely by acid, but that resulted in numerous sperm fertilizing the egg.

Partial Zona Dissection (PZD)

The first pregnancies and births have been reported using a technique called partial zona dissection. Dr. Jacques Cohen, of Reproductive Biology Associates of Atlanta, Georgia, reported seven pregnancies from PZD in the spring of 1989. Of the seven pregnant women four had given birth to healthy babies, including two sets of twins. At this writing the three other women had not yet delivered.

PZD is similar to zona drilling except instead of using acid the zona is pierced in two places using a sharp needle. The opened egg is then placed with washed and capacitated sperm and incubated. Cohen reported that in about 25 percent of cases more than one sperm fertilizes the egg and the resulting embryo dies.

Emotional Responses to Infertility

The reactions to the diagnosis of male infertility vary. Most men experience shock or disbelief when they learn about a poor sperm count or otherwise infertile sperm. But in the months or years following the diagnosis, how the information affects his life and emotions is as individual as the man himself.

A man's cultural background, his expectations and his sense of identity and self-worth may all play a role in his reaction. If he defines himself by his ability to father children, to pass on his genes, or to make his mate pregnant, it could become a life crisis. If he links his masculinity to his fertility, it is equally traumatic.

Some men talk openly about their infertility, but the majority do not. Men are less likely than women to discuss their emotions or feelings with others on any topic. Numerous studies have shown that most women more readily confide in friends or families about a whole host of issues, not just infertility. In addition, most people feel that male infertility is something that should be kept secret.

> *I was quite upset when I found out my sperm count was low, not because of some macho thing, but mostly because we really wanted children. But what made it harder was that I didn't feel able to discuss it with anybody, not my parents, not my friends—maybe that was a macho thing. It is a major event in your life and yet there was just this feeling that you keep it a secret, you don't bring it up over a beer with the boys.*

Unfortunately there has been an air of secrecy around male infertility more than female infertility. Perhaps that is rooted in the historical attitude that infertility is a woman's problem, so less acceptance was afforded men who were infertile. Secrecy about male infertility in general has been perpetuated by the fact that for years donor inseminatin was the only really successful therapy by which couples could overcome their childlessness. Donor insemination was kept a closely guarded secret; couples were instructed by the doctor not to tell anyone. A donor was selected who looked as much like the infertile man as possible so that no one would have to know.

The use of DI artificially hid the tremendous numbers of men who were infertile, preventing society from understanding the scope of the problem. It also made the individual man feel much more alone and unable to talk about his infertility. That secrecy and attitude has also contributed to the dearth of medical knowledge about male infertility, which in turn has hurt the cause of the infertile man. Fortunately those attitudes have been changing, but coping with male infertility is still difficult.

A study by Irish infertility specialists of infertile men and women's reactions to infertility found that men, in general, had a tendency to "fake good," as they called it, pretend that everything was fine while their partners showed the emotional distress. But the researchers felt the men's higher scores in what was called the "lie factor" and "motivation distortion factor" in standard personality questionnaires, showed that the opposite was true. They had significant stress and anxiety but were subverting it.

The same fears that strike the infertile woman can concern the infertile man. He can worry that his partner will leave him if he can not give her a biological child or that he should offer her a divorce. He can mourn not being able to pass on his family's genes or not seeing a child grow up with his hair or smile or eyes. He can feel deeply disturbed that his body has somehow let him down, that he is not the invulnerable man he thought he was. He can search his conscience and past actions for something that can explain why this has happened to him.

Infertility support groups can be as helpful to a man as to a woman, even if their actions in that group may be different, as one man describes:

It's my wife who does all the talking at the meeting, even though I'm the one who's infertile. I just sit and listen—that's the way with most of the men there; it's the wives who talk in the group setting. But I've noticed that during the breaks there'll often be a few of us in the wahsroom. We might just say a few words about what's been going on in the meeting, like what did you think about a certain part in a film we're watching, or crack a joke or something. But sometimes we've had a small discussion. I don't even think our wives know that happens. I can't open up in the group, but those few words in the washroom are a help. There is just a sort of understanding there.

Loss of Sexual Desire

It is common for men, after they learn they are infertile, to temporarily lose interest in sex and have difficulty getting an erection or performing during sexual intercourse. The impotence can be a result of depression, grief, loss of self-esteem, or less of motivation for sex because he knows it may no longer result in a child. It can be quite disconcerting for a man if he has never before had this experience and it may seem as a double blow—both fertility and sexual performance. It is estimated that as many as 75 percent of men who find out they are infertile have a temporary loss of sexual desire and an inability to sustain an erection. The loss of desire is usually temporary and libido and enjoyment of sex do return to normal. If impotence persists, couples should seek counselling.

Some men, however, react the other way, becoming more flirtatious with women other than their partners. Some may even begin to have affairs or one-night stands to prove to themselves and to others they are still desirable and have sexual prowess.

My husband was never the flirtatious type, but about half a year after he found out he was infertile I noticed at parties that his manner had really changed. He was really chatting up other women. I'd never seen him like that before.

Sexual problems or flirtation are usually short term, counsellors say. With time, the sexual relationship and behavior return to normal. The emotional responses to infertility, however, can linger and men can have a difficult time dealing with their grief. Men reading this chapter may benefit from reading Chapter 9 on donor insemination and the section on grief in Chapter 12.

CHAPTER 8
Cervical Mucus Factors, Recurrent Miscarriage and Unexplained Infertility

This chapter includes causes of infertility that do not have a linking theme. Cervical mucus factors, which affect about 10 percent of infertile couples, have little in common with recurrent pregnancy loss. Unexplained infertility is a category unto itself with no clues to tie it to other possible causes.

Cervical Mucus Factors

The Work and Structure of the Cervix

The fleshy, fibrous donut, the cervix, which sits at the top of the vagina, is not merely a narrow corridor into the uterus. This is no inert structure. It is an intricate organ on its own, that, with its mucous secretions, performs a host of jobs essential to the success or failure of conception.

1. *Gatekeeper* For most of the menstrual cycle the cervix acts as a barrier to sperm and other microorganisms, preventing their entry into the uterus and fallopian tubes. It produces a thick mucous plug that is impassable to most organisms and that helps protect the woman from infection. On a few days at the time of ovulation during the menstrual cycle when the cervix gets the "open-sesame" message from circulating estrogen, the mucus suddenly turns watery and hospitable and the cervix opens to allow passage of the sperm.
2. *Protector* At the time of ovulation, the watery fertile mucus protects the sperm from the otherwise hostile, acidic environment of the vagina and may also protect them from being engulfed, or phagocytosed, by the scavengers of the woman's immune system, the phagocytes.
3. *Nurturer* The mucus is a nutritious medium for the sperm and energizes them before they embark on their journey to the egg.
4. *Quality assurance* The cervix and mucus filter out poor or abnormal sperm, dead or immature cells, and other detritus in the man's ejaculate, separating the sperm from the seminal plasma and selecting the healthy, strong sperm to go on.

5. *Base camp* The many microscopic crypts and pits in the cervix seem to act as a reservoir for sperm, functioning as a base camp by keeping them in a protective, nuturing environment. From this safe position, the sperm can make ascents to the tubes in steady, continuous waves, increasing the chance that some will meet the egg.
6. *Capacitator* Either the cervical mucus, or the combination of mucus, cervical structure and timing, perform a job called capacitation of the sperm. Capacitation is a little-understood process by which sperm lose their acrosome cap, increase their metabolism and become able to fertilize an ovum.
7. *Pregnancy Gatekeeper* If fertilization and implantation take place and a pregnancy develops, the cervix closes down, keeping the pregnancy in and most microorganisms out for the duration of the pregnancy. Even as the fetus and uterus grow to weigh a number of pounds, the cervix holds strong. Then, when the baby is ready to be born, the cervix opens wide enough that the baby's head and body can pass through.

That so much activity can take place in a site no bigger than a matchbox is astonishing. But the cervix is well equipped to do its job. It has thick, strong walls surrounding the narrow corridor into the uterus. The passageway, the endocervical canal, is at least four or five centimeters long and runs from the external os, or opening at the vagina, to the internal os, or outlet to the uterus. The endocervical canal's walls are pocked and pitted.

The lining of the endocervical canal, the endocervical epithelium, is made up of different types of secretory cells. How much the cells secrete, and when, is dictated by the amount of estrogen and progesterone circulating during the woman's menstrual cycle.

Assessment of Cervical Mucus

To test whether the woman makes fertile mucus hospitable to sperm, the doctor takes a sample at the woman's predicted time of ovulation. The mucus is usually assessed on its own and in conjunction with the postcoital test to check the natural interaction of mucus and sperm. Other tests besides the postcoital may be used, such as the cross-penetration test described in Chapter 4, and mucus-capillary tests.

Standardization

To standardize the assessment of cervical mucus the World Health Organization set up a committee of international experts to come up with guidelines. The committee agreed on a classification system of mucus, which is now used as the general reference in assessing a woman's mucus. The WHO system gives point scores to five properties of cervical mucus that are seen to be essential: mucus volume, spinnbarkeit, ferning, viscosity and cellularity. Each item is given a score between zero and three. All five properties together enable a maximum, optimal score of 15. Fertile mucus is anything over a score of 10. Here is the breakdown of the scores for a mucus sample taken at ovulation.

1. *Volume* If 0.3 milliliters of mucus or more is extracted from the cervical canal, the maximum three points is given. Less than 0.1 milliliters rates zero points.
2. *Viscosity* Thick, pasty mucus rates zero points while watery, clear mucus gets three points.
3. *Spinnbarkeit* A drop of cervical mucus placed on a slide is immediately assessed for its ability to stretch. The WHO guidelines recommend a coverslip be gently touched on the slide and then lifted straight up. If a thread of mucus extends nine centimeters or more, the maximum three points are given. If it does not stretch farther than one centimeter, zero points are given.
4. *Ferning* When the sample of mucus has dried on a slide, it is examined under the microscope for characteristic crystallization in "stems" that look like a frond of a fern. The most fertile mucus has three or four stems, meaning a primary stem with smaller secondary stems, and then even smaller tertiary stems off the secondary stem. The maximum three points are given if three or four degrees of stems are found. One point is given if there is some crystallization with no distinct stems. If no crystillization occurs at all, zero points are allotted.
5. *Cellularity* The numbers of dead cells, white blood cells and amounts of other debris are graded. If no cells are found in a high powered field of the microscope, three points are given. If there are 11 or more cells in a high powered field, zero points are given.

A total score between five and 10 is considered to be generally unfavorable to sperm and a score of five or less is considered to be "hostile" cervical mucus.

The pH of the sample—the relative acidity—is not included in the total score, but it is also important for the sperm to survive. A woman's vagina is generally acidic, with a pH between 3 and 5, and sperm die in it quickly. The mucus, however, is more alkaline, with a pH between 7 and 8.5, and it buffers the top end of the vagina and the cervix. The alkalinity also enhances the sperm's motility. The pH of the mucus is tested by pH paper. A pH range between 6.4 to 8.5 is acceptable.

The Postcoital Test

The debate about the postcoital test, which is also known as the Sims-Huhner test, is described in detail near the end of Chapter 4.

Sperm-Cervical Mucus Contact Test (SCMC)

If a woman is suspected of having antibodies to her partner's semen she may be given the sperm-cervical mucus contact test (SCMC). The WHO guidelines suggest that a small amount of fertile mucus and an equal amount of fresh semen be placed together at one end of a microscopic slide and mixed well. At the other end of the slide a drop of fresh semen is placed by itself for comparison. Both are covered with a coverslip and placed in a moist Petri dish at room temperature. After 30 minutes the two samples are studied under a microscope. If more than 50 percent of the sperm in the semen-mucus sample are not motile and appear to be shaking in place, but the sperm in the semen-only sample still have good motility, the test is positive for antisperm antibodies, but it is not known whether the man or woman contributed the antibodies. The test will be followed with more specific antibody tests.

Causes and Treatment of Poor Cervical Mucus

A variety of conditions can lead to mucus that scores less than 10 by WHO standards. The most important cause to rule out first is improper timing. If the test was not well-timed to ovulation, even the most fertile women will get a low score. For some women even two days too early or too late can make the difference between excellent and abnormal mucus.

Causes

Once proper timing has been assured, the following are the usual causes of poor mucus.

Ovulation Disorders

If the woman is not ovulating, or if she has subtle ovulation problems, her mucus is usually poor. For example, if the follicles do not mature adequately, the estrogen levels do not reach the peak necessary to make good mucus. Ovulation defects are treated with ovulation drugs such as clomiphene citrate or human menopausal gonadotropin. Clomiphene citrate, however, may impair cervical mucus and so it is often combined with small doses of synthetic estrogen given up to day 15 of the cycle.

Anatomical Problems

Any disruption of the intricate structure of the cervix may alter its functioning. A small percentage of women may be born with a malformed or blocked cervix. Fibroids close to the cervix or polyps growing through the cervix (See Chapter 6.) may also interfere with mucus secretions. Any surgery on the cervix can damage or destroy the mucus-secreting cells. Conization (cone biopsies), cryosurgery, cauterization and laser surgery are used to treat a wide range of cervical problems or diseases. Pre-cancerous or cancerous cell changes, cervical erosion or chronic cervical infection, or cervicitis, are some of the cervical problems that may alter cervical mucus and lead to the need for surgery. Along with the mucus-secreting cells, the cervical crypts also may be destroyed by surgery. Doctors may refer to this condition as "dry cervix." Sometimes estrogen treatment stimulates the cells that are still functional to produce more mucus, but often there is nothing that can be done. Intrauterine insemination (IUI), described later in this chapter, or gamete intrafallopian tube transfer, described in Chapter 10, are now most often the recommended treatments to help a couple conceive.

Other factors that may lead to poor or hostile cervical mucus are not well understood.

Treatment of Hostile Mucus

Too Viscous If mucus is too thick and pasty at the time of ovulation, small doses of estrogens may be given to improve the consistency. The estrogens, usually in pill form, are taken from day five until day 14 or 15.

High Cellularity The presence of many dead cells, leucocytes or other debris in the mucus often signals an infection in the cervix, cervicitis, or inadequate estrogen stimulation. Antibiotics are usually given to treat the infection and estrogen or human menopausal gonadotropins (HMG) to treat poor estrogen stimulation.

Low Volume, Poor Ferning To increase the amount and quality of the mucus, estrogens may be given as in the case of viscosity, described above. If mucus quality does not improve, IUI or GIFT may be recommended.

Acidic Mucus Mucus is generally acidic when the general mucus score is less than 10 because it has not gone through the necessary changes to raise its pH. A cervical infection can also cause acidic mucus. The other problems will be treated first, as described above. Usually when the mucus quality is improved, the problem of acidity is resolved. In rare cases where the mucus remains acidic, some doctors recommend a precoital douche with bicarbonate of soda—two tablespoons in a liter of warm water. The patient is instructed to douche with the alkaline solution before having sexual intercourse.

New York infertility specialist Dr. Richard Bronson says in the rare cases that he suggests this treatment, he does a postcoital test after the first bicarbonate douche. "If the sperm are surviving after the douche then I feel this gives enough direction to recommend the couple try the douche for four or five months."

Sperm Antibodies

Like men, women can form antibodies to sperm that attack the sperm, coating them, immobilizing them or otherwise interfering with the sperm's fertility.

There are many unaswered questions when it comes to antibodies, sperm and fertility. The biggest question is why some women have them, but the majority do not. The puzzling aspect is that sperm are known antigens. If a woman is injected in the arm with a needle full of semen, as in a vaccination, she creates antibodies to the sperm. Sperm are foreign cells, with DNA different from the woman's. The immune system would have every reason to mount a response.

Why are most women protected from producing antibodies against their partner's semen? Researchers do not know, but there is the possibility that immunosupressive factors in the semen itself may stop the woman from forming antibodies, such as the prostaglandins and/or proteins in the seminal fluid. Perhaps the sperm in the epididymis are coated with blocking antibodies that "hide" the sperm from the woman's immune recognition. A theory that is still being investigated is that if the man lacks the immune suppressing factors, the woman might tend to become immunized.

Another theory, which has not been proved, is that the woman herself might have a greater tendency to become immunized. Her immune system may be more likely to become turned on, or, in a sense, allergic to her husband's sperm. Preliminary studies of women who have auto-immune diseases or allergies, however, have not shown that these women are more likely to become immunized by sperm. Perhaps there is some factor in the fertile woman's reproductive tract or in the cervical mucus that prevents an immune response.

There is some concern that swallowing semen or taking semen into the rectal passage, theoretically, could cause a greater likelihood that a woman would form sperm antibodies. The body might react as it does when a woman is vaccinated with sperm. Experiments with mice have shown that if their oral and rectal passages were exposed to semen an immune response followed. There is no concrete evidence for this in humans but it is seen as being a theoretical possibility.

It is believed that when a woman has formed antisperm antibodies she has formed them to all men's sperm, not just her partner's sperm.

When women form antibodies to sperm, the most common reaction is that the antibody causes the sperm to become stuck in the cervical mucus. The antibodies may also coat the sperm in the mucus and then somehow prevent the capacitation of the sperm.

Researchers say many women may have low levels of antibodies that never interfere with fertility. "We find a certain number of people have background noise—low level of reactivity," Bronson said. "We don't know how significant this is. It may not be completely normal, but it may also not be causing a problem."

When preliminary evidence suggests antisperm antibodies, such as sperm shaking in place in the cervical mucus, more specific tests may be performed to find out if antibodies are indeed present and which partner is contributing them. Antibodies cannot be seen on their own; it is the reactions that they cause that can be seen. Researchers, therefore, look for specific reactions from which the deduction can be made that antibodies are present.

Detecting Antibodies

To locate the problem, the man's semen must be tested to make sure it is not contributing the antibodies. An antibody test of his sperm is conducted, as is described in Chapter 7. When the sperm are found to be antibody free, a sperm sample is incubated with the woman's cervical mucus or blood. If the woman indeed has antibodies to his sperm, during the incubation period her antibodies hone in and attach themselves to her partner's sperm. Researchers can not see the antibodies coating the sperm so they introduce a marker, which might be a tiny plastic bead, a fluorescent molecule, an enzyme or a radioactive tag. All the markers are attached to an antibody that is specific to the sperm antibody. This antibody-to-the-antibody hones in only on the sperm coated with antibodies, taking the marker with it. Looking under the microscope, the doctor sees if the incubated sperm have plastic beads, fluorescent tags, or radioactivity associated with them. If so, the presence of the invisible antibody is confirmed.

Treatment

As the full understanding of antisperm antibodies is still in its infancy, so is the treatment. For a number of years the suggested treatment was condom therapy. The couple was instructed to use condoms for about six months in the hope that the woman's levels of antibodies against her partner's sperm would drop and she would become less sensitized to sperm. However, antibody levels did not fall in most women, and, furthermore, the couple was using contraception for six months, eliminating the chance that a spontaneous conception would occur. Condom therapy is no longer recommended. There may be benefit to using condoms at other times of the cycle, however, when the woman is not ovulating. "It is not clear to what extent the antibody levels may fall if a person is being exposed to sperm less frequently," Bronson said.

Corticosteriods, which cause immune suppression, have been tried as a treatment for antisperm antibodies, but there is not yet good data for its effect.

If the antibodies against the sperm appear to be only in the cervical mucus, bypassing the cervix by intrauterine insemination is now the most commonly recommended therapy. The antibody-coated sperm may first be tested by the hamster-egg penetration test (See Chapter 7.). It is not known, however, if women with antibodies in the cervical mucus have antibodies that attack the sperm higher up in the reproductive tract.

In vitro fertilization, because both the sperm and egg are removed from the body and meet in a Petrie dish, may be the best way to minimize the effect of antibodies. Some researchers have reported success when the egg is washed free of the cumulus cells surrounding it and the egg is also cultured in blood serum taken from a donor rather then using the woman's own serum. The rate of embryo division, called cleavage rate, however, appears to be lower in women with antibodies.

Now the tests for antibodies just say generally whether antibodies are present, but researchers hope in the near future that specific antibodies and how they undermine fertility will be identified by specific antibody tests. The technology is now available, using monoclonal antibodies, to develop tests to pinpoint the specific nature of the antibodies. More specific tests might enable a doctor to tell an infertile couple what kind of antibody they have and how to treat it. For example, the couple might be found to have an antibody that interferes with sperm motility but not with the sperm's ability to fertilize the egg and for that reason the couple should use IUI, GIFT or IVF. Another couple might find that their antibodies interfere with the capacitation reaction. That couple's option might have to be donor insemination or microinjection.

Intrauterine Insemination

In recent years intrauterine insemination (IUI) has become a recommended technique to take the sperm closer to the egg and possibly improve the chance of conception. This technique is most often used to treat poor sperm counts or poor sperm motility, cervical mucus hostility and antisperm antibodies and, occasionally, unexplained infertility and endometriosis.

IUI is done just before the woman is expected to ovulate. The man's sperm are specially washed and capacitated and then placed in a slender catheter. The catheter is guided through the woman's endocervical canal and into the uterus almost to the very top; then the sperm are released in the direction of both tubes.

Some infertility specialists claim poor results with IUI and say they establish very few pregnancies with the technique. But Dr. John Kerin, director of the Division of Reproductive Endocrinology and Infertility at Cedars-Sinai Medical Center in Los Angeles, says the technique can have good results if attention is paid to details. Kerin was the first to show in a controlled study that IUI improved pregnancy rates of infertile couples. While head of an infertility program in Adelaide, Australia, Kerin led an experiment comparing IUI to normal intercourse in couples with male infertility. One month the couples had normal sexual intercourse timed to ovulation by basal body temperature graphs. The next month they had intercourse more specifically timed to the woman's LH surge. The third month they had IUI timed to the LH surge. Each couple had all three treatments but they were randomized so that the treatments might have occurred in a different order. All the pregnancies that occurred during the study, except one, occurred from the IUI treatment (all in the first IUI treatment). One pregnancy occurred in a temperature-timed cycle.

Kerin says he feels there are three essential elements to successful IUI: good sperm preparation so the maximum amount of motile, capacitated sperm are brought near the egg(s); good placement of the sperm at the opening of the tubes; impeccable timing so fresh sperm are in the tube at the time of ovulation.

A fourth element has now been added to some IUI treatments that seems to be improving the pregnancy rates: stimulation of the woman's ovaries with fertility drugs, so that more than one egg is produced. The ovarian stimulation is similar to the method for in vitro fertilization or GIFT. (See Chapter 10.)

Sperm Preparation

As you know from the beginning of this chapter, the cervix and cervical mucus normally separates the good sperm from the poor ones. In the natural situation only the most motile healthy sperm make it to the fallopian tubes. For IUI, the sperm must be prepared and capacitated in the laboratory before they are placed in the woman's uterus. The sperm must first be separated from the semen—if semen is placed in the uterus the woman may experience extreme cramps because of the presence of prostaglandins in the seminal fluid. Originally, sperm were washed and spun down in a centrifuge with a commercial medium, Hamm's F10, a chemical powder full of nutrients mixed into solution. Hamm's F10 has been modified and calcium, sodium and human serum are added for sperm washing. The result is better motile, capacitated sperm. Others are trying another preparation media, the Test Yolk Buffer, which is modified egg yolk. It has also been shown to result in a higher percentage of motile, capacitated sperm.

Delivery System

Infertility specialists have been working on improving the catheters used to deliver the sperm to the top of the uterus. Now, directional cathers are being used that can aim a jet of sperm at both tubal openings, one at a time, when a plunger is depressed. Some catheters are even being tried that thread right into the tube so that placement is assured.

Timing

The more accurate the timing, the better the result, says Kerin. IUI is a one-shot deal, unlike the natural cervix, which holds a reservoir of sperm. The timing has to be right to make sure the sperm are in the fallopian tubes when the egg is ovulated. Kerin says many programs inseminate too early. If the woman's ovaries have been primed with fertility drugs, it is thought that insemination should follow about 38 to 44 hours after the shot of human chorionic gonadotropin. "Some people inseminate right after the HCG shot or about 24 hours after. But we know from IVF that if we give the shot and go in 36 hours later, the eggs are just ready to be ovulated. It makes sense that we should do IUI just a little bit after that," Kerin said.

With good preparation and accurate timing, IUI can have the same, or better, success rates of other assisted reproduction techniques such as IVF and GIFT, Kerin says. The advantage of IUI, however, is that it does not require surgery or egg removal by ultrasound. If IUI is used with ovary stimulating drugs, however, it does have the same risks of multiple pregnancies. Twins or triplets are 10 times more likely than in unstimulated cycles. Hyperstimulation syndrome, in which the ovaries are overstimulated with potentially dire consequences, is also a risk of drug stimulation. See Appendix B of Chapter 5.

Recurrent Miscarriage

The first pregnancy we were so excited. We were talking to it as if it was a real baby through my stomach, we were picking out names. We told all our friends. When I lost it, at nine weeks, we were devastated. It was horrible physically, because there was so much blood and that was shocking. But emotionally it was even worse. For the second pregnancy we were much more low key, more on edge. I lost that at 11 weeks and it was just as bad. Afterwards you think you can't possibly go through another pregnancy. But after a while you think maybe this time it'll work and you try again. My third pregnancy I was afraid to breathe or move. I spent a lot of time in bed. I was being watched closely but they didn't know what the problem was. I felt if I just made it past 11 weeks I'd be okay. I made it to 12 and then about three days later I woke up with pain and bleeding and I knew it was happening again.

Miscarriage is a physically and emotionally wrenching experience, a trauma for any couple; it cuts to their emotional core. What was real, the pregnancy, becomes unreal—but unforgettable. A single miscarriage is usually seen as a chance event, a random mutation of the embryo that makes it unable to survive. Simply bad luck, most doctors say. A single miscarriage is very common among fertile and infertile women. As many as 30 percent of embryos that implant may eventually miscarry, doctors have reported. The number might even be higher. The emotional and physical aspects of miscarriage for the infertile couple are discussed in Chapter 11.

For a small number of couples, miscarriage follows upon miscarriage. Their childlessness is not caused by a difficulty to conceive, but by the woman's difficulty in carrying the fetus to term. Almost 90 percent of these repeated miscarriages occur in the first trimester, before 12 or 13 weeks. It is estimated that one in 300 couples suffers from repeated loss, what doctors often call habitual abortion or recurrent spontaneous abortion. After one miscarriage the chance of having a second miscarriage is about 20 percent; after two miscarriages the chance of having a third miscarriage is estimated at about 32 percent.

Traditionally, medicine has not considered that a woman has a problem with spontaneous abortion until she has lost three or more pregnancies. The reason is that between 65 to 75 percent of women who have had even three miscarriages go on to have a successful pregnancy on their own. Many doctors say that couples who have two or more losses should see a specialist in case the miscarriage is caused by a treatable problem, such as an anatomical problem of the uterus or cervix.

Most recurrent miscarriages are poorly understood. There is a disagreement among specialists about what constitutes the major causes of spontaneous abortion and even more disagreement about how they should be treated.

The causes of recurrent loss are generally thought to fall into one of the following categories: genetic abnormalities of the embryo; anatomical problems in the mother; hormonal problems that fail to support the embryo; recurrent infections; and improper immune response from the mother. Different specialists allot varying proportions of loss into each category. For example, some researchers believe genetic abnormalities account for more than 60 percent of recurrent miscarriages. Other investigators believe abnormal immune reactions are behind more than two-thirds of recurrent losses. Still others believe hormonal problems—lack of progesterone support—account for a significant amount.

Adding to the medical puzzle is that the subject of repeated pregnancy loss has suffered from a lack of good research studies. Understandably, couples who have had three or more miscarriages are very reluctant to be assigned to a control group that does not receive treatment—a prerequisite for an unbiased study and for determining the true value of any treatment.

Couples want to know why they are losing their pregnancies and what can be done about it, but unfortunately for 40 percent of couples no cause will be found. In a commentary on the problems of recurrent abortion in the British *Journal of Obstetrics and Gynecology* in 1983, Professor Gordon Stirrat described the resulting problem.

> *The fact that, in most cases, neither question (why it's happening and what can be done about it) can be answered with certainty merely adds to the couple's distress. Those who look after them find this uncertainty equally hard to cope with and, as a result, may*

suggest and come to believe in causes and remedies for which confirming evidence is scant. Loose clinical associations are frequently cited as etiological (causing) factors on the slenderest of grounds.

Recurrent miscarriage is so distressing that some couples and doctors will try anything—even if it has not been shown to work and may even be dangerous—rather than doing nothing.

In areas where the cause is not known or where no proven treatment exists, it is wise for both couples and doctors to remember the lesson of DES. DES taught us that miscarriage treatments must proceed with caution, based on good scientific studies. It has been shown that 65 to 75 percent of couples who have had repeated loss will eventually have a successful pregnancy without treatment.

Suspected Causes of Repeated Loss

Anatomical Problems

Abnormalities in the shape or function of the uterus and cervix can cause a developing fetus to be expelled. A septate uterus, in which a membrane divides the uterus in half, polyps and fibroids can all cause recurring losses. The miscarriages can occur in the first or second trimester. These anatomical defects can often be repaired by surgery. Some uterine abnormalities, such as a double uterus, can sometimes carry a pregnancy successfully, so women should have other reasons for a miscarriages ruled out before undergoing major surgery. (See Chapter 6.)

Incompetent Cervix

During a normal pregnancy the strong cervix stays tightly closed until the time comes for the baby to be born. However, in some women the cervix opens spontaneously, the membranes rupture and the pregnancy is lost, usually in the second trimester when the fetus is growing larger. Unlike most other miscarriages, one caused by an incompetent cervix isn't necessarily accompanied by bleeding or pain. The pregnancy just loses its supporting floor and is released. It is very upsetting for the couple because the tiny fetus is usually born alive but dies soon after.

An incompetent cervix can be congenital or acquired. A woman whose mother took DES seems to have a greater incidence of cervical incompetence. Surgery or trauma to the cervix can weaken it and can cause it to open. Therapeutic abortions can also cause a cervix to become incompetent. It is not usually possible for a doctor to detect a woman's incompetent cervix by examination or hysterosalpingogram, but it is diagnosed usually by a woman's medical history—past abortions or cervical surgery plus the loss of a pregnancy in the second semester without accompanying labor contractions.

In the next pregnancy the doctor will examine the woman every two weeks to check whether the cervix is opening. At about 14 weeks, the cervix can be stitched shut by means of a purse-string suture, which, as its name suggests, closes down the cervix like a drawstring on a bag. At about 38 or 39 weeks the stitch will be removed to allow for a vaginal birth.

Chromosomal Abnormalities

A chromosome is a genetic blueprint, a long structure found in all cells that is comprised of genes linked together. A human being has 46 chromosomes, joined as sets of two, to make 23 pairs. Each pair has one chromosome inherited from the mother and one from the father. Together, the 46 chromosomes contain all the genetic information needed to oversee the growth and development of the embryo into a unique individual.

A chromosomal abnormality in the developing fetus—an extra piece or an entire extra chromosome, an irregular chromosome arrangement, or a defective gene—can cause it to stop developing and abort, most commonly before eight to 10 weeks gestation. This is believed to be the most common cause of miscarriage. The chromosomal error can arise at varying times in the reproductive process. One of the most common times is during meiosis, the prefertilization process in which the genetic material that forms the egg or sperm is halved, so that when an egg and sperm come together they have one complete set of paired chromosomes.

If an error occurs in meiosis, the result can be an embryo that has an extra chromosome or lacks a chromosome. An extra chromosome is called trisomy and it can happen to any pair of the 23 chromosomes. Sometimes a trisomy can result in a live birth of an abnormal child, such as a child with Down's syndrome, caused by an extra chromosome in the 21st pair. Most other trisomies cause spontaneous abortion. Studies have shown that if a couple's first miscarriage is caused by trisomy of a chromosome, the next miscarriage is frequently caused by a trisomy, too, perhaps of a different set of chromosomes. Researchers believe this indicates that some couples have a greater risk of abnormal meiosis resulting in trisomy at fertilization.

Errors that lead to loss of the pregnancy can also arise during fertilization if two sperm are successful in fertilizing an egg or if the egg or sperm did not undergo the meiotic division at all before being fused. The first few cell divisions of the embryo can also lead to chromosomal abnormalities. These embryos usually fail to develop and are expelled.

Either one or both parents may have what is called a "balanced translocation" on one of their chromosomes, in which a segment of the parent's chromosome has broken off and switched places with another chromosomal segment. The result will be a balanced set of chromosomes for the parent but may lead to unbalanced chromosomes for the embryo.

Parents may also pass on defective genes, the individual components of a chromosome. Some genetic defects can be determined by family history and a few can now be determined by chromosomal analysis. Although genetic analysis has been making big strides in recent years, in relation to what is unknown it is still in its infancy. Few medical centers have the ability to use genetic studies as a routine evaluation for aborting couples.

Diagnosing chromosomal abnormalities or genetic defects as being the cause of a couple's recurring miscarriages is difficult. When the miscarriage happens, couples should collect the expelled fetal material in a clean glass jar and take it to the hospital, a chore that is usually upsetting. Sometimes by examining the outward appearance of the fetal tissue, the doctor can be more certain whether chromosomal abnormalities are the cause. Some doctors, however, do not examine the fetal material because chromosomal abnormalities are common and some tissues yield no information. This can be equally upsetting for couples who have carefully collected it.

A karyotype, an expensive, time-consuming procedure in which the chromosomes are examined and arranged in order, can be performed only if the tissue is still living. But if fetal material is dead by the time it is examined, a karyotype is not possible. A karyotype may confirm a chromosomal error, but it may not be able to determine the source of the problem—for example whether the problem arises with the woman's eggs or the man's sperm; it may also not be able to determine if the error is most likely to arise again. However, in less than 1 percent of the time one or both partners will be found to have a chromosomal defect they are passing on to the embryo.

There is now no treatment for chromosomal abnormalities or genetic defects, but couples who are found to have recurring chromosomal abnormalities causing their micarriages can often have a normal conception occur by chance. If one partner is found to be passing on a chromosomal or genetic defect, donor sperm or donor eggs can be used. However, even some couples who are passing on a defect have a 30 percent chance of eventually having a normal pregnancy through the random fusion of a normal sperm and egg. In some cases the chromosomal abnormalities in the fetus may be caused by one or both partners' exposure to radiation or to toxic chemicals.

Hormonal Problems

Some investigators think luteal phase deficiency, in which the corpus luteum does not produce enough progesterone to support the endometrium, or the endometrium is not responsive to progesterone, is the source of the problem. (See Chapter 5.) Although the area continues to be a source of scientific controversy, many researchers claim very good results by supplementing pregnancies with progesterone suppositories.

Daily shots of human chorionic gonadotropin have also been given to support the pregnancy; however, this treatment is more expensive, not easy for the woman to administer herself and may not work. When poor progesterone level is thought to be the result of poor egg development, the fertility drug clomiphene citrate may be given to increase follicle stimulation.

Infection

If a pregnant woman becomes infected by one of a number of viruses or microorganisms, the infection, if severe enough, may cause the pregnancy to abort. This is thought to be a one-time occurrence. It is not known, however, if an organism can cause repeated miscarriages. Herpes, chlamydia, toxoplasmosis, and mycoplasma have all been suggested as possible causes of some women's repeated loss. After a pregnancy is lost, if the doctors find that the woman has an infection, she will be given antibiotics (if the organism causing the infection is treatable by antibiotics). It is not known whether this will make a difference to the outcome of her next pregnancy.

Immunology

Since the early 1980s an increasing emphasis has been put on the role of the immune system in repeated pregnancy loss. There is increasing evidence that a woman's inability to mount a protective immune response to her fetus may be one of the leading causes of habitual abortion.

Doctors' understanding of the intricate functioning of the immune system has been growing by leaps and bounds since the 1970s, helped by advances in other branches of medicine, such as organ transplants, cancer treatments and acquired immune deficiency syndrome. Nevertheless, it is only a fragment of the whole picture and the understanding of how the mother's immune system responds to pregnancy is particularly poor. A great deal of debate exists in the medical community over what is going on and there is even more controversy over how it should be treated. The most common mode of immune treatment for recurrent miscarriage—the injection of the woman with white blood cells from her partner or a donor—is still highly experimental.

Immune Model for Pregnancy

In theory, all mothers should reject the babies growing in their wombs, since the rapidly developing embryo is unlike her. The fetus derives half its genetic material from the mother and half from the father. It is a unique genetic entity, and the mother's immune system should see it as foreign and reject it as it would reject an unmatched organ transplant. But for most women, the rejection process does not take place. Instead, the pregnancy is protected and nurtured. Given that situation, some invesitgators believe women who suffer recurrent miscarriages may have a malfunction or inappropriate reaction from the immune system that causes rejection to take place.

The most current immune theory is that in a successful pregnancy, the outermost layer of cells that surrounds the embryo, the trophoblast, signals to the mother's immune system that the embryo is present. The trophoblast is what burrows into the endometrial tissue of the woman's uterus, nourishing the developing embryo and later giving rise to the placenta. How the trophoblast signals is not known. Some researchers have theorized it is the father's antigens or specific markers on the trophoblast that trigger the signal. Whatever it is that sends the signal, the signal itself is believed to call in components of the mother's immune system, T-lymphocytes and macrophages. Instead of rejecting the embryo, as one would expect, the T-lymphocytes and macrophages seem to have the opposite effect, protecting the pregnancy and making it grow. Recent research in Canada by Dr. Tom Wegmann in Edmonton, Alberta and Dr. David Clark in Hamilton, Ontario, has found evidence that the lymphocytes may secrete a growth factor, which stimulates the proliferation of the trophoblast and promotes fetal growth.

In a woman who repeatedly miscarries, one predominant theory is that she fails to have this protective immune response because she does not recognize her partner's antigens. The theory is that the couple may be too genetically similar or they may share too many of the same cell markers, the HLA markers (human lymphocyte antigens.) HLA markers are like the blood groups A, B and O but instead of marking blood types they designate tissue types. (In organ transplants when they tissue type the donor they are looking for a match of the donor's and recipient's HLA markers.) A man and woman could be from different backgrounds and still share HLA factors. The true role of HLA sharing in recurrent abortion has been hotly debated since the early 1980s and no agreement has been reached. Chicago specialist Alan Beer uses HLA-sharing by partners as a criterion for immune therapy in repeated abortions. Other groups, however, have found the same amount of HLA-sharing fertile couples who are able to carry pregnancies to term despite their similar antigens.

Perhaps there is a factor similar to HLA antigens but not exactly the same. A group in Indianapolis headed by Drs. Page Faulk, John McIntrye and Carolyn Coulam say they have found different markers that may relate to HLA on the trophoblast. They call the markers trophoblast-lymphocyte cross-reacting antigens (TLX-antigens), which they believe stimulate the immune response in the mother to protect the pregnancy. They believe if the mother does not react to TLX, or reacts inappropriately, the pregnancy aborts. The Indianapolis researchers say they have found that one of the richest sources of their TLX-antigens is the seminal plasma. They have put forward the idea that the woman becomes immunized to her partner's differences when the seminal plasma enters her reproductive tract. The group's research has been marred by the fact they have not used control groups in their studies. The validity of their findings remains to be confirmed by other groups.

Experimental Therapies

In the late 1970s when the first immune theories were emerging, a handful of researchers in England began giving women injections of their partner's white blood cells. The injections were meant to "immunize" a woman to the differences of her partner's antigens so that she would mount a greater response toward an embryo. The women who received the treatment were selected by a simple blood test, the mixed lymphocyte reaction, in which white blood cells from the woman were mixed with specially treated white blood cells from the man. If the woman's white blood cells did not grow, she was seen as not having an immune response to her partner's stimuli.

The researchers claimed good results from the injection of the partner's white blood cells (leukocytes)—women who had had recurring losses carried babies to term. But these studies, again, did not have good control groups and so the results were not widely accepted by others in the profession. A great deal of professional concern was also expressed about tampering with the woman's powerful immune system and the possible negative effects on the woman and her child.

Leukocyte injections have remained a controversial treatment, and London specialist Dr. James Mowbray is one of the few investigators who has given a large number of injections. By the end of 1987, he had injected more than 1300 women and reported an 80 percent pregnancy rate for those who received treatment. Mowbray is also one of the only researchers giving injections who has conducted a double-blind controlled study in which some of the women received their own cells rather than their partner's. The women who received their own cells had a 37 percent pregnancy rate compared to an 80 percent rate for those women in his study who received their partner's cells. Mowbray says he believes the procedure is safe for mother and child, although he is not sure why it works.

Faulk and his co-workers in Indianapolis who were developing the theory of TLX tried a different therapy. They believe that, because there was probably only a small group of TLX-antigens, immunizing with the male partner's cells might not be necessary and, instead, they could use leukocytes from third-party donors. Third-party donors were also used by other researchers if the partner's cells did not create the correct response. Faulk and others have also claimed a 70 to 80 percent success rate with third party donors. None of these studies, at this writing, used control groups and so others are reluctant to accept their findings.

Some doctors continue to be concerned about the possible side effects of injecting foreign white blood cells into a woman's body. Chicago researcher Alan Beer reported an increased rate of premature births, congenital abnormalities and growth retardation in the babies whose mothers had the treatment. Mowbray and others, however, have not reported these findings. It is simply not known what the long-term effect will be on the mother. In a commentary in the British *Journal of Obstetrics and Gynecology* in 1983, Prof. Gordon Stirrat expressed a number of concerns, one of which was the unknown effect on the mother: "Potent immune stimuli are being injected into healthy women without knowledge being available as to the possible effects in the long term," he said.

Primary and Secondary Aborters

Adding to the complexity of the immune basis for recurrent pregnancy loss is the fact that the women tend to fit into two categories—primary and secondary aborters. Primary aborters are women who have never had a pregnancy last beyond 20 weeks and have no surviving children. Secondary aborters have had their first pregnancy produce a child, or had their first pregnancy go past 20 weeks, perhaps having a premature delivery or a stillbirth.

Research seems to indicate that primary aborters do not react to their partner's antigens, which is taken to mean that they are too genetically similar and do not recognize their partner's differences. Secondary aborters seem to mount a very confused, broadly reactive response, which the researchers believe may signal a problem in the woman's immune system in the way she forms antibodies.

Some studies have shown that if primary aborters get a new partner or use donor sperm, the woman no longer has an infertility problem. If secondary aborters get a new partner, they usually continue to have problems.

Further research has shown that in women who are secondary aborters, leukocyte transfusion makes their problem worse; they become even more sensitized. The original problem seems to indicate their condition is like being allergic to pregnancy and the injection of more antigens makes the allergy worse.

Despite the apparent initial success with immune therapy, there are still many gaps in understanding and many controversies. The therapy is not readily available to couples unless they happen to be in a center conducting research. Couples should be cautious about accepting immune therapy from a doctor who does not have a strong background in immunology.

In an editor's note accompanying a 1988 text on various causes and treatments of recurrent spontaneous abortion, Dr. Miles Novy said, "A resolution of these controversies will require appropriate experiments in animal models, indentification and mapping of gene loci in human chromosomes and carefully designed clinical trials to prove efficacy (safety and effect) before immunologic therapy is universally adopted."

Auto-Immune Diseases

An auto-immune disease is one in which the immune system, instead of attacking foreign cells, turns and attacks healthy cells in the person's own body. Systemic lupus erythematosus, generally known as lupus, is an auto-immune disease that tends to attack women in their childbearing years. A woman with lupus has antibodies that attack her own cells. It is characterized by inflammation of the body's connective tissue with arthriticlike pain, fever, weakness, extreme fatigue and skin lesions. Women who have lupus symptoms have a miscarriage rate of 50 percent.

Doctors find that some apparently healthy women who have had repeated unexplained pregnancy loss actually have one or more of the same serum antibodies found in women with full-blown lupus. The most significant antibodies involved are lupus anticoagulent, anticardiolipin antibodies, and antiphospholipid antibodies. Although these antibodies might not be at a level in a woman to give her outward signs of lupus, the antibodies may be enough to interfere with her pregnancy. It is not known whether she will develop the disease in the future. Women with the lupus antibodies tend to have abnormal blood clotting in the vessels of the placenta. The clotting takes place where the placenta meets with "mother's" tissue, the maternal-fetal interface. Researchers believe this coagulation is part of an immune cascade triggered by the auto-antibodies. The picture that emerges is similar to the secondary aborters who were overly sensitized to the father's antigens.

A number of studies in North America and Europe are investigating ways of treating these lupuslike women, usually with a combination of low dose Aspirin (ASA) to stop blood clotting and high dose prednisone, a corticosteroid hormone that slows the production of antibodies. Some other groups use intravenous heparin to stop blood clotting and lower immune antibody activity. These treatments carry some risk to the mother. Prednisone can cause premature labor, facial swelling, acne and hypertension. Aspirin can cross the placenta and cause intrauterine bleeding, and excessive bleeding at delivery. Heparin may also cause uncontrolled bleeding.

Other Causes of Repeated Miscarriage

Cigarette smoking, use of household cleaning fluids or other toxic chemicals, emotional and physical stress, poor diet and high anxiety have all been linked to repeated miscarriage. Studies have shown that some women with repeated losses are able to carry their next pregnancy to term when they get a lot of care and attention from their doctors. With tender, loving care, but no specific treatment, they have as good an outcome as some women who get treatment.

Unexplained Infertility

For 10 to 15 percent of all couples going through the infertility work-up, at the end of it all, no reason will have been found to explain why they remain childless. They will endure blood tests, postcoital tests, hysterosalpingograms, endometrial biopsies, laparoscopy, semen analysis, no end of probing and prodding. Many couples endure the entire work-up two and three times, and still, no definitive cause is found.

Without it a cause of infertility, there can be no logical treatment—the doctors simply do not know what they should be treating.

One woman described it as purgatory: no sentence, no relief, but just an ongoing question mark.

> *After going through all those tests you can't believe they can't find anything wrong. You begin to feel like others are thinking, "Well they must not be having sex," or "It's all in their head, deep down they probably don't really want children." You begin to wonder yourself if it's something psychological, if you are inhibiting it in some way.*

If a couple has received the diagnosis of unexplained infertility, it should be backed by a full and adequate work-up by competent specialists. There are many stories of couples who were told they had unexplained infertility only to find out two or three years later there is a cervical mucus problem or antisperm antibodies or something that had been missed. It is also possible for a subtle ovulation problem or mild endometriosis to go undetected. Do not settle for the label of unexplained infertility unless all the tests mentioned in this book have been performed.

Couples should also determine whether somehow they are avoiding intercourse. It is rare, but there are stories of couples who knowingly avoid having intercourse when the woman is ovulating, or who have intercourse too infrequently to give themselves an adequate chance of pregnancy. This is an area where medical personnel will not probe too deeply. It will be assumed that after being given an explanation of how to time intercourse to ovulation, the couple will have regular intercourse at the fertile time. Couples should examine whether an avoidance of intercourse may be a factor before resigning themselves to the diagnosis of unexplained infertility.

However, most couples with unexplained infertility probably have a genuine abnormality that occurs in the multi-step reproductive process for which there is as yet no test. As you will recall from earlier chapters, many infertility tests are presumptive rather than conclusive. The tests of ovulation rely on factors that are known to occur when ovulation takes place: temperature rises, progesterone in blood, the endometrial changes. If the doctors see these secondary changes, it is assumed an egg has been released. If the tubes are open and an egg has been released, it is assumed the egg will find its way into the tube. If the sperm quality is good and the cervical milieu hospitable, it is assumed the sperm will make it to the far end of the tube to meet the egg. If the egg and sperm are together at the right time and place, it is assumed fertilization occurs. It is also assumed the embryo will begin to divide, and if the endometrium has gone through the necessary changes, it will implant and grow to a pregnancy. As you can see, a great many assumptions must be made based on secondary evidence.

Since the early 1980s, the procedure of in vitro fertilization has done much to illuminate possible problems with couples that have unexplained infertility. When the sperm and egg meet in the Petri dish outside the body, doctors for the first time can see whether fertilization occurs. Some couples who outwardly pass all the tests for fertility are found in IVF to actually have recurring problems with fertilization. The sperm meet the egg but they do not fertilize it. This points to a hitherto undiagnosed problem with sperm function. (The hamster-egg penetration test also points sometimes to problems of sperm function but is not as reliable.) Some couples in IVF have eggs fertilize but the embryos do not divide adequately. Because IVF shows these formerly undiagnosed problems, some infertility specialists recommend IVF not only as a treatment option of couples with unexplained infertility, but also as a diagnostic tool.

Treatment for Unexplained Infertility

It is hard for the doctors to treat what they do not understand. Giving treatment when there is no diagnosis goes against everything that is taught and stressed in medical school. "Do not treat what you do not know" is a fundamental rule of good medicine. Sometimes doctors give fertility drugs, bromocriptine, progesterone or other standard treatments for unexplained infertility. These are considered to be ineffective ways to treat the problem. The methods that are more successful in dealing with unexplained infertility are not really "treatments," but ways to get around the problem, helping the reproductive process. In vitro fertilization, gamete intrafallopian tube transfer (GIFT) and its variations such a tubal-embryo transfer are becoming the most common ways to manage longstanding unexplained infertility. These methods at least put the sperm and eggs, or embryo, at the right place at the right time to give pregnancy a greater chance of developing. IVF, GIFT and other assisted reproductions are detailed in Chapter 10. In some instances intrauterine insemination (IUI) is recommended for unexplained infertility.

CHAPTER 9
Donor Insemination

The use of donated sperm to help an infertile couple conceive is one of the oldest of the infertility treatments. In fact, donor sperm was first used in the late nineteenth century and then continued, sporadically, in the early half of this century.

Since the 1950s, however, it has become common. It is the main option, and often the only option for couples if the man is infertile. Donor insemination is also used when a man has a serious inheritable disease such as Huntington's Chorea or hemophilia, or when he has an untreatable illness or disability that prevents ejaculation. Donor sperm is also used when a woman is Rh-negative and severely reactive to an Rh-positive partner; when the man has antisperm antibodies in his semen; or when the couple suffers recurrent miscarriages that doctors believe may be solved by using donor sperm.

At least 10,000 children each year are born through donor insemination in the United States. In Canada, Britain, and Australia, a further 1000 to 3000 children a year are born in each country as a result of sperm donation. The true numbers of DI offspring in the world are not really known because of the secrecy maintained within the process for so long. Nevertheless, the rough estimate of children conceived by this technique in the last 30 years is several hundreds of thousands, if not a million or more, world-wide.

In the past it was predominantly known as AID—artificial insemination by donor, but when acquired immune deficiency syndrome came into the public consciousness as AIDS, the acronym was changed. Now many groups use the name therapeutic donor insemination (TDI), donor insemination (DI), or donor assisted pregnancy, DAP, although AID is still used, too. The American Fertility Society has recommended TDI. However, DI seems to be the most universal and that is the term used here.

As was mentioned in Chapter 7, DI is not really a treatment for male infertility. Rather, it is a way to get around the unfortunate consequence of male infertility: childlessness. Just like adoption, it cures the longing for a child and the longing for couples to be parents, but not the medical condition that prohibits conception. Unlike adoption, however, it allows at least the female partner to be genetically related to the child and also allows the couple to experience pregnancy, birth and breastfeeding.

Our child is the best thing ever happened in our lives. She is really a joy. We cannot imagine being without her.

The procedure itself is quite simple: the donor's semen is placed in the woman's genital tract about the time she is ovulating. Various methods can be used to put the semen in the right place at the right time.

Even if the procedure is relatively uncomplicated, the decision to have DI is not. It is a decision with powerful emotions and psychological factors, one that must be made carefully and deliberately, with full and open discussion with both partners.

Recently, the professional and cultural attitudes toward DI have been changing. For years, DI has been regarded as a treatment of male infertility, not a treatment of childlessness. Couples undergoing DI were advised to keep the nature of the conception a secret, to pretend that the child was both partners' genetic offspring. All efforts were made to match the donor's looks carefully to the man's so that no one would suspect he was infertile. Couples, usually, have been happy about this approach because of the unfortunate, but nonetheless real attitude that male infertility was not something to be acknowledged or discussed. Sometimes doctors mixed the man's sperm with the donor's so the couple could believe that perhaps one of the husband's sperm fertilized the egg.

Now, however, an increasing number of professionals and families who have used DI advocate couples no longer keep DI a secret and that the child be told of his or her unique origins and special place in the family. Although most professionals still believe the donor's identity should remain anonymous, increasingly, doctors and couples believe non-indentifying medical and personal information about him, such as his hobbies, skills and personality, should be made available to the child.

If you are considering DI, you may want to read American author Elizabeth Noble's book, *Having Your Child By Donor Insemination: A Complete Resource Guide.* Noble wrote about the emotional, practical and legal aspect of DI in exhaustive detail. She tells the story of her and her husband's decision to have a known donor for their child and to tell her the complete details of her conception. Noble has a particular point of view—avoidance of the medical system, complete openness, knowing full details about the donor—and some readers may not agree with her choices and personal opinions, and may be disturbed by her focus on the negative aspects of using anonymous donors. Nevertheless, the book may help couples forge their own beliefs about DI, help them decide how they want to use DI, and help them make decisions they can live with happily.

That last sentence, in essence, is the most important thing: you, as a couple and as individuals, must be happy about your decision. You must be able to live with it, balancing the pros and cons, without self-deception. Even more important, the child you create must live with your decision, too. If you are happy with the nature of your child's conception, the child will more likely be happy with it, too.

Preparing to Make the Decision

The central issue, of course, is how you both feel about conceiving, carrying, birthing, and raising a child who carries the genes of another man. From that central issue many other associated issues arise.

For example, a couple's decision may be complicated because many religious groups do not sanction donor insemination, including Roman Catholics, Eastern Orthodox, Orthodox Jews, Muslims, Lutherans, Methodists, Evangelical Christians and Jehovah's Witnesses. Among the groups that do not bar DI, such as Anglicans, Mormons, Baptists and Presbyterians, it is still highly controversial. Couples who are struggling with the DI decision often have to resolve their religious beliefs as well.

Professionals who have experience with DI stress that the decision must be given time; couples should not rush into it. Most health professionals say it must be a two-step process. First, the couple must deal with the diagnosis of their infertility. When the infertility is accepted and acknowledged, the couple are able to contemplate donor insemination or other methods to overcome their childlessness.

Dealing with infertility means dealing with the emotions that the diagnosis of infertility brings—shock, disappointment, grief, depression. Like getting over a death, it can take a long time to grieve the loss of fertility and be able to move on.

"The man needs to first mourn the loss of his fertility, his loss of biological offspring and express his fears about DI," counsels Patricia Mahlstedt, a Houston, Texas, psychologist who specializes in counselling the infertile. "This is very hard for most men to do because our culture generally doesn't allow for it. The tendency is for men to suppress those feelings and not acknowledge it." Mahlstedt says men who do not resolve their pain around their infertility may hide their feelings about donor insemination through guilt, letting their partners conceive, but resenting it later.

Couples also must deal with the way infertility puts stress on their relationship. The majority of couples emerge from the initial upheaval in the relationship stronger and more stable because of having had to deal with the stress of infertility. But that, too, takes time.

Before embarking on DI, the couple should pursue to their own satisfaction infertility treatment for the man. If the man's sperm count is low, but not nonexistent, the couple should probably try to conceive on their own for a reasonable length of time. As was detailed in Chapter 7, even a man with a sperm count of only five million per milliliter has a 23 percent chance of fathering a pregnancy in his first year after diagnosis. The longer a couple tries without success, the worse their statistical chance of fathering a pregnancy in the future. That means if a couple has been trying for five years their chances are low for a natural pregnancy. But before going on to DI, couples should feel satisfied that they have given nature an adequate chance. While discussing the option of DI, they should also discuss with equal attention the possibility of adoption and childless living. Only by comparing other choices can they decide if DI is truly the right choice for them.

How long it takes to feel ready to move on to DI varies. If a man has azoospermia with irrversible testicular failure, the couple may be ready to go to DI sooner than others are. Almost all professionals suggest allowing at least six months to elapse between getting the diagnosis of male infertility and going on to try DI.

"The partners' decision regarding the solution of DI must slowly mature. They must want DI treatment together—the DI child, the pregnancy, the delivery. The child must not be a stranger or the woman's child only... nor must DI be considered therapy for a couple having marital problems, especially if these problems are related to the man's sterility," says Belgain specialist Robert Schoysman in the medical text *Progress in Infertility.*

According to Canadian psychiatrist Dr. David Berger, couples who take time and deliberate over the decision have more chance of emotional happiness and family harmony when they finally decide to go ahead. "Of those patients who went on to donor insemination, those who took more time to arrive at their decision did considerably better than those who did not," Berger wrote in the *Canadian Journal of Psychiatry.*

Talk It Out

The biggest problem couples face in making a decision about DI, however, is simply finding the words to talk about it openly and honestly. Couples can not come to a mutually satisfying decision about DI if they can not discuss it.

"People just don't have the skills to talk about this," said Judith Bernstein, a clinical nurse specialist who for more than 10 years counselled and conducted inseminations for hundreds of infertile couples at the University of New Mexico's artificial insemination program.

"I wanted to talk about it, I really did," says one woman. "But I found it so hard to bring up. After his diagnosis he really kept his feelings to himself about his infertility. I was afraid of bringing up DI in case of hurting him, continually reminding him of his infertility. I knew he wasn't into DI, I wasn't even sure how I felt about it, but I wanted to talk about it so maybe we could become more used to the idea. But it would always have to be me that would initiate the conversation."

The most common factor that prevents open discussion is overprotectiveness of one partner for another, Bernstein says. The man may try to protect the woman from his real feelings because he feels guilty about denying her a child through his infertility. The woman may be reluctant to really probe her partner's feelings or help him deal with the issue of his infertility because she does not want to hurt his self-esteem, nor make him feel bad or remind him of his infertility.

Some women deliberately avoid talking about DI with their partners. They may be more intent on moving quickly to DI and may not want to take time to discuss it because they are eager to have a baby. They may be afraid to fully probe the issues, not because their partners may be hurt by the discussion, but because they may say no.

Mahlstedt says that as soon as a couple learns they have male factor infertility they should start discussing their attitude to DI, not necessarily because they plan to do it, but just so they can begin to become accustomed to the words and the idea. "They should talk about it and live with it for a while, talk about it again and live with it some more, then talk about it again, and live with that."

Common Responses

Each individual couple has a particular response to the option of DI, but couples tend to fall into a few general profiles, clinicians and counsellors observe. The profiles include the following.

1. Both partners want to get on with DI to hide the man's sterility and to have a child quickly. After the child is born they will pretend the infertility never happened.
2. The woman is eager for a child, concerned that her biological clock is running down and she pushes for DI while the man is less committed. His consent to the procedure may be based on guilt for being unable to give his partner a child. She may ignore his feelings because she wants a child so badly. He may harbor resentment towards her for this.
3. The couple has not fully talked about it, but they know they want a child and figure this is the only way to do it. They have not explored the issues or how they feel about them. They are not sure whether they will tell the child or others. They have an attitude of "let's try it and see what happens." They figure they will decide what to do as they go along.
4. The couple has spent time discussing the option. They both are sure this is what they want. They have anticipated potential problems, and discussed whether, as well as how and when, they will tell the child about DI. The man may decide to accompany his partner to the inseminations and take part, either by doing the insemination or by supporting her with his presence.

The last profile, of course, is the healthiest for the long-term outcome for the couple and the child. Counsellors tell stories of couples who did not work through the issues, who return for an abortion. The questions in the next section may help you go through the decision-making process to the last stage.

DI Checklist

The following questions pinpoint common issues and problems with DI. The questions may seem overly negative, but they are not meant to give a negative picture of DI or discourage couples from it. Rather, the questions are meant to highlight difficult areas. By exploring these issues together, you may be able to work through difficulties.

Man Have you accepted your infertility and accepted the fact that you cannot have a child that carries your genes? Are you happy with the role as a parent and nurturer of a child that is not genetically related to you? Will you feel jealous, resentful or hurt if your wife conceives by DI? Will a resulting child be a painful reminder of your infertility? Are you afraid of the child or of anyone else knowing that you are infertile? Do you feel obligated to allow your wife to have a child this way because you are infertile? Would you prefer adoption or childless living to DI? Do you have religious concerns about DI? Are you excited and happy about sharing pregnancy, birth and childrearing with your partner?

Woman Are you more keen to be pregnant than your partner? Do you know how your partner feels about the procedure? Are you worried whether he will accept the child? Will you interpret any lesser involvement with the baby by your partner to mean he does not accept the child? Do you feel guilty for wanting a child by DI? Will going through DI make you feel unfaithful to your partner, or adulterous? Will you be going against your religion? How do you feel about having semen from another man inside you at ovulation each month until you become pregnant? How do you feel about having a baby grow inside you whose genetic father you do not know? If and when you do become pregnant, will you be plagued by worries about whether the baby will be normal or what characteristics it inherited from the donor? Will worries prevent your excitement or happiness in the pregnancy?

Couple Are you both equally interested in pregnancy created by donor sperm? Do you plan to keep the nature of the pregnancy a secret or will you tell those close to you? If you favor secrecy, why? Is it because you are ashamed of using DI or are afraid of others' reactions to it? If so, why? Do you think you should tell the child of his or her origins? If not, is it because you are afraid the child will be hurt by the information? If so, when do you think you would tell the child? What words would you use to describe it to the child? Do you think you can tell the child and still have the child feel that you love and value him or her? If not, why not? What qualities would you like of the donor? What do you want to know about him? What do you think the child would like to know about his or her genetic heritage? Will you make that information available to the child if and when the child asks? If the baby has colic, temper tantrums or any other difficult behavior will you attribute the behavior to "bad blood" from the donor? Will you be able to accept and love the child, faults and all? How do you feel about the possibility that your child may have five to 10 half-siblings in your city or region?

By discussing some of these issues, answering together some of these questions, you may be able to explore more fully your attitudes to DI and understand areas that trouble you. You may never feel perfectly comfortable with all the issues, but unless you feel more comfortable than uncomfortable, perhaps you should take more time before making a decision.

If the issues have not been worked out beforehand, the insemination cycles or pregnancy may bring the issues to the fore. Donor insemination programs report a very high dropout rate, 20 percent or more. Some dropouts occur because the woman has not become pregnant after a number of inseminations. Other couples drop out because they conceive without insemination. (This can happen if the man has a low sperm count. But if the pregnancy happens during a treatment cycle, the pregnancy would be attributed to DI rather than to the partners.) A number of couples also drop out because of depression, worry or tension between them during the treatments. Studies have shown, however, that couples who have been counselled and supported during DI have a 2 percent dropout rate.

It is better to drop out and work through the problems than to go on when you have doubts. Mahlstedt and others can tell of couples who get pregnant with DI only to come back three months later asking for an abortion because they realize they can not go through with it. The pregnancy has aroused fears, worries, tensions or unhappiness.

There have been cases in which the man signed a witnessed consent form against his inner feelings and without wholeheartedly agreeing to DI. In subsequent divorce proceedings, the man has been found responsible for paying full support for the child because his signed consent makes him the legal father, even if he is not the biological father and even if he says he really did not want the pregnancy.

Some programs recommend that couples see a psychologist or counsellor before undergoing D! to be sure that all the issues have been raised and discussed. A few programs have a prerequisite that all couples receive at least one session of counselling. All programs require both partners to sign a witnessed consent form. This is a legal document and can and will be used in a court of law if necessary.

"If you have any doubts, do not sign the consent form—it can wait," Mahlstedt tells men and women.

Positive Results

Donor insemination is not all troubles and woe that lead to strife and tension between couples; many couples are made stronger by the experience. Divorce rates among couples who have used DI are reported to be well below the national average of other couples. Many women feel that their partner's consent to the procedure is a great unselfish gift, showing real love, and love him all the more for it.

> *I knew it was hard for him and he wrestled with it for a while. But when he said yes, let's do it, I just knew he was such a marvellous man and I felt so lucky to have him.*

Barbara and Alan Hayes are an Australian couple who have been very open about their positive results with donor insemination. Alan, 38, who is azoospermic, first had deep reservations about DI, but at a support group for infertile couples he saw a DI baby for the first time and saw the parents' obvious delight. That experience changed his mind.

"We finally decided that sperm was almost undetectable and someone else was donating a small part to aid us in becoming pregnant," Alan was quoted in a special 1988 issue of *The Australian Woman's Weekly* magazine devoted to infertility. "The pregnancy and the birth was something that belonged to us and no one could take that away. For us, donor insemination was the answer."

Selecting a DI Program

Donor insemination is, essentially, simple enough to be done anywhere by anyone. A number of women have inseminated themselves, using semen from a known donor that they released at their cervix with a syringe or a turkey baster. Some have placed donor semen in a diaphragm at the mouth of their cervix at the time of their ovulation. Some family doctors or gynecologists, who do not run a full-blown DI program, do a handful of inseminations a year for the few patients who need it. In fact, a recent study of DI practices in the United States shows that 25 percent of doctors doing DI do fewer than one insemination a month.

Even though DI can be done on an ad hoc basis, under those situations there is less assurance of good donor screening and an increased risk of sexually transmitted diseases or possible genetic problems. It is, therefore, wise for couples to seek out a good DI program that has quality control, accountability and follows set guidelines for dealing with both donors and couples.

American Fertility Society Guidelines

In 1986, The American Fertility Society adopted new guidelines for semen donor insemination to act as a reference for DI programs. The main purposes of the guidelines, as described by the AFS, were to improve the selection of donors, decrease the potential hazard of passing on infectious agents such as sexually transmitted diseases (STDs) and AIDS, update techniques, and highlight areas that need further attention such as follow-up studies and monitoring of programs.

The guidelines appeared in a 15-page supplement of the Society's journal, *Fertility and Sterility*, in October 1986 and have since been endorsed by the American College of Obstetricians and Gynecologists. The American Association of Tissue Banks also has put together guidelines for sperm banks, which are similar to the AFS guidelines. The guidelines, although voluntary, are now viewed as minimal acceptable standards for programs in the United States and Canada and many programs overseas. The guidelines detail the kinds of laboratory tests that couples and donors should have, particularly to screen for genetic abnormalities, STDs and poor health in the donors. The guidelines also recommend that doctors keep permanent confidential records on the donor, including genetic work-up and non-indentifying information, and to make that information available to the couple or to the offspring if it is requested.

Originally, for the first two years, the guidelines favored the use of fresh semen over frozen semen because of the superior pregnancy rates of fresh. But in February 1988 the AFS revised the guidelines in favor of frozen semen in efforts to further lower the risk of transmission of the AIDS virus in the case of a donor who is infected but is not yet testing positive for the virus. (His semen is frozen at the time of donation and kept for at least 180 days and at the end of that time the donor will be tested again for AIDS. If he is still negative, the frozen semen will be released for use.)

The AFS guidelines are straightforward, but in 1987 an American survey found that a significant number of DI practioners did not follow them. The most surprising finding of the study was that as many as 21 percent of doctors doing DI did not screen the donors initially for AIDS antibodies. The study, conducted by investigators at the University of Wisconsin and Trinity University in San Antonio, Texas, was reported at the 1988 AFS annual meeting. It sent questionnaires to 460 doctors randomly selected from a list of 1625 known to practice DI, of whom 268 replied. The study shows that 9 percent of doctors surveyed did not even determine the sex habits of their donors. The researchers concluded that although more programs were using frozen semen, "unfortunately there is still a small group of physicians who fail to adequately screen potential donors as well as a sizable group who do not keep creditable records."

Self-Protection

Couples can be their own best advocates when it comes to selecting a DI program, says Dr. Howard Jones, a leading American infertility specialist who pioneered in vitro fertilization in the United States and is often a spokesman for the AFS. Jones said, unlike in vitro fertilization in which it can be difficult for couples to determine the standards of a particular clinic or interpret success rates, donor insemination enables couples to ask specific questions and get specific answers.

"It's perfectly clear, either you freeze sperm and you test them or you don't. It's A, B, C," Jones said at the 1988 AFS meeting. He said couples having donor insemination should ask a clinic how long a donor's sperm has been quarantined and what the person has been tested for. "Consumerism can play a role because the guidelines, with respect to cryopreservation (freezing), for instance, are pretty clear, and the questions are not difficult to interpret."

Couples can draw up their own list of questions that are important, but the following are questions, based on the AFS guidelines, that couples might want to ask a DI program before undertaking inseminations.

1. Are donors' sexual habits screened?
2. Are donors tested for AIDs antibodies and all other STDs?
3. Are donors screened for other infectious diseases such as hepatitis?
4. Are detailed family genetic histories taken?
5. Is semen frozen for at least 60 to 90 days (180 recommended by AFS) at which time the donor is retested for AIDS and the semen then released?
6. Is there a limit to the number of offspring one donor can sire? (The AFS recommends 10 offspring per donor as the maximum for most populations, but the rate is based on population density. In areas of low population density or if the donor belongs to a cohesive ethnic group, the rate should be lower to minimize the chance of half-siblings meeting and marrying.)
7. Are permanent records kept on the donor and the couple?
8. Will non-identifying information on the donor be released to any adult offspring on request?

9. In the unlikely situation that one offspring should meet and wish to enter into a relationship with another DI offspring from the same program, will they be able to learn from the program's records whether they had the same donor father?

There have been two known cases in the United States of couples meeting by chance and almost marrying until they found they were half-brother and sister by DI. Although geneticists say the chance of two offspring meeting and marrying is very rare, some social biologists believe that the chance is greater than that which could be expected for a random meeting of unrelated adults. Like attracts like, the social biologist theory says. For example, in a university setting of 10,000 students, a donor offspring might notice another student who bore a strong resemblance to him- or herself more than he or she might notice a dissimilar student. Having noticed each other, been attracted to each other, there is a greater likelihood that they would meet, social biologists say.

Drawbacks of Frozen Semen

Although semen that has been frozen and quarantined for at least three months can reduce the risk of passing on AIDS, it also reduces the chance of getting pregnant in any one cycle. Freezing lowers the quality of semen. When the sample is thawed it is not as good as when it was fresh. Motility, concentration of live sperm and sperm shape all suffer from freezing. Even the quality of the best sperm sample is impaired. The result is that pregnancy rates for frozen semen are significantly less than those of fresh. Studies have reported a range of 17- to 35-percent-pregnancy rate for the first cycle of fresh compared with a range of 3.4- to 14-percent rate for frozen. Researchers hope that by improving techniques of sperm freezing the differences will be reduced, but until techniques are improved, when frozen sperm is used women will have to undergo, on average, more inseminations for a longer period—maybe a year or longer—for the same chance of pregnancy. There is some suggestion that programs that freeze semen themselves have better sperm quality after thaw than programs that rely on sperm banks.

Another drawback of frozen semen is that although it reduces the risk of sexual transmitted diseases and infection, it does not eliminate the risk completely. No DI program can guarantee 100 percent that infection will not be transmitted by semen, fresh or frozen. This fact means that some doctors have been reluctant to stop using fresh semen, particularly when they feel they have good, healthy, low-risk donors, because of fresh semen's superior ability to get women pregnant in a shorter period of time at less expense. Nevertheless, all American organizations, including the Centre for Disease Control, the Food and Drug Administration, the American Fertility Society and the American College of Obstetrics and Gynecology, recommend semen be frozen until donors can be retested. One sperm bank in the United States reported in 1987 that a donor who had previously tested negatively for AIDS was found to have tested positively at his retest, showing that the recommendations for frozen sperm have merit.

Fear of AIDS

The concern about AIDS and donor semen first became an issue in Australia in 1984 when eight women were exposed to a donor who carried the AIDS virus. Four of the women later developed AIDS antibodies. There has been no reported case of any woman yet developing AIDS from DI, but doctors are concerned enough about that possibility that strict screening and the use of frozen semen are seen as being necessary to reduce the risks.

Some women undergoing DI, even if precautions have been taken, become extremely fearful about getting AIDS from the inseminations.

> *After my second insemination I became preoccupied with the thought that I would get AIDS from the inseminations. It was a real, almost paralyzing fear. I phoned the clinic twice and both times they told me their donors were screened and I didn't need to worry. But I still was really worried. It was crazy but I didn't relax until I had an antibody test. Even though it was negative, I haven't yet been able to go back to the inseminations. The fear is still there.*

As long as the program screens donors for personal habits (not accepting homosexuals or drug users), quarantining frozen semen and testing for AIDS antibodies, the risk of a woman getting AIDS through DI is extremely remote, if not impossible. Studies have found that the incidence of AIDS antibodies among donors is negligible. Of 1009 potential donors screened during 1987 by the national sperm bank XYTEX Corp., not one was found to have AIDS antibodies, even after sperm quarantine and donor retesting a few months later. The study, reported at the 1988 AFS meeting, meant that there was a zero rate of AIDS antibodies among their donors. That rate is on par with the incidence of AIDS antibodies among blood donors to the Red Cross (0.012 percent) and below the incidence found in applicants to the United States military (0.15 percent), the sperm bank reported. The study concluded that donor sperm from the national sperm bank presented an acceptable risk for women.

The Procedure

When a couple first decides to undergo DI, the AFS guidelines recommend that both the man and woman undergo medical evaluation. Some couples will already have been through an extensive infertility work-up and in that case their charts are reviewed and a few tests may be reordered. If the couple has not had a complete work-up, particularly the man, such a work-up may be suggested. The man is also usually tested for sexually transmitted diseases and for AIDS antibodies. This is to avoid having him unknowingly pass an infection to his wife, which might be blamed on the donor.

The woman usually has a complete medical and reproductive history taken and a complete physical examination. She is usually tested for vaginal or cervical infections, sexually transmitted diseases, AIDS antibodies and, most doctors recommend, rubella antibodies to ensure that she has already had

German measles to avoid the complications that disease can cause during pregnancy. (If she has not had German measles, she is usually vaccinated for it before pregnancy.) If a complete infertility work-up has already been done, she usually does not need hormone tests, tests of ovulation or tests to ensure open tubes. But if the tests have not been done and there is suspicion of infertility, she will be further investigated.

During the first meeting the doctor usually discusses what physical characteristics couples want from the donor—the color of hair and eyes, the physical build, curly or straight hair, and the genetic lineage. The doctor may allow couples to choose from a list, usually provided by a national sperm bank, or the doctor may pick the donor himself based on the couple's specifications.

Timing Ovulation

Proper timing of the insemination, just before ovulation, is extremely important if the woman is to conceive. The woman's basal body temperature graphs and cervical mucus changes are the most common ways for doctors to time the inseminations, although luteinizing hormone surges (see Chapter 3) and ultrasound are also routinely used. Home ovulation (LH) detection kits are also used frequently and can be a help for the woman to know when she is ovulating. The woman should keep track of her cycles and make an appointment a few days before ovulation is expected. At that time, the doctor assesses her cervical mucus and cervical opening. Some doctors may also assess the ovaries for a developing follicle using ultrasound. If it appears that she is on the verge of ovulation, the doctor may do an insemination at that time or tell the woman to come back one or two days later. Some women may have only one insemination in a given cycle, but more often two or three inseminations are done, one every day or every other day, until the temperature on the BBT chart has unmistakably risen.

The actual technique of insemination has changed little in the 30 years of its use. The woman lies on the examining table as she does for a pelvic examination. A speculum is inserted into her vagina and the cervix is usually wiped clean with a cotton swab. The frozen semen will already have been thawed. If it was frozen in straws, the straws may be loaded into a special "gun" and ejected into the intracervical canal. The semen may also be injected into the cervical canal through thin polyethylene tubing or a blunt needle. Most of the sperm will go into the cervical canal but some will be also deposited around the outside of the cervix. Usually a cervical cap or non-absorbant sponge is placed at the cervix to keep the sperm in place. The woman usually lies on the examining table for 15 to 20 minutes to help the sperm in their progress to the tubes. About six to eight hours after insemination, the woman can remove the cap or sponge and wash it so it is ready for reuse.

Sometimes doctors teach a woman or her partner how to do the inseminations so they can be done at home. An increasing number of DI programs encourage (or at least do not discourage) partners to be present when the insemination is done. This can help them feel more a part of the pregnancy.

Once is Not Enough

Among women going through DI, there is the common belief, initially, that one insemination is all it takes to start a pregnancy. It can be discouraging to learn that, in fact, it usually takes a number of inseminations over a number of months for conception to take place. Reports state that usually after six months of insemination about 60 percent of the women will have become pregnant. That rate may become lower with the use of frozen semen and many more months of insemination may be required to get the same percentage of women pregnant. Doctors have recommended that if a pregnancy has not occurred after three to six months with fresh semen the woman should be investigated to rule out fallopian tube problems. The doctor usually schedules a hysterosalpingogram. The doctor may also confirm that ovulation is taking place, either by serum progesterone measurements or endometrial biopsy.

Some women undergo inseminations for 24 months or longer, a personal choice that other women might not be able to endure. The expense may also prohibit some couples from continuing. In some countries, the cost of DI is covered by health insurance, but in other countries couples must pay for each insemination. In Canada and the United States, for example, the cost for each insemination may be between $50 to $150.

If, after one year of inseminations you have still not become pregnant you might want to have further fertility tests or seek a second opinion to determine whether you have been receiving good quality sperm, and that the inseminations have been properly timed. The quality of sperm from commercial sperm banks can also vary greatly so couples might want to ask their doctor to check the quality of semen.

Common Reactions

Women vary in their reactions to the experience of insemination, but some reactions are common: fantasies about the donor; worry that the doctor mixed the specimen and the "wrong baby" will grow; depersonalization of the experience so that it is "just like getting blood." The following are some women's comments about how they felt after DI.

> *I kept thinking about this wonderful man who was donating his sperm. I pictured him as being really handsome and smart. I felt like I was having an affair with him. I felt a little guilty about it but it also made me feel good.*
>
> *I thought as little about the donor as possible—it was just a medical thing, like getting an injection of blood. It was no big deal.*
>
> *After the insemination for a couple of days I'd be walking around chanting under my breath "go sperm go" cheering them on.*
>
> *I just kept telling myself it was like getting a shot or a medical treatment. The only hard part was removing the cap and washing it. That is when it hit me that it was some other man's semen.*

Counsellors Patricia Mahlstedt and Judith Bernstein say that if the couple has worked through their feeling towards DI beforehand, their attitude towards the donors and the inseminations will be positive at the time of inseminations. Their experience of pregnancy will also tend to be more positive. During pregnancy, however, it is common to oscillate between excitement and fear that something may go wrong—all women during pregnancy have some worry that the baby will be abnormal.

> *I got pregnant after the second insemination and for the first few months everything was great. Then as my pregnancy went on, I got really afraid. I kept becoming really worried that the doctor might have made a mistake and I would have a child of a different race growing inside me or a deformed creature. I didn't relax, really, until I saw my daughter.*

The birth of the baby will usually make even the most worried parents finally relax.

Donors

Who They Are

Who donates sperm so that others can become pregnant? In the past, it was predominantly medical students, health professionals or other men in contact with the medical profession. They usually had been recruited, by word of mouth, or by the doctor running the DI program. It still is common for a representative of the DI program to give a talk to first-year medical students each year to try to bring a few new donors into the program. Although medical professionals and students at universities with medical schools still are well-represented in donors' ranks, the profile is changing so that men of more diverse backgrounds are also becoming donors.

In general, all sperm donors, whether recruited by local programs or national sperm banks, are under age 40 (although some programs accept up to age 45) with good health and average to above-average intelligence.

The use of frozen sperm in recent years has resulted in donor shortages as it requires more semen to achieve a pregnancy. The diversification of donors away from medical students is a result of broader-based advertising to address those donor shortages. In Melbourne, Australia, for example, the local sperm bank, operated from one of the infertility programs, regularly places ads on the sports pages of the city's daily newspapers. The ad attracts 50 or more new inquiries each time, and from that, a handful eventually pass all the screening to become donors.

Some DI programs, however, eschew general advertising because they believe it may attract men of questionable motives. Instead, many programs try to extend the reach of word-of-mouth by selecting places to meet men who might be open to the idea of becoming a donor. In an article on artificial insemination in the medical text, *Progress in Infertility*, the Belgian authors recommend that programs seek donors from new fathers in maternity wards, among husbands of successfully treated infertile women or among men of proven fertility who are planning to undergo a vasectomy. Word of mouth among donors is also used, encouraging donors to tell their friends about donation and to bring them in.

In most countries, single and married donors are equally acceptable, but France has a regulation that all donors be married men with at least one child and that their wives also sign a consent form showing their approval for the procedure. In France, doctors in the national DI programs have tried to promote the attitude that a sperm donation is "the gift of a happy couple to a less lucky one." The donors have often been brought into the program by infertile couples undergoing DI. French couples face at least a year's wait for insemination but if they recruit a donor, usually a friend, their wait can be shortened. (The donor does not donate to them; rather, his sperm goes to another couple higher on the list.)

Other countries also encourage men who are married with proven fertility to become donors, but have not gone so far as to make it a requirement. Many programs have a consent form to be signed by the wife or partner of a donor to be sure she is aware of the man's donations.

Television specials or newspaper reports on the plight of infertile couples often help to attract new donors.

A handful of surveys have been done to assess the type of men who become sperm donors. Belgian researcher P. Nijs and colleagues studied the psychological and medical aspects of 27 sperm donors and reported their findings in 1979 at a Paris symposium devoted to artificial insemination. The majority of Nijs's subjects were unmarried, from large families who had been motivated to donate because they personally knew someone going through infertility problems. All the donors strongly believed in anonymity and did not want, at any time, to be identified to their offspring.

Melbourne sociologist, Renata Rowlands, surveyed 67 donors for her 1983 study and, according to author Noble, found that their occupations ranged from gardener to computer analyst and their average age was 31. Most were middle class; one-third were married; and one-third had a university degree. The donors had two attitudes toward the infertile couples: 44 percent described them as "pathetic, lonely, desperate," while 33 percent called them "loving, strong, courageous."

Another Australian study, conducted by New South Wales social workers Julia Paul and Eva Durna, sent questionnaires to 50 sperm donors of the Royal North Shore Women's Hospital DI program in Sydney. About 35 replied. Their survey found that the majority were professional men with university degrees, in their mid-thirties who already had a wife and a family. Most had told their wives about their sperm donations and the majority of wives were happy with the decision. All the men (100 percent) said their motivation for donating was to help infertile couples have a baby, although 26 percent also added "other" motivation, most commonly the desire to "propagate my genes" or "contribute my family's genetic heritage." None of the donors reported that financial reasons were behind their donations, although in most Australian states it is now illegal to pay donors except for reasonable expenses incurred.

Although other studies have shown that donors wanted to remain anonymous and did not want to know anything about the outcome, the majority of NSW donors expressed the desire for information about the couples who received their sperm and also desired to be told if any pregnancies resulted. In a finding that was a surprise to the researchers and to others, the majority of donors (68 percent) not only said they felt non-identifying information should be made available to the couple and child, a full 59 percent said they had no objection if *identifying* information was made available and if offspring were to contact them. A full 70 percent felt that identifying information linking donor to offspring should be kept at the hospital and made available in the case of a medical emergency. Most of the donors, however, said it was up to the parents to decide whether the child should be told of his or her conception, although 31 percent felt the child should know.

Donors' Motivations

Why do men donate their sperm? The reasons vary, but the most common ones are these.

1. Primarily, an altruistic desire to help infertile couples, often because they know friends or family who have had trouble conceiving.
2. To gratify their ego, knowing their genes are desired and will be propagated. They will be able to produce a number of offspring with no strings attached.
3. To earn an extra $25 to $100 on a regular basis from donating their ejaculate to the program.

Studies have shown that all three motivations may play a major or a minor role at the same time. However most donors say financial reward is not a prime motivation, although it does cover expenses or the time required for the donation.

Toronto sociologist Rona Achilles interviewed 13 donors in the mid-1980s for her Ph.D. thesis on the social and cultural importance of biological relatedness in families with regard to donor insemination. Achilles's donors ranged in age from their twenties to early thirties and she found a variety of motivations behind their reasons to donate. She concluded that the motivation could not be brought down to a single unifying factor such as altruism or financial gain or a desire to populate the world—although those factors did play lesser or greater roles in each donor. Some of her subjects even expressed a sexual motive; they got sexual satisfaction knowing that their sperm was impregnating unknown women. One donor, Robert, described his feeling of a "power trip" to think his semen "was going into some strange woman" and "to get paid to jerk off."

Achilles's profiles of donors, particularly Robert, are more disturbing because it brings to light some donor's egotistical and less-than-altruistic motives. One donor jokingly told Achilles that he'd donate every week if he could: "God, I could start my own country." Robert told Achilles that when the doctor asked his motivation for donation, "I told him that I knew I wasn't going to get married for a while and that if I could help out some people who were having trouble, I wouldn't mind . . . but that is what I thought he wanted to hear."

Bernstein says that trained staff are usually able to weed out donors whose motives are questionable. Not all DI programs do personality screening of donors, but most report that the donors have a healthy sense of ego, an outgoing personality and are socially well-adjusted. Larry, 40, profiled in the Australian *Women's Weekly*, is perhaps typical of sperm donors in some respects. Divorced, and without children of his own, he had read an article in a magazine about the need for donors. He said it struck a cord with him, partly because in his marriage there had been fertility problems and his sperm count had been low, possibly because of stress and alcohol. He donated partly to confirm his own fertility and to help other infertile couples. "To me donating is just an act, there and then. I don't feel any emotion about it. When I'm told a pregnancy has occurred I suppose I am vaguely curious about the child, but it doesn't linger in the mind. It's just a fleeting thought. I am glad to know it has benefited someone and done some good, but for me it's pretty cut and dried. I just turn off."

Donor Screening

An increasing number of programs require donors to fill out four or five pages of medical and family history, including details of any incidence of infections, diseases or abnormalities in the donor or his family. Some programs, responding to the demand of couples undergoing the procedure, also ask for social information such as the donor's hobbies, special abilities and skills, and personality descriptions. Most programs do not accept donors who were adopted or any other men who, for whatever reason, do not know their family genetic history. The programs rely on donors truthfully filling out the questionnaire. It is practically impossible for the doctor to screen out donors who choose to lie, for example, about drug or sexual habits.

Some programs conduct laboratory genetic analysis (karyotyping) of donors, which arranges donors' chromosomes in descending order of size to help illuminate possible genetic problems. However, karyotypes are very expensive and the information is not always helpful, doctors say, as karyotypes can not pinpoint most genetic diseases that could be passed along. The American Fertility Society guidelines say karyotypes are "not thought to be an absolute requirement" as long as the recruiting doctor takes a proper family history and pays attention to possible genetic "hazards" within ethnic groups, such as cystic fibrosis in Caucasians, sickle-cell anemia in blacks, thalessemia in Mediterraneans and Tay-Sachs disease in Ashkenazi Jews. (There are laboratory tests for carriers of Tay-Sachs and sickle-cell anemia, but as yet no test for carriers of cystic fibrosis.) National sperm banks in the United States, which provide frozen sperm for a number of programs, routinely conduct karyotypes.

The AFS guidelines say that any history of developmental malformations, recessive chromosome-linked diseases or disease believed to have a genetic component in the donor or his family are cause to reject him as a donor. Development malformations include cleft lip or cleft palate, spina bifida, congenital heart malformations, congenital hip dislocation, clubfoot and/or genital tract malformations. A family history of hemophilia, high cholesterol, the "Elephant Man disease," neurofibromatosis or albinism indicates the donor might carry a gene for such disorders and makes him unacceptable. Some diseases are thought to have a major genetic component such as asthma, juvenile diabetes, rheumatic arthritis, high blood pressure and epilepsy and these, too, in the donor's history or in his close family render him unacceptable.

Screening also extends to the donor's health habits. He is asked how much he drinks, if he smokes or has tried any soft or hard drugs or if he has had any recent illnesses. He is asked if he has had any sexually transmitted infections such as herpes, gonorrhea or chlamydia, or any inflammations in his genitals. To screen out donors at higher risk for exposure to AIDS, the questionnaire asks if the donor has had any homosexual encounters since 1978, received a blood transfusion since 1978 or been in any situation that the donor feels might have put him at risk for AIDS.

After filling out the questionnaire, the donor is usually given a complete physical examination and blood tests, although not all doctors do this if the donor can provide records of an examination in the last year. Some doctors, however, say that physical examinations of all donors before they are accepted into the program should be mandatory. Couples may want to ask if all donors have been examined regardless of whether they have a recent medical report.

Blood tests are usually taken to test for syphilis, hepatitis and cytomegalovirus (CMV). Some doctors say that a positive test result for CMV antibodies will not necessarily disqualify a donor because 50 percent of the population is positive. If donors who have CMV were disqualified not enough donors would be available. Rather, the doctors say donors with CMV antibodies should be matched with recipients who test positive for CMV. The donor's semen is analyzed to make sure it has good to excellent count, shape and motility. The semen should also be cultured for STDs. When the donor is accepted into the program his health and semen may be periodically checked. Most programs reevaluate donors if they change partners or suffer an illness.

Since different programs have different questionnaires for donors, couples might wish to ask for a blank copy of the questionnaire to find out what kind of questions the donor must answer. A number of programs ask donors to fill out questions of a more personal nature, but which are still non-identifying.

"I think it is positive to have a sheet about the donor, non-identifying information that talks about himself as a person, what he is like, why he wanted to be a donor, what his hopes are for the child," psychologist Mahlstedt said. "This enables DI offspring, as adults, to have a feeling of wholeness."

Genius Sperm Banks

There are a few private sperm banks in the United States that actively seek out donors with high intelligence, proven scientific career or athletic ability, and otherwise "desirable characteristics." The most famous of these "genius" sperm banks is the Repository for Germinal Choice in Escondido, California. It was founded in 1980 by Dr. Robert Graham, an optometrist who developed the shatter-proof eyeglass. With the millions earned from his invention, Graham had the goal of increasing the number of intelligent children born in the world by providing a sperm bank of Nobel Prize winners for women and infertile couples of proven intelligence and character. Graham had long been advocating that intelligent people should have more children to "upgrade society." In his 1975 book *The Future of Man*, Graham made numerous comments such as "only man is so ignorant as to allow his worst animals to breed" and that "selective breeding" would "stop the pollution of the gene pool with non-producers." In 1980, in an interview with the *San Francisco Examiner*, Graham denied having similar genetic goals to Adolf Hitler and said: "I'm not thinking in terms of a super-race—only of ensuring a few more creative, intelligent human beings who otherwise would not have been born."

Donors for the repository have been hand-picked by Graham's staff and convinced to donate. The recruiting staff first sent a note to the accomplished man saying something like "Congratulations, you've been chosen." Then the recruiter later drops by the man's office or lab to complete the sale. Among the recruited donors was Nobel Prize winner William Shockley (who won the 1956 Nobel prize for physics for his role in inventing the transistor) who had been outspoken about his belief of the genetic inferiority of blacks. His vocal support of the sperm bank fueled criticism of the eugenic (perfect genes) goals of the bank and criticism of those couples who used it for "shopping" for the babies.

Now people no longer picket outside the repository's doors, but many still find the attitude behind the sperm bank offensive. As of the end of 1988, about 60 babies had been born in the eight years. Obviously, infertile couples have not been beating a path in large numbers to Graham's doors. A few of Graham's recruiters left the organization to start their own sperm banks and other small, elitist banks have also started. Couples can get a catalog that describes the donors by color or numbers and lists medical history, age, race, religion, national origin, profession, coloring, IQ, personality, skills and interests. Graham subsidizes the cost of running the bank with his millions, and couples pay a marginal fee, in line with the cost of inseminations charged by standard banks.

A few of the repository's parents and offspring have become world-famous through the media, most notably, single mother Afton Blake and her flaxen-haired son Doron, born in 1982 from donor #28, a professor of computer science who liked music, swimming, skiing and hiking. Media reports depict Doron as unquestionably a bright, intellectually advanced child. But even his mother admits it is difficult to determine how much of his abilities come from his genetic background and how much from the lavish, loving and undivided attention his mother gives him; she says she "immerses" herself with Doron.

Studies have shown that a high IQ is not a guarantee of success. A 1987 report about the repository in the *Los Angeles Times Magazine* quoted a Stanford University study started in 1921 that has followed 1500 children with IQs over 135 and found that their degree of achievement related more to their hard work and desire to succeed than it did to their intelligence rating. Other studies have shown that children born of intelligent parents who were adopted were more apt to be intelligent if they were placed in a supportive, nuturing intelligent family rather than in a less nuturing, less intelligent family. The environment of the child is as important as his or her genetic material.

Professionals have great concern about the eugenic goals of genius sperm banks, but just as important are concerns for the welfare of the individual children born of parents who "shop" for genius sperm. How good is the family environment for the child whose parents use the banks? It is feared that some of the parents may make unrealistically high demands of the child. The child will be expected to perform and live up to his or her genius genes. In an unfortunate example, another of the bank's famous, or in this case infamous, users was a Chicago woman who was found to have previously lost custody of two non-sperm-bank children for child abuse—abuse based, according to media reports, on her excessive demands for perfection of her children.

The desire for parents to choose the best donor possible is understandable and commendable. But health professionals recommend that parents temper that desire with a little common sense.

"I think, unfortunately, that a lot of parents come into DI thinking that it is second best," says nurse specialist Judith Bernstein. "They think, 'if we can't have a baby between the two of us then we want to be assured of getting things we might not otherwise get—we want to make sure the father is intelligent, musical, athletic, cream of the crop.' They are looking for more control than they otherwise might have. But if they were having a child between the two of them they would have to settle for the normal biological roulette. These couples have unrealistic expectations. You can't be assured that a biological child will be bright or athletic, you just have to accept the child the way it is."

Legalities

The legal relationship between the donor, the couple and the child has been of concern to many since the early years when DI first began to be used routinely. The legal questions were many. Could DI offspring claim to be an heir to the donor's estate? Could the husband of a wife who used DI to conceive a child be sued for child support in the event of the marriage break-up, even though he was not the child's genetic father? Could the donor petition for visiting rights to his genetic child? Could the mother sue for child support from the donor because he was the genetic father?

The legal permutations and considerations could be mind boggling. Because of the potential confusion, many countries and states have adopted legislation that spells out the rights and responsibilities of all parties. In the United States, 30 states have enacted laws covering the legal aspects of donor insemination.

Likewise, 15 European countries, as well as most Australian states, have legislation concerning DI relationships. Britain finally put a law in place covering DI in April of 1988. Until that time a DI child was effectively illegitimate in the courts, which encouraged couples to lie about the conception. In Canada two regions, Quebec and Yukon, have laws clarifying the arrangement.

In general, all the statutes confirm the following: If the husband or partner has signed the consent papers, the DI child is considered his legal offspring for purposes of legitimacy, inheritance and child support The donor, in signing his consent forms, gives up all legal rights and responsibilities to the child. He has no rights of visitation nor can he be sued for support or inheritance. These statutes, which protect all parties, seem to be the reason many donors are no longer worried about their identity being released to the child because they no longer will be seen as being responsible.

In places where DI laws are not in force, many people express concern over the uncertainty of the legal relationships. Critics say the situation encourages secrecy and poor medical records about the donor. Others, however, say legislation is not necessary because the participants enter into a contract by signing consent papers.

In its 1988 report on infertility to the U.S. Congress, the Office of Technology Assessment said that in states without laws, it is rightly assumed that contractual law will rule the arrangement. That means if the donor, recipient and recipient's husband have all signed consent papers specifying the rights and obligations of each party, those consents will hold up in court, despite not having state legislation. But the OTA report said that even with consent forms the outcome "would depend on court interpretation and future legislation."

The OTA report also brought up the point that even in states that did have a statute, if specific conditions set out by legislation were not met, the legal arrangement might be contested. For example, the OTA report says 21 of the 30 states with donor legislation rule that the offspring are legitimate children of the consenting husband, providing the insemination is done by "a licensed physician," "a certified medical doctor" or "person duly authorized to practice medicine." If the insemination is done by a nurse, a technician, or, as many couples are tending to do more often, the husband or lover, the OTA reports says the legislation might not be valid in an individual case. This sort of loophole might be successfully used by a formerly consenting husband trying to get out of paying child support in a subsequent divorce trial. In one case in the United States, the OTA reported, a donor successfully sued and won visitation rights to the child because the insemination was not supervised by a physician. (The case was complicated by the fact the mother was unmarried and living with another woman and the donor was a friend).

Couples undergoing DI should learn the specific legal situation in the region where they live before undergoing DI. Some groups, although small in numbers, are petitioning governments to clear up ambiguities regarding the legal relationship in donor arrangements.

Outcome of DI

The photographs of newborn or toddling DI babies on the bulletin boards of DI programs or on the desks of DI staff attest to the fact that DI children are as miraculous and beautiful as any child.

Unlike some other forms of infertility treatment, the birth outcomes in DI mirror those found in couples of the same age who get pregnant the standard way. Miscarriages occur at the same rate as in couples of the same age and health in the general population. Twins or multiple births are no more or less frequent. Birth defects occur at a rate of about 2 percent, which is also the rate found in the general population.

Studies have shown that many couples return to have DI for a second or third child, another indicator that the family has responded well to the birth.

As for the physical and mental development of DI children, all reports have been very positive and most have found that DI children are more advanced as a group than other children of the same age. Studies have shown that DI children tend to reach milestones, such as walking and talking, sooner than other children. As they develop, the children appear to maintain above-average speech and motor skills. Researchers say these characteristics may relate to the donated genes but are probably more a function of the fact that the children are loved, wanted and stimulated by their parents.

A study of 30 couples in France in the 1970s by Christine Manual and J.C. Czyba, has reported that the parents all tend to have a "deep emotional investment in the child." In a slightly less positive note, the researchers said this deep investment, in their opinion, caused some mothers to be "overly anxious" about the child and some fathers to be "overly involved" with the child and have "very maternal behavior patterns." The authors did not define what they meant by those terms.

Doctors reporting at the 1979 symposium on artificial insemination in Paris anecdotally reported couples coming back to the clinic for a doctor-requested follow-up with the child "held proudly in the father's arms." The French researchers, Gabriele Semenov and colleagues, reported that the "fathers appeared to be especially fulfilled. The birth had been intensely experienced by them and those who had been present stressed the happiness they felt. For them, the child's birth had clearly played a restorative role." The researchers said, however, that the couples held secrecy about the conception as being very important. The researchers said they wondered how this might affect the child's psychological development.

Secrecy

Until recently, more than 90 percent of couples kept donor insemination a closely guarded secret. They told no one, not their own parents or closest friends, and certainly not the child. Most pretended that the child was their natural offspring. Doctors supported and promoted this practice by keeping minimal records on the donor and by counselling that secrecy was in the best interest of all concerned.

"There is no benefit and considerable risk to informing friends, relatives, ministers, and offspring of the procedure," stated a 1980 report by the American Fertility Society Ad Hoc Committee of Artificial Insemination. The committee also stated that couples need not tell any other physicians who looked after the mother or the child that donor insemination had been used. In short, there was no reason to tell.

But is secrecy really in the family's best interest? No one honestly knows. The secrecy itself has made it almost impossible for doctors to do long-term follow-up studies of families who used DI. Apart from sending a photo of the newborn baby or coming back for one follow-up visit, DI families seem to want to put the whole thing behind them. When contacted, many DI families say "we don't want to talk about it, this never happened."

Toronto sociologist Rona Achilles tried to contact men and women who had used DI, their offspring and donors for her doctoral thesis on the impact of donor insemination and the importance of genetic relationship in families. She advertised widely on television, and printed write-ups in newspaper columns. Her Canada-wide efforts yielded 50 people: 19 DI mothers, 13 donors, five adult offspring and only three husbands of DI mothers. Two of the husbands had had vasectomies as the reason for their infertility, perhaps explaining their willingness to talk. Only one man was infertile without choice. Achilles's efforts showed that despite the thousands of people who have been involved with DI in Canada, very few were willing to talk about it.

Other researchers have had the same experience—they can not get people to open up. Researchers can not evaluate the long-term effects or whether secrecy is better than openness, because few will talk about their experiences. Couples who are considering DI often express the wish to talk to other couples who have gone through it, just so they can find out how they felt.

"I want to talk to families who actually have children about how they feel now and what they might do differently," said one woman contemplating the process. "I just want to hear from their mouths what the experience was like, how it has worked out. I asked around at the fertility support group but I still haven't come across anybody who will talk to me."

Does that mean the vast "silent" majority of couples who experienced DI are prefectly happy with their decision and the secrecy they have chosen?

All reports seem to indicate that the marriages of DI couples are more resilient than those of the average North American couple. American specialist Dr. S.J. Berhman and others have said that among their patients the divorce rate is almost non-existent in couples who undergo DI. Nurse specialist Bernstein has found the same thing. "My impression is that the marriages, by and large, are not just okay, but really strong." Bernstein says she has seen only one couple divorce in 10 years of her practice. The feeling on the part of physicians is that couples are brought together by the DI experience.

Author Elizabeth Noble surmises that some of those marriages may be held together by the bond of secrecy. "Is the secret the couple hides so powerful they will tolerate any marital situation rather than risk exposure?" she asks. Bernstein, too, is also troubled by what may lie beneath the surface. "We don't know if that huge silent majority is really happy or just afraid to open their mouths. Secrets can bind people together in a really dysfunctional way." Unfortunately, the couples who tend to talk openly about the DI experience are more often those who are separated or divorced: this can skew perceptions of the DI experience.

An increasing number of professionals, and many couples themselves, believe that the secrecy surrounding the procedure could be detrimental to the couple's relationship and to the family. The secret can be corrosive and can isolate the parents from the support of family and friends.

"What does secrecy imply? Shame, guilt, lack of trust, lack of openness," psychologist Mahlstedt said. "We all know that these things in terms of relationships can be poisonous. In marriage and family being able to be open is what it is all about."

It is the couple's ultimate decision, of course, whether they choose to keep their DI conception a secret or be open about it. Some couples appear to have no problem putting the details of the child's conception out of their minds and ignoring it for the rest of their lives. Other couples have a great deal of difficulty keeping the secret.

Secrecy and the Child

Before any couple makes the decision about whether or not to tell, they must take into account the welfare of one more person: the child.

Keeping the secret might be easier if only the man and woman were involved. But DI creates a new, unique individual. Parents can often have a hard time imagining that the child will grow up. They think in terms of protecting "the child" from the secret. But the child becomes an adolescent and the adolescent a young adult. Before long the "child" is a grown man or woman with a life of his or her own and usually a family and children, too.

Some couples undergoing DI have no problem with the thought that their child may believe he or she is genetically related to the man. "What difference does it make?" said one woman going through DI. "If you didn't tell the child they probably would never find out. But if you did tell them they might feel like they were an abnormality, it might make a great deal of difference."

Couples naturally want their child to feel loved and accepted. The reasons most couples give for not telling the child is that they don't want them to be singled out for being different, teased in the schoolyard, treated as somehow alien at family reunions or by narrow-minded relatives. Parents are also afraid the child may reject them, love them less, or search for the natural father. The parents want to protect their child and themselves from any possible negative outcome that telling about DI might have. So the attitude develops: "What the child doesn't know won't harm her."

British authors Robert and Elizabeth Snowdon, who conducted interviews with 70 DI families for their book *A Gift of a Child* (1984), found that those fears and attitudes were common among DI parents; but they also found the fears were groundless. Of the couples who did tell their children, there was no backlash, stigmatization nor rejection. In fact, the children seemed to respect their parents for their decisions, particularly the decision to tell them, the authors said. The children "were enjoying life and happy to be alive and they realized they owed their existence to DI. They were pleased to know that their parents had wanted a child so badly and they were the child who had fulfilled their wishes." The Snowdens said that by telling the child, the family seemed to have been strengthened. Not telling the child, the Snowdens concluded, was "somehow denying the child respect."

Noble and others say that children have a way of sensing there is something being held back, some huge secret involving them. The secret can alter family relationships and the way the parents interact with the child and deal with the child's questions and actions.

Shirley Pratton, a Nanaimo, B.C., woman who for the first three years of her DI child's life held the secret tightly with her husband, described one such interaction this way.

> *When we were keeping it a secret, pretending that my husband was her biological father, I found myself cringing inside any time her aunts, uncles and grandparents on his side were mentioned. I couldn't talk about them to her because I thought, they're not really her aunts and uncles. But when we decided that we would tell her, everything changed. I could talk about her relatives with her and feel that they really were her relatives. I wasn't keeping anything back from her.*

Pratton and her husband, now separated, have started a society dedicated to fostering openness about donor insemination, and to keeping complete donor records and nonidentifying medical information. Called New Reproductive Alternatives, the organization has been lobbying for changes in legislation and attitudes towards DI that they feel would protect all parties in the DI procedure.

Secrets, as well as hovering subliminally below the surface, also have a nasty habit of getting out, particularly during times when the secret-holders are angry, disappointed or simply petulant. "Everybody gets angry at adolescents," says Bernstein. "Some people don't have a vested interest in keeping it a secret and so they let it out. The results can be devastating."

Candace Turner, the founder of the California organization, Donor's Offspring, discovered her origins in the way detailed by both Noble and Achilles in their writings. Turner was told by her mother's second husband in anger when she was 13. She was not on as good terms with her stepfather as she was with her "Dad," whom she thought was her genetic father. She was packing to spend the summer with him when her stepfather said, "He's no more your father than I am."

Turner describes her illusions as being shattered by a single sentence. Counsellors say that parents who fear rejection if they tell the child the truth, or who fear the child will seek his or her biological father, may find that rejection is more likely to occur because the child feels deceived and no longer trusts them. Studies have shown that children are less upset by truth than they are by feeling that they have been lied to by their own parents.

Therefore, most professionals believe that keeping DI a secret can be risky to the family relationship. It is like building a house upon sand. The relationship may stay together by luck or providence, but any shaking of the foundations and it can come crashing down.

If couples do decide in favor of keeping the conception a secret from the child, professionals stress that it must be kept a secret from everyone else, too—the child's relatives, grandparents, the couple's friends or their new partners, if the marriage should break up. Apart from the inseminating doctor, only the man and woman must be party to the secret if it is going to be kept secret; tell another person and it will come out eventually. As Benjamin Franklin said, "Three may keep a secret, if two of them are dead." Couples must be committed to carrying the secret, literally, to their graves.

How and When to Tell

Couples may be in favor of openness and know that they plan to tell the child, eventually. But when it comes to actually doing the telling, they may be uncertain how and when to tell, even whom to tell. "What am I supposed to do?" asked one woman who was unsure how far openness should go. "Say someone says, 'What a lovely baby!' or 'Doesn't she look like her Daddy!' What do I say? 'Well, you know, she's a donor baby!'"

Deciding in favor of openness does not mean the couple is obliged to broadcast it to the world. They don't need to make sure all relatives know, or tell every inquiring stranger the details of the child's conception. Openness simply means the couple is not actively hiding it.

"If someone says 'beautiful baby,' and it's a stranger or someone you're not particularly close to, just say 'thank you'," Bernstein says. "You don't need to explain. The important thing is that the people who are emotionally close to the child and the child itself know about it so that is not a surprise or a shock."

In fact, most people recommend that couples be selective in whom they tell—if they do not feel close to a particular member of the family or they think the person would not understand or accept the child, do not tell that particular person. The most important aspect of the commitment to openness is being able to tell the child in words and a manner that the couple feels comfortable with. Making the child feel good about his or her origins matters most.

Just when the couple should do it has been debated. Some people say the offspring should know by the time they are 18. Many, however, feel that is far too late as children's identity has already been formed, and telling at that time can be a traumatic assault on who they think they are. Most believe it should be before adolescence, as almost all children go through an identity crisis during that unsettling time.

The experience of adoption has shown that if children are told between three and five they are able to accept and grow with their identity. Studies have shown that adopted children who are told early in life have little problem coping with the information compared to adoptees who are told in adolescence or later in life.

But telling the child at that age does not mean sitting down once and getting it over with, professionals say. Rather it is an ongoing process.

"As the child grows and learns, her origins will mean different things," Noble says in her book. "Parents need to help the child at various stages of growth, helping her assimilate the facts into her self-image."

Noble recommends that parents do not try to give too much information too soon, but to give only what the child can absorb. "Pre-school children need only a simple answer to their questions, not an elaborate biology lesson," she says. When a child starts asking about where she came from, then that is usually a good time to start telling her, she says. Noble told her then-three-year-old daughter when she asked where she came from: "Daddy didn't have any seeds to help grow you so we borrowed seeds from X." Later, in the garden, the topic about seeds came up again so Noble elaborated on it a bit more. At other discussions she and her husband told her how much they had wanted her; at another time they told her more about the donor.

"Rather than stressing the irregularity of the conception, stress your mutual love and commitment to have this gift, this extra life brought into your family," Noble suggests.

Psychologist Patricia Mahlstedt recommends that parents avoid starting disclosures with statements like, "I'm not your parent," which are negative. Rather, the couple should start with an affirming statement, "I am your parent (or Dad or father)." Then qualify the statement, "but there are a number of ways you can become a parent.... we got you this way," and then go on to explain.

A children's book has been written for parents who choose to tell the child of his or her DI origins. It was written by Sydney social workers for the Fertility Society of Australia because parents had been expressing the desire to tell their children but were not sure how to do it. Called *How I Began: The Story of Donor Insemination* (ed. Julia Paul), the book is based on the "Where Did I Come From" books, with explicit drawings and a simplified text telling children about male and female anatomy, sperm and eggs, how babies are made and, in this case, how DI babies are made. It is designed for children from age four to eight, but the authors say that younger and older children are still likely to get something from it.

Professionals stress that the words parents use in telling the child do not matter as much as the feeling behind the words. They believe children will accept any explanation as long as their parents do.

"There isn't one set of words that is right," says Judith Bernstein. "It is just whether the parents are comfortable with the words that matters. If parents haven't resolved their feelings around it, if they imagine it as too impossible, or too difficult to tell the child, then they probably have a lot they still have to work through themselves about DI. Nothing is more revealing to me about how parents really feel about DI than how they choose to express it to the child. If they can't find a way they are comfortable with, it probably means they themselves haven't yet found a way to accept it."

○ □

CHAPTER 10
In Vitro Fertilization and the New Technologies

○-□

In Vitro Fertilization

On July 25, 1978, just before midnight, Dr. Patrick Steptoe carefully lifted a slippery, 5 lb. 12 oz. baby through the Cesarean incision in her mother's womb. The infant, aptly born so close to the witching hour, was Louise Brown, the world's first in vitro fertilization baby. In his memoirs, *A Matter of Life*, written with his colleague and fellow IVF pioneer, Robert Edwards, Steptoe described the sight this way.

> *Glorious. She was chubby, full of muscular tone. The cord was pulsating strongly although it was hooked round the left thigh. I held the head low and we sucked and cleared the mouth and throat. She took a deep breath. Then she yelled and yelled and yelled. I laid her down, all pink and furious, and saw at once that she was externally perfect and beautiful.*

Since that extraordinary moment in the operating room of the small Oldham, England, hospital, IVF births have occurred with some frequency. In the first 10 years about 12,000 children started their lives in a Petri dish.

The word "in vitro" literally means "in glass" fertilization. The techniques used by Steptoe and Edwards are primarily the same today as they were then: eggs are removed from the woman's ovary and incubated with the man's sperm in a small flat-bottomed dish. Any resulting embryo is replaced in the woman's uterus where, with luck, it will establish a pregnancy. Scientists officially call the whole procedure in vitro fertilization and embryo-replacement (or embryo-transfer)—IVF-ER, or IVF/ET—but it will be referred to here as simply IVF.

At first, IVF was used to bypass the fallopian tubes, offering countless numbers of couples, infertile because of tubal damage, a chance to conceive. Now IVF, or variations of the technique, are also being used to treat unexplained infertility, male infertility, cervical factor infertility and endometriosis. The minimal requirement is that the woman have a uterus that can carry the pregnancy and that if she did become pregnant, it would not hurt her or her baby's health.

In IVF clinics around the world, the photographs of newborns are proudly framed. Each of the children were first seen by human eyes as a two-celled embryo under a clinic's microscope. The procedure has changed infertility medicine irrevocably. No doubt the ability to fertilize an egg in the laboratory to produce a pregnancy will rank among the more astonishing accomplishments of the twentieth century.

Bittersweet Victory

The discovery of IVF has not been an unmitigated success. In some aspects it has been a Pandora's box that, once opened, has let loose a host of other issues the infertile couple and society must wrestle with.

First, for the individual couple, IVF adds one more medical treatment they must endure in their quest for a baby—an expensive, stressful and demanding treatment at that. Before that July day in 1978 when the news shot around the world of the first "test-tube baby," couples knew when they had come to the end of the road. Even if it was unwanted, the end of the road forced a resolution of their infertility. They had no other options.

IVF is now a carrot dangling interminably in front of their noses. The enticement of IVF might be all right if the couples had a reasonable chance of having a baby at the end of the treatment. But at this writing at least eight of ten couples will emerge from IVF treatment as childless as when they started, and even when the treatment fails there is no sense of completion. Couples are still left with feeling "maybe next time." At many long-standing IVF clinics there are couples who have been there since the clinic opened, still trying for the elusive carrot.

It is the poor success rates of IVF that remain its biggest problem for couples. Although researchers are hard at work trying to improve the likelihood that any one couple will take home a baby, the improvements, as one leading IVF doctor described, are "nibble-throughs" rather than breakthroughs. It is expected that the improvements will continue to be gradual, not dramatic.

Of course it is unfair to expect IVF to have a 100 percent success rate while even the most fertile couples have at most a 30 percent chance of a natural pregnancy in any given month. But the uncertainty of the result of IVF, combined with its considerable financial cost, creates a huge dilemma for couples. Do they gamble and go for it or do they try to ignore the seduction of "maybe this time?" It *is* a gamble, IVF doctors readily acknowledge.

But IVF also has created a dilemma for society. The central issue is high technology's involvement in the creation of life. Many religions have been outspoken opponents of IVF and the associated reproductive techniques that involve manipulation or research on embryos or gametes outside the body. The techniques are immoral, they say. In 1987 the Vatican issued the document, *Instruction on Respect for Human Life and Its Origin and On The Dignity of Procreation*. It condemned IVF and any form of artificial conception and called for legislation to make some aspects of IVF research a criminal procedure.

Many feminists and sociologists have grave concerns about IVF and reproductive technologies. They fear the techniques exploit women and perpetuate the attitude that a woman is not valuable unless she bears children. They argue that the technology reinforces the attitude that a woman must experience pregnancy and birth and provide children for her partner to be considered a full woman. IVF reinforces that attitude at great physical expense to women who undergo it. Feminists are also highly concerned about the medicalization of the very natural process of conception and birth. The issue is compounded by the belief that the domination of male researchers and doctors in the field means men are co-opting the control of reproduction from women.

Still others are afraid that IVF has started society down the "slippery slope" towards a host of unpalatable reproductive practices described in science fiction such as Aldous Huxley's *Brave New World* or Margaret Atwood's *The Handmaid's Tale*. The practices of concern include IVF-surrogacy and embryo flushing in which a "gestational mother" carries the pregnancy, genetic manipulation and eugenics creating "perfect" babies.

Less futuristic, but still of ethical concern, is the paradox that thousands and thousands of dollars are spent trying to produce a single child in a world where millions of children are dying because they can not get enough food to eat.

For the infertile couple, the controversy around IVF adds to the stress and emotional strain of the procedure. Most couples undergoing IVF find the only way they can cope is to block out the criticisms and ignore the hypothetical "where-will-this-all-lead?" discussions being carried on by philosophers, legislators and academics around them. Nevertheless, the discussions are important and may determine whether certain techniques are available to infertile couples in the future. Some procedures that could help them may not be allowed unless infertile couples let their voices be heard in the debates. Just as important, infertile couples should decide for themselves how far science should go in helping them have a baby. Where are the limits? Understanding that society has problems with the reproductive technologies, the infertile couple can help society come to a realistic solution.

A History of IVF

Although Steptoe and Edwards were the first to produce an IVF birth, the trail leading to IVF starts a long time before Louise Brown let out her first lusty yell. Most people are familiar with Aldous Huxley's classic science fiction work, *Brave New World*, which depicts a future where babies were created outside the womb from eggs ripened in a mother liquor, fertilized in a bouillon of swimming sperm and hatched in incubators at the London Hatchery and Conditioning Centre. Huxley's novel was published in 1932 but even at that time it was not some totally implausible imagining. The seed of thought from his book may even have come from some casual conversation with his embryologist brother, Julian, or his scientific friends. Huxley could have learned that a few scientists had already tried to fertilize a mammalian egg outside the body.

The first reported attempt dates back to 1890 when Vienese embryologist, S.L. Shenck, tried unsuccessfully to fertilize rabbit and guinea pig eggs in the laboratory. In the years that followed, a handful of scientists continued to try to achieve in vitro fertilization in animals. In 1934, just two years after *Brave New World* startled the world with its stark and startling vision of the future, American scientist Gregory Pincus, the inventor of the birth control pill, published reports of successful IVF in rabbits. He had removed rabbit eggs from the ovary, placed them with sperm for 20 minutes in a watch glass and then transferred the egg to a surrogate rabbit's fallopian tube. At the time this was considered the first in vitro fertilization. Now the results are questioned because it is believed sperm could have been attached to the eggs when they were transferred back and fertilization could have happened in the tube.

In 1944, the late Dr. John Rock of Boston tried fertilizing two human eggs in culture. He reportedly watched one develop to a two-cell stage and the other to a three-cell stage, but since the sperm was not seen actually fertilizing the egg, his results are not accepted as the first human IVF.

M.C. Chang, an American researcher, is now accepted as being the first to successfully achieve IVF in animals. In 1960 he reported fertilizing rabbit eggs in vitro and transferring them back to the animal, resulting in the birth of a baby rabbit.

Overcoming infertility was not the central aim of these early experiments. It was predominantly scientific interest, an academic quest to see what was required to make a sperm fertilize an egg. The experiments were mostly used as a way of learning about the earliest stages of mammalian life and development. That intellectual attitude fit British physiologist Robert Edwards when he first became interested in embryology in the early 1950s. But over time Edwards began to see the potential application to infertility treatment.

The story of Steptoe's and Edward's long path to successful IVF is detailed in a fascinating account in their joint memoirs, *A Matter of Life*. Edwards, regarded by others as a brilliant scientist, describes himself in the early 1950s as an "ordinary" graduate of Bangor University in North Wales who had not done well on his final exams. Edwards wrote in his memoirs, "I was the clever, ambitious scholarship boy who looked now as if he had fallen flat on his face." Nonetheless, he still wanted to be a scientist and wrote a letter to the head of genetics at Edinburgh University applying to become a graduate student. He was accepted despite his academic standing and before long became immersed in the study of the reproductive cells, the gametes of mammals. He worked first with mice and then took a detour into immunology of reproduction for a few years. By 1960 he had returned to the study of human gametes. It was in that year, he says in his memoirs, that he wondered for the first time if human embryos could be fertilized in vitro and replanted in a woman's uterus to cure infertility.

Edwards was specifically studying the ripening process of eggs, the halving of the chromosomes to prepare for fertilization, called the second meiotic division. He learned that although eggs of each species take a different time to go through the specific ripening process, the eggs ripened with no special help in the laboratory dish just as they did in the ovary. He wanted to see if these eggs were normal enough to be fertilized by sperm in culture. By 1963, while at Cambridge, he tried to fertilize his first human eggs.

Despite four years of hard work, some of that time spent in the United States doing research and working with gynecological team Howard and Georgeanna Jones, he was unsuccessful. He thought the problem might be that the sperm needed to be exposed to the mucus and fluid in a woman's reproductive tract, so he devised a membranous chamber that allowed cervical fluid to bathe the sperm by not letting the sperm out. Women volunteers had the chamber inserted into their reproductive tract overnight during their fertile time. (Those were sleepless nights for Edwards who fretted needlessly that the sperm might escape.) Still no egg fertilized.

Constantly needing a fresh supply of eggs and wondering if the sperm might have to be collected from the fallopian tube to be capable of fertilization, Edwards was searching for an easy access to both tubes and eggs when he happened on an article in a medical journal in 1967 written by Patrick Steptoe. The article was on laparoscopy, at that time a revolutionary operative procedure developed in France and Germany. Laparoscopy was first developed in the late 1950s, but British doctors had been slow to adopt the new procedure and Steptoe had become its vocal, if somewhat unlikely, champion. The article hailed laparoscopy because it allowed viewing of the reproductive organs, sampling of tissue and conducting of a few minor surgical procedures, all with minimal trauma to the woman. In reading the article, Edwards recalls in *A Matter of Life*, "I wanted to shout out Eureka! . . . I was looking for just this expertise." He immediately phoned Steptoe to discuss the possibility of collaboration.

It was six months later in early 1968 when Steptoe and Edwards finally met by chance at a medical conference in London. Steptoe was then in his mid-fifties, a small-town doctor already well-established in his career. Years earlier, as an average medical graduate, he had failed to get a consultancy position in the competitive London scene. Instead, he had headed north to Oldham, a mill town outside of Manchester where he soon built a comfortable obstetrics and gynecology practice. He recalled in *A Matter of Life* that he had always been sympathetic to the special pain of women with tubal infertility, but in those days there was little that he could do for them. He also hated doing exploratory laparotomies on women complaining of pelvic pain; so often there was nothing seriously wrong and yet they had endured major surgery. He embraced the laparoscope when he first heard about it in 1959 as a way to quickly check out the situation. He practiced on female corpses in the morgue until he felt ready to try his first live patient in early 1960. By 1967, when he received Edwards's phone call, he had performed hundreds of laparoscopies while most gynecologists in the United Kingdom were still considering the new instrument a useless gimmick.

In fact, at that 1968 medical conference, laparoscopy was being so denigrated by some London physicians when Steptoe, in the audience, jumped up and yelled, "Nonsense!" He had brought colored slides with him and showed the disbelieving group his clear photos of ovaries, tubes and pelvic structure he had taken with the laparoscope. After the display, Edwards, also in the audience, approached him and said: "You must be Patrick Steptoe." The meeting started their 20-year collaboration.

Using woman volunteers who were undergoing hysterectomy or other pelvic surgery (who had been asked to have sexual intercourse before the operation) Steptoe took samples of eggs from their ovaries and sperm from the fallopian tubes. The gametes were passed to Edwards who had been given a small lab in the Oldham hospital's pathology department. Edwards tried to culture the egg and sperm to get the sperm to fertilize. The work meant Edwards had to drive more than 565 kilometers to Oldham from Cambridge on a moment's notice, sometimes more than twice a week for more than 10 years.

With the help of Cambridge Ph.D. student, Barry Bavister, who created a culture medium in which sperm and eggs thrived, the team was finally able to get sperm to fertilize eggs. Edwards had seen his first human in vitro fertilization one decisive day in March 1968 in his Cambridge lab. "All those years of striving for this and here it was: after ten hours in Barry's culture medium the human spermatozoa had wriggled their way through the membrane deep into the egg."

The sperm did not need to be taken from the fallopian tubes after all, the team learned. In February of 1969 they reported their successful fertilization of 56 eggs, all documented and photographed in the journal, *Nature*. The publication caused a flurry of scientific comment and criticism, and "Brave-New-World" headlines in the world's press. Thereafter, they conducted their research under the watchful and critical eye of the world.

Despite their success with fertilization, the next years proved frustrating for the Steptoe-Edwards team. In 1971 they moved to a new private hospital, Kershaw's Cottage Hospital, near Oldham, and assistant Jean Purdy joined the team. First Edwards and Purdy squashed and stained hundreds of fertilized eggs to view the chromosomes under the microscope. They found all were chromosomally normal and soon were confident that embryo replacement was ethical. Late that year they transferred the first embryo back to a patient, but it failed to take, like many after it. Although they were able to get the embryos to divide and grow, all attempts to transfer the embryos back to the many women volunteers were unsuccessful. They experimented with giving the women hormone shots and fertility drugs, and still nothing worked. Hampering their work was continual censure and criticism from other scientists and the media. They were refused funding for their studies in humans and had to rely on private funding, mostly from supporters in the United States.

After four years of attempts, in 1975 they had their first positive pregnancy test. Their jubilation was brief—it was an ectopic pregnancy and had to be removed. In 1977 they abandoned fertility drugs and returned to natural cycles.

Despite their lack of success, they had no problem finding women volunteers to undergo the experimental egg removal and embryo replacement. One couple sent to them for assessment in late 1976 was John and Lesley Brown from Bristol. John was a truck driver; Lesley, 29, was depressed about her inability to have children. On examining her, Steptoe found that an operation was necessary to clear her reproductive organs from adhesions. Finally, on November 10, 1977, Steptoe removed a single ripe egg from her left ovary. Close to midnight on November 12, an eight-celled embryo was gently replaced in her uterus and the team waited.

Australians Joins the Race

Around the time that Steptoe and Edwards first met, Australian gynecologist Dr. Carl Wood was frustrated in his attempts to help his patients who had blocked fallopian tubes. He first tried tubal transplants, taking a healthy tube from a woman undergoing sterilization and transplanting it into an infertile woman. Even though the surgery was technically a success, transplant immunology was in its infancy and the transplanted tubes were rejected in short order. Next he tried making an artificial fallopian tube of a plastic capsule that enclosed the ovary and two plastic tubes, one leading out of the woman's abdomen and the other leading to the woman's uterus. When the woman ovulated, the egg was theoretically caught in the capsule, the sperm was added through the outer tube, allowed to mingle with the egg for a few days and then the whole lot was flushed down to the uterus. An intriguing idea, but it did not work.

Wood had just finished reporting the failure of his artificial tube at the 1969 meeting of the Australian Society for Reproductive Biology when, reminiscent of the Steptoe-Edwards meeting, sheep embryologist Neil Moore approached him. "He asked me if I'd ever thought of bypassing the tubes altogether," Wood recounts. "Frankly, I hadn't. He told me he was working with sheep embryos at a small research station in New South Wales. He asked if I wanted to come up and see what they were doing."

Wood did, and what he saw excited him in its potential applications to human beings. Moore was working with his Ph.D. student, Alan Trounson, at Jerilderie, a remote 60,000-acre research ranch on the Victoria border. Trounson, who was later to head Wood's research team, recalls those early days. "It was just Moore and me. We were looking at embryos, flushing them out, trying to culture them, splitting them, looking at what controlled development rate, freezing and so on. Carl got interested in what we were doing and brought his team together to try it in humans."

Many North Americans are surprised to learn that Australia has been a pioneer in IVF technique, but the situation with Moore and Trounson exemplifies why Australia soon began to challenge Steptoe and Edwards in IVF research. Australia had a unique research environment, predominantly because of the country's multi-million-dollar sheep industry. Agricultural researchers were looking for ways to maximize the offspring of valuable stock—a single top-breeding Merino sheep can be worth as much as $300,000—and so techniques in artificial insemination and embryo transfer were being developed for agricultural use. Rather than put a prize ewe through the rigors of repeated pregnancy, the researchers were trying to do such things as flush the valuable embryos from her womb and transfer them to standard-brand ewes who would become the gestational mother. A few animal researchers like Moore and Trounson had developed an expertise in handling gametes.

It was 1970 when Wood, who by this time had heard about Edwards's work, spent time with Trounson and Moore at Jerilderie. In 1971 he established the first Austrialian team to start researching IVF, working out of two Melbourne hospitals. Key members of his team included physiologist Alex Lopata, John

Leeton at the Queen Victoria Medical Centre, obstetrics-gynecology colleague Ian Johnston and physiologist Jim Brown at the Royal Woman's Hospital. They first tried taking eggs from ovaries and putting them back into the uteri with sperm—much like the GIFT procedure of today—but it didn't work. Then they fertilized eggs in a Petri dish beforé replacement. They had done about 10 replacements when the group reported their first pregnancy in 1973, but it lasted not a week from first hormone detection to disappearance. (Although the group was sure it was a valid pregnancy, its brevity meant that much of the scientific world, including Steptoe and Edwards, do not accept it as the first IVF pregnancy.) A second pregnancy in 1973 under Johnstone at the Royal Women's, lasted 19 weeks only to be tragically miscarried following an infection caused by amniocentisis. This was the world's first legitimate IVG pregnancy.

The next five years were discouraging for the Australian team. "They were difficult years," Wood said. "It was hard to keep our spirits up—we didn't get a hint of a pregnancy—we didn't know why it wasn't working." Trounson had gone to study in Cambridge in 1972, ironically not far from Edwards's lab. "I knew Bob fairly well," says Trounson who was working on freezing cow embryos, "but at that time I had no interest in IVF, I was still thinking about agricultural systems." Wood wanted Trounson to come back to Australia to work with them and finally in 1977 he received a grant from the Ford Foundation to pay Trounson's salary in Melbourne. Trounson came home; Lopata eventually went to work with Johnston, and Trounson and Wood started their enduring collaboration.

Early in 1978, The Australian team began to suspect that Edwards and Steptoe had achieved a pregnancy.

"We'd heard rumors," Wood recalls. "About March of '78 Steptoe had come out to see us while Lesley Brown was pregnant. He wouldn't say that they had (achieved the pregnancy), but he wouldn't deny it either. At that meeting he talked to us about IVF, discussed everything about their techniques, but wouldn't tell us about their culture media—that was a big secret. After that meeting we were sure they had a pregnancy. We expected to hear any day."

Wood can't remember where he was when he heard the news that Louise Brown was born, but he remembers being both bouyed to know that IVF really could work, and slightly disappointed that they not accomplished it first.

"I guess it was a race, of sorts," Wood said. "We knew they were well ahead of us. Bob Edwards is an outstanding scientist. We said, 'Darn, they beat us,' but we weren't all that upset because it made us more confident that we could actually do it."

Six months after baby Louise, Steptoe and Edwards achieved the world's second IVF baby, a boy, Alastair Montgomery. But after that their luck ran dry for more than three years, perhaps because they had moved their operations to Bourn Hall, a beautiful sixteenth-century manor on the rolling green countryside about 15 minutes outside Cambridge. It is not known what interfered with their smooth procedures—different water quality? new equipment?—it is still a mystery. By 1981 Bourn Hall had pregnancies again and soon became one of the world's most famous and successful clinics.

Meanwhile, the Australian teams under Wood and Trounson, along with Johnston and Lopata, had been working on improving the pickup system for eggs; developing a standardized culture media to grow the embryos; and working on hormone regimes to super-stimulate the woman's ovaries to develop more than one egg. In 1980, two years after Louise Brown, the world's third IVF baby, Candice Reed, was born in Australia to mother Linda Reed, one of Johnston's and Lopata's patients. From that time on consistent pregnancies occurred there. The Australian team led the world in research developments and standardization of techniques. Most of the advances have come out of Trounson's and Wood's impressive team. Trounson applied the freezing expertise he developed in Cambridge for cow embryos to human embryos, and in 1983 the first baby was born from a frozen-thawed embryo in Melbourne. The group developed a way to mimic the natural menstrual cycle, allowing women without ovaries to have a nourished uterus ready to accept a donor egg. The first baby from an egg donation was also born in Melbourne in 1983. Trounson was the first to successfully try sperm micromanipulation—injecting the sperm into the egg—in mice, creating healthy mice offspring from the technique.

When IVF scientists are asked about the various teams' contributions to IVF, most summarize it something like this: Steptoe and Edwards showed the world that IVF could be done, and the Australian teams showed the rest of the world how to do it. Woods and Trounson invited interested scientists and physicians to learn their techniques. To date, most of the IVF specialists in the world have gone to Australia to be trained, including noted physicians in the United States, such as the Jones, Richard Marrs and Ricardo Asch, and Jacques Testart in France, as well as many Canadian IVF specialists.

Early in 1988, a few months before Louise Brown turned 10, the men who started it all, Steptoe and Edwards celebrated the birth of their 1000th baby at Bourn Hall. Louise Brown, then a pretty, chubby-cheeked girl with green eyes and long blonde hair, held baby number 1000 while her six-year-old IVF sister Natalie, Bourn Hall staff, friends and the world's press looked on. Two months later, in March 1988, Patrick Steptoe died of cancer at age 74 on the day before the Queen was to award him Commander of the British Empire. His modest grave is on the ground of the Bourn Hall Clinic with a simple headstone.

In August of 1988, Bourn Hall was sold to the pharmaceutical manufacturer Serono, which makes fertility drugs Pergonal and Serophene, two mainstays of IVF-ovarian stimulation. Serono continues to run Bourn Hall as an IVF clinic. Edwards, who still works out of Cambridge, is frequently seen in the labs and corridors of the rambling manor.

Deciding on IVF

Last Resort

The decision to try IVF should come at the end of a thorough infertility investigation, when it is clear that other treatment methods will be of no use.

There are three good reasons to keep IVF as a last resort.

1. IVF is expensive: in Canada it costs at least $3000 a cycle. ("Cycle" means one attempt at IVF.) In Canada, only Ontario's health insurance plan covers the cost of some hospital-based programs. In the United States the cost is about $5000 to $6000 a cycle, or more.
2. Its success rate is poor—the majority of people going through IVF do not become pregnant, and, the chance of success occurs only while undergoing the treatment cycle. (After undergoing successful surgery, a woman has a chance of pregnancy every month thereafter.)
3. IVF is psychologically and physically stressful. The fertility drug regimes and egg retrieval can take their toll on the woman's body, but even more stressful is the intense emotional experience of the treatment. Many couples find that the upheaval of the early stages of the infertility work-up leaves them with few emotional resources to endure IVF, if they begin too soon. "Although we could have gone straight on to IVF, we didn't feel at that time we could handle it; our relationship had gone through too many strains," one woman said. "We had to wait a few years until we felt strong again and could take whatever the outcome would be."

Couples should be sure they really need IVF and that their infertility can not be overcome by a simpler method before plunging into the procedure. Couples should also ask themselves whether, in the end, they will be happy they tried IVF, no matter what the outcome. After spending a few thousand dollars for the treatment, enduring the drug stimulation, the egg retrievals and replacements, and enduring the psychological stress, will they be able to say "We're happy we did it," even if the cycle failed and they had no baby?

If it has been determined that pregnancy by any other means will be unlikely, and if a couple feels emotionally ready, IVF is a legitimate choice. Some couples may be ready to make that choice soon after the infertility investigation starts, for example, if the woman is found to have blocked or distended fallopian tubes that cannot be corrected surgically.

IVF pioneer Prof. Carl Wood believes that IVF is also a legitimate choice for women for whom the value of surgery is uncertain. Wood believes IVF should be suggested to patients at the same time they are considering major tubal surgery, in cases where tubal surgery has a low chance of success and the woman is of advancing reproductive age.

"I believe that it would be an advantage to many women to come to IVF sooner, not waiting until after age 35—their chances would be better," Wood says. "Definitely, the simple things should be done first, but tubal surgery is not so simple. I believe both should be considered and the one with the best chance of success should be used."

Most women, however, continue to have tubal surgery before going to IVF. There may be some advantage to removing adhesions that restrict the reproductive organs before trying to become pregnant by IVF, although this is not fully known. But like Wood, others are recommending some women who cannot be helped by surgery go straight to IVF. Couples with male factor infertility and unexplained infertility usually try other treatments, including timed intercourse, for at least two or three years before entering an IVF program.

Many IVF programs have long waiting lists, particularly in Canada, Australia and Britain—as long as two or three years. Couples should find out if the IVF clinic they wish to go to has a waiting list and how long it is. Even if they are not ready to undergo the treatment, if the list is long, it is wise to list themselves early, so they can have treatment two or three years down the line. If they no longer want treatment when their number is called, they can always cancel.

In the future, IVF may no longer be an end-of-the-road treatment. If success rates can be improved, it may become a more realistic option earlier on in the infertility investigation, researchers say. IVF scientist Alan Trounson predicts there will soon come a day when IVF will be a much simpler procedure, akin to a trip to the dentist. He suggests a woman's natural menstrual cycle would be used without hormone stimulation; just before ovulation she would come in for 30 minutes for the egg retrieval; the next day the embryo would be replaced in less than 30 minutes. Each month the woman could come back until she conceived. "This would greatly reduce the cost and stress of IVF," Trounson says. The no-frills treatment, however, would be best for women still in their twenties who have tubal problems, because their cycles are more regular and fertile. It is believed that women in their mid- to late-thirties will still require ovarian stimulation.

Selecting an IVF Program

When you have decided that you want to try IVF, how do you know where to go? To which of the many IVF clinics should you pay you money and take your chance?

Those are not easy questions to answer. Finding a good IVF program that is right for you is a bit like shopping for a used car—IVF practitioners themselves acknowledge that. There are a lot of good IVF programs out there, but, unfortunately, there are also some that are not good. You have to know what you are looking for so that you are not swept up by the statistics of "success rates" and "pregnancy rates" recited by some IVF salesmen.

There is no handbook of IVF clinics to avoid; there are no consumer reports or specific ratings of programs available. Couples must do their own research, assess the reliability of the information they are being given, and rely on their instincts about a program and its staff.

Geographical Factors

Some couples, purely for geographical reasons, have a limited choice. If there is only one IVF program in your region, then that is likely the one you choose. You are usually referred there by the doctor that has been investigating your infertility. Sole IVF clinics in a state or province usually have long waiting lists, however, and couples may take a number of months to a year or more before undergoing treatment.

Some couples, however, decide to travel to distant IVF clinics. They save their money and their vacation time to book into an IVF clinic at a noted medical school or a clinic with a world-wide reputation. At Bourn Hall, the British clinic founded by Steptoe and Edwards, for example, at least 60 percent of the women staying at the English Manor come from overseas—Canada, the United States, the Middle East, Africa, Scandanavia, India. Dozens of languages are heard in the dining hall or TV room; women wearing saris and purda mingle with those in blue jeans and Christian Dior. But travelling a great distance to an IVF clinic, no matter which one, does not greatly improve one's chance of success. Even at Bourn Hall, three out of four women also do not get pregnant. It does, however, greatly increase the cost of IVF treatment and the emotional stakes. Having travelled so far the letdown can be even more acute.

For some couples who live in more populous areas, the choice among IVF clinics is greater. London, England, has 16 IVF clinics within the city's boundaries (in 1988 five of these clinics were new and had not yet received the stamp of approval from Britain's Voluntary Licensing Authority). In 1988, Southern California had 10 clinics in or around Los Angeles. New York City had six clinics in 1988 and three more in nearby communities. Baltimore and Bethesda, Maryland, combined, had six in 1988. The Boston area had six. The Chicago area had six. Even some less populated regions still have a wide selection: Southern Ontario, five; St. Louis, three; Cleveland, three. The list goes on.

Those numbers are likely to keep rising. Although IVF was slow to take off in the first years after Louise Brown's birth, when Steptoe and Edwards and the Australian team started showing that IVF births could be repeated, IVF clinics began to spring up like dealerships. In 1988 there were at least 500 IVF clinics worldwide: 170 in the United States, 15 in Canada, 20 in Australia, 40 in England and Scotland, and more than a hundred between Western Europe, Israel, South Africa and Asia. Some of the clinics have built fine reputations for both research and clinical outcomes and have continued to improve the scientific understanding and the practice of IVF, and some of the clinics have not. In fact, the 1988 report to Congress from the United States Office of Technology Assessment on infertility found that of 169 IVF clinics operating in the United States in 1987, as many as 50 percent had a few or no live births to their credit. "Some 70 to 80 medical teams in the United States have established a record of some success with IVF," the OTA report stated. "However, the remainder of the 169 IVF/GIFT programs, in this country have had little or no success to date."

The United States IVF Registry, a computer based system to which IVF programs voluntarily send their data, reported similar results. Of 96 clinics who sent their data to the registry, 86 programs reported that they had had "at least one delivery" resulting from IVF during 1987. The registry reported the figures in its second annual report, published in the January 1989 issue of *Fertility and Sterility.* This means that 10 of the programs that sent in data did not have a birth for that year! What does that say of the 63 clinics that did not bother to send in their results? The 86 programs that did have some success had a total of 991 deliveries, of which some were multiple births, producing 1260 babies. Of the 86 clinics, however, four clinics accounted for 34 percent of all the deliveries. A total of 10 clinics accounted for 50 percent of all the deliveries.

Sixty of the 86 clinics had fewer than 10 pregnancies that year. The report does not identify the results from individual clinics; for example, it does not state the names of the four clinics with the best results or the top 10. The names of the 96 clinics that contributed data, however, are acknowledged at the end of the report.

Dr. Alan De Cherney, president of the Society of Assisted Reproductive Technology (SART), which established the registry with the American Fertility Society and Medical Research International, said the membership decided that the results of individual clinics sent to the registry would not be released. "Because the registry is anonymous, we think that there is more honest reporting," De Cherney said in a press conference on IVF standards at the 1988 AFS scientific meeting. "Because clinics aren't identified, they are more willing to give their true data."

Although there has been some movement in SART to change the registry so that individual clinic results would be released on request, at this writing the move has not received approval from the majority of members of SART and the IVF registry.

The data from the IVF registry illustrates one salient point about IVF clinics: some have a great deal of experience and others do not. In fact, of the 13 clinics that had no babies, the maximum number of cycles was 26—other clinics had more than 200 cycles that year. That figure shows some clinics are just starting out and do not treat a large number of patients.

Granted, IVF clinics have to start out some time, but couples coming through their doors should know how long they have been operating. If a clinic is just starting out, many people, IVF practitioners included, believe couples should pay reduced fees.

Questions to Ask

Naturally, there is one question couples really want answered: are we going to a competent clinic where we have as good a chance of getting pregnant as can be expected? To get that answer you have to do some research before signing up.

First, the doctor who has conducted your initial infertility investigation should be aware of the availability of IVF treatment and the reputations of clinics in the region. Many IVF clinics, particularly in Canada, require patients to be referred by a physician and will not accept patients who come on their own. If you have consulted an infertility specialist, he or she can give you some assessment of the choices you have for IVF. Infertility support groups, which usually have a number of members who have tried IVF at least once, are also good resources for finding out about IVF programs.

Next, you can try phoning the IVF clinic, but most IVF programs do not answer in-depth patient queries over the phone. That is usually because their receptionists are not trained to answer many of the patients' questions. At some clinics a member of the staff will phone you back; others send you an information packet.

In general, the questions you should ask, either in a letter, over the phone, or by asking others, include the following.

1. How long has the clinic been operating?
2. Who makes up the clinic's IVF team? The American Fertility Society and the American College of Obstetrics and Gynecology have released statements of minimal standards for IVF/GIFT. According to AFS standards, personnel with four types of skills are required in an IVF program: a fully-trained reproductive endocrinologist; a pelvic surgeon with experience in laparoscopy and follicular aspiration; someone fully competent in semen analysis; someone with skills to handle and assess gametes and embryos. It is possible for one person to have one or more skills, such as endocrinology/surgery or semenology/embryology. It is recommended that clinics also have a psychologist associated with the program or someone who is able to provide emotional support.
3. How many cycles did the clinic perform in the last year? What is the maximum number of cycles performed a week? A cycle is one treatment of one patient. Because many patients may return for more treatments in a year, the number of cycles performed are a better reflection on the size of the program rather than the number of patients.
4. Of cycles performed in the last year, how many resulted in a live delivery? The number of live deliveries is more indicative of the clinic's success than is number of babies born as multiple births are more common with IVF.
5. Of patients treated, what percentage have solely tubal problems? What percentage would have other infertility causes such endometriosis, male infertility or combined problems? If the clinic treats a wider range of infertility problems, their live birth rate may be much lower than if they treated only tubal problems. Clinics that are treating more difficult patients can come out looking worse when, in fact, they are more advanced.
6. If the clinic is in the United States, is it a member of the IVF registry and did it submit data in the previous year? As mentioned above, the U.S. IVF registry is a voluntary organization that publishes anonymus compiled results of member clinics. The registry, in its way, is attempting to raise the standards and keep tabs on the practice of IVF. Although it would be more help to couples if individual clinics were identified, couples should consider refusing to patronize clinics that are not yet members. This would exert consumer pressure on all clinics to join. To verify if a clinic is a member, couples can check the list at the end of the registry's annual report published in Fertility and Sterility. Some clinics, however, may have joined since the last publication of data.
7. Does the clinic freeze embryos? What success has the clinic had to date with freeze-thawed embryos? If they do not freeze embryos, what will be done with leftover embryos? If embryo freezing is done, any embryos

not transferred back to the uterus in the first treatment cycle can be frozen for another try. Frozen-thawed embryos to date have had a very poor success rate with less than 5 percent ever producing a baby.

8. What is the estimated cost of one treatment cycle? If you must drop out before egg recovery (if stimulation of the ovaries is not adequate) what costs will you be expected to pay? If embryos are not replaced, is cost decreased? What is the cost of a frozen embryo replacement?
9. Is the clinic privately operated or is it associated with a university medical school? There are some fine commercial IVF clinics available, but in general, clinics that are at least partly associated with a university have a greater commitment to research and development of IVF; tend to be more up-to-date on new developments; and are more interested in sharing IVF statistics and less motivated by financial gain. Commercially operated clinics tend to be more expensive, but also tend to cater more to patients' comfort. Many patients find the commercial clinics are more responsive to their needs, are housed in nicer quarters and generally provide more attention—factors that do not improve the chance of success for a baby but improve the experience of IVF.
10. Is the clinic associated with a hospital? Most hospitals have peer review and ethics committees so that IVF programs running in a hospital would come under more scrutiny.

Getting all the answers you need may be difficult because some clinics are unreceptive or are unable to answer these queries. Some couples may sense hostility from clinic staff in the face of a list of questions. Fortunately, many clinics realize that patients not only want to know, but have a right to know details about the IVF program they are considering. Some clinics welcome questions and print an information sheet complete with up-to-date statistics of the clinic's practices. Many infertility support groups often invite a physician or spokesperson from local IVF clinics to talk to the group informally. This can be a good venue for couples to find out more information about the program.

Success Rates

You may have noticed that a question about success rates was not included in the list. That is intentional; success rates without some background or understanding can be meaningless or misleading.

Most clinics, when asked informally about success rates, say "Oh, about 20 percent" which is about the average rate that good IVF clinics claimed to have been maintaining in 1987 and 1988. The IVF registry shows that average rate across the board is really closer to 10 percent for live births. When a clinic quotes a success rate, the couple has to know where the success rate is coming from. How was it calculated? Even though they have not achieved that rate, many clinics quote the 20 percent success rate because that is what is quoted by others.

If a clinic quotes a success rate, or alternatively, a pregnancy rate, find out how the figure was derived. There are so many different steps in the IVF process that knowing the percentage of couples that eventually conceive is useless unless you know what it is compared to: the number of couples who signed up? the number who had eggs retrieved? the number who had embryos put back? the number of couples who had tubal obstruction only?

To illustrate, here is an example of what can happen to pregnancy rates, using nice, arbitrary round numbers that are factors of ten. (The percentages used here are actually based on the results of the 1987 IVF registry, so even though the numbers are concocted, the trend they show is real.) Suppose 1000 couples come to clinic X to have IVF. All 1000 women start ovarian stimulation, but after a week 100 have not responded to the hormones and therefore must drop out. That leaves 900 who go on to have eggs removed from their ovaries. All the eggs retrieved are mixed with the partner's sperm, but unfortunately 100 couples fail to have any eggs fertilize. That leaves 800 women who get embryos replaced in their uterus. All of them wait impatiently for 15 days for the pregnancy test result, but a total of 600 women are not pregnant; only 200 have hormones in their urine to indicate pregnancy. All 200 wait until a few more weeks pass until the tiny fetus can be assessed by ultrasound. Unfortunately 20 women who had hormone indication seem to have lost their pregnancy as no gestational sac can be found on ultrasound. That leaves 180 women with confirmed clinic pregnancies. As the weeks go by, 15 of those pregnancies are found to be ectopic. Then, unfortunately, a further 45 women lose their pregnancies in miscarriage before the twenty-third week. That leaves 120 women who have a live birth of a baby.

When you work out the pregnancy rate based on those figures, here are the different percentages you can achieve: if you compare the number starting out (1000) to the number having a live baby (120) the pregnancy rate is 12 percent; if you compare the number who had eggs retrieved (900) to the number who actually had a baby (120) it is 13.5 percent; if you compare the number who had embryos replaced (800) to the number with babies born, you have 15 percent. What happens to the pregnancy rate if, as at many IVF clinics, it is based on the number of women who showed a confirmed clinical pregnancy, regardless of how many pregnancies were lost? That means 180 of 1000 starting out, or 18 percent, actually became pregnant according to ultrasound, and 20 percent became pregnant according to hormone assay. If you compare only the number of embryo replacements (800) to the unconfirmed clinical pregnancies (200), a full 25 percent were initially told they were pregnant.

That long explanation shows how pregnancy rates really do not mean much unless you know how they are calculated. No matter how you slice it, 120 babies were born, but the "success rate" ranged from 12 to 25 percent!

Couples, naturally, want to know before they start what their chances are of emerging from the other end of treatment with a baby. The ability of IVF practitioners to actually tell you is confused by yet another factor: you as an individual couple. No one couple undergoing IVF is the same as another. The various combinations of age, type of infertility, male factors and responses of the woman's ovaries to stimulation all affect the chance of achieving a pregnancy. If a woman is under 30 and has tubal blockage only and the man is fertile, that couple has the best chance of pregnancy. As a woman becomes older, her chance of pregnancy decreases. (IVF pregnancies after age 40 are rare.) Women whose infertility is complicated by both tubal problems and other fertility problems such as polycystic ovarian disease or endometriosis, also have a lower success rate. Add a male factor into the equation and chances are reduced some more.

In the future, the problem of being assured of a competent IVF clinic may be solved, either by medical committees or by government legislation that would approve clinics. In 1988 the Ethics Committee of the AFS discussed the theoretical possibility of forming an independent body, similar in function to Britain's Voluntary Licensing Authority, that would certify that IVF/GIFT programs were complying to certain standards. Representatives on this hypothetical committee could come from groups such as the American College of Obstetrics and Gynecology, other medical and scientific groups, and consumer groups and other non-scientists. At this writing, however, no such group has been formed.

In Canada, the province of Ontario's hospital insurance plan pays the medical and hospital costs (not drug costs) of IVF if couples go to one of five approved programs. No other provinces, however, give approval to clinics or cover patients' costs. Most Canadian IVF clinics, however, are associated with university medical schools and the programs come under peer review and university scrutiny.

In Australia, IVF clinics are accredited by a committee established by the Fertility Society of Australia, made up of a cross section of representatives, including a consumer representative, which conducts site inspections of IVF clinics. All accredited clinics are required to submit data to a national IVF registry which now has collected detailed information on more than 2000 births. Non-accredited clinics do not get free supplies of fertility drugs from the government.

Starting IVF

The first step on the long road of IVF is to phone or write to the IVF clinic you have chosen and ask what you must do to enter the program. Usually the clinic sends forms you must complete and send back to them with a letter from your doctor or infertility specialist and a copy of your medical records. Some clinics ask for a referral from your doctor and deal more with him or her than with you. Usually before the treatment starts you meet with a member of the IVF team to discuss the procedure, to make sure you are fully informed and to go over questions you may have.

Male partners usually have to produce a semen sample at this time to have it analyzed for any potential problems in IVF. A test to determine whether the sperm is able to fertilize the egg in vitro, called a hamster-egg penetration test or a sperm penetration assay, may be performed. (See Chapter 7.)

Female partners usually are given a physical examination to assess general health before starting IVF. Often clinics require that couples undergo testing for the AIDS antibody and chlamydia. The female partner usually must have had, within the last year, a normal Pap test and a test of rubella titres in her blood (to insure that she has immunity to German measles before attempting pregnancy).

After the initial consultation, if the clinic has no waiting list, you will likely be instructed to phone the clinic the month before you wish to start. If the clinic has a waiting list you will be told where you are on the list and when you should expect to be called. When your number comes up, a member of the team usually calls the month before you start. Many clinics do not conduct the discussion and evaluation until your number has come on the waiting list. A doctor's referral, however, is enough to put your name on the list.

Cost of IVF

It is difficult to break down the costs of IVF, as it varies depending on the individual clinic, the needs of the individual couple and whether or not some aspects of the procedure are covered by insurance plans. In general, it is expensive. The procedure generally starts at about $3000 and can go as high as $7000, although some of that money may be recouped through insurance plans or drug plans. Drug costs alone can be about $1000 but some women may need more drugs than others. The majority of government and third-party health insurance plans specifically exclude IVF, essentially because IVF is not seen as being a medical need. If no coverage at all is available, costs can come from the infertility specialists who are consulted, the hospital or clinic itself, the anesthesiologists, the ultrasonographers and the drugs. Some clinics require that costs be paid up front before undergoing IVF. You may want to clarify all costs, possibilities for reducing costs (such as egg retrieval under local anesthetic rather than general) and possibilities for reimbursement before you begin. If you go to an out-of-town clinic, your hotel and meal expenses will be additional.

Consent Forms

Before you start treatment, both partners must sign consent forms to show you understand the procedure and the decisions you are making. Along with consenting to the procedure itself and the medical risks of ovarian stimulation you also have to decide what you want done with any surplus eggs and embryos collected in the procedure. Most programs replace no more than three or four embryos in the woman, but it is common to get five to ten eggs on a retrieval. If the program freezes embryos you may decide to have the extras frozen. Since the case of the famous Rios embryos, couples deciding to freeze eggs must also decide what will be done with the embryos should the parents die or separate. (Some clinics do not have couples sign consent forms for freezing until they know freezing will be used.)

Couples may also have to decide whether or not they consent to their extra embryos or eggs being donated to other infertile couples. They may also be asked to consent to entering into research projects being undertaken at the clinic. All decisions must be signed and witnessed. Consenting to the procedure itself is mandatory before starting IVF, but consenting to research or egg donation is voluntary and will not influence your treatment.

In some cases it may be anticipated that the partner's sperm may have difficulty fertilizing the eggs. The possible use of donor sperm may be discussed at the time of signing consents. If donor sperm is an option, a consent form must be signed, which usually takes place after the husband's sperm has failed to fertilize the eggs and the choice to use donor sperm is presented by IVF staff. Often couples have less than five hours while the eggs are sitting in the incubator to decide whether they want to use donor sperm. It is a good idea for all couples to explore how they feel about using donor sperm before undergoing IVF.

When all the paperwork and preliminary investigations are taken care of, you will be instructed how and when to notify the clinic to commence treatment.

Step One: Ovarian Stimulation

Although Steptoe and Edwards achieved the first IVF pregnancy using a single egg developed in Leslie Brown's natural menstrual cycle, it was not long before IVF practitioners found better results could be achieved by stimulating the woman's ovaries with fertility drugs to produce a number of eggs. The best pregnancy results were obtained when at least three or four healthy embryos were transferred to the womb. But while the fertility drugs increased the chance of a pregnancy, they also greatly increased the invasiveness of the technique and the risk to the health of the woman. Of most concern is hyperstimulation syndrome, a potentially dire occurrence when a woman's ovaries have been stimulated too much. The long-term effect of these drug regimens on the woman's health is not yet known. (See Appendix A and B of Chapter 5 for more on the fertility drugs.)

Since that time many different fertility drug regimens have been used. Common stimulations have included the use of clomiphene by itself, a combination of clomiphene and Pergonal (HMG), Pergonal by itself, a combination of Pergonal and pure follicle stimulating hormone (FSH), or FSH by itself. A number of programs have four or five different drug regimens, called protocols, that they are able to use. A woman is assigned to the protocol that is thought to work best for her and her particular medical history. (See Chapter 5.)

One of the most common protocols is the use of clomiphene citrate (CC—Clomid or Serophene) and human menopausal gonadotropins (HMG-Pergonal). In this protocol clomiphene, a pill, is taken by the patient starting between day three and eight of her menstrual cycle. Soon after, injections of Pergonal are given each day along with CC.

Whatever the protocol, the woman's reaction to the stimulation is assessed by ultrasound to check the number of follicles developing, and daily blood tests to assess the amount of estrogen being produced by the follicles. When the follicles on the ovaries have reached a certain size and estrogen levels in the blood have peaked, a shot of the hormone human chorionic gonadotropin (HCG) is given to spur the eggs to mature. About 36 hours after the HCG shot, the eggs are retrieved, a few hours before they would have ovulated on their own.

GnRH Analogues

In the mid-eighties, IVF researchers first started investigating the gonadotropin-releasing hormone analogues for use as a pre-treatment for women before they had ovarian stimulation. The effect of the GnRH analogues is to turn down, "down regulate," the woman's natural system to make it more responsive to fertility drug stimulation. (See Appendix D in Chapter 5.)

GnRH analogues are basically look-alike molecules of the long-chained GnRH molecule pulsed naturally from the hypothalamus to the pituitary. By giving a woman a GnRH analogue, the IVF physician can turn off the woman's normal hormonal stimulation of the ovaries and then take command of it himself, putting the woman in a pre-pubescent state—wiping the slate clean for artificial stimulation with the fertility drugs.

In 1987 and 1988 some IVF clinics began conducting clinical experiments with GnRH analogues in selected patients. The drugs used were Leupron, Buserolin, Leuprolide and others to first down-regulate the woman. Once the hormonal axis was quiescent, a combination of fertility drugs were used to stimulate the follicles. Consistently, the agonists showed improvement over standard fertility drug stimulation. In general, when the agonists were used, fewer patients had to be cancelled because of failure to stimulate properly; more eggs of better quality were retrieved and when pregnancies occurred there seemed to be a lower rate of miscarriage. By late 1988 and early 1989 some clinics had begun using the agonists for almost all their patients. Other clinics use the agonists for patients who have shown to be poor responders in the past. The drawbacks of the analogues are that they increase the expense of the IVF treatment; they can require higher doses of fertility drugs to stimulate the woman's ovaries and some women either did not respond well or developed too many eggs, as many as 30 or 40, which is seen as being excessive. The use of analogues may not be necessary for all women, and although researchers say GnRH analogues appear safe, the long-term effect of the drug is not yet known.

Method of Use The agonists can be injected, put under the skin in a pellet, or inhaled as a nasal spray. They can be given within the first week of the menstrual cycle in which the woman is undergoing IVF, called a follicular phase start. They can also be given during the last week of the menstrual cycle preceeding the cycle of IVF, from about day 21, called a luteal phase start. In some cases doctors using the follicular phase start use the "flare-up" to help stimulate the ovaries, or they may simply wait until the system has turned down before beginning stimulation with combinations of HMG, CC and FSH. When the agonists are used in the luteal phase, the stimulation with the fertility drugs starts when the system has turned down, usually about six to eight days later. Continued research will determine which regime is best for each patient.

Side-effects Because analogues create a menopause-like condition, women may experience hot flashes and dizziness. The standard fertility drugs can cause headaches, dizziness and fatigue, and many women report feeling moody, irritable and fragile while on the drug stimulations. Hyperstimulation syndrome is rare, but very serious. The long-term side effects of the drugs are not known.

Cancelled Cycles

If the hormone tests or the ultrasound scans do not show adequate egg development or a well-controlled cycle, the doctor may have to cancel the egg pickup and you will have to drop out of that cycle of treatment. This can happen to 10 percent to 35 percent of couples in their first IVF treatment, although it is believed that with the use of GnRH analogues the percentage will be no more than 10 or 15 percent. A cancelled cycle is emotionally difficult but there are advantages to getting out early when success is doubtful. There is no point going through the physical and emotional stress and expense of egg retrieval if there is little chance of getting eggs that will fertilize.

Step Two: Egg Pickup

The retrieval of the eggs from the follicles must be accomplished close enough to the time of ovulation so that the eggs are ripe, but not so close as to risk having them ovulate on their own and be lost into the pelvic cavity.

Originally, the ovaries were reached by laparoscopy while the woman was under a light general anesthetic. A long needle, made to suction and to flush, was used to puncture the follicle, suck out the fluid contents and then wash and suck the follicle to make sure the egg was retrieved. Although laparoscopy is still used in some circumstances, since the mid-1980s aspiration by ultrasound has become the more common method to retrieve the eggs. There are two ultrasound methods that are used: transabdominal aspiration or transvaginal aspiration, but the first method now is used very rarely. It is uncomfortable for petients and requires a general anesthetic. It has been largely replaced by the transvaginal approach.

Transvaginal ultrasound, developed in 1984-1985, is used in more than 90 percent of retrievals. Its ultrasound probe fits into the vagina and various models range in size from a man's index finger to those that are the size and shape of a singer's microphone. The aspirating needle nestles alongside the probe and is passed through the wall of the vagina to the ovary.

A light general anesthetic can be used but an increasing number of IVF physicians maintain that a local anesthetic and a sedative is all that is needed for transvaginal ultrasound retrievals. A local anesthetic allows the procedure to be done in an outpatient setting, decreasing the cost and the risk associated with general anesthetic. By this method, eggs can be retrieved in a matter of minutes. Many clinics allow partners to be present while the eggs are retrieved so that both the man and woman can watch the follicles on the ultrasound screen—they appear as large black dots on the grey-white scan—as they are punctured with a quick jab by the needle and then flushed with a solution to make sure the egg is sucked out.

Some women worry about the amount of pain they may experience if they are awake for the transvaginal procedure. Usually painkillers are given before the operation and then a local anesthetic, a paracervical block, is given to numb the upper vagina and cervix. Researchers at the University Hospital in London, Ontario, conducted a study of the level of pain experienced by 160 patients undergoing retrieval by transvaginal ultrasound. Using a scale of zero to 10, with 10 being the most intense pain a woman could imagine and zero being no pain, they asked the women to identify their level of pain during the procedure. A total of 55 percent of the women recorded a scale of three or less, 75 percent recorded the pain of five or less. Only six percent recorded pain of seven or greater. Dr. Albert Yuzpe, head of the London program said "the pain is extremely well tolerated." The group has now done more than 800 retrievals with transvaginal ultrasound and their findings still stand. "You don't need general anesthetic," Yuzpe says. "It's cheaper, quicker, you get the same access to eggs or better. And besides, doing with a local allows the husband to be there and to share the experience with his wife."

"It was like having dental work done, that's the closest experience that I can link it to," said one woman who had eight eggs retrieved transvaginally while she and her husband looked on. "I mean, it's not a picnic, it hurts, but it certainly doesn't kill you. And we really got into watching the follicles collapse and then hearing whether there was an egg there. That was really exciting. I was glad I didn't miss that."

Some clinics that use transvaginal ultrasound give the woman the choice of a local or a light general anesthetic. Regardless of the method used, as each follicle is punctured and flushed, all its fluid contents are collected in a small vial and are passed through a connecting window to the waiting lab technician in the laboratory. The contents of each vial is swirled in a Petri dish under the microscope until the egg is found. "Mature egg," the technician calls out to the physician if one is found. At that response, or when it becomes clear no egg is in the follicle, the doctor moves on to puncture and aspirate the next follicle until all possible eggs are retrieved.

Step Three: Culture and Fertilization

The laboratory work is one of the most critical stages of the IVF procedure. The process is out of the patient's hands and yet the culture and fertilization of the eggs may be the elements that determine whether an embryo successfully grows into a baby. Lab staff must be vigilant in every step of their work: they must be sure not a trace of detergent is left on the glassware; the temperature of the incubators must not raise a notch or two on a particularly hot day; the culture must not be contaminated. Even if every aspect of the lab has been diligently attended to, some couples' eggs will not fertilize or will fail to divide into a healthy embryo.

As the eggs are received from the operating room, a technician uses a microscope to assess each egg for its maturity and quality. According to Alan Trounson, the determination of egg quality is probably the single most difficult task of IVF. By looking under the microscope, the embryologist must assess whether the egg has ripened and all the egg's chromosomes have undertaken the necessary halving—the factors that enable the egg to be fertilized and a viable embryo to result. There is no easy way to do this and the assessment often relies on the size of the follicle the egg was taken from, with the larger follicles producing the better eggs.

Any immature eggs are placed in separate Petri dishes and incubated to see if they will mature further. Mature eggs are placed in Petri dishes, too, and incubated at 37 to 37.5 degrees Celsius for about eight hours.

Meanwhile, the male partner has produced a semen sample by masturbation. In the lab, the most motile sperm is separated from the rest by washing semen, and spinning it with a centrifuge which reduces the sperm to a pellet; and the motile sperm in the pellet swim into a different culture medium while the less motile stay behind in a process called "sperm swim-up." These procedures "capacitate" the sperm—remove the sperm's acrosome cap from the head and the sperm membrane undergoes changes that enable it to bind to the egg and penetrate it.

The sperm is added to the eggs when they reach the stage when they most likely would have been ovulated. After the sperm has been added to the culture, the egg and sperm are replaced in the incubator and are not disturbed to allow them to undergo fertilization in peace and quiet.

Research has shown that if the man's semen analysis is normal (more than 20 million sperm per milliliter, more than 40 percent motile, 60 percent normal shape), 70 to 80 percent of the eggs will be fertilized. If the semen has one or two variables that are abnormal, fertilization rates fall below 50 percent. If semen has defects in all three categories, the fertilization rates may be less than 10 percent.

After 12 to 20 hours in the incubator, the cultures of egg and sperm are removed and examined under the microscope for evidence of fertilization. The technician looks for the presence of two pronuclei—the sperm's genetic material and the egg's genetic material as two distinct spots in the egg that have not yet fused. That tells the technician the egg has been fertilized. At this stage (any time after fertilization) the result is called a zygote or a pre-embryo. Some IVF programs return the zygotes at this pronuclear stage. Others wait until the genetic material fuses and the embryo begins to divide before it is returned to the uterus.

Eggs that have not been fertilized may be reinseminated with the partner's sperm, or with donor sperm if the IVF physicians do not feel the partner's sperm will be successful. The decision to use donor sperm is not easy and patients should not make the decision just because eggs are there waiting in the lab. It is better to abandon a cycle of IVF than to go ahead with a donor sperm when couples have not had sufficient time to make a clear decision. (See Chapter 9.)

The evaluation of embryos is another of the more difficult tasks of IVF and there are no infallible criteria for what constitutes the best embryo that has the best chance of growing into a child. In general, however, the embryos that divide evenly, regularly and rapidly are considered to be the best. (Embryos in vitro are believed to divide much more slowly than those in the body.)

A worrisome factor for IVF researchers is that the rates of chromosomal abnormalities in eggs and embryos in IVF are very high—it is believed that from 20 to 50 percent of all embryos created in the lab have chromosomal abnormalities. This may be as a result of the process of superovulation, the IVF techniques or an exaggeration of what happens in the natural system. IVF researchers are actively working on a better way to assess the viability of embryos: by taking a piece of the dividing cells to analyze; or by designing a more quantitative measure of development such as measuring the quantity of nutrients the embryo consumes in its culture as it divides. These techniques have not been perfected. For now, only the three or four most healthy looking embryos are replaced in the uterus. Any leftovers are frozen in small capillary tubes in vats of liquid nitrogen at -196 degrees Celsius.

Step Four: Embryo Transfer

The Risks

There has been much discussion and debate among IVF practitioners and within the medical community about the number of embryos to replace in the uterus. It is known that the more embryos replaced, the greater the chance of pregnancy, but also the greater risk of multiple pregnancy, with its considerable risk to the mother and her babies. Most IVF groups, particularly those that have embryo freezing, put back no more than three, at most four, embryos into the uterus because of the risk of multiple births. Some places such as Great Britain have strict regulations stipulating that more than three embryos cannot be replaced, and if more are put back the clinic is censured. In regions where there are no regulations the doctor and the couple decide how many embryos should be replaced. Some clinics that do not yet have freezing put back six or more rather than discarding embryos or donating them to other couples. If you are in a situation where more than four embryos may be replaced, be sure you understand that multiple pregnancy increases the risk of premature labor and birth, perinatal complications such as low birth weight, physical and mental handicaps and perinatal death, as well as possible harm to the mother.

Some doctors argue that the risk of multiple pregnancy is dependent on the individual couple, not necessarily the number of embryos or gametes replaced and, therefore, the guidelines should be flexible. British IVF specialist Dr. Ian Craft has replaced up to 11 eggs in women over 40 undergoing GIFT because he believes it greatly increases the chance of a single pregnancy while not increasing the risk of multiple prgnancy. His practices, however, caused the British authorities to remove approval for his clinic until he complied with their guidelines and replaced no more than four. Craft has been vocal in his opposition to this policy. "We need flexible treatment policies to increase the prospect of pregnancy for the individual couples while avoiding the risks and consequences of multiple pregnancy," he said in a letter to *The Lancet* in November of 1988.

Couples faced with how many embryos to replace should talk over their decision carefully with their doctor and weigh the risks of each option. (See Chapter 11.)

The Procedure

The most dramatic moment when embryos are replaced in the womb lasts less than 15 minutes. When the time comes to replace your embryos, usually between the two- to eight-cell stage, you dress in a hospital gown and walk into the operating theater or examining room and get up on the table yourself. You place your feet in stirrups, as if for a pelvic examination, and the physician places a speculum into the vagina, and cleanses the cervix.

Meanwhile, in the lab the precious embryos are loaded into a narrow plastic catheter and then given to the physician who carefully threads the catheter through the cervical canal into the uterus. The catheter is pushed until the physician can feel it hit the top of the uterus, the fundus, and then it is brought back down a few millimeters so the doctor is assured the embryos are being released close to the top of the uterus. The plunger of the catheter is depressed and the embryos are ejected.

After embryo transfer, you are wheeled to a special room where you lie on your back with your feet elevated for a few hours. Once the embryos are replaced, progesterone suppositories or progesterone injections may or may not be given to sustain the endometrium for implantation. The waxy suppositories are placed in the vagina or in the rectum. It is not really known if the suppositories are necessary, as studies have shown the same outcome whether or not progesterone was used. Some clinics, but not all, continue to give injections of HCG until pregnancy has been established.

Then comes the hardest part for the couple: waiting to see if the embryos "take."

IVF Outcome

Pregnancy Detection

Despite all that has gone before, the most stressful time is from the moment the embryos are returned to the womb until the moment a couple find out whether implantation took place. Most couples describe themselves as "walking on eggshells" or "as tight as a wire." The conflict of emotions can be exhausting. Couples are full of hope and wonderful imaginings of pregnancy and birth—maybe even of twins or triplets—at the same time they are tense, anxious and fearful, afraid that maybe it is not working. The anticipation can be excruciating.

Women are afraid to do anything, wriggle, giggle or even sneeze, lest it somehow harm the pregnancy or cause the embryos to be lost. "I found myself holding my breath—really! I was so tense," one woman said. Rev. Tim Appleton, counsellor at Bourn Hall, laughs about the time a rumor went among the women who had received their embryos back that they should keep their legs crossed so the embryo would not fall out. "We had no idea about the rumor until one woman asked if it was all right if she didn't cross her legs," Appleton said. Doctors can reassure women that if an embryo is going to take, there is usually little that can be done to dislodge it—it is perfectly all right to breath or sneeze or uncross your legs. However, doctors do counsel women against strenuous activity, air travel, or sexual intercourse, at least until pregnancy has been confirmed. After that, women who are pregnant should take care of themselves to try to minimize the risk of losing the pregnancy although lifestyles need not be altered greatly. Margaret Brook, who gave birth to the world's first boy born from a frozen embryo, camped in the Australian outback in the early weeks of her pregnancy, certain that her embryo transfer had failed, only to come home and learn she was almost eight weeks pregnant.

IVF staff say the best job of all is telling a couple they are pregnant. It is always such a wanted, long-awaited pregnancy and not only the couple but the staff are exuberant. The worst job is telling patients that they are not pregnant. This scene, witnessed at Bourn Hall in the summer of 1988, is repeated time and again in IVF clinics around the world: five women, who had all received embryos 15 days earlier, sat tense and silent in the chairs at the base of the stairs near the nurse practitioner's office. All the women had had their blood drawn earlier that day to test for pregnancy. Three women sat with their husbands holding their hands; two had women friends undergoing the program sit with them. One by one the women's names were called and they climbed the stairs into the nurse's office. One by one, four out of five came down either cradled by a husband or comforted by a friend, dabbing their eyes with tissue and crying in disappointment. One came down with a look of immense emotion and conflicting expressions on her face—happiness, disbelief, fear and polite restraint so as not to cause more pain for others by the acknowledgment of her pregnancy.

It has already been stated that pregnancy rates are low for IVF—only one in five women receiving good news is typical for IVF. Knowing that, however, does not make it any easier for couples to receive the news if their attempt failed.

> *We knew that the pregnancy rate was low, but in the back of our mind there was always this feeling, we'll be the 10 percent, it's going to work for us. You have to have that hope or else you wouldn't do it—there is no point going through being certain you will fail. And yet that hope can make it even more difficult when you don't get pregnant. I don't know what the right mindset is to go through with it. I'm sure next time I'll be just as hopeful beforehand and just as disappointed if it doesn't work.*

Trying Again

If IVF does not work the first time should you go back and try again? Many couples who fail the first time do go back, some a few months later, some a few years later when they feel strong again. On the second try a new stimulation protocol may be used that will work better for you. But overall, the individual chance of pregnancy remains at about the same rate for the first few repeats and then becomes lower. Studies have shown, however, that the cumulative pregnancy rate increases. What that means is this: suppose 100 women all started IVF together; about 14 of those would become pregnant on the first attempt. That would leave 86 that were unsuccessful. If all 86 decided to try again, about eleven of those would conceive on the second try, leaving 75 of the original 100 who still had not had a baby. If all 75 women decided to try again, another 10 or so would conceive on the third attempt. Studies showed that if the unsuccessful women were prepared to undergo five attempts at IVF, about 50 percent of the original 100 would have had a baby by IVF at the end of five cycles. Over five attempts at IVF an individual has a 50 percent chance of pregnancy. Of course, you also have a 50 percent chance of no pregnancy. As many couples point out, anything less than the birth of a live baby is a failure, so in a sense each attempt is either a 100 percent success or it is a complete failure.

Some IVF clinics, particularly university or publicly funded ones limit the number of attempts a couple can make to three or four. The commercial operations, however, set no limits. Staff at such clinics tell stories of women who were unsuccessful for eight straight tries, only to become pregnant on the ninth attempt. Most couples would not be able to endure so many tries, financially or emotionally, and this book is not suggesting that couples keep undergoing IVF until they become pregnant. The decision must be left to each couple—only they know when they have had enough. Most IVF physicians say that after three tries couples can say they have given it a very good shot.

Improving the Odds

IVF researchers are working on ways to improve the chance of pregnancy. There are four parts of the process that remain stumbling blocks: consistently getting good quality eggs; improving the culture medium so that embryos will divide and grow as well in vitro as they do in vivo (the body); improving the ability to separate good embryos from poorer ones; and most important, understanding the qualities of the embryo and endometrium that enable embryos to implant.

One of the biggest enigmas in IVF is why embryos of apparently top quality fail to implant. "We have a problem with the womb," says Alan Trounson. "Some women can't get pregnant in a cycle because the condition in the uterus won't allow implantation. We are struggling to understand that. We've been getting closer to knowing what's going on by looking at women who don't have ovaries where we have been able to completely mimic a natural cycle. We know what the endometrium should look like—it shouldn't look like a thick woolly carpet, it should look flatter than that. We know there must be certain receptors, certain changes, but how they are actually programmed and how they can go wrong we don't really know. Until we know all the ingredients involved we won't know how to modify the uterus to make it more receptive to implantation."

Researchers around the world are trying to put together the puzzle of the unreceptive womb and find ways to manipulate it to make it more receptive. Blood flow to the uterus, hormone milieu, the affect of fertility drugs are all being examined as possible clues. Many researchers are experimenting with natural cycles to see if they can be used for some women. Researchers feel certain that bit by bit the IVF picture will improve, but no one is predicting dramatic breakthroughs overnight.

Pregnancy

Some IVF physicians recommend that women who do become pregnant by IVF undergo chorionic villus sampling (CVS) or amniocentesis during pregnancy to make sure there are no chromosome abnormalities in the developing fetus. Others feel it is not necessary. CVS can be performed by the tenth week of pregnancy and involves taking a small sample of what later becomes the placenta. The cells are cultured and the chromosomes are then analyzed for abnormalities. Amniocentesis can be done after the sixteenth week of pregnancy and involves taking a sample of the amniotic fluid that surrounds the fetus. Both techniques carry about a 5 percent risk of inducing miscarriage.

As was mentioned earlier, miscarriage rates are high in IVF pregnancies with as many as 25 to 35 percent ending in spontaneous abortion. The reason is not known, but it may be because the women undergoing IVF have tended to be 35 or older and this age group is known to have a higher rate of miscarriage. Chromosomal abnormalities in the embryo may account for many miscarriages and the factors that may have contributed to the woman's infertility, such as endometriosis or recurrent pelvic infection, might make the woman more prone to lose the pregnancy. Because the exact time of pregnancy is known in IVF, no pregnancy loss goes undetected, whereas women having natural pregnancies might not yet know they are pregnant and consider any bleeding as a delayed menstrual period. Ectopic pregnancies also occur in about 5 percent of IVF conceptions.

Since the first IVF births, IVF practitioners, parents of IVF babies and couples undergoing IVF have all had questions about whether conception outside the body affects the child. Do the fetuses grow as well in the womb? Are there more complications in pregnancy and are the pregnancies intrinsically higher risk? Do birth defects occur more often in IVF babies?

It has been difficult for individual clinics to answer those questions because the numbers of babies born per clinic were too small to notice any trends. To overcome the problem of inadequate sample size, Australia, again, led the way by establishing an IVF registry through that country's National Perinatal Statistics Unit. The central registry collected information on all the IVF pregnancies, including clinical pregnancies, miscarriages, ectopics, stillbirths and live births, recorded by the IVF clinics from 1979 to 1986 and the obstetrical outcome of those pregnancies. Based on 2000 births, the registry found some differences between IVF births and normal births, particularly a greater incidence of premature birth, multiple pregnancies, low birth weight and perinatal death. Perinatal death includes stillbirths and deaths soon after birth such as crib death (Sudden Infant Death Syndrome) within 28 days of birth. This rate was about twice as high as could be expected in the normal population, 30 per 1000 births as opposed to 15 per 1000. It is believed that the multiple pregnancies, increased premature labors and low-birth weight of the premature infants may have contributed to this higher rate of perinatal death.

The registry also found that congenital abnormalities, birth defects, were slightly increased over the general population, but whether this was because of IVF or because of the situations surrounding IVF (older women, reproductive tracts altered by disease) could not be determined. The average rate of birth defects is about 1.5 percent in the general population, but IVF births had a rate of 2.2 percent. A baffling finding was a greater incidence of two malformations, spina bifida and transposition of the great vessels of the heart. The registry reported six cases of spina bifida, three of which were terminated after prenatal diagnosis, when about 1.2 would have been expected in the general population. Transposition of the great vessels occurs when the major arteries out of the heart are reversed; this condition was reported in four of 2000 infants. No other groups have reported an increase in these two abnormalities.

The doctors in charge of the registry, epidemiologist Dr. Paul Lancaster and IVF practitioner Dr. Douglas Saunders, do not know whether the birth defects were related to the IVF procedure, or even if the finding was significant. "It is possible that (the number of congenital abnormalities) are not statistically different than the general population—we haven't got enough numbers to prove that the rate is really higher," Saunders says. "And, again, we don't know what the congenital abnormality rate would be of 34-year-old women who have had 10 years of infertility. It is hard to say what is normal or not in our population of women." The fact that the outcomes of the pregnancies were followed from the moment the pregnancies were recognized might also artificially inflate the incidence of problems that might have gone unreported in the general population, such as spina bifida cases that were terminated before birth.

As the number of IVF children born around the world increases, and more registries compile reports on the outcomes of births, the true picture will become more clear. But it is reassuring for parents of IVF babies to know that studies of the physical and emotional development of IVF children have shown no difference from the normal population. Like Louise Brown, the children are growing up happy, and healthy. In fact, the attention that some IVF children get can make non-IVF children a little jealous. Dr. Gab Kovacs, one of the doctors on the Monash Medical Centre/Infertility Medical Centre IVF team in Melbourne, took his two young children to the party celebrating the program's five-hundredth IVF birth. There was cake and balloons and all the IVF offspring had their pictures taken around Carl Wood and the team. In the car driving home Kovacs's two daughters asked, "Daddy, why couldn't we be IVF kids, too?"

Gamete Intrafallopian Tube Transfer and Other IVF-Related Techniques

In the years since the introduction of IVF, variations have been added to the standard IVF routine to suit couples' needs better. For example, as more couples began to undergo IVF who did not have tubal problems, such as those with unexplained infertility or hostile mucus, doctors began to realize there was no reason to bypass healthy tubes. Variations on the IVF were tried and they were described by a number of acronyms: GIFT, ZIFT, TET, PROST, TEST,

SOURCE and others. The different names generally describe where and when the gametes or embryos are returned to the woman's body. Until the time of egg retrieval, the treatment is essentially the same as IVF, in that all women receive a hormone regimen to stimulate their ovaries to produce more than one egg. The specific IVF variations are described.

GIFT

Gamete intrafallopian tube transfer is the most widely known and oldest of the new variations and has been performed since 1984 when it was pioneered by American specialist Ricardo Asch. His daughter came up with the name GIFT. A gamete is the scientific name for a sex cell, either a sperm or an egg. The name describes how the eggs are placed in the fallopian tubes with the sperm almost immediately after the eggs have been collected to enable the two to fertilize in the natural environment. Essentially, the procedure assures that a ripe egg and a motile sperm meet each other where they should in the tube. For this reason it is particularly recommended for unexplained infertility.

In the GIFT procedure, the ovaries are stimulated with hormones in the same manner as IVF and the HCG shot is given. When the eggs are aspirated from the follicles of the superstimulated ovaries, they are first examined under the microscope to make sure they are ripe and healthy. Then the mature eggs, usually no more than four, are loaded into a fine catheter, or tube. Next the partner's sperm, which has been collected a few hours earlier and prepared, is loaded into the catheter, separated from the eggs by an air bubble. The catheter is gently threaded through the fimbria of the fallopian tube to the ampulla where the contents are ejected. The egg and sperm mingle and, it is hoped, fertilize in the natural environment of the fallopian tube.

In GIFT, unlike IVF, the aspiration of the follicles is usually done under laparoscopy in order for the gametes to be returned to the fallopian tubes. Some doctors, however, are now using transvaginal ultrasound to remove the eggs and replace the gametes with a specially designed flexible catheter that can be fed into the tubes through the cervix and uterus, guided by ultrasound or fluoroscopy. At this writing "transcervical tubal catheratization" is being done in only a handful of centers, but it is expected to become more widely available as equipment becomes more refined and more doctors learn the technique.

GIFT is of use only to women who have open, healthy fallopian tubes. It is most commonly used for couples with unexplained infertility, low sperm counts, hostile cervical mucus or women in whom ovarian stimulation with regular intercourse has not achieved a pregnancy. Asch says that GIFT, done properly in patients with open tubes, should achieve at least a 30 to 35 percent pregnancy rate and many groups report equivalent success rates. Some groups, however, have reported much poorer pregnancy rates, although no one is sure why. In regions where there are long waiting lists for GIFT, some programs have reported as many, or more, pregnancies on the waiting list as those from the treatment. This is understandable in that couples undergoing GIFT have open tubes and some sperm so that they have a reasonable chance of a natural pregnancy. The longer they wait for GIFT the more opportunity they have to conceive naturally.

ZIFT

ZIFT stands for zygote intrafallopian tube transfer (TET, tubal embryo transfer; TEST, tubal embryo staging transfer are the same as ZIFT.). A zygote is the scientific term for the result of the fusion of sperm and egg and can be used to describe the embryo any time after the sperm has fertilized the egg. (*Zygo-* is the Greek prefix meaning joining or combining.) In the ZIFT procedure when the eggs have been removed, they are fertilized in a Petri dish with the partner's prepared sperm. From 20 to 48 hours after fertilization, the embryos, usually no more than four, are replaced in the woman's fallopian tubes. ZIFT differs from IVF in that the embryos are placed in the tube and not in the uterus. ZIFT is primarily used from male-factor infertility in women whose fallopian tubes are open. Its advantage over GIFT is that the fertilization of the eggs is assured before they are returned to the natural environment of the tube to develop and grow. The embryos can either be returned soon after fertilization or once cleavage has begun. It is also used to treat infertility caused by antisperm antibodies.

PROST

PROST stands for pronucleus stage transfer. The pronucleus is the name of the zygote after the sperm has penetrated the ovum before the genetic material of the sperm has merged with the genetic material of the egg and is one of the earliest stages of the embryo, sometimes called the pre-embryo. The genetic material will be two distinct dots in the ovum that will soon merge. PROST is identical to IVF with the exception that the zygotes are transferred to the uterus much earlier than in IVF. Its advantage may be that the embryo is not outside the body as long and it gives the IVF team more flexibility as to when the embryos are returned. The disadvantage is that the embryologist can not be sure the nuclei fused and that cell division took place. It is done for the same people who would have IVF. If the pronuclear embryos are returned to the fallopian tube, it is essentially ZIFT.

The state of the art in using these techniques, according to Dr. Ricardo Asch, the pioneer of GIFT who heads the program at the University of California, Irvine, is to first apply one technique to the couple and then if it does not work, try another form of the technique. For example, a couple who had unexplained infertility with open tubes should first be treated with GIFT. If GIFT failed, they should go to IVF or TET (ZIFT) to make sure the egg is being fertilized. If the man has a low sperm count but the woman's tubes are open, the couple should try TET first. If that fails, they can go on to GIFT and as a last resort try IVF. The cross-over technique may help couples conceive who failed the first time, Asch said. If a woman has blocked tubes, that is the only situation in which the cross-over cannot be used. In that case a couple's only choice is to repeat IVF.

The Stress of IVF

In the short span of time that one IVF cycle takes—a few weeks of a person's life—the emotions evoked can be startling in their intensity and extremes. Patients and IVF counsellors have so often used the phrase "an emotional roller coaster" to describe the fast ride of one IVF treatment that it has become a cliche. But the emotional ups and downs are like a crazy, tense, psychological ride that couples feel caught in as passengers, not drivers. IVF counseller Patricia Mahlstedt at Baylor College of Medicine's IVF program says emotions during this very brief period of time "swing back and forth from hour to hour between confidence and worry, elation and sadness, frustration and relief." Underlying it all is unrelenting tension. Many couples remain on edge for the whole cycle.

Why is it so stressful? Surely couples who are undergoing the IVF treatment have been through a great deal of the infertility mill already. They have had other treatments and in-depth investigations; they may have had major surgery, and they have certainly had disappointments, too. Why should IVF be any more stressful than any other part of infertility?

There is no clear answer. Perhaps many couples see IVF as their last chance; they have come so far already and IVF signals the end of the road. If this does not work, what is left? And there is the money—paying out $5000 or more for one shot, a gamble. For some couples the money may not be a great concern, but for others it may mean no vacation or no money for a down-payment on a house. The money spent would be worth it if one were sure of having a baby at the end, but one simply can not be sure. You pay your money and you take your chance.

And then there are the physical and emotional ups and downs of the treatment itself. "Each phase of treatment seems to have a particular set of emotions," says Nancy Newman, counsellor for the University of British Columbia's IVF program. In the winter of 1988 Newman conducted a study of couples undergoing IVF in Vancouver to determine the emotional experiences common in the six stages: ovulation induction, egg retrieval, embryo transfer, the two-week wait until the pregnancy test, the test result and waiting to start a new cycle. The survey confirmed the pendulum swing of intense emotions.

Newman's study found that during ovulation induction anxiety mingled with optimism seemed to be the most common emotional experience. Couples described themselves as being tense, worried, sleepless, anxious and irritable as they went through the stimulation, but they were hopeful, too. Almost no couples reported depression or sadness at this time.

The feelings of tension, worry and anxiety continued through to egg retrieval, but optimism was still combined with those feelings. Separate from the study, many couples say egg retrieval is quite exhilerating: "You have something tangible at last, three or four eggs, your eggs." If, however, the egg retrieval should fail to get a good yield, or worse, none, it can be a devastating time.

When the gametes were in the lab, the most common feeling was loss of control, "having life on hold," Newman said. One woman said about the lab stage, "I couldn't get it out of my mind. I kept thinking of the sperm and egg in the dish, and in my head I was saying 'Please fertilize, please, please fertilize.' It was like a mantra."

In Newman's survey, embryo transfer was the highest point of positive emotion in the whole treatment. The reality of getting embryos back was marked by confidence and optimism, but combined with that was also the feeling of having no control.

Following quickly on that high point of embryo replacement was the two-week wait for the pregnancy test. Newman's couples confirmed what others have noted; the wait is one of the hardest times for couples. Anxiety and loss of control were both at their highest peaks. (Couples tell of swinging between the feelings of I-must-be-pregnant, I-can't-be-pregnant, like a pendulum.)

The final stage, the pregnancy test, was one of sadness, depression, disappointment and frustration for the majority of couples. Most did not become pregnant. Those that did become pregnant, it is assumed, were thrilled. But because pregnant couples are out-numbered five to one in all IVF programs their positive comments are not reflected in studies of the emotional stress of IVF. Taken together as a whole group, the couples' experience is largely frustrating and disappointing.

Couples who do become pregnant, however, say the positive result makes the stress of the previous stages worth it. "Yah, IVF was stressful, when I think back on it, but none of that seems to matter now that we've got this little guy," said one woman as she held her IVF boy. "It definitely wasn't easy. I know I was tense and anxious, on edge, throughout the treatment. But that has all faded into the background now. I'd do it all again if I knew he'd be the result."

Couples who do not become pregnant often describe the experience as "devastating" or "heartbreaking." "I couldn't believe how it affected me," said one woman who failed to get pregnant in her first cycle. "I have never felt so deeply depressed. So emotionally and physically exhausted. I never thought it would get me down like that."

Her husband said, "For me the hardest part was the lack of control. You just can't do anything about it. You feel so helpless."

The depression and disappointment can linger for a few months after an unsuccessful IVF attempt. Couples often say they felt "flat" or lifeless. But in time couples generally begin to see the experience in a more positive light. A study by Dr. William Keye, chief of reproductive endocrinology and infertility at the University of Utah in Salt Lake City, found that couples going into IVF feel good about themselves and view IVF as a possible solution to their problem. When the attempt fails the immediate reaction is anger, depression, resentment and bitterness. But six months later they are back to their baseline optimism, he reported.

The Shock of Failure

One of the most common reactions couples express, particularly after their first failed treatment, is shock that it did not work for them. "Couples start out overly optimistic and the problem with that is it makes the negative outcome more difficult to deal with," said Newman who also runs an IVF support group. "They just can not believe it didn't work."

Louise Bowen, IVF counsellor for Carl Wood's team in Melbourne, says even if couples know intellectually that the statistics say only one or two in ten couples will have a live birth, it is mentally and physically impossible for them to truly accept it. "Each couple who goes through IVF thinks, 'We are going to be the one in ten,'" Bowen says. "They have to; you cannot go through it believing you will fail."

Many couples have what can best be called a Tinkerbell theory of IVF: if they believe hard enough, it will work for them. Women who have become pregnant by IVF often credit their positive mindset for contributing to its success. "I just knew it was going work," said one woman who got pregnant on the first cycle. "There was no doubt in my mind it was going to work. You just have to have the right attitude. That's all. I was very determined."

The trouble with that mindset, however, is that most women believe just as strongly; they fill their mind with positive thoughts, and yet it does not work. The disbelief and disappointment, then, are devastating. And doubt may creep in: "Did I somehow sabatoge the cycle by thinking negative thoughts? Did my faith falter enough so it didn't work?"

There is no magic. There is no train of thought, or way of thinking that will make IVF work. No amount of believing will guarantee it will work.

How to Cope

So, what is a couple supposed to do? On the one hand, you need the hope and positive outlook to undergo IVF; you have to believe you have at least some chance or it is not worth doing. But on the other hand, if you have too much hope and faith dealing with a negative result becomes so much more difficult. How do you walk the line of realism? How do you keep a healthy mental attitude?

There is no pat answer, but counsellors do have some suggestions about how to make coping with IVF easier, no matter what the outcome.

1. Do not take great risks for the treatment. If undergoing IVF means that you have to sell your house, take on a heavy debt or quit your job, it may not be worth doing. "I have been surprised by the risks that couples take—women who quit their jobs before the cycle; couples who take their names off adoption lists," Newman said. "When it is over, they

have left themselves with nothing to fall back on." When a great deal is riding on a positive outcome, the tension and worry is more extreme and the failure that much harder to deal with.

2. Try not to let your self-esteem and sense of self-worth become wrapped up in the success or failure of the treatment. If you do not become pregnant you are not the one who failed; the treatment failed.
3. Make positive alternative plans in case you do not conceive. You could go back to school, take a pottery course or a painting course. Perhaps planning a trip is the thing to do, or perhaps training for a marathon or getting back into exercise. Or maybe you would enjoy just planting a garden. By having something to look forward to, even if it is a small thing, you do not put yourself in the position of thinking, "If it doesn't work, I don't know what I'll do."
4. During the treatment cycle occupy yourself with things you like to do to help you cope with emotional swings. You may have to spend a lot of time waiting—waiting for blood test results, waiting for the eggs to fertilize, waiting after the embryos have been returned—which gives lots of time for worry cycles and emotional tension to build. A good book may be all you need, but some people find concentrating on reading too difficult. Many women bring knitting, small puzzles, a sketch pad, or a diary to write down their feelings.
5. Seek help from the program's counsellor or ask to be referred to a counsellor if you are having a hard time coping with emotions during the treatment cycle. "Many couples are afraid to come and tell me they are not coping too well," Bowen says. "They are afraid that we may cut them off the program or tell them we think they should stop. But we never judge them, we never are assessing their 'fitness' for treatment, we never say you should quit. It always is their own decision. We may help them clarify how they are feeling. But they decide when to start and stop. We are just here to talk to, if they need it."
6. Be honest with yourself about your desire to undergo IVF. If at the end of the treatment you emerge unsuccessful, will you still be glad you tried it? Is spending the money and the time only worth it to you if you can have a baby at the end? No matter what the outcome, will you still think it was a good thing to do?
7. Do not become frustrated by trying to control what you can not control. Understand that you have no control over how many eggs develop, how well they fertilize, or if they develop into a pregnancy. Accept that it is out of your hands.
8. Keep your chance of success in perspective. Approach IVF treatment with the attitude that it gives you more chance of pregnancy than you would probably have without it. Acknowledging that it improves your chance of pregnancy but does not guarantee it will probably help you have the needed optimism without creating expectations that are out of line.

First Is Worst

The first IVF treatment is often the worst, couples and IVF counsellors say. It is all so new; patients are never sure what to expect from the drugs or the procedures. Will the drugs make you feel bad? Will egg retrieval be painful? Will the sperm be able to fertilize the eggs? Nothing is routine. Everything and anything can be unsettling.

Subsequent treatments are usually easier to handle, couples say.

> *The first cycle I was overly optimistic and I just didn't know what to expect. I was shattered when it didn't work. The second time I had it all in better perspective. I was optimistic, but not overly, overly optimistic. I felt more relaxed. It wasn't going to kill me if it didn't work. I knew I'd be really disappointed, but I'd get through it.*

Counsellors say they can tell who is on the first cycle and who is back for another try, just by the way the people interact with the staff and with other patients. "The people on their first cycle tend to keep to themselves. They're not apt to strike up a conversation or joke with others, they seem more tense," Newman said. "Women on their second cycle seem much more relaxed."

Many couples do not want to talk about any of the emotional aspects during the first treatment. "They want to know when she should get her shots, when they have to be where, how the program works, how long it will take to do this or that. Nuts-and-bolts stuff. They want information and that is all."

It is only after a few cycles, particularly when cycles have not worked, that couples seem more ready to talk about it, Bowen said. "It is the realization tht they probably are not going to be successful. It usually takes a few tries for people to start to think, 'I don't think this is going to work for me.' That's when they really want to talk."

Deciding When It Is Time to Stop

Some clinics limit the number of tries a couple can have at IVF to three or four. Other clinics leave it open-ended. But most counsellors recommend that couples have some idea how much they will endure for IVF. How much money? How many times? When will they feel that they can stop and say they gave it a good try?

"We suggest that couples set time frames," Bowen said. "We don't tell them when they should stop or when they can't come back. People have to make that decision themselves. But if they set time frames they can review the decision when the time is up."

Making the decision to stop can be extremely difficult. "It is a huge emotional decision," Bowen said. "They have invested a lot of time and money and they feel like they have nothing to show for it. It represents the crunch, the end after years of pills and tests and surgery. And at the end there is no consolation prize." But despite the difficulty of stopping IVF, many couples experience a sense of relief, counsellors say.

Rev. Tim Appleton, who counsels patients at Bourn Hall, recalls one couple who had had six attempts and came to see him when they were considering their seventh try. "They said they would have to sell the house and get something smaller but they were prepared to do that. But as I talked to them I could sense that one of them—the man—had a much stronger desire to undergo IVF again. I told them what I sensed and I told them to go away and talk about it. And sure enough they said, you're right. He was prepared to sell the house because he thought she really wanted it. She, frankly, had had enough and wanted their life to get back to normal but was doing it because she thought he really wanted to do it. When they both realized how each other felt it was a great relief for them to stop."

Many couples, when they stop, are philosophical, Bowen said. "A lot of them say to me, 'After all this time we're pretty good at dealing with disappointment.' They can sit back and say, 'We tried.'"

Surplus Eggs

The use of fertility drugs to stimulate the woman's ovaries has enabled the IVF team to get multiple eggs, increasing the chance that one will produce a baby. But the ability to get so many eggs creates a new problem: what should be done with the leftovers? They certainly couldn't be thrown away.

Embryo Freezing

Freezing (also known as cryopreservation) seemed the most logical answer. In the early 1970s animal embryologists began freezing mouse embryos in the early stages after fertilization to see if they could then be thawed, implanted and eventually result in a live birth. The first live mice born from frozen embyros were reported in 1972. It wasn't until late 1980 that Alan Trounson in Australia began experimenting with freezing human embryos in IVF, using the expertise he had gained when he developed methods to freeze cow embryos at Cambridge a few years earlier. "We came up with freezing at the same time we came up with superovulation," Trounson said. "We had to—we had to do something with all the eggs."

Embryo freezing offered a number of advantages for the couple undergoing IVF. First, it increased chances of pregnancy from the same IVF cycle and egg retrieval. The three best embryos in IVF treatment could be transferred to the woman's uterus in the IVF treatment cycle and the rest could be frozen and replaced at a later time, saving the trauma and expense of another treatment. Most important, since the eggs were replaced in a natural cycle the endometrium would not have to be altered by drug stimulation and it might therefore be more receptive to implantation. Trounson and his Ph.D. student Linda Mohr began experimenting with cryopreservation by placing embryos in protective solution (cryoprotectant) and slowly cooling the embryos before placing them in liquid nitrogen at −196°C.

In March of 1984 the world's first frozen embryo baby was born to a Victoria couple, Lorreto and David Leyland, who were in Wood's and Trounson's program. The eight-cell embryo had been frozen for a number of months with five other embryos created in vitro. A baby girl, Zoe, was born, a perfectly normal little girl, and a few months later the world's first frozen-embryo boy, John, was born to Margaret and Brian Brooks. The pregnancy had come as a total surprise to the Brooks because Margaret had already undergone a number of IVF attempts and frozen egg replacements with no success. The replacement of the two embryos, one of which eventually became John, did not look promising because they had been considerably damaged by the process. One embryo had only two out of six cells still living; the other embryo had only one out of four cells still living. The doctors decided to replace the two embryos anyway.

"I thought there is no way this is going to work," Margaret Brooks recalls. Two pregnancy tests after the replacement were negative and so the couple went on a camping trip into the outback. When her period still had not come she got her husband to drive 100 miles to pick up a pregnancy kit, which Margaret set up in the tent. To their amazement it was positive and she was eight weeks pregnant. Despite its slow beginning, the developing fetus soon caught up and John was born August 16, 1984, completely normal and healthy in every way. He has since grown into a precocious, charming little boy, the center of the Brooks' life. "I look at him and I still just can't believe it. It seems like such a stroke of luck."

In 1985 Bourn Hall announced its first frozen-embryo births and soon after many other IVF clinics began to adopt freezing programs. Now a substantial number of IVF programs arund the world freeze the excess embryos. The standard process involves placing the embryos in one of three cryoprotectants in small glass ampoules, slowly lowering their temperature degree by degree until it reaches -80 degrees Celsius and then placing them in liquid nitrogen at -196 degrees Celsius.

The benefits of freezing are hampered by the problems: as many as half of the frozen embryos, once they are thawed, are no longer viable, though some may divide and grow despite damage. The frozen ones that are replaced in the womb tend to have the same or slightly worse success rate compared to fresh embryos replaced in the IVF cycle. In 1987, for example, the Monash IVF program under Trounson thawed 272 embryos for 136 patients, but only 115 embryos (42 percent) survived the thaw. Of the 81 patients who received thawed embryos, only nine developed viable pregnancies (11 percent) compared to a 16 percent pregnancy rate for fresh embryos. Only 7 percent of patients in the program who had stored frozen embryos ended up with a pregnancy from them in 1987. The frozen embryos do, however, give women more chances at pregnancy from one single treatment of IVF.

Researchers around the world are working on ways to further improve the outcome of frozen embryos. Many feel the habit of replacing the best IVF embryos during the treatment cycle and freezing the rest has unfairly biased the results of freezing since the ones frozen were not as good to begin with. If the best embryos were frozen and replaced in a natural cycle, the results might be the same as or superior to fresh and frozen embryos, researchers say. Other research has shown that if embryos are frozen at the pronucleus stage, the thawing survival rate and the pregnancy rate are higher, perhaps as much as 20 to 25 percent pregnancy rate in patients who receive embryos back. The reason is not known but one explanation may be that because pronuclear embryos have not yet begun to divide, an equal number of embryos of top quality and lesser quality are frozen, removing the bias from selecting the best to remain fresh.

Researchers have been trying to develop ways of freezing embryos faster. In 1987 Trounson came up with a new method, ultrarapid freezing, which he feels may be a superior and significantly cheaper method. Embryos are combined with a special mixture of cryoprotectant and buffer solution, sealed in the ampoule and plunged directly in liquid nitrogen. He did not expect this experiment to work, but he found the results to be superior. In mouse embryos frozen by the ultrarapid technique, no difference could be found between the fresh and thawed embryos. "It just takes a couple of minutes to do, there is no extra cost or fancy equipment, it's very efficient and if it works in mice it should work in humans," Trounson said. Clinical results of ultrarapid freezing, however, in human IVF are not yet available. Prof. Ian Johnston, of Melbourne's rival IVF program at Royal Women's Hospital, said his group has been able to freeze eggs and have more than 85 percent survive the thaw. He believes, however, that the practice of leaving the best embryos fresh and freezing the rest should be reviewed and studies should compare the outcomes when the best embryos are frozen and replaced in natural cycles.

The Famous Rios Embryos and Other Legal/Ethical Dilemmas

While embryo freezing helps to solve the problem of what to do with excess embryos, the practice has created ethical and legal dilemmas. Some pro-life groups have adopted the stance that freezing embryos is the same as freezing children and because as many as half do not survive the process, it amounts to killing children. Although most people's stance is not so extreme, there is no doubt that embryo freezing can create legal and ethical problems.

The most famous frozen embryo dilemma to date concerns the "orphaned" Rios embryos. Mario and Elsa Rios were a wealthy Californian couple who flew to Melbourne in June of 1981 to undergo IVF at Wood's and Trounson's program. Three of Mrs. Rios's eggs were fertilized. One embryo was transferred to her womb and two were frozen, a process the team had just started. Mrs. Rios became pregnant but miscarried early on. But the couple decided to return home and the embryos were to remain frozen until they returned to have them replaced. The couple and their adopted child were tragically killed in 1983 in a plane crash in Chile. They left a million dollar estate, no will and two frozen, orphaned embryos.

A big debate arose—were the embryos the rightful heirs to the estate? If they were implanted in a surrogate mother could any resulting child claim the estate? Should they remain frozen indefinitely? Should they be thawed and given anonymously to an infertile couple? Should they be thrown out?

Anti-abortion groups protested any disposal of the embryos. More than 100 women in Australia and the United States offered to be the gestational mother of the embryos. Mario Rios's son by his first marriage, Michael, applied for guardianship of the embryos, but in a complicating factor it was learned that Mrs. Rios's eggs had been inseminated by a donor and so Michael Rios had no right to them. Trounson and Woods felt in some ways the controversy might be a non-issue because the embryos had been frozen so early in their freezing program there was only a 5 percent chance that either embryo would survive the thaw.

Nevertheless, the embryos remained in storage while courts and ethical committees in Australia and the United States debated the issue. In December 1986 Carl Wood asked the Victoria minister of health for direction about what they should do with the embryos. The issue was referred to the ethical committee and debated some more. At the end of 1987 the minister announced the embryos could be thawed and implanted anonymously in an infertile couple. (In December of 1987 a California court declared Elsa Rios's mother to be the guardian of the embryos, but she told them she would not make a claim.)

But a catch-22 situation arose by the spring of 1988 that now makes it seem unlikely the embryos will ever be thawed and implanted, says Wood. The Rios had never been tested for AIDS antibodies—the test didn't even exist and the disease was barely known in 1981. But in 1988 no gametes or embryos can be donated without the donor being tested for AIDS antibodies. "We really can't implant them now," said Wood. It seems the embryos are destined to stay frozen in the liquid nitrogen forever.

The Rios embryos are not the only ones in the center of a legal dilemma. In Tennessee, a couple has been waging a custody battle over embryos frozen during an IVF attempt before their divorce. The woman wanted to have the embryos implanted but the ex-husband did not. At this writing the case has not been resolved.

To minimize the problems of what to do with frozen embryos, all programs require couples to sign consent forms detailing how the embryos will be disposed of should divorce, death or illness interfere. Consent forms also allow for embryo donation to another infertile couple should the original couple decide they do not want all the embryos to be transferred back, particularly in the case of women who have many eggs harvested.

"We had one woman who had 31 eggs fertilize. We transferred four embryos and froze the rest and she had the nerve to get pregnant on the first replacement!" said Dr. Richard Marrs, a Los Angeles IVF practitioner. "She wants a big family, but not that big. That leaves us with the problem, what are we going to do with all those embryos? Fortunately our consent forms allow for donation if the couple does not want all the eggs."

Theoretically it is possible the embryos could be frozen indefinitely, giving rise to such strange possibilities as an embryo being conceived today and implanted 100 years from now in a woman three or four generations removed from the original parents; or a mother leaving her frozen embryos to her daughters or granddaughters to implant if they like, allowing them technically to give birth to a sister or aunt. To avoid problems like this, most programs stipulate a time frame after which the embryos will be destroyed or donated, such as when the woman turns 45 or 10 years after freezing.

When the couple wants to try for another pregnancy again, they notify the IVF clinic that they would like to have one or two embryos thawed and replaced. The woman's natural menstrual cycle is followed closely. After her LH surge occurs the embryos are removed from the liquid nitrogen, thawed and then assessed for quality. If more than 50 percent of the cells are still viable, the embryos are returned to the uterus in the same manner as IVF embryo replacement.

Egg Freezing

Many of the problems associated with freezing embryos could be avoided if eggs could be frozen before fertilization. The eggs would not be considered potential babies just as a sperm cell can not be considered a potential human being. The eggs could simply be thawed and fertilized when needed, just as frozen sperm is today. Oocyte banks for donations could be set up and young women could potentially bank eggs for the future to protect against disease, aging or other events that might impact on fertility.

Researchers started trying to freeze mouse and rat eggs in the early 1950s and research continued off and on for the next 30 years. But frozen eggs have always had poor fertilization rates after thawing. A number of people tried fertilizing frozen-thawed human eggs in the 1980s, also with poor success. Only one researcher, Dr. Christopher Chen, reported any real success in freezing eggs. He reported the first IVF twins, male and female, born from frozen eggs in South Australia in 1986. A baby girl was born from another egg frozen in Chen's program in 1987. The only other place where egg freezing has been successful is in Germany where three pregnancies were established, one that ended with a live birth and two miscarriages.

The limited success of egg freezing has been accompanied by a great deal of concern in the research/medical community because of the possibility of damaging the genetic material of the egg during freezing. The biggest concern with egg freezing is that it creates too many chromosomal abnormalities. When the egg is being frozen it is undergoing the precise process of halving its chromosomes, called the second meiotic division. This is such a delicate and important step of egg maturation that if the freezing or thawing or the cryoprotectant interferred with the process, significant abnormalities such as too many chromosomes or breaks in chromosomes or absence of chromosomes could result. As well, any cracks in the outer shell of the egg, the zona pellucida, could allow more than one sperm to enter and fertilize the egg, leading to more chromosomal problems that are usually fatal to the embryo. Trounson and others at the Monash program have tried oocyte freezing but stopped when they found too many chromosomal abnormalities. "I have been very critical of the business of freezing eggs because from all our work we think it is too dangerous. We are worried because we have had to terminate some pregnancies," Trounson said.

Although freezing eggs is theoretically desirable, it is far away from becoming widely available in IVF practices.

Egg Donation

A final option for dealing with surplus eggs is to donate them to another couple. The donated egg would be fertilized with the recipient's partner's sperm and the developing embryo would be transferred to the recipient's uterus.

Couples undergoing IVF at a clinic that has an egg donation program are asked if they consent to having any of their surplus eggs donated to another couple. There are a number of reasons why a woman's own eggs are not usable: she may have had premature menopause; she may have been born without ovaries; she may have had her ovaries removed through surgery; or she may be at risk of passing on an inheritable genetic disease; or she may have ovaries that do not respond to stimulation.

Donation of eggs is anonymous, but the physical characteristics of the mother and the donor are matched and non-identifying information is given about the donor and the recipient to both couples, if wanted. Some women undergoing IVF find it hard to imagine their eggs going to another woman when they themelves are trying to get pregnant. "If I knew for sure that I would get pregnant with IVF than I think I'd be able to donate without any trouble," said one woman who decided not to do it. "But if I didn't get pregnant I might wish I had those eggs to fall back on. And what if the woman got pregnant on one of my eggs and I didn't?"

Other women, however, put themselves in the other women's shoes and, knowing how much they want a baby, imagine how grateful they would be if someone did that for them. "I didn't have any problem donating," said Margaret Brooks, the Melbourne woman who gave birth from a frozen embryo and donated three times during her five IVF treatments. "I had met so many wonderful women in the hospital undergoing IVF that I thought if I can maybe do something to help you get pregnant, I will. I knew how much I'd want someone to do it for me."

A woman who donates eggs can decide how many of the eggs retrieved she wants to give away and is assured that the best eggs are kept and used for her own IVF attempt. Women can also decide whether to allow their eggs and embryos to be used for research.

On the Receiving End of Egg Donation

Until egg donation became a reality, women whose ovaries were absent or not working had no hope of bearing a child. But egg donation has changed all that. Since the mid-1980s a number of babies have been born as the result of egg donations. The first donor egg baby was born in 1984 in Melbourne.

The procedure for donations varies among clinics, and even among women, depending on such things as whether the woman has a natural menstrual cycle, open fallopian tubes and whether the partner has fertile sperm.

Most clinics require that all couples receiving donated gametes in IVF first talk with an independent counsellor to discuss the relevant issues. "I want to make sure they are both equally happy with it," said Rev. Tim Appleton, independent counsellor for Bourn Hall. "I want to make sure that it isn't going to present any problems for them later, that they have discussed the issues. If they do have problems sometimes it is something we can work through." Some counsellors say that egg donation usually presents fewer problems than sperm donation because the woman carries the fetus and gives birth so both parents feel equally involved.

Making the Switch

The synchronization of egg retrieval from the donor and the transfer of the embryo to the recipient is a bit like jumping from one fast moving train to another. It takes some coordination and finesse on the part of the IVF clinic. There are a few ways the switch can be made. If the recipient woman has a natural cycle, the women's cycles can be lengthened or shortened slightly by fertility drugs so that they coincide. If the recipient woman does not have a natural cycle, the doctors can create one by giving her estrogen and progesterone. Estrogen is given in increments in the first half of the cycle and progesterone in the second half. Some women stay on this sort of artificial cycle for a number of months until a donor egg becomes available. Another option is to fertilize the donor egg as soon as it becomes available with the recipient husband's sperm, freeze the resulting embryo and then wait to thaw it until the woman's cycle is ready.

The embryo is usually returned between day 15 and 20, but GIFT has been done with donor eggs so that the egg and sperm are introduced together in the recipient's fallopian tubes and allowed to fertilize there. If the woman has open fallopian tubes, there is no reason why TET or other variations of IVF could not be performed as well.

Known Donors

The majority of egg donors are woman who are infertile and undergoing IVF. (Volunteer donors or women undergoing sterilization also become donors but they are not many.) Some clinics, however, allow known donors, enabling a woman to bring in a sister or a friend to donate an egg for her, but this practice is controversial. Unlike the attitude toward sperm donors, where there is almost unanimous medical and ethical opinion that the donor should be anonymous because of the psychological problems of using a brother or a friend, the attitude for known egg donors is split into two camps, for and against. Many clinics have strict rules forbidding it, either because that has been decided by the clinic's ethical committee or by the regulations of the state or country.

The opposition arises from concerns that a sister or friend might feel obligated or coerced into donating eggs because of her relationship to the infertile women. In addition, the resulting child might create tension, disharmony or rivalry between the mother and the donor woman over how the child is being reared. Competition for the child's affections might occur or the child might be confused about his or her identity. Adding to the issue is the fact the donor must undergo the risks and physical stress of ovarian stimulation and egg retrieval.

In Britain, the Voluntary Licensing Authority, which oversees the practice of IVF, does not sanction known donors. One IVF practitioner, Professor Ian

Craft, had his clinic approval removed in 1987 when the VLA found out he had allowed sister donations. The VLA reinstated his approval when he stopped the practice, but Craft remained upset that he could not provide this option to his patients who wanted it.

"I don't see anything wrong with it," Craft said. "I think it is wonderful if a sister wants to donate an egg to another sister, if they've talked it over very carefully and know what is involved. I would be very upset if I were a woman with ovarian failure who had sisters who wanted to donate to me and someone prevented me from doing so. On whose authority do they speak, I ask you?"

Craft said although people express the concern over the negative aspects that could arise between sisters from the donation, no one seems to consider the positive aspects. "It could just as easily bring them even closer together, really strengthen the family. It could be very good for the child to have two women who shared a deep commitment to him. I don't know where people get these ideas it would be all negative. And shouldn't the sisters be the judge of that?"

Dr. Ricardo Asch, whose University of California, Irvine clinic has a large egg donation program, said in 1988 they had already had 15 sister-sister donations. All the sisters have to undergo psychological evaluation and discuss issues such as child rearing, but no one really knows how it will impact on the family in the long run. "We have no experience with it," Asch said. "I still don't think that means we should prevent people from doing it. That seems very dictatorial to me."

The controversy over known egg donors is likely to continue. Women who want this option will have to seek out those clinics who will do it for them. Any sisters contemplating this route, however, should carefully discuss all the issues and know what is at stake. Professional counselling for both sisters should be considered to make sure that all underlying feelings and complicating factors are brought to the surface before undergoing the procedure.

The Controversial Frontiers of IVF

IVF Surrogacy

A highly controversial area of IVF is that of IVF surrogacy, or host womb, a process in which an embryo created by a couple is transferred into the womb of a surrogate mother who carries the baby to term and gives it back to the genetic parents after birth. IVF surrogacy enables a woman who has functioning ovaries but is unable to carry a pregnancy to have a child who is genetically related to both her and her partner. A typical candidate is a woman who has been born without a uterus, has had a hysterectomy, or has uterine abnormalities. The obstacle: finding a woman willing to undergo nine months of pregnancy and birth only to surrender the baby at the end.

In the handful of publicized host-womb births, the surrogate mother has usually been a sister or, in one famous incident, the mother of the infertile woman. In 1987, 48-year-old Pat Anthony, of South Africa, gave birth to triplets created from her daughter's eggs and her son-in-law's sperm, becoming the first woman in the world to give birth to her own grandchildren. Her daughter, Karen Ferriera-Jorge, then 27, had been forced to have a hysterectomy three years earlier after the birth of her first son. Anthony knew how distressed her daughter and son-in-law were at not being able to have more children. On her own initiative, she found an IVF clinic in Johannesberg that would allow her to be the surrogate mother for their embryos before she presented the idea to them. The surrogacy arrangement met with a great deal of opposition, ethical debate and media coverage. When the triplets were born, all normal and healthy, a judge ruled that Ferriera-Jorge and her husband Alcino had to adopt them to be their legal parents in the eyes of the law. In most countries the legal mother is the woman who gives birth to the baby and courts have not yet come to grips with genetic and gestational mothers.

In Australia in 1988 two sister-sister surrogacy arrangements made a big splash in the news. One resulted in the birth of a baby girl in Melbourne, the other in the birth of triplets in Perth. The Melbourne case involved Linda and Maggie Kirkman. Maggie, 40 and childless, had undergone a hysterectomy a number of years earlier. Linda, 32, had two children and wanted to help her sister have a baby. They approached IVF physicians Carl Wood and John Leeton and over a number of meetings convinced the doctors to allow Linda to carry embryos for Maggie. (Maggie's husband was also infertile so donor sperm would have to be used to inseminate her eggs.) What made the Kirkman's surrogacy arrangement particularly controversial was that when Wood and Leeton approached their hospital's ethics committee for permission to transfer the eggs to Linda, the committee would not allow it. Victoria law says that only infertile women can receive medical treatment to establish a pregnancy. "(The committee) felt the law was unclear and so rejected it," Wood says. Wood and Leeton circumvented the committee by having Leeton carry out the embryo transfer at a small private hospital outside Melbourne. "We were a bit naughty doing that," Wood admits. "But we thought it was the right thing to do. The more we saw the sisters the more impressed we were that they could handle it and they knew what they were doing. They had intelligence, compassion. If we waited until the law was worked out they would be too old to do it. So we made the decision to circumvent the hospital."

Linda's sacrifice for her sister was great indeed. The pregnancy ran into trouble at week 29 and for eight weeks Linda had to lie in a hospital bed so the pregnancy would not be lost. Still, at the end of it all, Linda said it was worth it and she had no regrets giving the newborn Alice to her sister. "I feel no maternal bond, she is genetically not my baby, I just carried her," Linda told the media. The state government, however, ruled that Maggie would have to apply to adopt Alice to become her legal mother. It also ruled that further IVF surrogacy arrangements were illegal in the state.

IVF surrogacy arrangements are rare and many clinics will not do them either because of the ethical and legal debates that surround the practice or because other authorities will not allow it. However, most people can identify with the plight of a woman who has been forced to have a hysterectomy and still wants a family. Perhaps IVF surrogacy with a willing surrogate who is acting out of love or devotion should be a legitimate option. But the fear is that once IVF surrogacy is accepted, it will become distorted until it is used by women for convenience rather than need, that one woman will hire another woman to undergo pregnancy for her because she would rather not be pregnant, but she still wants a genetic child. In all likelihood the host womb hired would be that of a woman needing money. Like the nurse-maids in the Middle Ages who breastfed babies of the nobility because breastfeeding was "below" the upper class, a child-bearing class of women could emerge to carry other women's pregnancies, not out of love or devotion, but to earn a living.

The procedure would not have to be limited to IVF. Embryo flushing, a procedure in which the egg is fertilized under natural conditions and then flushed from the woman's body and implanted in another woman, would be the easiest method. Embryo flushing is already performed in top breeding animals, such as show horses, so that less valuable animals carry the offspring.

Some states and countries already have regulations in place, or at least have made policy recommendations to restrict or prevent surrogacy on a commercial basis. A survey of IVF directors in the United States reported in *Fertility and Sterility* in 1981 that 59 percent of those who responded to a questionnaire opposed IVF surrogacy. Some doctors and policy advisors in a number of countries, however, believe the problems can be avoided if arrangements that involve payment to the IVF surrogates are banned. When altruism is the motivation, some people feel IVF surrogacy should be allowed for the Linda Kirkmans and Pat Anthonys of the world to willingly make their own choices.

Embryo Biopsy

Embryo biopsy is another area now being pioneered in IVF. One or two cells are taken from the developing embryo at the eight-cell stage and are examined for genetic and chromosomal defects. If the embryo is healthy, it is replaced in the womb. (The cells taken do not interfere with the development of the early embryo at this stage and it would grow normally after it is transferred to the womb.) If there is evidence of defects, the embryos are discarded. Scientists in Cambridge have already been able to biopsy mouse embryos for a specific defect. Embryologists in Australia, Europe and North America are also working on the techniques.

Although embryo biopsy is still undeveloped, many scientists say before long embryos will be successfully biopsied for chromosomal abnormalities. Only a fraction of all possible diseases that have their origins in a single gene or set of genes can now be identified because science has not yet discovered the genetic codes for these defects or where they reside on the chromosomes. But mapping the human genome—the complete set of genetic instructions encoded on the 23 pairs of chromosomes—has become a focus of considerable scientific effort. In January of 1989 the United States National Institute of Health launched a $3 billion project to map the human genome, bringing together a wide range of scientists from a multiplicity of areas: computer science, molecular biology, genetics, engineering, biochemistry and others. The leader of the project is Dr.

James Watson, famed Nobel laurete who with Francis Crick in 1953 discovered the code of DNA. The group predicts that in as little time as 15 years most of the genome could be mapped. Such a development would allow gene probes to be developed that would screen more precisely the cells of an embryo for hereditary diseases.

Although such a tremendous scientific effort could reduce a great deal of disease and suffering, many critics are concerned that embryo biopsy would create a world where only the perfect would be tolerated. The question arises: how far do we go in deciding what is genetically undesirable?—allergies or asthma? a tendency towards heart disease? a propensity for alcoholism?

Australian social scientist Ditta Bartels calls efforts to weed out genetic defects the new eugenics. "The old eugenics was to achieve a perfect population, a perfect race," she said in a lecture on the hazards of reproductive engineering in 1987. "On the whole this has given way to the individualistic goal of avoiding genetic blemishes in one's offspring. But the objectives remain much the same, namely the eugenic ambition to achieve genetic perfection with an in-built bias against those who are considered not to be perfect."

Choosing Gender

Sex selection in which embryos would be discarded depending on what the couple wanted, is also a concern expressed by those opposed to the technique. There may be some advantages to sex selection in the case of inherited diseases such as hemophilia that reside on one of the sex chromosomes. Already researchers in Edinburgh have been able to determine the sex of eight-day old embryos by embryo biopsy. Critics like Bartels and others, however, are concerned the sex ratio of a population could be distorted by such practices, particularly in cultures where a great deal of emphasis is put on the birth of a boy.

Those in favor of the embryo biopsy technique say both chromosomal screening and sex selection is already available through chorionic villus sampling and amniocentesis in the first trimester of pregnancy. Many couples, particularly in later reproductive years, routinely have amniocentesis to screen for abnormalities. The proponents of embryo biopsy say not replacing an eight-cell embryo is certainly more desirable than aborting a 16-week-old fetus. According to reports, amniocentesis is already used for sex selection in a number of cultures where it is available. In an article on gender selection, American anthropologist Melvin Konner describes a survey of 700 women who underwent amniocentesis at a hospital in Poona, India, during 1976 and 1977. The survey found that of the 450 women who learned they were carrying daughters, 430 chose to abort the pregnancy. Of the 250 women who were carrying boys not one chose to abort, although some were shown to have genetic defects, Konner said.

Other Ethical Concerns

While IVF surrogacy and embryo biopsy are the most immediate, and, at this point, the most realistic of the IVF concerns, they are by no means the limits of the technology. IVF and embryo manipulation have placed what was science fiction a decade ago into the realm of science fact.

The following have become more technically feasible because of IVF.

Cloning The identical duplication of individuals can be as simple as splitting an early embryo in two with a microscopic scalpel to make identical twins, a process already used in animal embryology. This embryo twinning could be used in IVF to create two embryos and increase the chance that one would "take" in the uterus. Of more concern is the cloning of a large number of identical offspring en mass from a single embryo.

Cloned cows and sheep are already romping in pastures of some breeding farms. They have been created by first giving the top-quality mother fertility drugs to produce a number of eggs, inseminating her with the semen from a prize bull and flushing out the resulting embryos. The embryos are then examined for the desired characteristics—in the case of cattle being male—and the embryo that is selected to be cloned is allowed to grow to a certain number of cells. Then, using microscopic instruments, the nucleus of each of the cells, which contain the genetic blueprint for the calf, is removed. The genetic material is dropped into the de-nucleated unfertilized eggs of standard-brand cows. It is like taking the yolk out of an egg and transferring that yolk to another egg which has had its yolk removed. The result is equivalent to a fertilized egg that soon divides into an embryo. The embryos are transferred to surrogate cows, which give birth to identical offspring all at the same time. The animal husbandry industry is interested in cloning because it gives livestock a uniform quality and production value, like a manufacturing plant that turns out the same product.

Although cloning is technically possible in human beings there is no persuasive argument why anyone would want to do it. Still, it is a concern and in those countries or states where laws or guidelines involving IVF are in place, cloning research for humans is not allowed.

Transgenics This process is the injection of new genes into the embryo so that it is born with specific qualities. South Australia researchers have injected a gene for growth hormone into a sheep embryo and produced a larger, faster growing sheep. The ability to inject genes presents the specter of creating super human beings in the lab.

Mixed Species, or Chimeras The fusion of embryos from different species is an attempt to create a new species. At the University of California, Davis, the first geep, part-goat, part-sheep was born in 1985 from the fusion of two embryos. Will some scientist try to make a half-man, half-beast just to see if it can be done?

Ectogenesis The complete gestation of a fetus outside the uterus is another "fringe" that IVF makes more plausible. As neonatologists learn how to keep smaller and smaller premature babies alive and embryologists learn to grow embryos longer, the two areas may move closer and closer together. Right now a mere 21 weeks in the womb separate the embryo from the youngest premature baby that has been kept alive. The big question is why would we want ecotgenesis in the first place, just to see if it could be done?

Fetal Spare Parts Some scientists believe "farming" embryonic tissue to grow various organs, body components or needed tissue, such as kidneys for transplantation, is a possible off-shoot of IVF. Because each cell of the early embryo has the ability to differentiate into all the organs of the body, it is theoretically possible that organs, or at least needed body chemicals such as interferon or immune cells, could be farmed in the laboratory and used for medicinal purposes.

Government Controls

It is not hard to understand why in recent years a great deal of public backlash and concern has been expressed about IVF and the new reproductive technologies. Society is afraid of where these techniques may lead. The technologies are going too fast, outstripping society's moral or ethical ability to understand them and deal with them.

"It took human beings a long time to work out the customs, ethics and laws appropriate to the traditional forms of human reproduction," says Canadian ethicist David Roy. The frontiers of IVF have the potential to change longstanding traditions rapidly. Some groups call for a moratorium on all IVF development; others have called on legislators to put policy in place to restrict the growth and speed of development.

Some countries and states have already adopted controls. The state of Victoria in Australia, was the first in the world to regulate IVF and embryo research with the Infertility (Medical Procedures) Act 1984. The act makes counselling of all IVF patients and gamete donors mandatory, along with complete records of all births from IVF and donor insemination and a central registry where information on those births can be obtained. It prohibits any advertisements that either solicit or offer surrogate mothering and makes illegal any payment of money for surrogacy. Any surrogate contract is void and unenforceable in the courts. Cloning and interspecies fertilization is banned. All other embryo research must be approved by the Standing Review and Advisory committee. Embryos cannot be created for research purposes only. Destructive, non-therapeutic experiments may be approved only where spare or excess embryos are formed in an IVF program. Those IVF researchers who go against the act are guilty of a criminal offence.

IVF researchers in Victoria have problems with parts of the law, particularly the restriction on experiments destructive to embryos. In micromanipulation experiments in which sperm were injected into an egg, Alan Trounson wanted to do chromosomal analysis comparing 40 embryos created by micromanipulation with 40 normal embryos to see if the micromanipulated embryos had a greater proportion of chromosomal abnormalities. The experiment would involve destroying the embryos to examine them. The research was not allowed, but it would have been legal to transfer the embryos to women and then do amniocentesis if a pregnancy had been established and abort any malformed babies. "Ethically I could not replace the embryos without knowing if those women were at an increased risk of a miscarriage or might be faced with a decision whether to terminate a pregnancy," Trounson said. Other researchers, however, decided to go around the problem by replacing the micromanipulated eggs into the wombs of informed participants. Prof. Ian Johnston, who chose that route, was philosophical. "It doesn't make sense for a woman to have to undergo amniocentesis because a researcher is not allowed to destroy an embryo in the lab. But it might just take a very well-publicized abortion of such a case to get people to see how ridiculous some aspects of the law are."

Despite the scientific opposition to the way the law has been worded, Trounson and Johnston both believe that limits to IVF and embryo research are important. In fact, the public perception of scientists working in their labs with no concern for the impact on society is wrong. Most IVF scientists agree that some control of the process is needed. However, they favor guidelines rather than legislation. Guidelines can be changed, but laws must be ammended, which takes a long time, scientists say.

In Britain, voluntary guidelines have been set up by a committee. Those IVF doctors who do not follow the guidelines will have their approval withdrawn from the committee. In 1982, the Government set up a committee of inquiry into embryo research and practices of IVF under the direction of Dame Mary Warnock. In 1984 the committee released its report, known as the "Warnock Report." One of the report's key recommendations was that a licensing authority be set up to regulate research and IVF-related infertility treatments. The authority would oversee and approve each IVF program operating in the country. The report recommended the authority be statutory—created by legislation in an act of Parliament. But because government legislation takes some time to pass, the report recommended that, in the interim, a voluntary licensing authority be set up to oversee IVF practices. In 1985 the 16-member Voluntary Licensing Authority, generally known as the VLA, was established. Its members include a few professors of gynecology, a pediatrician, a theologian, four research scientists, a rabbi, an actress, an author of child-care books, a magistrate, and a retired conservative MP. All research projects must be approved by this group, and all IVF programs are screened for approval. The VLA will eventually be replaced by a Statutory Licensing Authority, but to date the passage of the bill has been continually delayed in Parliament.

Twenty-three states in the United States have legislation forbidding fetal or embryo research but there have been calls there for federal policy on new reproductive technologies. In Canada a number of groups banded together to convince the government to create a Royal Commission to explore the issues and establish policy and set legislation; the government announced plans to call a Royal Commission in April of 1989.

Some of the concerns may not be really legitimate, according to Australian IVF pioneer Ian Johnston, particularly techniques like ectogenesis and cloning. "Ectogenesis and cloning really aren't going to go anywhere as far as human beings are concerned," Johnston says. "There is no need for it. It is economics and need that drive these things. Why should we create babies outside the womb when there are already human models that do it much better and much cheaper? What's the point of having identical human beings? It is much more realistic that instead of ectogenesis it will be a bearing class of poor women —that truly should be of concern."

But groups calling for legislation or policy say that we must not let the technology be dictated simply by economics or need. "Neither the push of consumer wants nor the pull of market strategies are acceptable guides for the development of these technologies," says Louise Vaillancourt, president of the Vanier Institute of the Family, one of the groups in Canada that requested a royal commission.

Many groups have used the catch-phrase "the desperation of the infertile" to describe the force that is behind the continued developments of these techniques and they stress that the desires of the individual couples should dictate such far-reaching changes for society.

What role does the infertile couple have in all this? What does it all mean to them? To be sure, not one couple would undergo IVF or any of the other reproductive techniques if they could have a baby without medical help. No infertile couple intends to alter the nature of reproduction or lead society on the tracks to *Brave New World*. They just want to have a family. There are no easy answers. Policies that restrict or prohibit certain practices may have a direct affect on preventing someone from having a child, and yet it must be obvious even to infertile couples that some policies are needed. Infertile couples can help the process by supporting discussion and open debate on the topics; by supporting a process that allows the adoption of reasonable guidelines and reasonable, workable limits to the techniques. Couples can also help by setting their own limits, by figuring out how far they should pursue their goal of having a child. In doing so they help the new technologies proceed at a pace and in a direction that most people in society can accept.

CHAPTER 11
Pregnancy After Infertility

When they called from the clinic they said: "Are you sitting down? And I could tell from her tone that it wasn't bad news. My heart just began to pound so hard and I could hardly breathe. She said: "You're pregnant!" And I can hardly remember what I did next, except I think I began to cry, and I remember saying to her, "Are you sure?"

At last! The event that you have wanted for months or years: A positive pregnancy test! You are pregnant! You may feel like laughing and crying at the same time, to sing from your lungs: "We're pregnant! We're pregnant!" The joy is among the most heady you have ever experienced. You are full of disbelief and elation, and you feel like hugging everyone and anything.

Becoming pregnant is something to celebrate. However, for couples who have struggled to overcome infertility, becoming pregnant has its unique stresses and strains. The experience of pregnancy, for those who have tried so hard to achieve it, may be different than that experienced by couples who conceived without difficulty.

Of course, we were so delighted to be pregnant—ecstatic! But I was also really afraid, anxious. After taking five years to get pregnant, after going through so much, the pregnancy was so important to me. I was so afraid that something would happen. I don't think I ever really relaxed and enjoyed the pregnancy. I didn't relax or believe it until the baby was born and safely in my arms.

Common Worries

Fear and worry is normal in any pregnancy. Every pregnant woman experiences moments of trepidation and anxiety about the new process, the health and well-being of the developing fetus and the health of the pregnancy itself, but those moments of anxiety may be more intense and more frequent for previously infertile couples who have crossed the threshold into pregnancy. The longer it has taken a couple to become pregnant, the more anxiety they may experience.

"Formerly infertile couples know all too well that many pregnancies end in loss. So they worry and worry," says Chicago infertility counsellor Judith Calica, who herself struggled with infertility and two miscarriages until her third pregnancy resulted in the birth of her son. "Women search for signs that all is well. Many women report being afraid to go to the bathroom, fearing to find blood where none should be."

> *When I found out I was pregnant, I was feeling this is great, it's wonderful, we're so happy. But at the same time I was afraid to be happy. It was my third one and I'd been devastated by the first two losses. I'd be doing something and all of a sudden a feeling of pure dread would sweep over me. It was panic. It shouldn't be like that, but you've been conditioned for so long you think that something has to turn out negative.*

Calica says friends and family of infertile couples who finally become pregnant are often perplexed by the couple's subdued or overly-anxious approach to the pregnancy. They want to celebrate and share the couple's joy, but the couple may want to play it cool, not get their hopes too high until the birth is over, and they may suppress their emotions and happiness to protect themselves from disappointment or loss.

The couples themselves may be perplexed by their mixed emotions. They may have believed that becoming pregnant would solve their problems; the ordeal would be over and the infertility battle won. "Many couples assume that a positive pregnancy test will bring their prolonged crisis to an end and restore them to their former selves," Calica says. Instead, some may find it presents new issues and worries, some of which are common.

Miscarriage, stillbirth, ectopic pregnancy or other complications Until a pregnancy is confirmed in the uterus, infertile couples may worry about the possibility of an ectopic pregnancy. All pregnancies are also at risk of ending in miscarriage, particularly in the first trimester, whether the couple is infertile or not. Although estimates vary, the generally accepted figure for miscarriage after a pregnancy has been recognized is between 15 to 25 percent for the general population. (Miscarriage before a pregnancy is recognized has been estimated to be as high as 40 to 50 percent.) Some infertile couples may be at greater risk for miscarriage because of advancing maternal age, fertility drugs or other factors contributing to their infertility.

Genetic screening Many infertile couples are over 35 when pregnancy occurs and may be faced with the decision to undergo amniocentesis or chorionic villus sampling. If the tests show an abnormality, couples may be faced with the painful decision to abort a very much wanted child, not knowing if or when pregnancy may occur again.

Maternal age Pregnancy during the later reproductive age can carry a higher risk of complications such as difficult birth, premature labor or placenta previa (the placenta implants in the lower portion of the uterus and may cover the cervical opening). But most doctors believe good general health, nutrition and prenatal care are more important than age.

Multiple pregnancy With infertility drugs or reproductive techniques such as IVF and GIFT multiple pregnancies are common. Of course, this increases the risk of various complications surrounding the pregnancy, and also presents a logistical problem for the couple. How will they manage, financially? How will they take care of two or three infants at once? Where will they put the cribs?

Multiple pregnancy may also present the couple with the difficult choice of selective reduction, described in more detail later in this chapter.

Reluctance to complain After wanting a pregnancy for so long women may feel they have no right to say anything negative about the pregnancy experience —feeling exhausted, sick, having aching legs, emotional swings or general difficulties. While it is normal for other pregnant women to share these stories, the formerly infertile woman can be afraid to lament the downsides of pregnancy lest she be met with a chorus of "you wanted it" or lest cruel Fate, as if judging her ungrateful, takes the pregnancy away. Without sharing the full range of her experiences, she may lack helpful support from friends, family and medical professionals.

Over-protectiveness and high expectations for the baby The preciousness of the child and its meaning to the couple can confuse parenting. The couple may feel somewhat let down when they compare their vision of what life would be like with a baby with the reality of a crying child, lack of sleep and the changes in their life.

A Strategy to Combat Worry

Regardless of the new issues pregnancy brings forward, it is truly a wonderful event. Do celebrate. Revel in it. Enjoy your pregnancy to the fullest. Pamper yourself, and do not worry. Worry and anxiety are so consuming and yet they serve little purpose. We all can imagine any number of horrible events occurring in our lives, but worrying about them bears no relationship to whether they happen. As Tucson counsellor Lee Schnebly said in her book, *Out of Apples*, there is no "magic" quality imparted by worrying, that if one worries enough it will not happen. Nor does worry "rehearse" us in ways to deal with bad events should they indeed happen. A tragedy like a miscarriage is not lessened or easier to handle because one worried about it beforehand—in fact it probably makes it worse because one has to deal with both the imagined and the real miscarriage. In short, worry has very few redeeming qualities. It creates fears and anxieties that often turn out to be unfounded. As Mark Twain once said, "My life has been full of problems, most of which never happened." Do not let your imagination create anxieties in your pregnancy where no problems exist.

All that is easier said than done, of course. For a woman who has struggled to overcome her infertility, convincing herself not to worry is about as effective as telling bees not to buzz. But counsellors do have suggestions for reducing worry. Convert the worry into positive steps that may be able to help you feel more in control. In the circumstance of finally becoming pregnant after struggling with infertility, you can deal with worry by putting it to work for you.

1. Find out from your doctor what you do need to worry about and what you do not need to worry about. Your infertility specialist may refer you to your obstetrician or to your general practitioner. Find out from your doctor if there are any particular activities you should or should not do; if there are any increased risks you face because of your type of infertility

and treatment. Learn what you should do in the case of an emergency, such as bleeding or contractions. Regular prenatal visits to the doctor will help reassure you and will help keep worries in check.

2. Funnel whatever anxiety or worry you have into taking care of yourself, making sure you eat a nutritious, well-balanced diet, that you sleep well and exercise moderately in activities such as swimming or walking. Cut down on coffee and alcohol, or better yet, cut them out completely. If you still smoke after all your attempts to become pregnant, for the sake of the health of the baby and the pregnancy, quit now.
3. Buy a good, informative book about pregnancy (there are dozens) and read about the changes that are happening to your body, the emotions you may experience and how to prepare yourself for labor and birth.
4. Try different strategies to cope with worry. One good method is to set aside 15 minutes a day to completely devote to worry. If worries crop up outside that time tell yourself you will deal with them in the designated time slot and postpone those worries until then.

Another strategy is a formula to replace bad feelings with good feelings, described by Schnebly in *Out of Apples*. She credits the four-step formula to Dr. Maxine Ijams.

1. *Where did this feeling come from?*
2. *What am I getting out of it?*
3. *How long do I want to keep it?*
4. *What am I going to put in its place?*

Here is how that formula works if it is applied to anxiety during pregnancy. Suppose you have morning sickness and feel tired and nauseated throughout the day. You begin to worry that something is going wrong with the pregnancy; you dwell on all the things that could go wrong and imagine being infertile once again. Every wave of nausea makes you feel more depressed and afraid.

Now try applying the formula to deal with that feeling. 1. Where did this feeling come from? From the morning sickness, of course; and the uncertainty, whether the pregnancy is normal. 2. What are you getting out of it? Perhaps self-pity. "Nothing ever goes right for me" or "I know something has to be wrong with this pregnancy because I'm always disappointed." Maybe a little "magic," as Schenbly calls it: "If I worry enough about it maybe it won't happen or else if it does happen maybe it won't hurt so much." 3. How long do I want to keep it? Probably not another second—you want to feel good and excited about the pregnancy, you want to feel happy. 4. What can I put in its place? Reassurance that nausea is normal in pregnancy; it is a sign that hormonal changes are taking place in your body to allow it to nourish the baby. Replace it with: "I'm feeling this way, not because something is wrong, but because I'm pregnant. Hoorah, I'm pregnant." If you cannot convince yourself that the nausea and fatigue are normal, talk to your doctor or others about it for reassurance.

This saying is worn out but it works: Take each day as it comes. Celebrate the little landmarks: the ultrasound scan that shows the fetal sac in the uterus; passing the first trimester; making it to the second trimester, making it to 30 weeks, the home stretch. Do not worry about what may come in the future, live in the present. Only allow yourself to worry if, and when, there is something to worry about.

Expectations of Pregnancy

After trying so hard to become pregnant, couples can be shocked or let down when they finally reach their elusive goal. Psychologists call it the "destination syndrome" and it is best summed up by the adage "Beware of what you desire most, you may achieve it."

The reality of pregnancy, birth and parenthood can be quite different from the expectations. The glow of pregnancy may be more hot flushes and bone-weary fatigue. The fulfillment of labor and birth may be more an endurance of pain. The joy of parenting may be tempered by the reality that the child irrevocably changes one's life.

I think there's a great conspiracy out there that brainwashes women into thinking pregnancy is wonderful. I feel awful. I ache, I'm tired, I had terrible morning sickness. I've spent six years waiting for this and now I can hardly wait to get it over with. (comments of a woman who became pregnant after IVF)

Nurse coordinator Carol Wiggins, recently of Bourn Hall IVF Clinic in England, says it is common for women to have their expectations of pregnancy clash with the reality. "I often get calls from women during their pregnancy with them saying, I never knew it was going to be like this. The pregnancy is not what they expected. It is not all wonderful and sometimes they think, I don't even like this. After spending eight years in pursuit of a child it can be quite a shock."

Guilt can be a by-product of the realization that it is not all rosy. The pregnant woman can berate herself for having negative thoughts. "How can I be feeling this way? I must be a bad person to have negative thoughts about pregnancy; maybe I don't deserve this." But pregnant infertile women can reassure themselves that these ambivalent feelings during pregnancy are normal. Writing about the psychological changes of pregnancy, Dr. Samuel Brown, a professor in the departments of both psychiatry and obstetrics and gynecology at Emory University, said "The couple is delighted about finally being able to conceive, but for the woman there may be a sense of disappointment. The expected euphoria is absent and she is left to cope with her fatigue, nausea and vomiting.... The general psychological sign in this period is emotional withdrawal." Remember, Brown is referring to pregnant women in general, not just those who have struggled to overcome infertility.

Brown says that one of the most difficult aspects of early pregnancy, for almost all women, is their emotional instability, caused by surging hormones. "These new effects may be experienced as a feeling of being out of control. With so many changes, and the feeling of having little physical or mental control, depression may occur," he said.

Survivors' Guilt

The previously infertile couple may experience another type of guilt when they become pregnant, particularly if they have infertile friends who are still trying to conceive. It can best be called "survivors' guilt."

> *I had prayed for a normal pregnancy but now that I had got what I wanted I felt as if somehow all the other struggling women in my position had somehow been cheated. I know they are as deserving as I, so why should my prayers be answered and not theirs? Instead of making me feel privileged it made me a little suspicious and sad . . . . It is so strange to pray so hard for yourself, all the while fighting envy for others who have what you want, and then to be granted your wish. Along with the relief can come a slight shame. (Comments of a woman quoted in a column by F. Forrester Church in the* Chicago Tribune*)*

If you belong to an infertility support group, you might worry about how you will tell your infertile friends about your pregnancy. You know, of course, that other couples will be happy for you, but all the same you may be afraid your good luck will deepen their own pain and make them feel their void all the more. You may be afraid that once the original basis of your friendship, shared infertility, is removed the friendship itself may falter. You know how hard it was to be with friends when they were pregnant.

There is no easy way to deal with those feelings, except, perhaps, to reassure yourself that everyone is truly happy for your good fortune. Your success can give others the renewed hope that the same good fortune could come to them.

Expectations of Parenthood and of the Child

Couples who have children after so many years of effort can have unreal expectations of themselves as parents, says infertility counsellor Patricia Mahlstedt. "They expect to be perfect parents all the time. They are reluctant to complain about the daily hassles of raising children because others will say "You got what you wanted . . . ."

All parents, at times, doubt the wisdom of having children, Mahlstedt says. Children are demanding, and can be bratty and ill-humored. They can take up every available minute in the day so that it feels as if you'll never have a private moment to yourself again. Parents who were once infertile may be reluctant to express any reservations about parenting and to share those very normal feelings with others. They may have difficulty allowing themselves to be angry at a naughty child, disciplining or setting limits on behavior.

Parents who were once infertile also are at risk of having unreasonably high expectations of the child, Mahlstedt says. "A child born of science and intense devotion can hardly turn out to be average. But no child, however brilliant and gifted, can ever make up for what some parents go through to have him or her." The child can also have unreasonably high expectations, Mahlstedt said. "The parents worked so hard to have her, she may perceive she has some debt to pay."

The Too-Precious Child

A book released in 1987 detailed the pitfalls of parenting for those who have strived to have children. Called *The Too Precious Child: The Perils of Being a Super Parent and How to Avoid Them*, it was written by Lynne Williams, M.D., Henry Berman M.D. and Louisa Rose, a pediatrician, a child psychiatrist and a journalist, respectively. The authors described a syndrome of over-involved parenting and the problems it creates for the child, psychologically and socially. "We believe the parental attention springs from loving and well-intentioned impulses but we have seen significant problems created by the pressures at home and in school for children to perform," they said.

The authors listed 12 situations that might lead parents to produce a too-precious child, and the first four and the twelfth could directly relate to infertile couples.

- A very wanted child
- First child while parents were in their thirties
- Obstacles to conceiving the child
- Adopted child
- Child with extraordinary meaning to parents and/or grandparents

They described Karen, a first-time mother at age 35, as a typical super parent. When Nicky was born she took a leave of absence from her career and devoted herself to his care. She spends the child's every waking minute singing with him, playing with him, reading to him. He always wants more attention and she admits that she is going crazy but she wants him to have every advantage and a perfect mother. The authors ask, why would she not put him in the play-pen for an hour and let him amuse himself? She could not do that because he would cry. It is a small price to pay, she says, for seeing that he has lots of love and attention. She plans to feed him only health food, expose him only to good music, buy him only good books to read, take him to museums on the weekends.

But the authors say she is setting Nicky up for a difficult life. "How will Nicky find out who he is and what he wants for himself if his parents won't let him experiment and make mistakes, if his parents deny him the experiences of boredom, anger and sorrow?"

Although Nicky and his mother are an extreme, the authors say they have been seeing the syndrome more and more frequently; dedicated and concerned parents who do too much for their children. The child is never permitted to be bored or messy or average or sad or left alone to amuse himself. Nothing is too good for the child. The child is indulged, entertained, stimulated and "every gurgle gets lavish attention."

Infertile couples who have children also tend to be over-protective, these authors say. The parents have a hard time separating themselves from the "miracle child." They may have a hard time letting the toddler explore and take his tumbles and falls, or to let the child learn to swim, or go off camping with friends, or pet the neighbor's dog. Such over-protectiveness breeds a timid, restrained child.

When too-precious children grow up, they may respond in a number of ways to their parent's over-involvement. They may be "unhappy narcissists" who do not know how to give and take, how to postpone gratification, how to nurture or share, or how to reciprocate. Instead, they may carry an attitude of entitlement and so find themselves lonely and alone. Too-precious children may be shocked to learn that they are average and in the big world everything they do does not receive lavish attention and praise. Their self-esteem, built on being the center of attention, may crumble. Some of these children, on the other hand, when they grow up may make a violent break from their parent's control by rejecting the parents' mores or in extreme circumstances, by committing suicide or joining a cult.

To avoid the pitfalls of super parenting the authors recommend that parents set clearly defined limits, mix conditional love with unconditional love, not always put the child first and help the child distinguish between wants and needs. Children, of course, need love and attention, but there is a difference between raising a precious child and a too-precious child.

"Precious children have parents who spend time with them, (and time away from them), who enjoy them (but also enjoy time away from them), who care about their education (but don't insist on competitive performance), who help them discover their unique abilities (but don't insist they be stars)."

Multiple Pregnancy

We thought it was great having twins. I mean, it's so efficient. After all the time and money, finally paying $5000 for in vitro, we get one pregnancy, one labor and two babies! What a bargain!

Women who have had fertility drugs to stimulate a number of follicles or who have had IVF or GIFT are ten times as likely as the general population to have more than one baby develop in the womb. Of the 991 IVF deliveries reported by the United States IVF registry for 1987, 17.2 percent were multiple pregnancies (14 percent sets of twins, 3 percent triplets or more). Of the 362 GIFT deliveries reported for that year, 22 percent were sets of twins and 5.8 percent were triplets or more. Figures from the Australian and New Zealand registry showed comparable rates with 18.7 percent of IVF deliveries twins, 3.5 percent triplets and 0.1 percent quadruplets.

Twins and multiple births (here triplets and more will be called "multiple") may create special problems. Most infertile couples see twins as a double blessing, two for the price of one. But when the ultrasound scan starts picking out three or more distinct fetuses developing in the uterus, the palms begin to sweat and the future seems daunting. How will we manage? How will we pay the bills? How will we care for multiple newborns all at the same time? The couple may be faced with the ethical dilemma of "selective reduction."

Twins

By far, twins are the most common pregnancy "side effect" of infertility treatment. Long before the days of Clomid, Pergonal and IVF, twins occurred regularly in the general population. Identical twins, called monozygotic twins, occur when one egg is fertilized by one sperm forming one single zygote (hence monozygotic.) During early cell division, the embryo splits in two, forming two identical offspring. Identical twins are always of the same sex and share the same genetic makeup. Fraternal twins, called dizygotic twins, are formed when two eggs are fertilized by two sperm at the same time and both implant in the uterus and grow. Fraternal twins can be of different sex and are essentially no more genetically similar than any other brother or sister.

Identical twins occur naturally at a constant rate of about four of every 1000 births, regardless of the woman's race, age, or health. But the rates of fraternal twins seems to vary with race or maternal age. Orientals have the lowest rate; only one set of fraternal twins in about every 460 births. Caucasians have fraternal twins under natural conditions about one in every 105 births, and Blacks one in every 75. One black African tribe, the Yoruba of Nigeria, have the highest rate of fraternal twinning in the world, one in every 23 to 25 births.

Infertility treatments usually result in the birth of fraternal twins, particularly in IVF and GIFT in which separate embryos or gametes are replaced. But identical twins can still occur if one embryo splits in two. Identical twins are more susceptible to problems in utero because their division may not be complete. They may share the placenta or fetal sac, even part of the umbilical cord. In rarer cases twins can share a complete umbilical cord or still be partly joined, as in the case of Siamese twins. In some cases one identical twin may develop at the expense of the other twin. Fraternal twins usually have fewer developmental problems because each has its own placenta and fetal sac. Occasionally, in both types of twins, one twin may die in utero while the other develops normally.

All twin pregnancies are considered high risk, but usually the pregnancy develops smoothly. The mother may have a longer duration of morning sickness and she will feel twice as much movement. As the pregnancy progresses she usually becomes more uncomfortable, and movement becomes more awkward simply because of her size. She is at a greater risk of iron deficiency, miscarriage and toxemia (called pre-eclampsia), which includes high blood pressure, swelling in hands and feet and protein in the urine, an indication of kidney trouble. She is more likely to deliver smaller babies a few weeks before term and have a more difficult delivery. If the babies are born close to term, after 35 or 36 weeks, they usually are fine, but if they are born too prematurely or too small, they may have a number of problems that require a special care nursery until they are big enough to go home.

Women expecting twins may want to obtain a copy of Elizabeth Noble's book, *Having Twins: A Parents Guide To Pregnancy, Birth and Early Childhood.*

Multiple Births

The risk to the mother and her developing babies is in direct proportion to the number growing in her womb. The more fetuses, the greater the risk of spontaneous abortion, premature birth, low birth weight and even death as a result of the prematurity. The premature labor occurs usually because the mother's uterus can no longer contain the expanding pregnancy. The birth is usually very difficult because of the malpresentation of the fetuses, and there are numerous opportunities for accidents with the umbilical cords causing damage or death to the fetuses. The infants that are born of a multiple pregnancy can have numerous health problems, usually related to their tiny size and premature development. Breathing problems, blood poisoning, physical and mental handicaps are all more common. Multiple pregnancy also takes a great toll on the mother. She is at greater risk of pregnancy complications such as pre-eclampsia, post-birth hemorrhage, anemia and premature rupture of the membranes. Weeks or months of bed rest may be necessary to maintain the pregnancy. Any activity for the mother—even breathing—may become very difficult because the developing babies take up so much room.

In recent years the media has reported the drama and tragedy of a few incidents of multiple births, usually caused by fertility drugs, IVF, or GIFT. In England in 1987 the world watched as septuplets born 15 weeks prematurely to an infertile couple in Liverpool died one by one. Other cases have been less tragic as one or two of the babies survived.

There have been, however, some celebrated successes when the babies in multiple births lived. A Michigan couple, Michele and Raymond L'Esperance, gave birth to the first IVF quintuplets in the United States in January 1988. Michele had seven eggs fertilized in IVF and she decided with her doctor to have all seven replaced. Her pregnancy lasted seven and a half months, four months of which she spent in a hospital bed. It was anything but easy, particularly near the end, as she told *People Magazine.*

> *I was miserable . . . . I had string bean arms and string bean legs and a humongous stomach. When I stood up, if I wasn't on balance, I could fall forward. I couldn't sit up. I couldn't lie down because Veronica and Danielle had their heads on my diaphragm . . . . Erica was on my left side and she wasn't real thrilled about it. She would get violent. It hurt when she kicked. I'd get sick, actually throw up, from her hitting me. One baby was underneath my bladder and had my cervix pushed way back to where I couldn't even be examined . . . . I couldn't walk. The last few days I could hardly move. There is no such thing as sleep during that kind of pregnancy, one of the babies was always up and I'd just lie there watching the clock all night long . . . .*

When the babies were born all were under 3.5 pounds, and the smallest, Raymond, weighed less than one pound. They spent a number of months in incubators in the hospital's special care nursery before they were allowed to go home. Although the L'Esperances told *People* they weren't sure how they would manage, they viewed their babies as a blessing from God and a special task that He must think they can handle.

Most doctors, however, view such multiple births not as gifts from God but as a medical mishap to be avoided whenever possible. Not only do multiple births put the mother and her babies at serious health risks, they also cause a tremendous financial drain for the hospitals and society (not to mention the parents) as the babies and the mother often have to spend a long time in hospital under intensive care. If the infants are severely premature, they may grow up with significant developmental handicaps that require special schooling or medical care, further increasing their cost to society.

Since most of the multiple births are the result of treatment for infertility, a great deal of controversy has erupted. Numerous editorials and case reports in medical journals have stressed that no more than three or four embryos or eggs should be transferred in IVF and GIFT procedures because of the risk of multiple births. The clinics that do return more than four eggs or embryos usually have their reasons, often because the patients beg them to.

> *None of those factors is a reasonable excuse for putting a woman or her babies at the risk of the severe complications of a quintuplet or larger multiple pregnancy, and there are even grounds for concern for triplet and quadruplet pregnancies. Instead of replacing large numbers of eggs and pre-embryos, IVF practitioners should carefully consider the reverse trend of replacing fewer eggs and embryos. (Editorial in* The Lancet, *October, 1988)*

Some IVF practitioners disagree with the stand taken by *The Lancet* editorial because they feel it would greatly reduce the chance of even a single pregnancy. "Infertile couples rightly expect to maximize their chance of achieving a single pregnancy with every attempt at treatment. . . ." wrote Prof. Ian Craft, of London's Humana Hospital, Wellington, in reply to the editorial. "The editorial's attitude discriminates against certain infertile couples by assuming that infertile couples with different clinical features have comparable pregnancy potential. This is not so."

The Controversy of Selective Reduction

At the center of the ongoing debate over the creation and management of multiple pregnancies is the issue of selective reduction, also known as selective termination. It refers to a procedure in which the physician reduces the number of fetuses in a multiple pregnancy down to triplets or twins to improve the chances that the remaining fetuses will develop and be born healthy and survive. The procedure is carried out in early pregnancy by injecting a solution into the fetal heart which instantly stops the heart and kills the fetus.

The procedure was first used in the early 1980s to abort defective fetuses in twin pregnancies, for example where one fetus was normal but the other had a major chromosomal disorder. By 1987-1988 it was being used more frequently to reduce apparently healthy individual fetuses in multiple pregnancy who, by virtue of their collective number, put all of them at risk. By the end of 1988 a hundred or so cases of selective reduction in multiple pregnancy had been reported in medical literature from centers around the world. It is believed, however, that the actual incidence of selective reduction is much higher because instances of its use go unreported.

There have been mild variations in techniques since it first started in the early 1980s, essentially using different approaches and different methods to stop the fetal heart. The most common method by 1988 was to use either transvaginal ultrasound (using a vaginal probe) or transabdominal (using an abdominal probe) under local anesthetic. The procedure is carried out when the fetuses are large enough that their hearts are clearly visible on ultrasound, usually between eight and 13 weeks. When ultrasound has pinpointed the flickering beat of the fetal hearts, a long, thin needle is passed through the uterine wall into the uterine cavity. One by one, the most accessible ones are punctured by the needle and injected with .25 to .50 cubic centimeters of potassium chloride. The killed fetuses, at this stage between one and three inches long, are then absorbed by the woman's body over a number of weeks, giving the remaining fetuses room to grow. The fetuses selected to be killed are the ones that are easiest to reach.

The procedure is not easy and it carries the risk that the entire pregnancy will be lost, either by inducing bleeding, uterine contractions or infection. In a report of the procedure in *The New England Journal of Medicine* (NEJM) in April 1988, Dr. Richard Berkowitz and colleagues at Mount Sinai Medical Center in New York detailed the reduction of 12 multi-fetal pregnancies (the largest with six fetuses.) Four of the 12 pregnancies were completely lost after the procedure although only one loss could be directly blamed on the reduction, the doctors said.

Doctors at the Tel Aviv University in Israel reported in a letter to the NEJM following Berkowitz's report that they had reduced the pregnancies of 13 patients using either transabdominal or transvaginal ultrasound. Seven patients had transabdominal reduction and of those, three lost the entire pregnancy. (Of the seven women, one had nine fetal sacs, one had six, two had five, two had four and one had three.) Six women had transvaginal reduction (one had seven fetal sacs, one had six, one had five and three had four). One entire pregnancy was lost using the transvaginal approach.

Selective reduction is not pleasant and it has fueled an ethical and moral debate among the medical profession. Some, like IVF pioneers Alan Trounson and Ian Johnston in Australia, have been vocally opposed to it because they believe not only does it risk the entire pregnancy but it is a medically created situation in the first place. As well, they are concerned about the psychological impact of the procedure on the mother, the couple and the surviving offspring, should the parents tell them that their siblings in the womb were killed to allow them to be born.

"I am against the use of selective reduction as a management tool," says Trounson. "It's a scatter gun approach. We should be trying to solve the problems and putting fewer embryos back. Having an abortion is a traumatic event and this, I imagine, would be even worse. We know absolutely nothing about how the woman and the children subsequently feel."

Johnston's comments mirror Trounson's. "We don't solve a problem by creating a new one. We must attack the problem of multiple pregnancies head on by finding ways to put fewer embryos back that we know will work. It is a terrible emotional stress for couples who have tried so hard to get pregnant. They feel tremendous guilt. It simply is not good medicine, it is crisis management."

The doctors who do selective reductions agree that it is an unpalatable option, but faced with having a multiple pregnancy end in premature delivery of infants that are too small to survive or have severe handicaps, it is the lesser of two evils.

"I hate the term of selecting fetuses to be killed—although I suppose in reality, in essence, that is what happens," says London infertility specialist Craft who has patients referred to him for the procedure. "It is a very difficult decision to do and at the end of the day I don't think there is any one of us who likes it.... The consequences of a complication of the technique weighs heavily on the doctor's mind and on the patient's mind.... None of us wants to see selective reduction used frequently, and all physicians would agree that prevention is better than cure. But the problem will not go away completely. Are we to turn our back on the women that need it?"

Doctors who believe selective reduction has its place in infertility medicine argue that without it couples may be forced to have a therapeutic abortion of the entire pregnancy. "Since couples with multiple pregnancies have the legal right to terminate their entire pregnancy, we see selective reduction as a way to save some lives that would otherwise be lost," Berkowitz and colleagues replied to critical letters in the NEJM.

Couples who are faced with the unfortunate circumstance of multiple pregnancy and the difficult decision of selective reduction should be aware of all the benefits and risks of the procedure. They should be aware that they risk losing the entire pregnancy through selective reduction and that there is no information, scientific or anecdotal, about the emotional and psychological effects of the technique on couples or their surviving offspring. (No couples who had undergone selective reduction would speak about their decisions for this book.)

To avoid being in the situation of needing selective reduction, couples would be wise to have no more eggs or embryos transferred in IVF or GIFT than they are prepared to carry in pregnancy. In the case of ovarian stimulation with fertility drugs without egg retrieval—such as Pergonal stimulation for ovulation problems—the women can choose not to have a shot of HCG to spur ovulation or not to have sex at the fertile time if ultrasound shows that numerous follicles have been stimulated. This may be a hard decision to make if previous IVF or GIFT treatments have failed, or if fertility drugs have not yet worked to produce a pregnancy. The couple may feel they have little chance of success and so opt to have the maximum number of eggs or gametes transferred in the hope that one will take. The desire for pregnancy outweighs the specter of the possible outcome.

Before making the decision, for example, to replace seven or eight embryos in IVF, you must examine what you would do if all, or many of them, developed.

Would you be able to undergo selective reduction without remorse? Would you be able to risk losing them all? Would you be able to endure giving birth to multiple premature infants without knowing whether they would live or die, or be normal if they did live? The ultimate decision about going ahead with treatment in the face of a possible multiple pregnancy always rests on the individual. Think it over while the eggs are still in the Petri dish or in their follicles. It is this author's opinion that couples should avoid at all costs the crisis, six or eight weeks into pregnancy, of having multiple fetuses that must be selectively reduced, terminated completely or carried into an uncertain future.

Pregnancy Loss

Miscarriage

> *The night I started spotting I phoned the doctor four times and said, Do something! Do anything! He told me to stay in bed. I've never been that scared before and it just freaked me right out. I was especially floored by all the blood. I bled heavily for four days—I never expected to bleed that much. By the end of it I was really drained—mentally, emotionally and physically. I was numb. Someone could have stuck a pin in me and I wouldn't have felt it. In fact, I'm still numb from it and that was more than a year ago.*

The loss of a wanted pregnancy is a tragedy. It is devastating and, unfortunately, it is also very common. It is estimated that as many as one in four recognized pregnancies ends in loss, for all couples, not just those who have had difficulty conceiving. In Chapter 8, the especially difficult situation of recurrent miscarriage was detailed from a medical perspective. The couples who experience loss after loss are not infertile because they are unable to conceive, but because they are unable to carry a pregnancy to term. Theirs is an extraordinarily difficult road because each new pregnancy is like an invitation to pain, a gamble between the hope of finally having a baby and fear that yet another pregnancy will end in a flow of blood.

Any miscarriage, whether it is the first or the fifth, is a traumatic and emotionally agonizing experience. Studies have shown that there is a slightly greater chance that a pregnancy will end in miscarriage for infertile couples, perhaps because they tend to be of older reproductive age or because they may have used fertility drugs or other medical interventions to become pregnant.

A 1988 study reported in the *New England Journal of Medicine* looked at women trying to conceive and found that those who experienced a pregnancy loss tended to eventually establish a successful pregnancy. Those women who never experienced a miscarriage tended to be less fertile and not conceive at all. The researchers concluded that a miscarriage is a positive sign that a couple will eventually have a baby. Miscarriages are emotionally difficult for infertile couples because they do not know if they will become pregnant again. The loss throws them back into the medical world of more treatments of Pergonal or Clomid, or perhaps cycles of intrauterine insemination, or another expensive go at IVF.

When a miscarriage occurs the burning question most couples ask is, Why? What went wrong? But there is often no clear-cut answer. Doctors think a miscarriage shows there is an error in the basic constitution of the embryo or fetus that prevents it from developing properly. Such an error, such as a chromosomal abnormality or genetic defect, is seen as a random mistake of nature for which nothing can be done. Given that every pregnancy starts as a single cell and then divides millions upon millions of times as the pregnancy grows, it is understandable that an error in early cell division might create a problem with the placenta or embryo. If the error arises early in the pregnancy and leads to miscarriage, it is often called a blighted ovum, meaning a fertilized egg that failed to develop. Other causes of miscarriage in the first trimester may be infection, uterine abnormalities, a maternal illness or an environmental cause such as exposure to radiation.

In the second trimester, miscarriages can be caused by an incompetent cervix or uterine abnormalities, multiple pregnancies, maternal illness or infection, separation of the placenta or chromosomal abnormalities that failed to miscarry in the first three months. (See Chapter 8.)

A couple experiencing the first or second miscarriage has difficulty accepting that doctors do not know why it happened. Nor is it easy to accept that when the bleeding starts and the pregnancy is threatened there is very little that the doctors do to stop it. The usual recommendation is that the woman rest in bed and abstain from sexual intercourse. Thereafter, it is a matter of waiting to see whether the bleeding stops of its own accord and the pregnancy continues or whether it continues and the pregnancy is lost.

Finally, couples have difficulty believing that after one or two miscarriages doctors and even friends and family can see it as simply "bad luck," a normal, commonplace, albeit unfortunate, occurrence, playing down the significance of the loss. For the infertile couple who has tried so hard to become pregnant, miscarriage is a great deal more than bad luck. It is a tragedy.

The Physical Experience of Pregnancy Loss

The emotional pain of losing a pregnancy is considerable, but the physical experience can also be very frightening. The amount of blood lost can be shocking, with clumps of blood and tissue being passed. Labor-like pain and contractions can occur. Sometimes a live fetus is expelled, either in the hospital or while the couple is still at home, a very upsetting experience.

Bleeding and spotting in early pregnancy are common and do not mean an inevitable miscarriage. Usually bleeding settles down and the woman goes on to have a normal pregnancy and delivery. When the bleeding becomes heavier and tissue is passed a miscarriage usually becomes inevitable. According to Gillian Lachelin, a senior lecturer in Obstetrics and Gynecology at University College London, intermittent uterine contractions may start that are like labor contractions. The contractions may be painful but the amount of pain varies, Lachelin says in her book *Miscarriage: The Facts*. As the bleeding becomes heavier, clots of blood may be passed as well as fetal membranes, the placenta and the fetus itself. If the fetus has died in the uterus before the miscarriage takes place, it may be partly dissolved and not recognizable. Any tissue that is expelled should be collected in a clean container and brought to the hospital for examination.

Some pregnancies are completely expelled from the uterus, called a complete abortion, and if this is the case bleeding gradually slows down and stops over a few days. Complete abortions usually occur in pregnancies lost before seven weeks. In later miscarriages, some remnants of the pregnancy may remain in the uterus and continue to cause bleeding or even cause infection. Incomplete abortions require a dilation and currettage (D&C) in hospital to scrape the remnants from the womb.

In some circumstances the fetus may die in utero but not be expelled in a miscarriage. This is called a missed abortion and usually a miscarriage eventually follows. The doctor may recommend that the pregnancy be terminated through a therapeutic abortion so that the woman does not have to sustain the emotional difficulty of carrying a dead fetus or if there are medical reasons to remove the fetus immediately. In most cases the woman can decide whether or not she wants to have an abortion or wait until the fetus is miscarried naturally.

The later the miscarriage occurs into the pregnancy, the more physically and emotionally difficult it is. Janet and Gordon, both in their late thirties, were at home asleep when Janet's second miscarriage started, caused by separation of the placenta. Janet, who had undergone Pergonal treatments, was 20 weeks pregnant and had been bleeding off and on since the beginning. "I woke up early one morning about 6:00 A.M. and I had a pain in my abdomen, like contractions. I went to the washroom and I was bleeding again, this time quite hard. I tried to go back to bed but the pain and bleeding was getting worse. So we went to the hospital and it wasn't long before my water broke and I went into labor. It was only a matter of minutes before I delivered a live baby, a little girl. She died within 10 minutes."

"There was such an incredible sense of helplessness," Gordon said about the miscarriage. "Here this baby was born alive and you can't do anything about it. There is nothing you can do—it is so upsetting. I found it to be a totally devastating experience. I wouldn't ever want to go through that again."

Stillbirth

In some circumstances a pregnancy may proceed normally but near delivery or during delivery itself, the baby may die. Although stillbirth is much less common than miscarriage, it does happen.

"This is particularly shocking for a couple," says Toronto psychiatrist Dr. Gail Robinson. "After nine months of expectations all of a sudden they are faced with emptiness."

Robinson said that usually there is no way to predict a stillbirth will occur and so the couple has no chance for anticipatory grieving. "The woman comes in for a routine examination and finds out the baby is dead, or during the delivery something goes wrong and the baby will be born dead. It is truly shocking."

A lack of oxygen to the fetus is usually what causes its death. The umbilical cord may be compressed or may separate from the placenta. The placenta itself may separate prematurely, causing hemorrhage to the mother as well as threatening the baby's life. During birth the oxygen supply may be cut off during a cord accident, or a fetal abnormality may prevent the baby's heart or lungs from taking over when the baby is born.

Emotional Aftermath

Following a miscarriage or stillbirth, couples experience a wide range of emotions such as grief, disappointment, anger, self-pity, helplessness, failure, guilt and depression. Individual couples vary in the amount and intensity of emotions they experience, as will the man and woman themselves.

A miscarriage or stillbirth is a death, and the reactions couples have is like the reactions to the death of any loved one. But unlike a friend or family member's death, the lost baby has elements of unreality, which often makes it more difficult to mourn. The baby being mourned is an unknown entity. There are no memories to treasure and no knowledge of the personality or characteristis of the lost child. And yet the loss is real and the baby, even though it never lived in the parents' lives, lived in their hopes and dreams and expectations during the pregnancy. There is a great need to mourn and yet no familiar person for whom to mourn.

For many couples seeing the baby or fetus helps the grieving process, particularly if the loss has occurred in the later months of pregnancy. Some may find this morbid, Robinson says, particularly if the fetus has abnormalities, but it can help in dealing with the loss and finalizing it. "It helps reinforce the reality that there was a baby and there was a loss," Robinson says. About 90 percent of couples choose to view the baby if given the option. Medical staff wash the baby and wrap it in a blanket. Couples who have viewed their babies say it is not a horrible experience, but rather a deeply meaningful experience that gave them a sense of peace and finality.

"They had put a bonnet on her and wrapped her up and then left us alone," said one woman whose baby was born anencephalic, without a brain, and so died immediately after birth. "It wasn't awful, in a way it was really good. The rest of her body was perfect, her feet and her hands were incredible. We had a quiet moment with her and we said good-bye. After all we'd gone through, that was really important to say good-bye. In the months after that my husband and I were so glad we had done that. I know that it helped us grieve."

Ritualizing the loss also helps couples deal with it. That can mean having a memorial service or burial, giving the miscarried or stillborn baby a name, asking the doctors for a footprint or lock of the hair. Some hospitals will take pictures of the baby. This can be helpful if at the time of death the couple did not wish to view the baby and later regret their decision.

In the case of an early miscarriage it can be hard to finalize the loss as there is nothing to view. Couples may find, however, that if they ritualize the loss in a way that has meaning to them it may be easier to grieve and leave the loss behind. One woman, for example, made a doll that represented the lost pregnancy and then buried the doll.

Guilt

One of the most common reactions women have is to blame themselves. They go over what they ate, drank, or did for the weeks preceding the loss and plague themselves with worry over anything they perceive as having contributed to the outcome.

I had a tremendous sense of guilt. Guilt for staying up late the night before the miscarriage happened, guilt for working out in the garden and cutting the lawn. I kept going over and over maybe if I hadn't done this or that it wouldn't have happened.

According to Robinson, women blame themselves for negative thoughts, for somehow not being worthy of motherhood, for perhaps not calling the doctor sooner or for having sexual intercourse. "She will keep wondering what it was she did wrong—she was the baby's caretaker. She feels very bad because she was not able to protect her baby when other women can."

Women must reassure themselves that it is highly unlikely any of their actions during pregnancy caused the loss. A healthy pregnancy is very resilient to almost any insult—horseback riding, a fall or even a car accident will not necessarily precipitate a miscarriage. And, conversely, if a pregnancy is going to miscarry there is very little that can be done beforehand to prevent it from occurring and little that can be done to stop it once it has started.

Others close to the woman can feel guilty, too, for something they did or did not do.

A friend of mine lent me her maternity clothes when I was pregnant—really nice clothes—and when I miscarried I gave them back. She lent them to another woman and she miscarried, too. My friend felt so bad. She took the clothes and she threw them all out. She felt those clothes were bad luck and she felt awful for having lent them to us.

Although guilt and remorse are powerful emotions they come, in part, from trying to make sense of the often incomprehensible reasons behind pregnancy loss. Shouldering the blame or laying blame is often easier for people than accepting that there is no rhyme or reason to the tragedy.

Effects on the Man

When a miscarriage happens the man's first concern is for his partner's welfare. He may be frightened by the amount of bleeding and may be afraid her life is in danger. When the crisis has passed and the grief sets in he may have a hard time getting in touch with his own feelings because the pregnancy was less real to him, or he may be unsure how he should react because he does not want to hurt his partner.

He may try to hide his feelings of disappointment from his partner, thinking that she may become more depressed if she knows how disappointed he is, but if he does this she may think he is insensitive. (Lachelin)

The man may try to minimize the loss and try to get the couple's life back to normal by not dwelling on the loss. He may try to keep conversation light to "keep her mind off it," changing the conversation when she wants to talk about it. He may immerse himself in his work to stave off his own feelings of disappointment and sadness. He may feel inept at expressing his own grief and so contain it.

The miscarriage can be difficult for the man because it is his partner who gets all the condolences; she is the one given the implicit permission to grieve. She gets more attention and sympathy from the medical staff and family and he may feel he stands on the periphery and that no one acknowledges that it is his loss, too.

Effects on the Family

If the couple already has other children, the miscarriage can also affect them. Young children may have been eagerly asking questions about the baby in Mommy's tummy, the brother or sister that is on the way, when suddenly the miscarriage happens.

Our six-year-old daughter had come with me to the doctor and had seen the baby's heart on ultrasound and she'd listened to it with the doctor's stethoscope. She had really identified with the baby and was always talking about it. When we lost it, it was terribly difficult for her. She didn't understand death and she wanted to talk about it all the time. . . . "Why did the baby die, Mommy? Where did the baby go?" Her questions were non-stop. The doctor said it was best to let her talk it out, and we did, but it finally got so hard on me I had to say, "Mommy can't talk about it anymore." But she still is talking about it, though. She told one of her playmates' mother the other day that I had lost my baby.

Even if children in the family have not known about the pregnancy, they will be aware of their parent's grief and may feel that they have done something to cause it. Lachelin recommends talking with the child about what has happened in ways they can understand, letting the child know he or she had nothing to do with it and letting the child talk and ask questions. Although a child's incessant questions may be hard on the grieving parents, it may also help the parents deal with the loss themselves.

Insensitive Comments

Couples who have undergone miscarriage always remark on the people who told them "It's all for the best" or "It was God's will" or any number of platitudes meant to console them but irritate them instead.

I was in one of the beds in the emergency department and I was crying really hard. I guess one of the doctors must have asked a nurse what I was in for and she told him. He walked over to me and put his hand on my arm and said. "Don't worry dear, they'll be other pregnancies. You're still young." Then he lifted up my wrist and read the bracelet and said: "Oh . . . . not so young." I just wailed all the louder—can you believe it? I laugh now because it was such a stupid thing to say. But I just couldn't believe it at the time.

The inappropriate comments are attempts, albeit inept, to recognize that you have suffered a loss. People are uncomfortable with death and with grieving and often do not know the words or the approach that is most comforting. It takes experience with death to know that when someone is mourning others can often comfort best by a well-timed hug, or by giving permission to "cry it out" in their presence, or by simply being willing to listen. Do not be too hard on your family and friends for saying or doing the wrong things—they may not know what to do. Instead, try to help them comfort you by letting them know what it is you want to hear and how they can help you mourn and put the loss behind you. Tell them when their comments are inappropriate and why; that way they will learn how to comfort you and others.

Attempting pregnancy Again

For medical reasons, it is a good idea to wait a few months after a miscarriage before trying to become pregnant again. Your body has been under stress with the miscarriage or stillbirth, and it may take a few months for it to get back to normal.

Emotionally, however, it may take even longer. Individuals vary in the length of time it takes to grieve. Some may feel ready to try pregnancy right away. Others may want time to deal with the loss and heal.

> *After the second miscarriage I found myself saying I can't go through it again. I can't go back to the regular trips to the doctor for Pergonal. Every day for shots, forget it. It is such a drag. I can't bear to get pregnant and lose another. But after a while you can feel your attitude starting to change. I don't know what happens but you begin to think, well, may be I could take one more try. What have I got to lose? So you feel yourself coming around. And the hope starts creeping back . . . maybe I'll eventually get pregnant. And before you know it, you're going back for more treatment.*

Hope springs eternal, and eventually the pain of the loss will fade. You may be reminded of it each year when the date the baby would have been born passes on the calendar, or there may be something in the air one night that reminds you of the night you miscarried and drove to the hospital. Little reminders will bring back the memory but the grief will pass and eventually you will feel ready to try again or you will have moved on to another stage.

CHAPTER 12
Enough Is Enough

There are three things that are never satisfied.
Four things never say, "It is Enough"
The grave
The barren womb
The earth that is not satisfied with water
And the fire that never says, "It is Enough."

Proverbs 30:16

That proverb was written sometime between 2200 to 3000 years ago in the Middle East. It is attributed to Agur, an unidentified author about whom nothing is known. There were no fertility drugs in Agur's time and no scientific treatments for infertility. There was no real understanding why a couple might be infertile, except, perhaps, the displeasure of God. And so, as Agur alludes, a couple's hope for a child would continue unabated, never satisfied until either a child was conceived or until death or infirmity removed the hope completely. The longing was insatiable, like fire, like the thirsty earth, like the inevitability of death.

Much has changed since Agur's time. Pills or hormone shots now can make most women ovulate. Medical work-ups can tell most couples why they are not conceiving. Advanced techniques such as in vitro fertilization give hope of conception and birth to couples who, in any other period of history, would have had no hope at all.

And yet, in some ways, nothing has changed since Agur's time. While couples then turned ceaselesssly to God, now they turn to science and medicine for their salvation. The hope is just as strong that an answer will be found some day in a lab or clinic. There is often no finality to infertility treatment. If a couple chooses, they can go on and on with more tests, more treatment, one more try of IVF. It must be the couple who finally says "It is enough." They must reach a stage where they are satisfied with the decision to no longer pursue conception and birth.

For some, getting to the stage of saying "enough" happens more quickly than others. When hope is removed completely, such as in the case of hysterectomy or complete testicular failure, the finality of the diagnosis compels couples to move on.

I would never say that I'm glad I had a hysterectomy—having a hysterectomy at 27 is nothing to be glad about. But in another way it has forced me to come to terms with it. I couldn't get caught up in the hope that I might get pregnant. I grieved it and then I had to accept it and find alternatives that would fulfill my desire for children. Sure, there are times when I still say, if only . . . and I feel sad. But for the most part I have now put it behind me. When I see other women who have been trying to get pregnant for 10 or 15 years—some for their whole reproductive life, then I think I may have had it easier.

When conception and pregnancy are still theoretically possible—when some swimming sperm are present, when tests show that an egg is being ovulated either naturally or through stimulation, when the fallopian tubes are open, or when there is no known reason why IVF should not work—then the decision to stop trying can be much harder to make. There is always the hope that something will still work. It is this open-endedness of infertility treatment that drives many couples crazy. One can keep going around and around in medical treatment, like a gerbil in a wheel, with no definitive end. Perhaps, for that reason, it is even harder for infertile couples now than at any other time in history.

Knowing When to Stop

How do you know when it is time to say "enough"? How do you know that you no longer stand a reasonable chance of getting pregnant through medical treatment? What are the signs that the time to stop is near?

The 1988 United States Office of Technology Assessment report said that many couples assume the medical profession will tell them when the time has come to stop, but physicians, in their desire to help patients conceive, may not pause often enough to consider whether it is best for a particular couple to stop trying. If couples have enough money, theoretically, they could continue indefinitely with treatments such as IVF.

Many infertility specialists, however, now voice the opinion that the medical profession should do more to help couples decide to end treatment. "Since as many as half our patients may not get pregnant, I believe we have an obligation to find ways to help patients stop and to accept their infertility," says Dr. John Collins, Chairman of Obstetrics and Gynecology at McMaster University in Hamilton.

"There are two cures for infertility," says Dr. Patrick Taylor, former director of Bourn Hall IVF Clinic and now the head of the University of Manitoba's infertility program. "One is to help the couple have a baby, the other is to help them cope with the results of not having a baby. I think sometimes it would help if we spent a little more time on the latter."

Even if more infertility specialists are beginning to help couples in their decision to stop, it will always be the couple themselves who must ultimately choose when the time is right. Deciding to stop is never easy but here are some questions, based on comments from infertility counsellors, infertility specialists and couples themselves, that couples may ask themselves to assess if that time is approaching.

1. Have treatment options and medical knowledge been explored and given a reasonable chance of working? It makes no sense to stop seeking help before completing the diagnostic work-up or before trying some of the suggested therapies. "That's dumb," says Dr. Michael Soules, chairman of the division of reproductive endocrinology at the University of Seattle. But each treatment, once tried, has its logical end point, he says. Couples can reassure themselves they have given medical therapies a good trial, for example, after six to nine months for each method of ovulation induction; one good microsurgery operation for tubal problems with a two-year period to try to establish pregnancy; six to 10 intrauterine inseminations with the partner's sperm; three or four attempts at IVF. Studies have shown that longer durations of treatment do not significantly increase the chance of pregnancy.
2. Is infertility treatment making you postpone other things you would like to do, or making you change decisions? Have you delayed plans to move because it might take you away from your infertility specialist? Have you postponed vacations and trips because you might be pregnant by the time the trip rolls around? Have you thwarted plans to return to school, to make a career change or otherwise change your life because you are waiting for pregnancy? If you can answer yes to these questions it is time to evaluate how much you want infertility to continue to put your life on hold.
3. Is the pursuit of infertility treatment straining your financial resources? Will another try at IVF force you to mortgage or sell your house? Are drugs or treatments leaving you with a minimal savings account so that you can not afford to do other things you would really like to do? Do you resent the money you have to pay out for infertility treatment? If financial worries and pressures of infertility treatment are putting undue stress on your life, it is a good time to assess whether further expenditure is worth it. It is unfortunate that money should be the limiting factor in whether some couples continue treatment, while the rich have unlimited treatment. However, financial restriction can be a blessing in disguise. It gives a tangible, convincing reason to stop and may be part of the painful but necessary task of resolving and accepting infertility.
4. Has your relationship with your partner drifted or become strained by continued medical investigations and treatment? As you know, infertility creates stress on relationships. Couples can lose sight of each other's qualities and lose sight of the positive aspects of their relationship. The sexual aspect of relationships is often what suffers most, degenerating to the point where sex is no longer enjoyable, no longer an expression of love or intimacy, or no longer even worthwhile unless it creates a baby. Discontinuing infertility treatment can allow couples to get their sexual relationship back on track.

5. Do you hate what your life has become? Do you resent the treatments and loathe going for shots or more investigations? Do you long to feel happy again, to feel like your old self? If you feel as though you do not want to go through infertility treatment anymore, even a new therapy the doctor suggests, you are ready to stop.
6. Are alternatives to biological parenthood, such as adoption, foster parenting or childless living becoming acceptable options? If other ways of living your life, which do not include having a biological child, now seem plausible to you, you may be ready to call a halt to medical treatment.
7. If you are not ready to stop now, when will you be? Is there a logical end point to your treatment? Can you establish a plan? By setting a time frame and deciding when you will be ready to stop, you will be able to determine better when the appropriate time has arrived.

Examining your reasons for wanting children may be helpful. During the years of infertility treatment it is easy to lose sight of the real reason you are going through it: pregnancy and having a baby can become a goal in itself, like climbing a mountain. Once you are on the mountain you want to make it to the top. You may not ask yourself why you are climbing the mountain. Sometimes the more obstacles put in the way of a goal, the more we desire it and the more determined we are to reach it.

More than any other factor, the passage of time itself is what leads couples to become ready to stop infertility treatment. In the first few years while they are still actively trying to overcome their infertility most are not ready yet to accept their infertility. Nor should they force a resolution or force themselves to stop treatment if the feeling is not there. With the passing of time other options will present themselves and will appear more acceptable. Couples will know when they are ready to stop because it will feel right.

Strategies for Stopping

It would be nice if there were a quick, easy recipe for dealing with the pain of continued infertility, resolving it and moving on—a checklist of do-this-and-then-do-that and then everything will be fine. Simple solutions do not exist. When the time comes that couples begin to feel they are ready to stop, they must struggle to reconcile their vision and dream of what might have been, with what is. That means changing the vision of the future so that it does not revolve around the birth of a biological child.

One couple, described by IVF counsellor Louise Bowen, began the process of changing the map of their future just as they were deciding whether to undergo another attempt at IVF. They checked themselves into a nice hotel for the weekend, away from any of the distractions of home. With no phone calls, no household chores, the couple focused on each other and on their eight-year struggle with infertility. They cried about the past and about the future. They talked about their relationship and admitted that they had grown apart during the process of infertility investigation and treatment. They got back in touch with what it was that they really liked about each other. They drew up a list of what they wanted to have accomplished in five, 10 and 15 years. They talked about individual goals and goals they would share as a couple. They talked about where they wanted to travel and when. They swam in the pool and went for walks and ate good dinners. And at the end of the weekend they were resolved that the IVF attempt would be their last and they would move on.

The couple, of course, did not resolve the pain of infertility in one weekend. They did not successfully jump to a whole new life vision all at once and never look back. Resolution takes time. No doubt they had further tears and resolutions. But they did make a good, positive start in the direction of reconciling their future without a biological child.

Other couples have also found that writing lists is helpful. One couple drew up a list of all the things that a child would have fulfilled in their life. The list included items like giving and receiving love, being an integral part of a child's growth and development, a sense of family, nurturing and having someone need you, being loved and having security in old age, having young children around when you are old, making a contribution to the future, having a purpose to life, and simply enjoying a child for who he or she is. And when the list was done, the couple then looked for ways they could achieve those things in their life without having their own child. For this couple it meant being closer to their brothers' and sisters' children and being a greater part of their lives. They decided to become a special aunt and uncle to the children, taking them to the zoo or making special outings for the weekend.

Each person has a particular set of reasons that can be listed for wanting to have children. Some reasons may be hard to intellectualize or rationalize. It is just "there." Maybe it is a biological urge, maybe it just feels like something you should do. Ask anyone who has easily had children why they had them and they will usually have a hard time answering. "We just wanted to," is the common answer. It is only the infertile couple who find themselves figuring out just why they want children.

If we are really honest with ourselves we may find that one of the compelling reasons for wanting children is that they will give us something meaningful to do with our lives. They will need us. They will need us to get them off to school, to feed them, to play with them, to be there when they cry in the night. They will give us a reason to work at a nine-to-five job, to make a salary and spend it in the grocery store. In a way, they define our future for us, placing the path out ahead in a straight line.

If one does not have children, the future becomes wide open. It is a blank page on which anything can be written. An undefined future is frightening. Psychologists have studied the reactions of men who retire after having worked as long as 45 years, day after day, earning a wage to support their family. The men often feel lost when they retire. What do they do now? They can do anything they want and yet usually it takes a period of adjustment to find a new direction. The same thing is true of women who have spent their adult life raising children. When the last child leaves home their time is suddenly their own. What should they do with it? Their lives may seem aimless until they find a new focus, a new interest, a new way to have a meaningful existence.

The same adjustments are required to face infertility. The loss of direction takes place prematurely, in the height of adult life, and something is needed as a replacement. For some people it might be coaching a youth sports team or running a Girl Guide company; others may try adopting an international child or special-needs child; others may find that travel, career aspirations, community activities, volunteer work, or working with animals fills the vacant spot. Still others may find fulfillment in other activities meaningful to them, such as environmental issues, or creative pursuits such as writing a book or painting. The solutions will be as different as the people who choose them. You need to figure out what solution works for you.

Grief

I had been trying to get pregnant for 13 years and I thought I would be prepared for the grief that would follow my fourth attempt at IVF. I knew I wouldn't become pregnant. But when the telephone call came telling me I wasn't pregnant, the grief was uncontrollable. I was numb. I sobbed for hours. I didn't believe the blood test could be correct. The next four days I was in a fog and when my period came I cried all day . . . . I felt as if I would never rejoice in anything again, nothing in life would ever give me pleasure. What was the use of doing anything when what I had wanted all my adult life could not be fulfilled? (Adapted from the News Letter of the Australian support group, Concern.)

The word, grief, comes from the Latin word for "burden" and the French word for "heavy." As such, it aptly describes the emotional weight of working through grief. It is a painful process, but to resolve their infertility and accept it, infertile couples must work through their grief.

Grief is the reaction to loss. It is universal. All people—men, women and children—in all cultures repeatedly experience shades of grief whenever they encounter loss. It may be as monumental as grief at the sudden death of a loved one in the prime of life or as small as grief over losing a toy or valued possession. Death, divorce, changes of home or job, fights with friends, a breakup with a lover, retirement all have greater or lesser elements of loss. Whenever there is loss, some form of grief reaction is to be expected, whether it is recognized or not. It may be delayed or avoided, but it will be there. Even positive events, such as a promotion or a wedding, can trigger a small grief reaction. New brides or new division managers can feel bewildered at a sense of sadness or letdown they experience in their new life. They do not realize they are experiencing a mild grief over the loss of their former life or former job.

"Grief is the process that allows us to let go of what was and be ready for that which is about to come," wrote Dr. Therese Rando, a Rhode Island clinical psychologist specializing in grief and loss. Rando is the author of the clinical text *Grief, Dying and Death*, which outlines many theories around grief and its resolution. Rando says Sigmund Freud was one of the first theorists to recognize the purpose of grief in his classic 1917 work, *Mourning and Melancholia*. "Mourning has a quite precise psychological task to perform: its function is to detach the survivors' memories and hopes from the dead," Freud said.

For infertile couples there is no corpse, no deceased, no "dead" to be the focus of the grief. But there is a tremendous loss. What has died is their dream of the future. Their grief reaction varies in intensity, depending on how much they feel they have lost and what dreams they can put in its place. But some form of grief will be there all the same. For the infertile couple the process of their grief has more in common with the grieving experienced by a person with a terminal illness like cancer. An infertile couple's grief usually begins when they are given the diagnosis of infertility and may be drawn out for years, waxing and waning, until the final "death" or until the finality of the loss is acknowledged.

According to Rando, two kinds of losses can occur, physical loss or symbolic loss. A physical loss, for example, is the death of a loved one, the amputation of a leg or arm, the removal of a breast for cancer, or a stillbirth. A symbolic loss is an abstract concept: a loss of identity or status, a loss of ideals, a loss of a specific relationship, and so on. Symbolic losses are often less easy to indentify than physical losses, but they elicit strong grief reactions, nonetheless.

Infertility gives rise to both physical loss and symbolic loss. The physical loss is the loss of the fertility itself and the loss of a child that, although never born, was very real to the couple. Associated with that are a variety of symbolic losses—the loss of the creation of a family, the loss of a shared biological child between a loving man and woman, the loss of the experience of motherhood and fatherhood, and the loss of a vision of the future. The symbolic losses of infertility often cause the most grief.

Grief Work

American psychiatrist Erich Lindemann, a pioneer in grief investigation, coined the term "grief work" in 1944 for the process of getting through grief. The term is apt because grieving is hard physical and emotional labor. Counsellors specializing in grief say that most people, because they do not perceive grief as work, are not prepared for the intensity of their own emotional reactions and do not understand the importance of accepting the emotions and expressing them.

In its intensity, grief creates very similar physical reactions in most people. Lindemann identified the uniform physical picture of grief this way: feeling of acute distress that comes in waves lasting 20 minutes to an hour; a tightness in the throat; choking with a shortness of breath; a need for sighing; an empty feeling in the stomach; a lack of muscular power or physical energy; and subjective distress described as tension or mental pain. The griever often has trouble eating and food lacks taste or sits heavy in the stomach. Any physical task, even climbing the stairs, feels exhausting.

The physical feelings can be so uncomfortable that one avoids experiencing grief because it opens one up to feeling pain, emptiness and sorrow and to the fear those emotions bring.

In the depths of grief work it is common for those grieving to believe they are going crazy. Australian IVF counsellor Louise Bowen says numerous couples come to her when they have decided to stop IVF with the fear they are going mad. "They are struggling with so many emotions that they just have to let them pour out. They have to sob with a box of tissues. There is nothing you can say; they just have to get through it. All I can do is reassure them they are not crazy and that it will end. It won't always feel this bad."

Rando confirms that confronting grief often causes people to think they are going crazy. "The reactions are so different, uncontrollable, unexpected and intense that some mourners believe they have actually lost touch with reality," she said. Grief is craziness but grievers are not crazy.

Keeping yourself healthy is important during grief work. Special attention should be given to maintaining a healthy diet, sufficient sleep and regular physical activity. Calcium, vitamin D and phosphorous can become depleted by the stress of grief, Rando said.

Many psychiatrists and psychologists have presented stages and schemes for the process of grieving. Elizabeth Kubler-Ross's five stages of grief—denial, anger, bargaining, depression, and acceptance—are well-known and were published in her book *On Death and Dying* in 1969. Lindemann in 1944 said grief entails a three-step task: freedom from the bondage of that which is lost; readjustment to life without that which has been lost; and reinvestment of emotional energy into someone or something else.

Rando says that despite all the different labels and descriptions, all the theories cover the same basic feelings. All the schemes can fit into three broad categories that comprise grief: avoidance, which includes shock, denial and disbelief; confrontation, a highly emotional state wherein the grief is most intense and the psychological reactions to the loss are felt most acutely; and reestablishment, in which there is a gradual decline of the grief and the beginning of an emotional and social reentry into the everyday world.

However, grieving does not follow structured stages, such as Kubler-Ross's five stages, in a certain order. Each person has a unique experience of grief and may move through all the stages a few times, or may be in two stages at once. People may feel they have resolved their grief only to find themselves back at an earlier stage. "It is a choppy one step forward two-step back experience," Rando said.

During the infertility work-ups and treatment, all the stages of grief may be experienced a number of times over. For example, when the first diagnosis is made there may be shock at learning you are infertile, you may go through the denial of the problem, confrontation of the grief of not being fertile and acceptance of the need of infertility treatment. When you begin treatment, shock may occur again when treatment does not work, you may go through denial over the failure (maybe-they're-wrong-and-I-am-pregnant), confrontation of the sorrow and depression, and then acceptance of the failure of that treatment. For each IVF treatment the cycle may repeat itself. Acceptance and recovery will improve until the couple feels ready to undergo IVF one more time. Then the grief cycle may repeat itself again.

Unresolved Grief

Some infertile people have trouble getting through the grief work and emerging at the other end. They become caught in a stage of continually mourning their loss without finally accepting it and moving on. The woman may find that although she knows she is infertile, she can not eliminate her desire for babies. She avoids friends or relatives who have babies; she cannot speak about her infertility or her desire for a child without her voice cracking. Yet she cannot enjoy other people's children. She is trapped in her grief.

One of the reasons that grief remains unresolved, counsellors say, is if the loss is an extension of the self. When the grievers place such a high value on the loss, when they define themselves by the loss, they cannot recognize it and let go because it would be losing part of themselves. Couples or individuals who are infertile often fit this model because many men and women define themselves by their fertility. A woman may not feel she is a woman unless she can have a baby. A man may not feel like a man unless he can make his partner pregnant. They must change their self-definition to completely work through their grief. If they can not do it, they remain stuck there.

Some people may have resistance to mourning because they do not permit themselves to grieve. Some do not grieve for fear of losing control or appearing weak. They do not want to experience the "crazy" emotions of acute grief so they push them away. This can often happen to men, who in Western society are conditioned to remain controlled and to avoid the expression of feelings. In the process of grief a man may experience conflict in his emotions and may have difficulty resolving his grief because it is contrary to his sex-role conditioning.

Emotional restraint can affect both men and women. Some people are afraid if they open up to grief they will start to cry and never stop. Others are afraid to work through the grief because it still binds them to that which was lost and they want to keep tied to it. It is like a man or woman who, having lost a partner, keeps the closest with the deceased's clothes so the bond with the partner does not have to be severed. If he or she works through the grief, that which is lost is left behind. In the case of the infertile couple it means separating themselves from their dream of a biological child.

There can be social/cultural factors that also prevents individuals from grieving. If society in general, or those close to the griever, do not consider the loss to be very significant, the griever does not receive the needed permission to grieve. This often happens in the case of miscarriage when others fail to recognize the loss as a real entity and a significant loss to the couple. Infertility, because there is no overt loss, is often negated by others who make comments like "if you'd tried getting pregnant earlier maybe you wouldn't be in this situation," or any other statement that diminishes the loss. Infertile couples and those around them need to give themselves permission to grieve.

Uncertainty surrounding the loss also prevents people from dealing with it and moving on. Couples with unexplained infertility or men who have a low sperm count are never sure whether some day they may conceive. It is like a kidnapped child, a soldier missing in action or a boater lost at sea—there is never any certainty over the loss and so the grief can't be completed. Couples who hold out the hope their infertility may respond to future treatments may get stuck because of the uncertainty of their future prognosis.

To resolve grief, individuals or couples should try to identify the reason they are stuck. Sometimes on their own they can let the emotional ties go, endure the pain and say good-bye to the feeling. Sometimes, however, professional counselling may be needed to move through grief.

The final grief of infertility occurs when couples decide to stop treatment completely.

> *I'd had eight failed attempts at IVF and I realized I was very depressed. My depression after my eighth failure was the worst I have ever experienced. I'd set a limit way back at four attempts but I kept extending it—one more time because there was always a new reason—a new drug protocol, a new piece of equipment. Ironically, I was asked by the support group to talk about how to know when to stop. As I was writing my speech I began to look at myself. I realized I had to stop. The decision felt like letting go from the edge of abyss and falling in. It seemed that if I let go of my grip on IVF, that fingernail-hold on having a baby, I'd fall and fall and never stop falling. It was bad for the first little while—it was that letting go that was so hard. But soon there was this tremendous release. Real relief. I didn't fall forever.*

To grieve your inability to have a baby, you must release the emotional ties that bind you to your dream of a baby, despite the discomfort and sorrow it causes. You must yield to the painful process of grief and accept the pain of looking realistically at the loss. Grieving can be delayed or postponed, but it can not be escaped. If you allow yourself to grieve, eventually you will emerge from the emotional harangue. It is not an all or nothing emergence, "rather it waxes and wans. It never arrives all at once and it may co-exist with many of the previous reactions," Rando says. But when that acceptance comes the grievers are changed by the experience. They will never be the same again, they never get back the innocence of the period before the grief, but the grief over that particular loss will never affect them so dramatically again.

"The loss is not forgotten, but merely put in a special place which, while allowing it to be remembered, also frees the mourners to go on to new attachments without being pathologically tied to the old ones."

Resolution

Resolution does not mean that you reach a stage where you forget that you ever wanted your own biological child and go blithely on with never a look back. Resolution, instead, means that you accept the loss and incorporate it into your life. You always remember your infertility and desire for a child, but the pain diminishes.

Psychologists and psychiatrists have come up with some behavioral criteria that they feel establish that the grief process has been worked through. These have been modified here to relate to the circumstance of infertility.

- Depression lifts and functioning returns to the level experienced before the infertility.
- Sadness changes from being bitter to sweet.
- There is acceptance of the infertility and loss of a biological child. It can be talked about with composure, without eliciting emotion.
- There is a positive and realistic attitude toward the future.
- There is an ability to cope with future loss.
- The ability to socialize and relate to others returns, including those with children or those who are pregnant and might remind the griever of the infertility.
- General self-esteem returns.

The acceptance of the loss into the life process is the result of the grieving process. Rando quotes one New York psychiatrist, G. Caplan, who describes a 1974 study of the grieving process of widows who had lost their husbands: "After a time they were no longer actively mourning, but their loss remains a part of them and now and again they are caught up in a resurgence of feelings of grief. This happens with decreasing frequency as time goes on but never ceases entirely."

That description is reminiscent of a quote from a woman describing the sweet sadness of her infertility. It first appeared in a newsletter of the American support group *Resolve*, and then in Barbara Eck-Menning's 1978 book *Infertility: A Guide for the Childless Couple.*

> *My infertility resides in my heart like an old friend. I do not hear from it for weeks at a time, and then, a moment, a thought, a baby announcement, or some such thing, and I will feel a tug—maybe even be sad and shed a few tears. And I think: "There's my old friend." It will always be a part of me.*

Adoption

> *I have been comforted in my infertility by thinking that maybe the reason all this happened is that I have the ability to love another person's child. I would have liked to have had my own if it had all worked out, but I don't need to, because I can love a child that is not genetically mine just as much.*

Until 10 or 15 years ago, adoption was the way infertile couples satisfied their desire for children. In fact, adoption is one of the oldest remedies for childlessness. Roman law recognized adoption as a legitimate arrangement more than 2000 years ago. Statutes in the United States enabled couples to become the legal parents of an unrelated child through a judicial process since the mid-nineteenth century. In Canada, all of the provinces had passed adoption acts by the early 1920s. Long before laws recognized adoption, foundling homes and orphanages, set up in Europe as early as the eight century, provided a steady supply of infants and young children to those who wanted them, although many of the children were wanted for cheap labor. Oliver Twist and Anne of Green Gables are but two of the many characters in literature whose story included adoption.

Adopting a baby has become increasingly difficult in recent years. Many couples are unable to adopt because babies are simply not being given up in the numbers that they were in years past. The same story is repeated in almost every jurisdiction: couples wanting to adopt now outnumber the infants available by more than 10 to one. The number of adoptable infants, in most regions, peaked in the late 1960s and early 1970s and has been steadily declining ever since. The province of British Columbia is typical. In 1987-1988 only about 300 healthy infants were given up for adoption while about 3000 couples were on a waiting list. In 1971, almost 1000 infants less than a year old were placed in adopting homes in British Columbia. The state of New South Wales in Australia mirrors this trend. In 1972, 2000 children were surrendered for adoption but by 1983 the number had fallen to 155.

The decrease reflects a number of social trends. The social stigma of out-of-wedlock and teenage pregnancy has largely disappeared. Women are no longer shamed or pressured into giving up their babies, and they no longer disappear for a year or go into homes for unwed mothers. In some inner city areas having a baby and raising the child has become a trend among teenage girls. Children are no longer given stigmatizing labels such as "bastard" or illegitimate if they are raised by an unwed mother. Government social assistance programs have enabled single mothers to keep their children. With access to safe abortions, teenage girls and women can terminate an unwanted pregnancy in the early months. In 1987 in Canada more than 60,000 women terminated an unwanted pregnancy through a legal abortion.

These social trends have been positive for women and have given them more control over their own reproduction, but the result means there are fewer babies for infertile couples to adopt.

Private adoptions, with the relinquishing mother and a couple making their own arrangements, have begun to outstrip the number of agency or government-arranged adoptions. Some couples are aggressively advertising, hiring lawyers as baby brokers, sending hundreds of copies of their "resumes" to doctors or schools in the hope that it will come to the attention of a pregnant teenager willing to give up her child privately.

Adoption agencies have waiting lists of five to seven years, but if a couple is willing to adopt a child of a mixed race, an international child or a child with special emotional, mental or physical needs, the wait may be shorter. But those special adoptions require a great deal of time and effort to arrange. Children with special needs, such as those with physical or mental handicaps, troubled backgrounds or behavioral problems, often require special parenting skills and many couples are not prepared for that.

Despite the long waits, the paper work and red tape, thousands of couples attest to the joy that their adopted child or children have brought them when the adoption finally comes through.

Both our adoptions have been so positive. It is hard to believe when you are waiting that it will ever happen, but when the child comes it is well worth the wait.

Deciding on Adoption

The first step for an infertile couple is to determine, honestly, whether adoption is what they want. Infertility counsellors, social workers and psychologists all stress that couples must have come to terms with their infertility before moving on to adoption. They must have satisfied themselves that medical treatment has been adequately explored. Grief over their infertility should be resolved. They must want to love and raise an adopted child.

Adoption is not right for every one, but the worst scenario is for a couple to discover it is not right for them after the process is completed. Adoption breakdowns, fortunately, are infrequent, but when they happen they can be devastating to the child. Social workers tell stories of profoundly damaged adoptees who were rejected by their adoptive parents after the adoption. One infertile couple adopted a boy as an infant and then four years later the woman became pregnant. Their favoritism for their biological child was obvious and their relationship with the boy, who was difficult and acted out against his sibling, began to deteriorate. When the boy was 10, the couple returned him to government social workers saying they could no longer raise him and he was put in foster care. At 16, psychiatrists found that the boy was significantly disturbed. The doctors felt his psychological and behavioral problems had germinated in his early rejection and adoption experience.

Most adoption agencies make it clear that their purpose is not to help childless couples get children to raise, but to help children have a good family that will love them. The focus must be the needs of the child. Couples considering adoption must look at all the angles and consider whether they can give the child the kind of love and support he or she needs. Couples should also be in good health and have enough financial resources to provide a secure environment for the child. The issues are similar, in some respects, to those faced by couples undergoing donor insemination.

Here are some questions, suggested by social workers and adoption agencies, that you should consider before going through with adoption.

- Can you love, whole-heartedly and with full commitment, a child that is not genetically related to you?
- Have you considered all the various physical needs of a child, such as schooling, food, shelter, clothing, medical attention and dentistry and are you willing to meet the child's needs until he or she reaches independence?
- If you happen to have a child by birth after adopting a child, will you value and love your adopted child the same?

- If the adopted child should have some difficulty, be it a learning disability, trouble in school, illness or unruly behavior, will you still love and accept the child?
- Will you blame any undesirable characteristics in the child on bad genes and be less committed to working through the problem?
- Will your extended family of brothers, sisters and parents accept and love the child?

Most professionals involved with adoption believe that it is very important that children know they are adopted from an early age so that they can incorporate this information into their indentity. An adopted child, like any child, needs to feel confident of her adoptive parents' love and acceptance.

Adoption often has wonderful results; many solid families have been built on adoption. For couples who have carefully weighed their decision, there are few, if any, regrets. Studies have shown that adoptive parents and children form strong, resilient bonds.

Our two children are 15 and 17 now and I simply can't count the times I have thanked God for bringing them into our lives. Our infertility was hard, but I really have forgotten about that now, it was so long ago. We feel so fortunate to have had these kids to raise. The infertility is something way in the past but these kids are what happens day to day. I feel sorry for other couples who may be unable to adopt now. I wouldn't have wanted to miss out on our kids for the world.

Adoption procedures vary from province to province and state to state. Couples wishing to adopt must research the procedures in their own area to become familiar with the regulations.

Essentially adoption is a legal procedure that creates a court-recognized relationship between the parents and the child. The rights and duties of natural parents are conferred on the adoptive parents. Through adoption, the child is given the legal rights of any biological child. The child, for example, has rights to the family name, inheritance and support.

Despite the differences between regions a number of elements are the same. Couples basically have the choice to go through traditional adoption agencies, arrange a private adoption, adopt internationally or adopt a special-needs child.

Adoption Agencies

Government-operated adoption programs, children's aid societies and church affiliated agencies have traditionally acted as neutral third parties, linking birth mothers to adopting parents for the benefit of the child. The agencies have staff and social workers who process applications, counsel birth mothers, conduct home studies to approve couples for the placement of a child and generally do the paper work and leg work to match a birth mother's child with a good home. The agencies generally conduct their business without ever having the two parties meet, although non-identifying information on both birth mother and adopting couple will be exchanged.

In the past, the majority of adoptions were conducted through such agencies and there are many advantages to using them. They are non-profit organizations whose concerns are for the placement of a child that will ensure a good match and a safe and happy upbringing. Costs of agency adoptions are low, at most a few thousand dollars. The risks of adoption failure through agencies are minimal. Mothers who have gone through agencies rarely change their mind once a baby has been placed because they have been counselled beforehand. Social workers usually anticipate problems and do not begin negotiations with adopting parents, nor place a child if the birth mother is unsure of her decision. Couples can be assured the baby has not been "bought" nor the mother coerced to give up the child. Relinquishing mothers can be assured their babies are going to safe homes that are approved and that have had detailed home studies.

The drawbacks to agencies are that their waiting lists are long and their procedures are criticized by some couples and birth mothers as being bureaucratic. The agencies control the reins of the adoption. Many agencies have age limits for adopting parents (generally both partners under 40) or restrict adoptions to married couples only. Church-affiliated agencies may restrict adoptions to parents who share the agency's religious faith. Fewer babies are being given up to agencies because many birth mothers want more control and less hassle in the placement of their child, and so bypass agencies and select parents themselves. Some agencies have been getting too few babies to be able to keep their waiting lists open. In Ontario in 1988 a number of children's aid societies said they would be closing their waiting lists because more mothers were going through private arrangements than through agencies. One children's aid society outside of Toronto had more than 250 couples on their waiting list but had fewer than 15 babies to place in 1988.

Despite the trend away from agencies, they are still a good vehicle because of their commitment to good, well-researched placements. If you are interested in going through an agency you must first contact the specific agency and find out how to apply. Many agencies have regular informational group meetings with a social worker or staff member who details the steps of the adoption process. Many agencies allow couples to put their names on other agencies' lists, too.

One of the first steps is to fill out a detailed application and possibly a questionnaire. The application, if it is accepted, puts you on a waiting list for further assessment, including a detailed home study and medical examination of both partners. You will usually be asked to provide personal references.

A home study involves a number of interviews and meetings with the social worker to determine what kind of home environment you would give a child. It is not really a study of your home so much as it is a study of the interpersonal relationship between you and your partner, your attitudes and beliefs, your past experiences and your future plans. The study is a way the social worker can learn to know you better so that he or she can recommend your home without reservations. The initial meetings may take place in a group setting with other couples. Later meetings and interviews will be conducted with you and your partner and individually. The social worker may drop by unannounced to be sure of seeing the real "you" in your typical setting.

Some couples are surprised or taken aback at the level of detail and the personal questions the social worker asks. Your relationship is probed as is your struggle with infertility. Your attitude to your own parents and your relationship with your family is questioned. You may feel you are under a magnifying glass, but the social worker's goal is to get to know you to help with the best selection and placement of a child. This process is also an opportunity for you to determine whether adoption is right for you. From the home study the social worker will prepare a detailed description of you and your home to give to birth mothers.

When the home study is complete and approved, your application is kept on file until your spot is reached on the list and a child who is suited to you becomes available. Most agencies present the birth mother with a few non-identifying portfolios of approved couples from which she makes the final selection. She reads through descriptions of the couples, their relationship and attitudes and chooses the one to whom she wants her baby to go. For that reason some couples who have been approved by the agency may never have a baby placed with them because the mother does not select the application. The couple's age, particularly if they are close to the age of her own parents, may be the factor that prevents a birth mother from selecting an application.

Most agencies do not contact prospective parents until the birth mother has signed the papers and selected the couple so as to not falsely raise a couple's expectations. A call may come out of the blue one day that a baby is waiting if your application is selected by a mother. Your social worker discusses the details of the child's background with you and most agencies allow the couple to see the child and meet with the birth mother's social worker before the final decision is made. Couples can also discuss the child's medical information with their doctor. It is important that you not feel pressured into accepting a placement if somehow you feel the child is not suited to you. Many couples are afraid to turn down an offer, social workers say, because they are afraid they will never be offered another child. But it is much better to turn down a child than to accept one with doubts; adoption is a life-long arrangement.

After you have accepted the child and have taken him or her home, the social worker may make a few follow-up visits. Some regions allow the birth mother to change her mind within a certain number of days of the child's placement, others require that after the papers are signed the birth mother must petition the court within six months to rescind the arrangement. Such court petitions are usually not successful for the birth mother unless she can prove that she was coerced into signing the papers or did not know what she was signing. In most regions the adoption usually becomes legal after a waiting period of about six months, at which time the couple signs legal documents that are submitted to the court. In some regions couples must attend court themselves to legalize the adoption; in other regions social workers or lawyers attend court on the couple's behalf. After the court grants the order of adoption, the child is legally yours.

Our two children were adopted through (the government agency) and we have nothing but good to say about the process. The social workers were professional, thorough. I am amazed when I look at our children because they seem to have been selected to fit right in with our temperment. The match is perfect. We never once worried that the adoption would break down. It took a long time—three years for the first and four for the second—but there is no doubt in our mind that the wait was worth it.

Private Adoption

Since the early 1980s private adoptions have begun to outstrip agency adoptions. The trend has been fueled by adopting parents who are frustrated with drawn-out procedures and agency restrictions such as the age of the adopting parents. Birth mothers tend to give their babies up more often through private channels than through agencies because it gives them more control of over who gets their baby. Since babies are in such demand, the birth mother can often dictate the arrangement she wants. Under private agreements, she can sometimes demand to meet the prospective parents or to carry on correspondence with the child or to get periodic news of the child through the adoptive parents.

Our birth mother told our lawyer she wanted to meet us before she decided. Three or four years ago we would have said no. But we thought, this is the age of rights, if this is what she wants, if this makes her happy, this is what we'll do. We stipulated that there would be no last names and no contact afterward, which she agreed to. We met in our lawyer's office for about 30 minutes.

Private adoptions can have significant drawbacks. The most significant one for the adopting couple is that the private arrangements have a much greater tendency to fall through. Because the arrangement is often made through an inexperienced intermediary, such as the birth mother's grandmother, a doctor or a lawyer, the birth mother may not have been professionally counselled and may be more likely to change her mind. Some adoptions even fall through after the child has been taken home, a devastating experience for the adopting couple.

We've had four private adoptions fall through. You hear about it before the baby is born and then you get your hopes up and then it doesn't happen. Fortunately we hadn't taken any of the babies home, but it was hard all the same. Usually it's because the mother has changed her mind and wants to keep the baby. But we had one where the mother decided she wanted another couple after she had originally picked us—they had a pony.

Private adoptions have more potential for exploitation of both the adopting parents and the birth mother. An unscrupulous intermediary may illegally demand money from the couple or charge inflated "expenses." The birth mother may be pressured into relinquishing a child, giving her grounds to reverse the adoption in a court challenge later on. Child welfare professionals are concerned that children may be placed without adequate screening (or any screening at all) of the adoptive parents. Lawyers, doctors or the birth mother's grandmother may not be the best judge of a home environment. A lawyer, for example, may give a couple a relinquished baby not because they would make good parents but because they can pay their legal bills. Many critics are concerned that private adoptions may tend to favor couples with money and connections. A deserving couple may be unable to attract a birth mother, not because they would not be good parents, but because they do not have a swimming pool.

Despite the significant concerns about private adoption, it has become the current trend. Many couples, who have their names on agency waiting lists, also decide to pursue private adoptions to increase their chance of getting a baby.

Couples who are intent on adopting privately must let everybody know they are looking for a child—that means everybody. They never know where a child might come from. Successful couples tell colleagues at work, the woman who works in the coffee shop, the mailman, their neighbors and friends of friends. Couples also put together "resumes" that give details about themselves to send out by the hundreds to doctors, priests, school nurses, lawyers—anybody who might have contact with a pregnant woman wanting to relinquish her child.

At first I was uncomfortable letting everybody know that we were looking for a baby. I'd considered our infertility a private thing and it wasn't really something I wanted to announce to everybody and anybody. But after a while we got used to telling everybody. And it worked. We got our baby from a contact with a neighbor's cleaning lady whose friend had a granddaughter who was pregnant.

Many couples have become very aggressive in tracking down potential mothers. Couples have been known to put together glossy packages with a multipage personal letter to the potential birth mother describing themselves, their attitudes and beliefs and the kind of home they would give a child. The package is often accompanied by pictures of themselves, their house, their yard and even pets, boat, cottage, or whatever they think the birth mother might like to see. The package, with a covering letter, is then sent to dozens, even hundreds of possible contacts such as doctors in small towns or Catholic priests. The covering letter asks the contact to bring the package to the attention of any pregnant woman thinking about giving her child up for adoption. Some couples have even put together a tape of themselves, addressing their comments to the potential birth mother. Couples have sent such information packages to university health clinics, high school nurses, and clergy members of a number of denominations. No doubt in the future, some couples will make home videos of themselves to send a birth mother.

Other couples have tried advertising in newspapers (in some areas such ads are illegal), in flyers placed under car windshield-wipers in parking lots or distributed in subdivisions, and through notices on campus bulletin boards. The techniques some couples use to track down a birth mother rival the resourcefulness of public relations firms.

Many couples who are looking for a private adoption hire a lawyer to act as an intermediary and to help with the legal procedures of the adoption. Some lawyers locate birth mothers for the couple and do all the paper work to make it legal—for a fee. A Los Angeles legal firm guarantees a baby to couples who can afford the hefty $30,000 fee for "expenses." Most adoption lawyers do not cost that much, but private adoptions, in general, are more expensive than agency adoptions. Legal fees are higher and the birth mother's medical and legal costs are also absorbed by the couple. Some regions do not allow intermediaries to charge fees, however, which keeps costs down.

In private adoptions a lawyer is needed for the legal documents. Before hiring a lawyer, however, you should contact a local bar association to find out what expenses are legitimate and what are not. An ethical lawyer experienced in adoption procedures in your area can often be located through adoptive parents associations or infertility support groups such as Resolve.

Unlike agency adoptions, many private adoptions place the baby in the adoptive parents' home before the mother has signed the papers removing her rights to the child. This can be uneasy time for the adoptive parents.

We picked the baby up three days after she was born and took her home, but the mother didn't sign the papers until a week later. That was emotionally a very difficult week—it was a lot harder than our first adoption which was through the ministry. You are always aware that it may fall through. It was difficult for us and our relatives and friends. We told everybody don't visit, don't send presents, don't call us, we'll call you.

When a baby has been found by private adoption and placed in the home, most regions require that a social worker conduct a home study before the arrangement is finalized by the court. As in agency adoptions, the arrangement must be legalized through a court procedure, usually about six months after the placement.

Private adoption isn't easy—it isn't simple, straightforward and unemotional. But for us it worked. And it will be really nice to be able to tell our daughter so much about her birth mother, to show her pictures and tell her about our meeting. I think that our daughter will appreciate that.

International Adoptions

In recent years many couples desiring adoption have turned to foreign countries to find children. Since the 1980s Vietnam, Thailand, Korea, Peru, Colombia, Mexico, El Salvador, Brazil, India, Hong Kong, and other countries have provided infants for North American couples wanting to adopt. Both the adoptive parents and the child's life can be enormously enriched by the arrangement.

Couples should pursue international adoptions with their eyes open. A "lady bountiful" attitude of rescuing poor little children from grotty slums and indoctrinating them into a white, middle-class culture may not be the best thing for the child. Some professionals are critical of international adoptions because they feel the time, effort and money would be better spent giving the support and means to help children stay with their natural parents in their own country. Because poverty and social stigma are the reasons why most international children are placed for adoption, addressing those issues in the country might better serve the child, critics say. If international adoptions seem appropriate and good for the child, most professionals believe the couple should be committed to maintaining links with the child's culture and country of origin so he or she can grow up aware of roots and with a sense of identity.

My husband and I have always been very interested in Latin American culture. We both speak Spanish and we have made a number of trips to Central and South America. When we first considered international adoption, we knew immediately it should be a Latin American country. We chose Colombia because, at the time, its waiting list was short and we both knew and loved the country. We now have two children from there. We speak Spanish and English to them, we play the music, we tell them about the country and when they're old enough we'll take them back there so they can see it.

International adoptions are not easy and are not necessarily faster than private or agency adoptions. Placements can take up to three years or longer. Each country has its own red tape. One month a country may accept applications for international adoptions and the next month it may have closed its doors. The situation can change overnight. Couples may have completed all the paper work for an adoption with a country only to find that it has placed an indefinite moratorium on international adoptions and the couple must start at square one with a new country. Many countries do not allow a couple to be on a list for another country at the same time. Foreign adoptions can also be expensive, as couples may have to fly there to pick up the infant or pay for the child and an escort who delivers the child to North America. Legal fees and other costs can also escalate. Some countries require the couple to go through court proceedings in the child's country to obtain custody. The cost of an international adoption may range from about $3,000 to $10,000, depending on such things as whether the couple has to fly to the country or stay there while the adoption is being finalized.

Newborn babies from foreign countries are practically impossible to adopt. A child is considered young at four or five months old. Often the child may be a year or older by the time it reaches you. If a couple is willing to adopt a child who is three or four years old, the wait can be considerably reduced. Older children may have had a difficult early life, with illness or malnutrition, factors the couple should weigh before adopting.

To find out about international adoptions, you should contact adoption social workers working for your provincial or state government, local adoptive parents' associations or local infertility support groups. Each country has its own set of requirements but most have a liason in regional or national government departments who can help you with the procedure. An international child needs a permit to enter Canada, so the Department of External Affairs must be contacted. Most countries require a home study, which will usually be conducted by local social workers.

International adoptions can also be done privately through contacts in the country. One couple adopted a little girl from an orphanage in India after the wife's parents saw the child while they were working in the region. The paper work took nearly 16 months, so the child was almost two years old by the time she came into her adoptive parents' care. Some people have used a lawyer, doctor, church group or aid program as a contact in a country. Direct contact with a specific orphanage is also possible.

Couples should be careful, however, of whom they are using to arrange the adoptions. The demand for babies is very high and there are many concerns of baby black markets, baby selling, or exploitation of poverty stricken parents. Early in 1988, Sri Lanka suspended all international adoptions because of allegations of an illegal baby trade with Europe. Couples should not be part of an arrangement that has any hint of illegal dealings or the buying or selling of babies. The babies may have been kidnapped from their natural parents or obtained through exploitation or even torture. If couples come across a suspect arrangement in their search for an international child to adopt, they should notify government authorities.

Some organizations, such as Toronto's Families For Children, bring destitute children out of war-torn or impoverished countries. These children are often suffering from an illness or malnutrition and if uncared for would die. The adopting family may receive an urgent call saying, "We have a baby—she has her hearing and eyesight but otherwise we know nothing about her. She is sick. If she lives, will you take her?" Couples who open their hearts to such children know that they are giving a child a chance at life. But they also are taking the child without knowing whether malnutrition, early childhood experience or illness may have caused permanent damage to the child's development.

International adoptions, however, can be highly rewarding for couples who are willing to make the effort and commitment to go through with it.

Special-Needs Adoption

A child who is described as having "special needs" may be a baby or a teenager, but always has some factor that makes his or her care and parenting requirements greater than other children given up for adoption. The child may be physically or mentally handicapped with a disability like Down's syndrome, cerebral palsy, spina bifida or brain damage. Or the child may have emotional or behavioral problems, the result of a neglected or abused background. A group of siblings who all want to be placed together are also in the special-needs category. Sometimes children may have more than one factor contributing to their designation of special needs. A special-needs child needs a special set of parents.

Unlike other adoptions, special-needs children usually outnumber the parents who are willing to adopt them. As a result, government agencies advertise and promote these children for adoption. Many regions run profiles of children in a regular newspaper column or publish adoption bulletins featuring children with special needs who are available for adoption. The children sometimes require parents who have particular child-rearing skills or a particular home environment that includes other children. Infertile couples, who usually have no parenting experience, do not often apply to become the adoptive parents of a special-needs child, adoption officials say.

Rather than having a general home study that applies to any placement, couples are assessed for their suitability to parent a specific child. Often agencies put couples through an in-depth training course for special-needs parenting before a placement occurs so that the couple is fully aware of all that may lie ahead. Often the prospective parents and child have a few pre-placement visits, even a few weekends together to see if the couple and the child can relate to each other. There are usually no costs to special-needs adoptions.

Foster Parenting

Foster parenting is another option an infertile couple should consider. It isn't adoption, but it is a way to have a significant and meaningful role in a child's life. It is temporary placement, not a permanent one, but it can have a stabilizing role for a needy child.

Children come into foster care because of neglect, abuse, family breakup or some situation that requires that the children be placed with another family while their own family situation is worked out. Unlike children put up for adoption, foster children have not been relinquished by their natural parents. Foster child arrangements can be short-term or long-term. A short-term placement may be for only a few weeks when a family is in crisis, such as when a single mother is sick in hospital. A long-term placement can last for months or years. Some foster children are eventually put up for adoption if family problems cannot be corrected.

Foster parents take a child knowing that some day the child will probably be reunited with his or her family. It can be hard on some couples to give the child back but some foster families keep strong bonds with the children they have taken into their homes, keeping in touch and having regular visits. Some couples will have cared for more than 20 children in a lifetime. One foster couple in British Columbia has already had more than 20 foster children. They have three adopted children and up to six foster children in their home at one time. "Some of our earliest foster children are now in their twenties," says the mother. "They come back and see us, tell us about the job they're doing, the boyfriend they're seeing. One has even gotten married and he brings his newborn child to see us. They are all my children, whether they were here for a month or five years."

Foster parents often require special parenting skills. Some government child welfare departments will train couples to become foster parents. For more information about foster parenting contact the government department responsible for child welfare in your region.

Surrogacy

Surrogate parenting, in which a woman is contracted to bear a child for another, has become one of the most controversial and thorny issues related to infertility. The notorious custody case of Baby M in the United States, in which surrogate mother Mary Beth Whitehead refused to surrender the child to contracting parents William and Elizabeth Stern, propelled the formerly closeted arrangements into the public spotlight. Debate has raged ever since about whether a surrogacy arrangement should be a legitimate way for a childless couple to get a baby or whether it represents the worst of baby selling and exploitation of women.

The Baby M case seemed to give the impression that surrogacy was a relatively new twist on a couple's pursuit of a child. As adoptions became less available, it appeared, more were willing to take the risks of surrogacy. But surrogacy has probably been around, in its clandestine fashion, for centuries. In fact a surrogate mother was recorded as early as Genesis, the first book of The Bible. Her name was Bilhah and she was Rachel's maidservant. She bore Rachel's husband, Jacob, two sons, Dan and Naphtali, because Rachel was barren. Genesis actually records the first two biblical surrogate arrangements in quick succession. When Jacob's first wife, Leah, saw that Rachel's maid had produced two sons for Jacob, she offered him her maid as well. Leah's maid, Zilpah, bore Jacob two sons, too. (Jacob had six sons and a daughter with Leah, four sons with the two surrogates and two sons, finally, with Rachel.)

These days a surrogate is most likely to be a married woman in her mid-twenties who has already had one or more children. She is found by an agency for a commissioning couple, usually well-off professionals in their mid-to-late-thirties who are unable to have a child because the woman is infertile or unable to carry a pregnancy. The surrogate signs a contract saying she will abide by certain requirements during the pregnancy, such as no drinking, smoking, drugs or X rays, and in return she will receive payment for medical costs, maternity clothes and living expenses. She is inseminated with the commissioning husband's sperm, creating a fetus that carries half her genes and half his genes. When the baby is born she surrenders the child to the couple and signs away all her maternal rights, at which time she receives the balance of payments from the couple.

As an alternative to being inseminated by the male partner, the surrogate may agree to carry the embryo created by the commissioning couple's sperm and egg. In this situation, often called host womb or IVF surrogacy, the surrogate mother has no genetic relationship to the child.

In the time of Genesis, Jacob and his clan obviously accepted surrogacy as a practical arrangement that ensured lots of offspring to tend the flocks and beget more offspring. But in recent years opponents of surrogacy have found much to criticize about the modern arrangements. Some opponents call it highly immoral and unethical, others simply say it is bad for the child and for the woman contracted to bear the child. It reduces children to commodities and the women who bear them to containers, mere vessels for babies.

Those in favor of surrogacy, or at least those who do not oppose it, see it as an issue of individual rights. Why should informed, consenting adults not be able to enter into an arrangement that benefits both parties? Should not an individual have the right to make personal decisions about procreation? Those in favor of surrogacy argue that unless society can actually prove that surrogacy arrangements cause harm to the child or society the state should not pass laws that limit individual freedoms.

The rest of society, befuddled by the novelty and the scope of it all, sits uncomfortably astride the fence. Many have a vague feeling of uneasiness, an intuition that something is not right with surrogacy. "It seems... well, so dangerous. It has so much potential to go wrong." Yes, people should have individual freedoms; a woman should have the right to choose if she wants to use her body to make a baby and to make money. But there is no doubt that poor women are the ones who will become surrogates. What is there to stop them from being exploited? But if being able to bear a child is a skill that a woman can do well, why should she not be paid handsomely for it? A woman might be able to find real fulfillment and meaning knowing she was helping an infertile couple. And the couple might provide a terrific home for the child. So, how do we get a grip on what is right or wrong in surrogacy?

There are no right or wrong answers. Perhaps surrogacy is right for some involuntarily childless couples who would make loving, good parents. Perhaps some surrogate mothers have an ability to carry a baby and give it up knowing that they are giving a childless couple one of the greatest gifts in life. But then there are all those instances that horrify—the cases where a couple acquires a baby as they would acquire a piece of furniture or a piece of modern art, as long as it fits their lifestyle and their particular tastes; the cases where a poor woman, needing the money, is exploited into becoming a breeder because that is the only job open to her.

The worst fears of the sort of couple who might enter a surrogacy contract were borne out in a news story in the *New York Daily News* on April 24, 1988. According to the report, a couple hired a woman to bear their child and the surrogate was inseminated with the contracting man's sperm. When the woman gave birth to healthy twins, a boy and a girl, the couple refused to accept the twin boy. It seems they only wanted a girl and the extra baby was not in the contract. The boy was first placed in foster care, but then the surrogate and her husband decided to raise him.

What is Legal

The legality of surrogacy, in most regions, is up in the air. In the United States half the states have introduced legislation relating to surrogacy but, according to the Office of Technology Assessment report to Congress, by mid 1988 most of it was still pending. The four states that had passed legislation by 1988, according to the OTA, had all taken different directions. Louisianna made the arrangement unenforceable (meaning any contract would not stand up in court and was not valid). Arkansas endorsed the validity of the contractual arrangement. Kansas exempted it from laws prohibiting adoption agency advertising. And Nevada exempted it from provisions prohibiting payment for babies.

In most regions the legality is now left to court decisions. The custody case of Baby M has blazed the path for other court decisions to follow. Mary Beth Whitehead's contract with the Sterns was a typical surrogacy arrangement.

Inseminated with William Stern's semen, she was to receive $10,000 when she handed over the baby. But Whitehead became distraught at giving up her newborn daughter. She fled to Florida where, despite a court order to surrender the baby to Stern, she remained for four months until Stern regained custody.

An eight-month court case ensued in New Jersey to determine if the contract Whitehead signed was enforceable. In March of 1987 the trial court judge, basing his decision on strict contract law and what he thought was best for the child, awarded custody to the Sterns, terminated Whitehead's parental rights and cancelled her visitation privileges. Almost a year later the New Jersey Supreme court reversed the decision of the trial court. Chief Justice, Robert Wilentz, found that the surrogacy contract violated New Jersey law against baby-selling, adoption and termination of parental rights. He reinstated Whitehead as the legal mother, gave her back visiting privileges, and halted the adoption procedure by Elizabeth Stern. He still, however, gave custody of Baby M to the Sterns, on the basis of what he thought was best for the child. But his condemnation of payment for surrogacy arrangements rang like a bell: "[it is] illegal, perhaps criminal, and potentially degrading to women .... There are, in a civilized society, some things money cannot buy."

In Canada there is no formal legislation against surrogacy and as yet there has been no test of surrogacy in the courts. There has been no national dialogue although the federal government in April 1989 announced in its throne speech that a Royal Commission would be called to address the issue of surrogacy and other reproductive techniques. The Royal Commission announcement was in response to repeated calls by public interest groups for Canada to come to some decision on surrogacy and other reproductive issues.

In 1985 the Ontario Law Reform Commission's Report on Human Artificial Reproduction and Related Matters found commercial surrogacy to be ethically acceptable and recommended that the family law courts supervise the screening and counselling of the surrogate mother and the commissioning parents. (The Ontario Law Reform Commission's Report is one of a few in the world to make such recommendations as most other regions, which have looked into surrogacy, have decided payment is unethical.) It appears most Canadian couples who enter into surrogacy arrangements do so through agencies in the United States, hiring an American surrogate. The total number of surrogacy cases in Canada to date are not known but a Canadian study commissioned by the Law Reform Commission of Canada estimated that by 1988 a minimum of 104 surrogacy arrangements had been carried out. The study's researchers, however, believed that the actual numbers probably greatly exceeded the estimates.

Some countries have taken the approach that if payment to surrogates is prohibited, the abuses and exploitation will not take place. A woman who wants to bear a child for another couple on purely altruistic grounds should be able to do what she likes with her body. It is reasoned that very few women would decide to be surrogates without some reimbursement. In the United Kingdom commercial surrogacy is banned and private contracts that are disputed have been made unenforceable. France has also made surrogacy contracts unenforceable and agencies providing commercial surrogacy arrangements are illegal. Any agency or individual in France who uses an agency services to obtain a surrogacy contract can be subject to prosecution. Only one state in Australia, Victoria, has passed legislation banning commercial surrogacy outright but committees that advise the government on reproductive matters in four Australian states have recommended rejection of any surrogacy arrangements. It is illegal in New South Wales for a mother to designate to whom her baby should go in adoption and so surrogacy is effectively illegal there, too.

In areas where there are no laws, one of the pivotal factors affecting court decisions will be the issue of informed consent. Many legal experts believe a contract signed before the birth of the baby cannot be considered a document signed with informed consent because the woman, even if she has borne children before, cannot know how she will feel after the baby is born. The OTA report noted that if a surrogate mother decides to break the contract by not giving up the baby, legal opinions say she forfeits her right to payment but then she has equal rights as the commissioning father to custody of the child. The decision would then rest with the court as to which parent would provide the best home for the child.

Other Issues

There are many issues in surrogate parenting: What happens if the child is born with a mental or physical handicap—who then takes custody of the child? What if the commissioning couple demands amniocentesis and the surrogate refuses? What if the woman undergoes amniocentesis and the fetus shows a defect or is somehow undesirable to the couple, perhaps because it is not the right sex? Can the couple force the woman to have an abortion? If the surrogate decides not to undergo an abortion, can the couple walk away from the contract, refusing to accept the child or pay her the money, and leaving her with the pregnancy? Or what if the couple wants the woman to undergo a Caesarean section to minimize the risk to the baby during birth? Can the couple make demands on the surrogate's behavior such as not to have intercourse with her husband during the insemination cycle, or not having a glass of wine, or even compelling her to eat a diet the couple dictates?

The complications and permutations of surrogacy contracts are mind boggling. Some surrogacy agencies stipulate that the complete obligations be set out in writing and signed by both parties. Such contracts set out what happens in the case of miscarriage, stillbirth or disability, whether or not the woman must submit to prenatal testing or a Caesarean section, what behavior during pregnancy will be allowed and what will not. The surrogate and couple agree to conditions before undertaking the inseminations.

These sorts of contract specifications only prove to reinforce that surrogacy arrangements are like hiring a contractor to renovate one's bathroom or hiring a manufacturer to make a customized piece of machinery. The contract simply stipulates how the job will be done. No big difference, except for one enormous difference—the product is a child.

And what about that child? What impact will it have on an individual child's psyche? No doubt there will be some children who will thank their parents that they wanted them so much they hired a surrogate to have them. But there will be others who will be disturbed to know their mothers bore them for money or their fathers paid a woman a lump of cash in exchange for his or her life. And when surrogacy arrangements turn sour, what will happen to the children then? What will Melissa Stern think when she is old enough to understand the world-publicized fight over her custody? Or what will go on in the mind of the twin girl when she learns her parents would not accpet her brother? Will some children despise their parents for their choices?

What to Do?

What is an infertile couple desiring a baby supposed to do? Should you venture into a surrogacy arrangement? There is enough concern about the legality and social issues surrounding commercial surrogacy that this book cannot recommend that couples swim in these murky waters—they are shark infested. You do it at your peril. You may be fortunate to find a surrogate with whom you can enter into a mutually satisfying relationship with no problems, no exploitation and a great result. And then again you may not. You may be able to find a friend, relative or unknown woman willing to carry a baby for you out of altruism with no payment. But that still does not mean you will not have problems if she decides she wants more access to the child. Paid or unpaid, if she chooses to sue for privileges or custody you have no legal ground. Everything could work out fine, but then again it might not. It is a risk you take.

Everyone knows the problems of surrogacy will not stop couples who really want to pursue it. According to the OTA more than 600 couples in the United States had entered into such arrangements by the end of 1987. The numbers are likely to stay the same, if not increase, as couples explore it as an alternative to adoption. Ironically, the publicity about the hazards of surrogacy that came out around the Baby M case did not deter couples from seeking a surrogate. In fact, the OTA report said that in a survey of surrogacy agencies in the United States most stated that inquiries increased after the case.

Society, no doubt, will continue to grapple with the issue and further legislation or clarification on surrogacy is to be expected. But infertile couples must grapple with the issue, too. After all, it is you, the infertile couple, who drives the machinery.

Living Without Children

There is one more option that infertile couples may choose, and that is to remain childless. That may seem no choice at all to a couple that has desired children and tried hard to get them. How can it be a "choice" when it has been thrust upon you?

But a choice it is. It may not be the same kind of choice that a fertile couple has when they plan their future, weighing the pros and cons of having children. If they choose to remain childless it is not scarred by the disappointment of having first tried for a child. Your first choice has been to try to have a child. When infertility treatment failed, when you worked through your grief, the time comes for the second round of choices. Placed in front of you are the various forms of adoption, perhaps artificial insemination or surrogacy, and childlessness. While you consider the pros and cons of the other options, you should do the same for childlessness. You may find that its benefits are considerable and it makes the most sense for you.

"Less" May Be More

Some people have trouble with the word childless, especially the "less" part. It seems to imply an incomplete state, less than being whole, but for many people there is nothing "less" about living without children. They lead very full, meaningful lives.

It was seven years ago when we decided that we'd forget about trying to get pregnant, put away the thermometer and the Clomid. I look back over the last seven years and I know we'd never have done the things we've done if we'd had young children. We decided there was nothing holding us here and so we went and worked in Africa for two years on a development project. We took our time coming back home, hopping from one country to the next—that was great. We both have interesting jobs here but at the same time we don't feel slaves to them because we don't really need the security. I've had time to take a Spanish course and I've started to do some volunteer work on a crisis line. My husband and I have a great relationship—really close. My life feels very full.

Those who are happy in their childless life will give you all sorts of reasons. They have a much greater disposable income, they do not have to work so hard to make ends meet, they have more time for everything—their partner, their friends, their careers, their hobbies—more time to spend on special projects. They have freedom to go where they want, when they want. And they have more emotional and physical energy.

To the couple who wanted children in the first place, all those things may sound hedonistic. The talk of "more money" and "free time" can sound selfish and insignificant. But deciding to remain childless does not mean you are being selfish.

When we were deciding whether we would go without children I wanted to know what childless couples' lives are like. I had always thought, I guess, that choosing to be childless was selfish and self-centered, not contributing to society. I began to pay attention to people who didn't have any children—acquaintances, people at work, people I read about in magazines. I would just take note of whether they had children or not. And I noticed that a lot of the people who didn't have children were living very interesting, productive lives. Many had more time to do "good works," like volunteer work. In fact I began to realize that some of the most self-centered people I knew were those whose lives revolved around their children and only their children. That really made me see things in a different light.

It is odd how childlessness has somehow been perceived as being selfish and non-contributing. A look back through history does support that contention. There are countless names of famous men and women who have made lasting contributions to society, yet never had children. In fact, Francis Bacon (himself childless) may have been right when he said that children (and wives, too, he noted) are "impediments to great enterprise." Queen Elizabeth I was not the only great leader who remained childless. George Washington sired no offspring although he adopted Martha's grown children from her first marriage. A number of literary figures never reproduced: George Bernard Shaw, Jane Austen, the Bronte sisters, Louisa May Alcott, Virginia Woolf, Katherine Mansfield, to name but a few. Great composers such as Beethoven and Haydn put their creative energies into music rather than offspring. The list goes on: prima ballerina Anna Pavolva, chanteuse Edith Piaf, screen stars Mary Pickford and Katherine Hepburn, pilot Amelia Earhart Putnum, philosopher Jean Paul Sartre and his companion Simone de Beauvoir, Leonardo da Vinci, Michelangelo, Raphael, Vincent Van Gogh, Susan B. Anthony, scientist Isaac Newton (considered by scientists as the greatest intellect who ever lived). Even some people whose names are closely associated with children remained childless: Beatrix Potter, Lewis Carroll, Hans Christian Andersen and the founders of the boy scout and girl guide movement, Robert Baden-Powell and his sister Agnes.

Finding Meaning

That illustrious group isn't meant to be a yard stick by which to judge yourself. It does not mean that if you choose to live without children you should write the twentieth-century equivalent of *Pride and Prejudice*, paint a modern-day Mona Lisa or finish the Tenth Symphony to have lived a worthwhile life. All that is important is that you feel your life has meaning and satisfaction if you do not have children. What makes you feel satisfied does not matter; nor does it matter what anybody else thinks about how you find your satisfaction. There is no yard stick. All that matters is that you feel good about it.

For many people where they should put their energies may be unclear. If they have always imagined themselves with children it may be hard to figure out what to do. They may feel obligated to find a reason for being, a passion, to give their life meaning.

> *It is a dreadful pressure—I feel I must now accomplish great deeds so that I haven't wasted my life. I feel I must find purpose to my life or else I'll have failed. It seems so much more simple for people who can have children.*

Some people may find that by examining the option of a childless life it becomes more clear to them that they want to parent. They want that role and that vocation. Discovering that, they can then pursue a form of adoption, foster parenting or surrogacy confirmed in their decision that a childless life is not for them.

If you decide to remain childless you do not have to strive to achieve great things. You are under no more obligation than anyone else in the world to be or do a certain thing. You do not have to accomplish more than others because you do not have children. You may feel like striving and throwing your energies into a project or into something that would be deemed to be a contribution to society. That may be your heartfelt choice. But you do not need to feel obligated to do that. You can give yourself permission to be normal.

Mythologist Joseph Campbell, in talking about how one finds fulfillment, says you must "follow your bliss." That means you pay attention to what in your life makes you feel whole and good, and then follow that path. Following one's bliss does not mean feeling good in the hedonistic sense of indulging in sex or food or drugs or alcohol. It means feeling good in the spiritual sense. It means feeling good inside, not just feeling pleasurable sensations. All people—men, women, young, old, fertile and infertile—seek fulfillment and meaning in their lives. To find their bliss they must be on the look-out for it. No one can tell you where it is or how to find it. Each person's bliss is different.

Childless But Not Without Children

Deciding to remain childless does not mean that your life therefore must be without children, unless you choose that. There are many ways of being involved with children and to be an important person in their lives without being their parent. You can coach a sports team or become a Big Sister or Big Brother to a needy child. You can run a girl-guide company or build a special relationship with the child of a sister or friend. Marsha Dubrow, a Washington, D.C. dancer and writer, wrote about the pleasures of being a some-time parent to her two nieces in the April 1989 *New Woman* magazine. "Most of the time being an aunt instead of a parent means being a companion rather than a disciplinarian, making a child laugh but rarely hearing her cry," she said. She took each niece on her ninth birthday to Manhattan for a weekend, as much an adventure for nervous Auntie with her charges as it was for her nieces. When the girls were seven and five she took them together to Club Med in Guadeloupe. "You're my best friend," one niece told her. "I can tell you things I can't tell anybody else," said the other.

The desire to nurture is a strong component of wanting a child, but many have found that they do not need fatherhood or motherhood to do it. "Nurturing is a normal part of making the world a better place," said Claire, 36, a Sydney doctor interviewed by Australian *Woman's Weekly*, who with her husband had decided childless living was for them. "I think medicine is partly a way of nurturing for me. But it's vital not to do what some parents and doctors do—confuse nurturing with wanting to be in control."

Others have found that by helping other infertile couples, such as by starting a support group, they can resolve their own infertility and achieve some fulfillment knowing their own experience with infertility is helping others. "When I see some of the couples coming into the group for the first time and I think back how I was in the first couple of years, I think if in some way I can help this couple get out of the really black stage, then I am doing something of value," said Jennifer Hillman, co-leader of the Vancouver infertility Peer Support group.

Infertility support groups can be a great help to couples in the midst of the infertility crisis, but many find that once they have resolved their infertility and accepted childlessness they no longer need to go. "Infertility support groups are tremendously helpful but they do have one central issue—being infertile. Sometimes it gets to a point where you don't want to dwell on it anymore," said Jerry Steinberg, a childless teacher who in 1984 formed the first social group for childless couples in Canada, called No Kidding! The Vancouver group of 60 members meets for regular dinners, dances and parties. "Our activities are not child-centered so you don't feel the loss. We don't sit around talking about how we don't have children. We talk about our careers or our travels or our hobbies—things of interest. It's not taboo to talk about children, but you just don't feel the need to."

Courage

Connecticut psychiatrist Dr. M. Scott Peck wrote a wonderful book, *The Road Less Travelled*, first published in 1978, and its opening line is this: "Life is difficult."

The second page says this: "What makes life difficult is that the process of confronting and solving problems is a painful one. Problems, depending on their nature, evoke in us frustration or grief or sadness or loneliness or guilt or regret or anger or fear or anxiety or anguish or despair.... Yet the whole process of meeting and solving problems is what gives life its meaning. Problems are the cutting edge that distinguishes between success and failure. Problems call forth our courage and our wisdom. It is only because of problems that we grow mentally and spiritually."

Confronting and working through the pain of infertility may be the hardest problem you ever face in your life. It forces you to make decisions you do not want to make, to live a life you otherwise would have not chosen, and it takes courage to do it.

Courage is defined as the ability to conquer fear or despair. It does not mean you do not feel those emotions, it just means you go on in spite of them. Coping with life after infertility requires courage, whether you choose to adopt children, enter into a surrogacy arrangement or remain childless. It takes courage to face and embrace the future when you are not sure what it holds. It takes courage to allow yourself to be imperfect. It takes courage to live a full life, to not be defeated even when you have met with disappointment, sadness and loss.

Courage is a strengthening word, a comforting word. There have been many good words written about courage, many of which can be applied to infertility: "Bear with a good courage that which hath befallen thee," advised the Apocrypha, the hidden scriptures that were left out of the Bible. Writer Añais Nin said "Life shrinks or expands in proportion to one's courage."

But there is something about the poem "Courage," written by pilot Amelia Earhart, who died just before age 40 in 1937 when her plane was lost over the Pacific, that captures the essence of life after infertility.

Courage is the price that life exacts for granting peace
The soul that knows it not, knows no release
From little things
Knows not the livid loneliness of fear
Nor mountain heights where bitter joy can hear
The sound of wings

Sources
Chapter 1

The first chapter is a synthesis of interviews with dozens of couples, counsellors, and health professionals. The following interviews, articles, and books helped in putting it all together.

Articles and Books

Aral, Sevgi and Cates, Willard. The increasing concern with infertility: why now? *Journal of the American Medical Association*, Vol. 250, No. 17, November 4, 1983.
Benson, Dr. Herbert. *The Relaxation Response*. New York: William Morrow and Co. Inc., 1975.
Bernstein, Douglas and Borkovec, Thomas. *Progressive Relaxation Training*. Champaign, Illinois: Research Press, 1973.
Bloomfield, Dr. Harold; Vitesse, Sirah; and Kory, Robert. *Lifemates: The Love Fitness Program for a Lasting Relationship*. New York: NAL Books, 1989.
Debrovner, et al. 1975. Sexual problems in the infertile couple. *Medical Aspects of Human Sexuality* 140-150.
Elstein, Dr. Max. Aspects of sexual medicine. *British Medical Journal*, August 2, 1975.
Ethical considerations of the new reproductive technologies. Ethics Committee of the American Fertility Society. *Fertility and Sterility*, Supp. 1, February, 1988.
Infertility: Social and Medical Choices, U.S. Congress Office of Technology Assessment, OTA-BA-358. Washington, D.C.: U.S. Government Printing Office, May 1988.
Johnstone, Patricia Irwin. *Understanding: A Guide to Impaired Fertility for Family and Friends*. Fort Wayne, Indiana: Perspective Press, 1983.
Luthe, Dr. Wolfgang. *Autogenic Therapy*, Vol. 1 of *Autogenic Methods*. J.H. Schultz, Wolfgang Luthe, eds. New York: Grune and Stratton Inc., 1969.
Mahlstedt, Dr. Patricia. The psychological component of infertility. *Fertility and Sterility*, Vol. 43, No. 3, March 1985, 335-346.
Predictions of reproductive failure starting to ring true. *Medical Post*, May 17, 1988.
Rantala, Maija-Liisa and Koskimics, Aarne. 1988. Sexual behavior of infertile couples. *International Fertility* 33:26-30.
Salzer, Linda P. *Infertility: How Couples Can Cope*. Boston: G.K. Hall and Co., 1986.
The billion dollar infertility biz. *USA Today*, May 8, 1988.

Interviews

Louise Bowen, infertility counselor, Monash Medical Centre, Melbourne, Australia.
Dr. John Collins, Chairman of the Department of Obstetrics and Gynecology, McMaster University, Hamilton, Ontario.
Dr. Patricia Mahlstedt, psychologist, IVF Program at Baylor College of Medicine, Houston, Texas.

Dr. Arnold Relman, Editor of the *New England Journal of Medicine*, Press Conference, 1988 American Fertility Society Meeting, Atlanta, Georgia.

Dr. Michael Soules, Director Division of Reproductive Endocrinology and Infertility, University of Washington, Seattle, Washington.

Dr. Patrick Taylor, Head of Endocrinology, Infertility and Reproductive Sciences, University of Manitoba, Winnipeg, Manitoba.

Louis Waller, Professor of Law and Chairman of Victoria Standing Review and Advisory Committee on Infertility, Melbourne, Australia.

Carl Wood, Chairman of Obstetrics and Gynecology, Monash Medical Centre and the Infertility Medical Centre, Australia.

Sources
Chapter 2

Biographical and Historical

Asimov's Biographical Encyclopedia of Science and Technology, New York: Avon, 1976.
The New Columbia Desk Encyclopedia, 4th ed., 1975.
New Encyclopedia Britannica, 15th ed., 1980.

Religion and Mythology

The Bible. The New King James Version, Thomas Nelson Inc., 1980.
Carlisle, Richard, ed. *Illustrated Encyclopedia of Mankind.* London: Marshall Cavendish Ltd., 1978.
Grimal, Pierre, ed. *Larousse World Mythology.* London: Hamlyn Publishing Group Ltd., 1965.
Man, Myth and Magic: The Illustrated Encyclopedia of Mythology, Religion and the Unknown. Toronto and New York: Mars' l Cavendish, 1983.

The Tudor Age

Hoffman, Ann. *Lives of the Tudor Age, 1485-1603.* New York: Barne's and Noble, 1977.
Johnson, Paul *Elizabeth I: A Study in Power and Intellect.* London: Weidenfeld and Nicholson, 1974.
Smith, Lacey Baldwin. *This Realm of England.* Lexington: D.C. Heath & Co., 1976.

Fertility Goddesses

Cotterell, Arthur, and Morgan, David *China's Civilization.* New York: Praeger Publishers, 1975.
Ghalioungui, Paul. *Magic and Medical Science in Ancient Egypt.* London: Hodder and Staughton, 1963.
James, E.O. *Cult of the Mother Goddess.* London: Thames and Hudson, 1959.

Infertility in the Roman Empire

Tannahill, Reay. *Sex in History.* New York: Skin and Day, 1980.
Walsh, James J. *Old-Time Makers of Medicine.* New York: Fordham University Press, 1911.

Medical Discoveries

Boorstein, Daniel. *The Discoverers: A History of Man's Search to Know His World and Himself.* London and Melbourne: J.M. Dent and Sons Ltd., 1984.
Castiglioni, Arturo. *A History of Medicine.* New York: Alfred Knopf, 1947.
Gomel, Dr. Victor. Odyssey Through the Oviduct. Transcript of speech for the 1982 American Fertility Society.
Schmidt, J.E. *Medical Discoveries: Who and When.* Springfield, Ill.: Charles C. Thomas, 1959.

Causes and Treatment of Infertility

Child, Dr. Charles Gardner. *Sterility and Conception.* New York and London: Appleton and Company, 1922.

Gibbon, Robert Alexander. *Sterility in Women, Its Causes and Treatment.* Toronto: The MacMillan Company of Canada, 1923.

Meyer, George; Blum, Kenneth; and Cull, John. *Folk Medicine and Herbal Healing.* Springfield, Ill.: Charles C. Thomas Publishers, 1981.

Mondat, Chevalier Vincent. *Sterility in the Male and Female.* Translated from the 5th French Edition by Chevalier Vincent. New York: Clinton Hall, 1844. (Courtesy of the Academy of Medicine Rare Book Collection in Toronto.)

Ricci, Dr. James V. *One Hundred Years of Gynecology: 1880 A.D. to 1900 A.D.* Philadelphia: The Blakiston Co., 1945.

Sielger, Samuel. *Fertility in Women.* Philadelphia: J.B. Lippincott Co., 1944.

Sources
Chapter 3

Reproduction

Dawkins, Richard. *The Selfish Gene.* New York: Oxford University Press, 1976.
Golanty, Eric. *Human Reproduction.* New York: Holt, Rinehart & Winston, Inc., 1975.
Madaras, Lynda, and Patterson, Dr. Jane. *Womancare: A Gynecological Guide to Your Body.* New York: Avon, 1984.
Ritchie, David. *Human Biology.* Reading, Mass.: Addison-Wesley, 1983.
Sherman, Irwin and Vilia. *Biology: A Human Approach.* 3rd ed. New York: Oxford University Press, 1983.

Interviews on Male Reproduction

Dr. David Cummings, Vancouver, British Columbia.
Dr. David Dekretser, Melbourne, Australia.
Dr. Timothy Hargreave, Edinburgh, Scotland.

Interviews on Female Reproduction

Prof. David Baird in Edinburgh, Scotland.
Dr. David Cummings, University of Alberta (interviewed in Vancouver).
Dr. Jerilynn Prior, University of British Columbia, Vancouver.
Dr. Michael Soules, University of Washington, Seattle.

Speeches on Female Reproduction

Dr. Richard Blandau, Keynote Speech, Society of Obstetricians and Gynecologists, Vancouver, June 1988.

Detecting Fertility

Billings, Dr. Evelyn and Westmore, Ann. *The Billings Method.* London: Allen Lane, 1981.
Dr. Jerilynn Prior, University of British Columbia, Vancouver.
Becton-Dickinson BBT Thermometers
Information on ovulation detection kits was researched through company literature and interviews with company personnel.
Information on freezing First Response vials came through private communication with Tambrands, the manufacturer.

Male Fertility

Barlow, S.M., and Sullivan, F.M. *Reproductive Hazards of Industrial Chemical.* New York: Academic Press, 1982.

McGrady, A.V. 1984. Effects of psychological stress on male reproduction: a review. Archives of Andrology, 13:1-7.

Whorton, D. et al. Infertility in Male Pesticide workers. *The Lancet,* Dec. 17, 1977.

Interviews on Male Fertility

Dr. Gordon Baker, Melbourne, Australia.

Dr. David deKretser, Melbourne, Australia.

Dr. Tim Hargreave, Edinburgh, Scotland.

Dr. Larry Lipschultz, Houston Texas, American Fertility Society Meeting, October, 1988.

Female Fertility

Cummings, Dr. David. 1987. The reproductive effects of exercise and training. In *Current problems in Obstetrics, Gynecology and Fertility* 10(6):225-285. Chicago: Year Book Medical Publishers.

DeCherney, A.H. 1983. In *Principles and Practices of Clinical Gynecology.* New York: John Wiley and Sons.

Environmental effects on animals used in biomedical research. 1982. *Biological Review* 57:153-156.

Frisch, Rose. Fatness and fertility. *Scientific American*, April 1988.

Seibel, M. and Taynor, M. 1982. Emotional aspects of infertility. *Fertility and Sterility* 37:137-145.

Preventing Infertility

Canadian Pelvic Inflammatory Disease Society Handbook.

Infertility: Medical and Social Choices, May 1988. U.S. Congress Office of Technology Assessment, OTA-BA-358. Washington, D.C.: U.S. Government Printing Office, May 1988.

Interview with Dr. Richard Bronson at the 1988 American Fertility Society Meeting in Atlanta, Georgia.

Sources
Chapter 4

Articles and Books

Alexander, N.J. Semen Analysis: The Method and Interpretation. In *Gynecology and Obstetrics*. Edited by J.J. Sciarra. Philadelphia: J.P. Lippincott Co., 1988.

Berger, David. 1980. Infertility: a psychiatrist perspective. *Canadian Journal Of Psychiatry* 25:553-559.

Blackwell, R.E. et al. 1987. Are we exploiting the infertile couple? *Fertility and Sterility* 48:735-739.

Collins, John A. Diagnostic Assessment of the Infertile Female Partner. In *Current Problems in Obstetrics, Gynecology and Fertility* 11(1):1-42. Edited by Robert Barbieri. Chicago: Year Book Medical Publishers, Inc., 1988.

Collins, John A. 1983. Treatment-independent pregnancy among infertile couples. *New England Journal of Medicine* 309:1201-6.

Collins, John A. et al. 1984. Postcoital test as a predictor of pregnancy among 355 infertile couples. *Fertility and Sterility* 41:703.

Coulehan, J.L., and Block, M.R. *The Medical Interview: A Primer for Students of the Art*. Philadelphia: F.A. Davis Co., 1987.

Hammond, Mary G. Evaluation of the Infertile Couple. In *The Infertile Woman*. Edited by Roger Kempers. *Obstetrics and Gynecology Clinics of North America*, Vol. 14, No. 4, December 1987. Philadelphia: W.B. Saunders, 1987.

Infertility: Medical and Social Choices, U.S. Congress, Office of Technology Assessment, OTA-BA-358. Washington, DC: U.S. Government Printing Office, May 1988.

Lee R.D., and Lipshultz, L. Evaluation and Treatment of the Infertile Male. In *Infertility: A Practical Guide for the Physician*. 2nd ed. Edited by M.G. Hammond and L.M. Talbert. Oradell, New Jersey: Medical Economics Books, 1985.

Male Patient History/Female Patient History. Serono Pharmaceuticals. (Physician Handout)

Moghissi, K.S. 1981. Prediction and detection of ovulation. *Fertility and Sterility* 34:89-98.

Noyes, R.W.; Hertig, A.T.; and Rock, J.A. 1950. Dating the endometrial biopsy. *Fertility and Sterility* 1:3-5.

Richmond, J.A. 1987. Hysterosalpingography. *Infertility, Contraception Journal* 136:829-832.

Wentz, A.C. 1980. Endometrial biopsy in the evaluation of infertility. *Fertility and Sterility* 33:121.

World Health Organization. *Laboratory Manual For the Examination of Human Semen and Semen-Cervical Mucus Interaction*. Cambridge: Cambridge University Press, 1987.

Seminars and Presentations

Baker, Gordon. Initial Investigation of the Infertile Couple: The Man. At the seminar The Infertile Couple. Clayton, Victoria, Australia, August 24, 1988.

Berg, Barbara. Psychological Functioning Across the Phases of an Infertility Work-Up. American Fertility Society 44th Annual Meeting, Atlanta, Georgia, October 1988.

Berger, Henry. The First Interview: Initial Assessment of the Infertile Couple. At the seminar The Infertile Couple. Clayton, Victoria, Australia, August 24, 1988.
Coulam, Carolyn. Role of Endometrial Biopsy in Diagnosing Luteal Phase Defect. Poster presentation at the American Fertility Society 44th Annual Meeting, Atlanta, Georgia, October 1988.
Jones, Howard. Infertility and Ethics. Press Conference, American Fertility Society, Atlanta Georgia, October 1988.
Lipshultz, L.I. and Sherin, R.J. Diagnosis and Treatment of Male Infertility. American Fertility Society 44th Annual Meeting, Atlanta, Georgia, October 1988.
Lipshultz, L.I., Investigation of the Subfertile Male. Keynote presentation at workshop, Male Subfertility: Update on Management. British Columbia Urological Association Annual Meeting, Vancouver, B.C., April 29, 1989.
Mattox, J.H. and Bernat, S. Routine Dilation and Curettage With Laparoscopy for Infertility. Poster presentation, American Fertility Society Annual Meeting, Atlanta, Georgia, October 1988.
Talbot, Mac. Initial Investigation of the Infertile Couple: The Woman. At the seminar, The Infertile Couple. Clayton, Victoria, Australia, August 24, 1988.
Wallach, Edward. Infertility and Ethics. Press Conference, American Fertility Society Annual Meeting, Atlanta, Georgia, October 1988.

Interviews

Dr. Richard Bronson, Department of Obstetrics and Gynecology, North Shore University Hospital, Cornell University Medical School. Interviewed at the American Fertility Society Annual Meeting, Atlanta, Georgia, October 1988.
Dr. John Collins, Chairman of the Department of Obstetrics and Gynecology, McMaster University, Hamilton, Ontario. July 1988.
Mr. Timothy Hargreave, Urologist and Director of the Infertility Clinic, Western General Hospital, Edinburgh, Scotland. July 1988.
Dr. Gab Kovacs, Clinical Director, Infertility Medical Centre, Epworth Hospital, Richmond, Victoria, Australia. August, 1988.
Dr. Timothy Rowe, Associate Professor, Department of Obstetrics and Gynecology, University of B.C., Vancouver, B.C. (Observation of history taking of couples in initial infertility work-up, Infertility Clinic, St. Paul's Hospital.) June, 1988.
Dr. Michael Soules, Professor and Director, Division of Reproductic Endocrinology, and Infertility, University of Washington, Seattle, Washington. July 1988.
Dr. Patrick Taylor, recently of Bourn Hall, now Chairman of Infertility Medicine at the University of Manitoba. Bourn, England. July 1988.
Dr. M.S. Wolochow, diagnostic radiologist, Vancouver B.C. July 1988.

Sources
Chapter 5

Polycystic Ovarian Disease

Franks, S. et al. Ovulatory disorders in women with polycystic ovary syndrome. *Clinic in Obstetrics and Gynecology,* Vol. 12, No. 3, September 1987.

Gindoff, Dr. Paul R., and Jewelewicz, Dr. Raphael. Polycystic ovarian disease. *Obstetrics and Gynecology Clinics of North America, The Infertile Woman,* Vol. 14, No. 4, December 1987, 931-955. W.B. Saunders.

Greenblatt, Dr. E.M. and Casper, Robert F. Polycystic ovarian disease—a review. *Society of Obstetrics and Gynecology of Canada,* November/December 1987.

Lobo, Dr. Rogerio. Androgen excess and the infertile woman. *Obstetrics and Gynecology Clinics of North America, The Infertile Woman,* Vol. 14, No. 4, December 1987, 955-977. W.B. Saunders.

Clomiphene Citrate

Clomid. Merrell Dow Compendium of Pharmaceuticals and Specialties, Canadian Pharmaceutical Association, 1988.

Corenblum, Dr. Bernard, and Taylor, Dr. Patrick. 1987. Clomiphene citrate. *Current Problems in Obstetrics, Gynecology and Fertility,* Vol. 10 #7:287-326. Year Book Medical Publishers Inc.

Dodge, Dr. S.T. et al. 1986. Ovulation induction with low doses of clomiphene citrate. *Obstetrics Gynecology* 67:63S.

Kenney, Dr. Janet, and Adashi, Dr. Eli. Ovulation induction. *Obstetrics and Gynecology Clinic of North America, The Infertile Woman,* Vol. 14, No. 4, December 1987, 831-865. W.B. Saunders.

Serophene. Pharmascience Compendium of Pharmaceuticals and Specialties, Canadian Pharmaceutical Association, 1988.

Human Menopausal Gonadotropin

Benadiva, C.A. et al. 1988. Ovarian response of individuals to different doses of human menopausal gonadotropin. *Fertility Sterility* 49:997.

Fedorkow, D. et al. Septuplet gestation following use of hmg despite intensive monitoring: case report. *Fertility Sterility,* Vol. 49, No. 2, February 1988.

Pergonal. Serono Pharmaceuticals, Compendium of Pharmaceuticals and Specialties, Canadian Pharmaceutical Association, 1988.

The Role of Pergonal Therapy in Infertility Management: Full Proceedings of Round Table Discussion. Washington, D.C., January 7, 1986. Transcript of discussion between six leading American Reproductive endocrinologists on HGM use.

High Prolactin

Archer, Dr. David. Current concepts and treatment of hyperprolactinemia. *Obstetrics and Gynecology Clinic of North America, The Infertile Woman,* Vol. 14, No. 4, December 1987, 979-998. W.B. Saunders.

Check, Dr. Jerome. Use of bromocriptine in mildly hyperprolactinemic women with follicular maturation defects. *Advances in Therapy,* Vol. 2, No. 6, November/December 1985.

Hammond, Dr. C.B. Bromocriptine mesylate in hyperprolactinemia fertility: a review. *Advances in Therapy,* Vol. 1, No. 4, July 1984.

Hyperprolactinemia: a brief review with case presentations. *Society of Obstetrics and Gynecology of Canada Bulletin,* January/February 1987.

Molitch, Dr. Mark. 1985. Pregnancy and the hyperprolactinemic woman. *New England Journal of Medicine* 312:1364-1370.

Molitch, Dr. Mark et al. 1985. Bromocriptine as primary therapy for prolactin-secreting macroadenomas: results of a prospective multicenter study. (Conducted at 11 universities in the United States, Canada and the United Kingdom) *Journal of Clinical Endocrinology and Metabolism,* Vol. 60, No. 4, 698-705.

Luteal Phase Defect

Annos, T. et al. 1980. Luteal phase deficiency and infertility: difficulties encountered in diagnosis and treatment. *Obstetris and Gynecology* 55:706.

Soules, Dr. Michael et al. 1981. The function of the corpus luteum of pregnancy in ovulatory dysfunction and luteal phase deficiency. *Fertility Sterility* 36:31.

Soules, Dr. Michael. Luteal phase deficiency: an underdiagnosed and overtreated reproductive endocrine disorder. *Obstetrics and Gynecology Clinic of North America, The Infertile Woman,* Vol. 14, No. 4, December 1987, 865-886. W.B. Saunders.

Interviews on Ovulation and Menstrual Disorders

Prof. David Baird, Department of Obstetrics and Gynecology, University of Edinburgh, Centre of Reproductive Gynecology, Edinburgh, Scotland.

Dr. David Healy, Medical Research Centre, Prince Henry's Hospital, Melbourne, Australia.

Dr. Michael Soules, University of Washington, Seattle, Washington.

Interview on Luteal Phase Defect

Dr. Georgeanna Jones, at the 1988 American Fertility Society Annual Meeting, Atlanta, Georgia.

Interview on: Ovarian Cautery for Polycystic Ovarian Disease Success Rates of Ovulation Treatments

Dr. Gab Kovacs, Infertility Medical Centre, Richmond, Australia.

Seminars and Presentations Attended

American Fertility Society Annual Meeting on Ovulation Induction, Menstrual Disorders and Corpus Luteum Function.

Society of Obstetricians and Gynecologists of Canada, Vancouver, June 1988.

Sources
Chapter 6

PID, STDs and Tubal Disease

Chlamydia now reportable disease. *The Globe and Mail*, November 8, 1988.

Greer, Germaine. *Sex and Destiny.* London: Martin Secker and Warburg Ltd., 1984.

Infertility: Medical and Social Choices. U.S. Congress Office of Technology Assessment Report, OTA-BA-358. Washington, D.C.: U.S. Government Printing Office, May 1988.

Madaras, Lynda and Patterson, Dr. Jane. *Womancare.* New York: Avon Books, 1984.

Moore, M. PID: The silent epidemic. *Healthsharing*, Spring, 1985.

Routine screening for chlamydia would cut the PID rate. *The Medical Post*, December 8, 1987.

Sellers, J., Mahony, J., Chernesky, M., and Rath, D. Tubal factor infertility: an association with prior chlamydial infection and assymptomatic salpingitis. *Fertility and Sterility*, Vol. 49, No. 3, March, 1988, 451.

Westrom, Dr. L. 1980. Incidence prevalence and trends of acute PID and its consequences in industrialized countries. *American Journal of Obstetrics and Gynecology* 138:80.

Pelvic Microsurgery

Filmar, S., Gomel, V., and McComb, P. The effectiveness of CO2 laser and electromicrosurgery in adhesiolysis: a comparative study. *Fertility and Sterility*, Vol. 45, No. 3, March 1986.

Gomel, Dr. Victor. *Microsurgery in Female Infertility.* Boston: Little, Brown and Co., 1983.

Minton, J.P., and Absten, G.T. Surgical lasers: how they work. *American College of Surgeons Bulletin*, Vol. 72, No. 8, August 1987.

Reich, Dr. H. Laparoscopic treatment of extensive pelvic adhesions, including hydrosalpinx. *Journal of Reproductive Medicine*, Vol. 32, No. 10, October 1987.

Use of Interceed (TC-7) Absorbable Adhesion Barrier to Reduce the Extent and Severity of Adhesion Reformation in Women Undergoing Infertility Surgery: A Clinical Update. Oral presentation of results of multi-center trial.

Ectopic Pregnancy

Coutifaris, C. Transvaginal Ultrasonography in Visualization and Diagnosis of Very Early Ectopic Pregnancy. Pennsylvania School of Medicine poster presentation, 1988 American Fertility Society Annual Meeting, Atlanta, Georgia.

Curtis, L.R., Curtis, G.B., and Beard, M.K. *My Body—My Decision: What You Should Know About the Most Common Female Surgeries.* Tucson, AZ: The Body Press, 1986.

Easley, H.A. et al. Contemporary evaluation of suspected ectopic pregnancy. *Journal of Reproductive Medicine*, Vol. 32, No. 12, December 1987, 901.

Infertility: Medical and Social Choices. U.S. Congress Office of Technology Assessment Report, OTA-BA-358. Washington, D.C.: U.S. Government Printing Office, May 1988.

Oelsner, G. et al. Salpingectomy by Operative Laparoscopy for Tubal Pregnancy. Department of Obstetrics/Gynecology Chaim Sheba Medical Center, Tel Aviv University. Israel poster presentation at the 1988 American Fertility Society Annual Meeting, Atlanta, Georgia.

Stoval, T.T. et al. Outpatient Chemotherapy of Symptomatic Unruptured Ectopic Pregnancy. (University of Tennessee Medical School, Memphis) Poster presentation at the 1988 American Fertility Society Annual Meeting, Atlanta, Georgia.

Vermesh, M. et al. Management of Unruptured Ectopic Pregnancy by Linear Salpingostomy: An Extended Prospective Clinical Trial of Laparoscopy Verses Laparotomy. (Department of Obstetrics/Gynecology, University of Southern California School of Medicine, Los Angeles, California) Oral presentation at the 1988 American Fertility Society Annual Meeting, Atlanta, Georgia.

Uterine Abnormalities

Buttram, V.C., and Reiter, R.C. Uterine leimyomata: etiology, sumptomatology and management. *Fertility and Sterility* 36:433, 1981.

Damewood, Dr. Marian, and Rock, Dr. John A. Reproductive uterine surgery. *Obstetrics and Gynecology Clinics of North America, The Infertile Woman*, Vol. 14, No. 4, December 1987, 1049-1068. W.B. Saunders.

Hogden, Dr. Gary. Progesterone Antagonists: Physiological Basis for Clinical Application. Plenary session speech at the 1988 American Fertility Society Annual Meeting, Atlanta, Georgia.

March, C.M. 1988. Update: leiomyata uteri. *Endocrine and Fertility Forum*, Vol. IX, No. 3.

Schlaff, et al. Leuprolide in the treatment of uterine myomata. (Department of Obstetrics, Gynecology, Johns Hopkins University Medical School, Baltimore, Maryland) Poster presentation, 1988 American Fertility Society Annual Meeting, Atlanta, Georgia.

Endometriosis

Audibert, F. et al. Responsibility of Endometriosis in Infertility: IVF Results. Co-study Norfolk, Virginia and Montpellier, France. Presented at the 1988 American Fertility Society Annual Meeting in Atlanta, Georgia.

Bayer, S.R.; Seibel, M.M.; Saffan, D.S.; Berger, M.J.; and Taylor, M.L. Efficacy of danazol treatment for minimal endometriosis in infertile women: a prospective randomized study. *Harvard Medical School Journal of Reproductive Medicine*, Vol. 33, No. 2, February, 1988, 179.

Chong, Augusto, and Baggish, Dr. Michael. Management of pelvic endometriosis by means of intraabdominal carbon dioxide laser. *Fertility and Sterility*, Vol. 41, No. 1, January, 1984.

Chong, A.P. et al. Comparison of Three Modes of Management for Minimal Pelvic Endometriosis in Infertility. (Division of Reproduction, Endometriosis and Infertility, Department of Obstetrics/Gynecology, Mount Sinai Hospital, Hartford, Connecticut; and University of Connecticut School of Medicine, Farmington, Connecticut) Presentation at the 1988 American Fertility Society Annual Meeting, Atlanta, Georgia.

Dawood, M.Y. et al. Bone Mineral Content in Women with Endometriosis: Effect of Buserilin and Danazol. (Department of Obstetrics/Gynecology, University of Illinois, Chicago, Illinois) Presentation at the 1988 American Fertility Society Annual Meeting, Atlanta, Georgia.

Eisermann, et al. Tumor Necrosis Factor (TNF) Mediates Spermicidal Activity of Peritoneal Fluid from Infertile Women with Endometriosis. (Department of Obstetrics/Gynecology, University of Washington School of Medicine, St. Louis, Missouri) Presentation at the 1988 American Fertility Society Annual Meeting, Atlanta, Georgia.

Endometriosis. Presentation by the Reproductive Endocrinology and Fertility Committee, Society of Obstetrics and Gynecology of Canada Bulletin, Vol. 9, No. 5, September/October, 1987.

Ory, Dr. Steven J. Pelvic endometriosis. *Obstetrics and Gynecology Clinics of North America, The Infertile Woman*, Vol. 14, No. 4, December, 1987, 999-1014. W.B. Saunders.

Sims, J.A. et al. The Effects of Peritoneal Fluid on the In Vitro Cleavage of One-Cell Mouse Embryos. (University of Oklahoma Tulsa Medical College) Poster presentation at the 1988 American Fertility Society Annual Meeting, Atlanta, Georgia.
loped less well in peritoneal fluid taken from patients with endometriosis as opposed to peritoneal fluid from patients with pelvic adhesions.)

Vercellini, P. et al. Presacral Neurectomy During Conservative Surgery for Endometriosis. (Department of Obstetrics/Gynecology, University of Milan, Italy) Poster presentation at the 1988 American Fertility Society Meeting, Atlanta, Georgia.

Weiss, Dr. Gerson, ed. *Book I: Endometriosis: Nature and Recognition; Book II: Approach to Management; Book III: Clinical Experience with and Use of Danazol.* Proceedings of the Endometriosis Symposium, October, 1985, New York University Post Graduate Medical School. New York: Winthrop Laboratories, 1987.

Interviews on Tubal Disease and Anatomical Problems

Dr. Ian Craft, Humana Hospital, Wellington, London, England.

Dr. Robert Franklin, Obstetrics/Gynecology, Women's Hospital of Texas and Baylor College of Medicine, Houston, Texas, at Atlanta, Georgia, at the 1988 American Fertility Society Annual Meeting.

Dr. Victor Gomel, Department of Obstetrics/Gynecology, University of British Columbia.

Dr. David Healy, Infertility Medical Centre, Richmond, Victoria, Australia.

Dr. Gab Kovacs, Infertility Medical Centre, Richmond, Victoria, Australia.

Dr. Bernie McLeod, University of British Columbia Health Sciences Centre Hospital.

Dr. Patrick Taylor, University of Manitoba, at Bourn Hall, Bourn, England.

Dr. M.S. Wolochow, radiologist, Vancouver.

Prof. Carl Wood, Infertility Medical Centre, Richmond, Victoria, Australia.

Sources
Chapter 7

Articles and Books

Bernstein, G.S. Male Factor in Infertility. In *Infertility, Contraception and Reproductive Endocrinology*, 2nd ed. Edited by D.R. Mishell, Jr. and V. Davajan. Oradell, NJ: Medical Economics Books, 1986.

Harrison, R.F.; O'Moore R.R.; and Moore, A.M. Stress and fertility; some modalities of investigation and treatment in couples with infertility in Dublin. *International Journal of Fertility* 31(2):153-159.

MacLeod, John, and Gold, R.Z. The male factor in fertility and infertility: II. Spermatozoon counts in 1000 men of known fertility and in 1000 cases of infertile marriage. *Journal of Urology*, Vol. 66, No. 3, September 1951.

Makler, A. Evaluation and Treatment of the Infertile Male. In *Reproductive Failure*. Edited by A.H. DeCherney. New York: Churchill Livingstone, 1986.

Ross, L.S. 1983. Diagnosis and treatment of infertile men: a clinical perspective. *Journal of Urology* 130:847-854.

Silber, Sherman J. *Reproductive Infertility Microsurgery in the Male and Female.* Baltimore: Williams and Wilkins, 1984.

Vance M.L., and Thorner, M.O. 1984. Medical treatment of male infertility. *Seminars in Urology* 2:115-134.

Urry, R.L. et al 1986. A simple and effective technique for increasing pregnancy rates in couples with retrograde ejaculation. *Fertility and Sterility* 46:1124.

World Health Organization: *Laboratory Manual For the Examination of Human Semen and Semen-Cervical Mucus Interaction*. Cambridge: Cambridge University Press, 1987.

Yates, C.A. and de Kretser, D.M. Male Factor Infertility and IVF. Manuscript in progress.

Seminars and Presentations

Baker, Gordon. Investigation of the Infertile Couple—The Man. At the seminar The Infertile Couple. Clayton, Victoria, Australia, August 1988.

Belker, A.M. Infertility is Significantly Associated with Vasovasostomized Men. Poster presentation American Fertility Society Annual Meeting, Atlanta, Georgia. October 1988.

Gordon, J.W. The Human Oocyte Blocks Polyspermy At The Zona Pellucida. American Fertility Society Annual Meeting, Atlanta, Georgia, October 1988.

Lipshultz, L.I. and Dr. Richard Sherins. Diagnosis and Treatment of Male Infertility. American Fertility Society Annual Meeting, Atlanta, Georgia, October 1988.

Odawara, Y. et al. Assisted Fertilization Of Human Oocytes Using Zona Opening and Low Sperm Concentrations. Annual Meeting of Fertility Society of Australia, Newcastle, New South Wales, Australia, August 1988.

Southwick, G.J. Microsurgical Epididymal Sperm Aspiration From Azoospermic Men For IVF. Fertility Society of Australia, Newcastle, Australia, August 1988.

Silber, Sherman. Fertilizing Capacity of Epididymal Sperm in the Human. American Fertility Society Annual Meeting, Atlanta, Georgia, October 1988.

Interviews

Dr. Richard Bronson. Interviewed at the American Fertility Society Annual meeting Atlanta, Georgia, October 1988.

Prof. David de Kretser, Andrologist and Head of the Department of Anatomy, Monash University. Interviewed at the Centre of Reproductive Biology, Monash University, Victoria, Australia.

Timothy Hargreave, urologist. Interviewed at the Western General Hospital, Edinburgh, Scotland, July 1988.

Sources
Chapter 8

Cervical Factor Infertility

Davajan, Dr. Val. Post Coital Testing: The Cervical Factor as a Cause of Infertility. In *Infertility, Contraception and Reproductive Endocrinology*, 2nd ed. Edited by Dr. D.R. Mishell, Jr. and Dr. Val Davajan. Oradell, New Jersey: Medical Economics Books, 1986.

Laboratory Manual for the Examination of Human Semen and Semen-Cervical Mucus Interaction. World Health Organization. Singapore Press Concern, 1987.

Moghissi, Dr. Kamran. Cervical and uterine factors in infertility. *Obstetrics and Gynecology Clinics of North America, the Infertile Woman*. Richard Kempers, ed. Vol. 14, No. 4, December 1987, 1099-1113. W.B. Saunders.

Intrauterine Insemination

Kerin, John et al. Improved conception rate after intrauterine insemination of washed spermatazoa from men with poor quality semen. *The Lancet*, March 10, 1984.

Kerin, John. Supracervical Placement of Spermatozoa—The Utility of Intrauterine and Tubal Insemination. In *Controversies Obstetrics and Gynecology Vol. I*. New York: Science Publishing Co. Inc., 1989.

Recurrent Miscarriage

Boue, Dr. Andre. Spontaneous Abortions and Cytogenic Abnormalities. In *Progress in Fertility*, 3rd ed. Edited by Dr. S.J. Berhman; Dr. R.W. Kistner; and Dr. G.W. Patton, Jr. Boston: Little Brown and Company, 1988.

Haxton, M.J., et al. Unexplained infertility: results of secondary investigation in 95 couples. *British Journal of Obstetrics/Gynecology*, Vol. 94, June 1987, 539-542.

McDonough, Dr. Paul. Recurrent aneuploidic and euploidic abortion. *Obstetrics and Gynecology Clinics of North America, the Infertile Woman*. Richard Kempers, ed. Vol. 14, No. 4, December 1987, 1099-1113. W.B. Saunders.

Novy, Dr. Miles, ed. *Recurrent Spontaneous Abortion: Seminars in Reproductive Endocrinology*, Vol. 6, No. 2, May 1988. Thieme Medical Publishers, New York.

Rock, Dr. John. Investigation and Management of Habitual Abortion. In *Reproductive Failure*. Edited by Dr. A.H. DeCherney. New York: Churchill Livingstone, 1986.

Stirrat, Gordon. Recurrent abortion—a review. *British Journal of Obstetrics/Gynecology*, Vol. 94, June 1987, 539-542.

Interviews at the American Fertility Society 1988 Annual Meeting, Atlanta, Georgia

Dr. Richard Bronson, Department of Obstetrics/Gynecology, North Shore University Hospital, Cornell University Medical College.

Dr. John Kerin, Director of Reproductive Endocrinology and Infertility, UCLA School of Medicine.
Dr. Gilbert Haas, Jr., Associate Professor and Director of Reproductive Endocrinology and Infertility, University of Oklahoma.

Interview at the Fertility Society of Australia 1988 Scientific Meeting, August 1988, Newcastle, New South Wales, Australia.

Dr. Tom Wegmann, Department Immunology, University of Alberta, Edmonton.

Seminars

Immunologic Causes of Recurrent pregnancy Loss: Diagnosis and Treatment. Drs. Carolyn Coulam, W. Page Faulk, and John McIntyre. 1988 American Fertility Society Meeting.
Immunology of Reproduction: Dr. David Billington, Department of Pathology, University of Bristol: "Maternal Immune Response to Pregnancy"; Dr. Tom Wegmann, "Animal Models for Recurrent Abortion"; Professor James Mowbray, Dept. Of Immunopathology, St. Mary's Hospital, London: "Genetic and Immunology Factors in Human Recurrent Abortion"; Bill Hendry, St. Bartholomews Hospital, London: "Antisperm Antibodies in Infertility"; Professor Shinzo Isojima, Dept. of Obstetrics/Gynecology Hyogo Medical College, Nishinomiya, Japan: "Characterisation of Epitopes of Seminal Plasma Antigens Stimulating Human Monoclonal Sperm in Mobilising Antibody." 1988 Fertility Society of Australia, Newcastle, New South Wales, Australia.
Recurrent Abortion. James Mowbray, Dr. Tom Wegmann, and Warren Jones, Department of Obstetrics/Gynecology, Flinders Medical Centre, Bedford Park, Adelaide, Australia. 1988 Fertility Society of Australia, Newcastle, New South Wales, Australia.

Sources
Chapter 9

Articles and Books

Achilles, Rona. *The Social Meaning of Biological Ties: A Study of Participants in AID.* (doctoral thesis) Toronto: University of Toronto, 1986.

Alexander, Nancy and Ackerman, Steven. Therapeutic insemination. *Obstetrics and Gynecology Clinics of North America, The Infertile Woman,* Vol. 14, No. 4, Dec. 1987, 905-929. W.B. Saunders.

Berger, Dr. David. Infertility, a psychiatrist perspective. 1980. *Canadian Journal of Psychiatry,* Vol. 25.

———. Psychological aspects of donor insemination. 1982. *International Journal of Psychiatry in Medicine,* Vol. 12 (1).

Berger, Dr. David et al. Psychological patterns in donor insemination couples. *Canadian Journal of Psychiatry,* Vol. 31, December 1986.

Clayton, C.E. and Kovacs, G.T. 1982. AID offspring: initial follow-up of study of 50 couples. *Medical Journal of Australia* 1:338-339.

Hammond, M.G. et al. 1986. Factors affecting pregnancy rates in a donor insemination program using frozen semen. *American Journal of Obstetrics and Gynecology* 155:480-485.

Huerre, P. Psychological Aspects of Semen Donation. In *Human Artificial Insemination and Semen Preservation.* Edited by G. David and W.S. Price. New York: Plenum Press, 1980.

Infertility: Social and Medical Choices. United States Congress, Office of Technology Assessment, OTA-BA-358. Washington, D.C.: United States Government Printing Office, May, 1988.

Kovacs, G. et al, Artificial insemination with cryopreserved donor semen: a decade of experience. *British Journal of Obstetrics and Gynaecology,* Vol. 95, April 1988, 354-360.

Lowry, Katherine. The designer babies are growing up. *Los Angeles Times Magazine,* November 1,

Manuel, C. and Czyba, J.D. Follow-up Study on Children Born Through AID. In *Human Artificial Insemination and Semen Preservation.* Edited by G. David and W.S. Price. New York: Plenum Press, 1980.

New Guidelines for the Use of Semen Donor Insemination. 1986. *Fertility and Sterility* (Supplement by the American Fertility Society), Vol. 46, No. 4, October, 1986, 95s-101s.

Nijs, A.; Steno, O.; and Steppe, A. Evaluation of AID Donors: Medical and Psychological Aspects: A Preliminary Report. In *Human Artificial Insemination and Semen Preservation.* Edited by G. David and W.S. Price. New York: Plenum Press, 1980.

Noble, Elizabeth. *Having Your Baby by Donor Insemination: A Compete Resource Guide.* Boston: Houghton Mifflin, 1987.

Paul, Julia, ed. *How I Began: The Story of Donor Insemination.* Paddington: The Fertility Society of Australia, 1988. To order, send cheque in the amount of $10 (Australian) made payable to Fertility Society of Australia to: Julia Paul, Social Work Dept., Royal Hospital for Women, 188 Oxford St., Paddington, NSW 2021 Australia.

Revised new guidelines for the use of semen-donor insemination. *Fertility and Sterility,* Vol. 49, No. 2, February 1988, 338-339.

Schoysman-Deboeck, A.; Van Roosendall, E.; and Schoysman, R. Artificial insemination. In *Progress in Infertility*. Edited by S.J. Berhman; R.W. Kistner; and G.W. Patton, Jr. Boston: Little, Brown & Co., 1988.

Snowden, Elizabeth and Robert. *Gift of a Child*. Boston: George Allen & Unwin, 1984.

Wannan, Sue, ed. Profile of a sperm donor; Why I'm generous with my genes; Coming to terms with another man's child. In *The Baby Chase*. Sydney: *Australian Woman's Weekly* and Australian Consolidated Press, 1988.

Presentations

Brown, C.; Boone, W.; Shapiro, S. A Comparison of Fresh and Frozen Semen for Donor Artificial Insemination. (Department of Obstetrics/Gynecology, University of Wisconsin) 1988 American Fertility Society Annual Meeting, Atlanta, Georgia.

Keogh, E.J. et al. Should Sperm Donors Be Examined by a Medical Officer? (Reproductive Medicine Research Institute, Nedlands, WA, Australia) 1988 Fertility Society of Australia Annual Scientific Meeting, Newcastle, NSW, Australia.

Tawny, L. et al. Incidence of Human Immunodeficiency Virus (HIV). (Xytec Corp.) 1988 American Fertility Society Annual Meeting, Atlanta, Georgia.

Interviews

Rona Achilles, sociologist, Toronto, May 1988.

Judith Bernstein, phone interview and correspondence.

Dr. Gab Kovacs, Director, Prince Henry's Hospital DI Program, Melbourne, Australia.

Patricia Mahlstedt at the 1988 American Fertility Society Annual Meeting and phone interview in 1989.

Shirley Pratton, DI mother and founder of Reproductive Alternatives, a Canadian group lobbying for legislation regulating the practices and legal arrangements of DI, interview in 1987, phone interviews and correspondence.

Sandor Shapiro, Dept. of Obstetrics/Gynecology, University of Wisconsin, at 1988 American Fertility Society Annual Meeting.

Sources
Chapter 10

General

Diamond, Dr. Michael and DeCherney, Dr. Alan. In Vitro Fertilization and Gamete Intrafallopian Transfer. In *The Infertile Woman, Obstetrics and Gynecology Clinics of North America*, December, 1987. W.B. Saunders Co.

First, Second and Third Report of the Voluntary Licensing Authority for Human In Vitro Fertilization and Embryology (1986, 1987, 1988). London: The VLA Secretariat, The Medical Research Council, 1986, 1987, 1988.

First Report to the Minister for Health. Melbourne, Australia: Standing Review and Advisory Committee on Infertility, September, 1988.

Infertility: Social and Medical Choices. U.S. Congress Office of Technical Assessment, OTA-BA-358. Washington, D.C.: U.S. Government Printing Office, May 1988.

In Vitro Fertilization and Embryo Transfer in Canada. Report of the Reproductive Endocrinology and Fertility Committee, *Society of Obstetricians and Gynecology Bulletin*, May/June 1987.

In Vitro Fertilisation in Australia. Council of the Royal College of Obstetricians and Gynecologists, *RACOG Bulletin*, August 1988.

Navot, Dr. Daniel, and Laufer, Dr. Neri. Update on infertility, a symposium. Edited by Dr. Alan DeCherney. In *The Journal of Reproductive Medicine*, Vol. 34, No. 1, January 1989.

Speirs, Andrew. The changing face of infertility. *American Journal of Obstetrics and Gynecology*, June, 1988, 1390-1392.

History

Biggers, J.B. In Vitro Fertilization in Historical Perspective. In *In Vitro Fertilization and Embryo Transfer*. Edited by Alan Trounson and Carl Wood. New York: Churchill Livingston, 1984.

Edwards, Robert, and Steptoe, Dr. Patrick. *A Matter of Life*. London: Hutchinson, 1980.

IVF Standards and Results

Blackwell, R.E. et al. Are we exploiting the infertile couple? *Fertility and Sterility*, Vol. 48, No. 5, November 1987, 735.

Experts access a decade of in vitro fertilization. *New York Times*, April 11, 1989.

Minimal standards for programs of in vitro fertilization. American Fertility Society. *Fertility and Sterility*, Vol. 41, No. 1, January 1984.

Pappert, Ann. Success rates not what they seem. *The Globe and Mail*, January 1989.

Soules, Dr. Michael. The in vitro fertilization pregnancy rate: let's be honest with one another. *Fertility and Sterility*, Vol. 43, No. 4, April 1985.

Statement on In Vitro Fertilization and Embryo Transfer. Committee on Endrocinology and Fertility. *Society of Obstetrics and Gynecology of Canada Bulletin*, May/June 1984.

Taylor, Dr. Patrick. IVF—is enough enough? *Society of Obstetrics and Gynecology of Canada Bulletin*, Vol. 9, No. 1, January/February 1987.

IVF Techniques

Anderson, R.E. et al. Evidence Supporting the Routine Use of a GnRH Antagonist During Ovarian Stimulation for In Vitro Fertilization. Poster presentation, American Fertility Society Annual Meeting, Atlanta, Georgia, October 1988.

Barlow, David et al. Transvaginal compared with transvesical ultrasonography for recovery of oocytes for IVF. *British Medical Journal*, Vol. 296, March 12, 1988.

de Kretser, D.M. et al. The use of IVF in the management of male infertility. *Clinics in Obstetrics and Gynecology*, Vol. 12, No. 4, December 1985.

Frydman, Rene et al. 1988. Programmed oocyte retrieval during routine laparoscopy and embryo cyropreservation for later transfer. *American Journal of Obstetrics and Gynecology* 155:112-117.

Fuerst, Mark. Sperm tests being designed to predict success for IVF. *Medical Post*, September 13, 1988.

———. Successful IVF rate low in cases of male factor infertility. *Medical Post*, October 11, 1988.

Imoedemhe, D.A.G. et al. Outcome of in vitro fertilization and embryo transfer after different regimens of ovarian stimulation. *British Journal of Obstetrics and Gynecology*, Vol. 94, September 1987, 889-894.

Kerin, J.F. and Warnes, G.M. 1986. Monitoring of ovarian response to stimulation in IVF cycles. *Clinical Obstetrics and Gynecology* 29:158-170.

Marrs, Dr. Richard. A Comparison of Leuprolide Acetate Verses Conventional Stimulation for Controlled Ovarian Hyperstimulation. American Fertility Society Annual Meeting, Atlanta, Georgia, October 1988.

Marrs, Richard et al. Effect of variation of in vitro culture techniques upon oocyte fertilization and embryo development in human in vitro fertilization procedures. *Fertility and Sterility*, Vol. 41, No. 4, April 1984.

Marrs, Richard et al. Effect of time of initiation of clomiphene citrate on multiple follicle development for human in vitro fertilization and embryo replacement procedures. *Fertility and Sterility*, Vol. 41, No. 5, May 1984.

Remohi, J. et al. Controlled Ovarian Hyperstimulation for IVF/GIFT Cycle: Use of a GnRH Analogue and Gonadotropin Therapy. American Fertility Society Annual Meeting, Atlanta, Georgia, October 1988.

Shatford, L.A. and Yuzpe A. et al. Assessment of Experienced Pain During Transvaginal Ultrasound Guided Oocyte Recovery for IVF. Poster presentation, American Fertility Society Annual Meeting, Atlanta, Georgia, October 1988.

Outcome

Andrews, M.C. et al. An analysis of the obstetrical outcome of 125 consecutive pregnancies conceived in vitro and resulting in 100 deliveries. *American Journal of Obstetrics and Gynecology* 154:1223-1224.

High incidence of preterm births and early losses in pregnancy after in vitro fertilization. 1986. Australian in Vitro Fertilization Collaborative Group. *British Medical Journal* 291:1160-1163.

In Vitro Fertilization Pregnancies, Australia and New Zealand. Sydney: National Perinatal Statistics Unit, Fertility Society of Australia and New Zealand, 1987.

Yuzpe, A. et al. Rates and outcome of pregnancies achieved in the first four years of an IVF Program. *Canadian Medical Association Journal*, Vol. 149, January 15, 1989.

Gift

Asch, R.H. et al. Pregnancy after translaparascopic gamete intrafallopian transfer. *The Lancet*, Nov. 3, 1984, 1034-1035.

Craft, Ian et al. Analysis of 1071 GIFT procedures—the case for a flexible approach to treatment. *The Lancet*, May 14, 1988.

Jarrett, J.C. et al. Limiting Multiple Pregnancies in GIFT: The Importance of Number of Eggs Transferred. Poster presentation, American Fertility Society Annual Meeting, Atlanta, Georgia, October 1988.

Psychological Stress

Fagan, P.J. et al. 1986. Sexual functioning and psychological evaluation of IVF couples. *Fertility and Sterility* 46:668-672.
Mahlstedt, P.P.; Macduff, Susan; and Bernstein, Judith. Emotional factors and the in vitro fertilization and embryo transfer process. *Journal of In Vitro Fertilization and Embryo Transfer*, Vol. 4, No. 4, 1987.
Reading, A.E. and Chang, I.C. An Evaluation of Psychological Processes over the Course of IVF-ET. Poster presentation, American Fertility Society Annual Meeting, Atlanta, Georgia, October 1988.
Reading, A.E. et al. Anxiety Levels and Attitude Ratings in Relation to an IVF Pregnancy. Poster presentation, American Fertility Society Annual Meeting, Atlanta, Georgia, October 1988.
Stanley, Fiona. In vitro fertilization—a gift for the infertile or a cycle of despair? *Medical Journal of Australia*, Vol. 148, May 2, 1988.

Surplus Eggs and Embryos

Ashwood-Smith, J.J. The cryopreservation of human embryos. *Human Reproduction*, Vol. 1, No. 5, 1986, 319-332.
Chen, C. 1986. Pregnancy after human oocyte cryopreservation. *The Lancet* 1:884-886.
Rozenwaks, Z. 1987. Donor eggs: their application in modern reproductive technologies. *Fertility and Sterility*. 47:895-909.
Tounson, A. 1986. Preservation of human eggs and embryos. *Fertility and Sterility* 46:1-12.
Trounson, A., and Freeman, L. The role of Cryopreservation of Human Oocytes and Embryos in an IVF Program. In *Progress in Infertility*. Edited by S.J. Berham; R.W. Kistner; and G.W. Patton Jr. Boston: Little Brown, 1988.

Ethics

Bartels, Ditta. The Engineering of Reproduction: Is It Heading off the Rails? Fifth Keith Roby Lecture in Community Science, Murdoch University. October 14, 1987.
Bonnicksen, Andrea and Blank, Robert. The government and IVF: views of IVF directors. *Fertility and Sterility*, Vol. 49, No. 3, March 1988.
Corea, Gena. *The Mother Machine*. New York: Harper and Row, 1985.
Dawson, Karen. In vitro fertilization: legislation and problems of research. *British Medical Journal*, Vol. 295, November 7, 1987.
Ethical considerations of the new reproductive technologies. American Fertility Society Ethics Committee. 1986. *Fertility and Sterility* 46:1S-94S.
GIFT fertilization gets Vatican ok. *The Vancouver Sun*, March 23, 1987.
Goldman, Brian. Infertility giving birth to new problems for doctors and lawyers. *Canadian Medical Association Journal*, Vol. 138, January 15, 1988.
Gray, Charlotte. High-tech conceptions: can Canada afford them? *Canadian Medical Association Journal*, Vol. 138, May 5, 1988.
Instruction on Respect for Human Life in its Origins and on the Dignity of Procreation. Vatican City: Congregation for the Doctrine of the Faith, 1987.
Test-tube fertilization denounced. Canadian Press. *The Vancouver Sun*, November 2, 1987.
Vaillancourt, Louise. Regulating Human Reproduction: Legal Dilemmas and Human Responsibilities. Vanier Institute of the Family, May 17, 1988.
Vatican raps test-tube conception research. Associated Press. *The Vancouver Sun*, December 24, 1988.

Frontiers

Gordon, J.W. et al. Assisted fertilization by zona drilling: a mouse model for correction of oligospermia. *Journal of Experimental Zoology* 239:347-354.

Jaroff, Leon. The gene hunt. *Time Magazine*, March 20, 1989.
Konner, Melvin. The gender option. *The Sciences*. November/December 1987.
Laws-King, A. et al. 1987. Fertilization of human oocytes by microinjection of a single spermatozoon under the zona pellucida. *Fertility and Sterility* 48:637-642.
Man-made bulls stir debate: conveyor-belt cattle point to human clones. New York Times News Service. *The Vancouver Sun*, October 15, 1988.

Interviews: Australia

Louise Bowen, IVF counsellor, Infertility Medical Centre, Richmond, Victoria.
Dr. David Healy, reproductive endocrinologist, Infertility Medical Centre, Richmond, Victoria.
Dr. Gab Kovacs, Infertility Medical Centre.
Dr. Christine Kirby, Director of IVF, Reproductive Medicine Unit, The University of Adelaide.
Prof. Ian Johnston, Chairman of the Reproductive Biology Unit, Royal Women's Hospital, Melbourne.
Dr. John Leeton, Director of Donor Egg Program, Monash Medical Centre/Infertility Medical Centre.
Dr. David Livingstone, Perinatal Statistics Unit, National Health Service, Sydney.
Prof. Douglas Saunders, Department of Obstetrics and Gynecology, Royal North Shore Hospital, Sydney.
Dr. Robert Seamark, reader in endocrinology, University of Adelaide, Reproductive Biology Unit, Adelaide.
Dr. Alan Trounson, Director of the Centre for Early Human Development.
Louis Waller, professor of law, Monash University and Chairman of the Standing Review and Advisory Committee on Infertility.
Prof. Carl Wood, gynecologist, Chairman of the Infertility Medical Centre, Richmond.

Interviews: Canada

Dr. Victor Gomel, Chairman Department of Obstetrics and Gynecology, University of British Columbia, Vancouver.
Dr. Arthur Leader, IVF coordinator, University of Ottawa.
Nancy Newman, social worker and IVF counsellor, University of British Columbia IVF program, Vancouver.
Dr. Al Yuzpe, Chairman Department of Obstetrics and Gynecology, University of Western Ontario, London, Ontario.
Dr. Christo Zouves, Director of the IVF Program, University of British Columbia, Vancouver.

Interviews: United Kingdom

Rev. Tim Appleton, patient counsellor, Bourn Hall, Bourn.
Ian Craft, director of IVF, Humana Hospital Wellington, London.
Dr. Rajit Goswamy, gynecologist, Bourn Hall, Bourn.
Jennifer Gunning, executive director, Voluntary Licensing Authority, London.
Mike Macnamee, PhD., embryologist, Bourn Hall, Bourn.
Dr. Patrick Taylor, Medical Director, Bourn Hall, Bourn.
Carole Wiggins, nurse coordinator, Bourn Hall, Bourn.

Interviews: United States

Dr. Ricardo Asch, Director of the University of California—Irvine American Medical International Center for Reproductive Health Care, Irvine, California.
Dr. Alan De Cherney, John Slade Ely Professor of Obstetrics and Gynecology, Yale University School of Medicine, New Haven, Connecticut.
Dr. Howard Jones, Director and Founder, Jones Institute for Reproductive Medicine, Eastern Virginia Medical School, Norfolk, Virginia.

Dr. John Kerin, Director Division of Reproductive Endocrinology and Infertility, Cedars Sinai Medical Center, UCLA School of Medicine.

Dr. Larry Lipshultz, Scott Department of Urology, Baylor College of Medicine, Houston, Texas.

Patricia Mahlstedt, psychologist, Baylor College of Medicine, IVF program, Houston, Texas.

Dr. Richard Marrs, IVF Director, Good Samaritan Hospital and UCLA Medical School, Los Angeles, California.

Dr. Michael Soules, Director Division of Reproductive Endocrinology and Infertility, University of Washington, Seattle, Washington.

Sources
Chapter 11

Articles and Books

Alexander, Terry P. *Make Room for Twins.* Toronto and New York: Bantam Books, 1987.

Berkowitz, Dr. Richrd et al. Selective reduction of multifetal pregnancies in the first trimester. *New England Journal of Medicine*, Vol. 318, No. 16, April 21, 1988.

Borg, Susan and Lasker, Judith. *When Pregnancy Fails.* Boston: Beacon Press, 1981.

Brown, Dr. Samuel. Psychological and Psychiatric Disorders. In *Signs and Symptoms in Disorders of Pregnancy.* Edited by Edward Bishop and Robert Cifalo. Philadelphia: J.B. Lippincott Co., 1983.

Calica, Judith. After all that trying we're going to have a baby. *Chicago Parent*, October 1987.

———. The perfect birth. *Today's Chicago Woman*, October 1987.

Church, F. Forrester. She accepts her fate and finds she is free. *Chicago Tribune*, June 10, 1988.

Craft, Ian et al. Multiple pregnancy, selective reduction and flexible treatment. *The Lancet*, No. 8619, Vol. 2, November 5, 1988.

Friedman, Rochelle and Gradstein, Bonnie. *Surviving Pregnancy Loss.* Boston: Little Brown and Co., 1982.

Lachelin, Dr. Gillian. *Miscarriage: The facts.* Oxford: Oxford University Press, 1985.

Lipovenko, Dorothy. Multiple-pregnancy fetuses aborted to improve survival odds of others. *Globe and Mail*, January 19, 1989.

McCauley, Carole Spearin. *Pregnancy after 35.* New York: E.P. Dutton & Co. Inc., 1976.

Schnebly, Lee. *Out of Apples? Understanding Personal Relationships.* Tucson: Fisher Books, 1984.

Selective fetal reduction. *The Lancet*, Vol. 2, No. 8614, October 1, 1988.

Selective reduction of multifetal pregnancies (six letters). *New England Journal of Medicine*, Vol. 319, No. 14, October 6, 1988.

Thankful for five tiny blessings. *People Magazine*, April 1988.

Weber, Susan. Controversy caused over 'selective reduction' technique. *The Medical Post*, January 31, 1989.

Williams, Dr. Lynne; Berman, Dr. Henry; and Rose, Louisa. *The Too Precious Child.* New York: Athenum, 1987.

Volkart, Carol. Ethical guidelines sought for fetal deaths. The Vancouver *Sun*, January 19, 1989.

Interviews

Judith Calica, counsellor, Chicago.

Ian Craft, Humana Hospital Wellington, London.

Dr. Christine Kirby, Director of IVF, Reproductive Medicine Unit, University of Adelaide, Australia.

Patricia Mahlstedt, psychologist, Houston, Texas.

Prof. Ian Johnston, Royal Woman's Hospital, Melbourne, Australia.

Dr. Gail Robinson, psychiatrist, Toronto General Hospital (workshop on pregnancy loss, Society of Obstetricians and Gynecolgists of Canada, June 1988, Vancouver).

Dr. Michael Soules, Chairman Division of Reproductive Endocrinology and Infertility, University of Washington.

Alan Trounson, Centre for Early Human Development, Monash Medical Center, Clayton, Victoria, Australia.

Prof. Carl Wood, Infertility Medical Centre/Monash Medical Centre, Clayton, Victoria, Australia.

Sources
Chapter 12

Articles and Books

An Open Life: Joseph Campbell in Conversation with Michael Toms. New York: Larson Publications, 1988.

The baby chase. *The Australian Woman's Weekly,* Australian Consolidated Press, Sydney, 1988.

Casselton, Valerie. Private adoption: new trend worries some experts. *The Vancouver Sun,* September 10, 1988.

Couple rejects ordered baby. *New York Daily News,* April 24, 1988.

Dubrow, Marsha. Aunt Misbehavin'. *New Woman,* April 1989.

Hepworth, Philip. *Foster Care and Adoption in Canada.* Ottawa: Canadian Council on Social Development, 1980.

Infertility: Social and Medical Choices. U.S. Congress Office of Technology Assessment, OTA-BA-358. Washington, D.C.: U.S. Government Printing Office, May 1988.

Kubler-Ross, Elizabeth. *On Death and Dying.* New York: Macmillan, 1969.

Leidel, Pat. No kidding: adults who stay childless by choice. *The Vancouver Sun,* September 3, 1988.

Lindmann, Erich. Symptomatology and management of acute grief. *American Journal of Psychiatry,* Vol. 101, 1944-1945, 141-148.

McKay, Nina. Desperately seeking a baby! *New Woman.* April 1989.

Peck, Scott. *The Road Less Travelled.* New York: Simon and Schuster, 1978.

Rando, Therese. *Grief, Dying and Death: Clinical Interventions for Caregivers.* Champaign, Illinois: Research Press Co. 1984.

Silversides, Ann. Heavy demand for adoption forces closing of waiting lists. *Globe and Mail,* September 16, 1988.

Snarey, John. Men without children. *Psychology Today.* March 1988.

Stainsby, Mia. Adoption: it is all in the name of love. *The Vancouver Sun,* March 26, 1988.

Surrogate Parenting: Analysis and Recommendations for Public Policy. New York State Task Force on Life and the Law, May 1988.

Veevers, Jean. *Childless by Choice.* Toronto: Butterworths, 1980.

Interviews

Rev. Tim Appleton, counsellor, Bourn Hall.

Louise Bowen, infertility counsellor, Infertility Medical Centre, Richmond, Victoria, Australia.

Dr. John Collins, Chairman Department of Obstetrics and Gynecology, McMaster University, Hamilton, Ontario.

Rhea Flamer, adoption social worker, Grace Hospital, Vancouver.

Sally Greer, president, Adoptive Parents Association, British Columbia.

Dr. Patrick Taylor, Chairman Division of Reproductive Endocrinology and Infertility, University of Manitoba.

Dr. Michael Soules, Chairman Division of Reproductive Endocrinology, University of Seattle.

Jerry Steinberg, founder of No Kidding!, Vancouver, British Columbia.
Louis Waller, Professor of Law and Chairman Standing Advisory Committee on Infertility, Melbourne, Australia.
Hank Vanderpol, Co-ordinator Adoption Services, Ministry of Social Services, Government of British Columbia.

Resources

Infertility Support and Information

The American Fertility Society
1608 13th Ave. S., Suite 101
Birmingham, AL. 35256 U.S.A.
An association of medical specialists with interest or expertise in infertility treatment and research, which also publishes the medical journal *Fertility and Sterility*. The society will provide a list of doctors offering infertility treatment in your region but will not make recommendations.

Canadian PID Society
P.O. Box 33804, Station D
Vancouver, B.C., Canada V6J 4L6
604-684-5704

Canadian Fertility and Andrology Society
2065 Alexandre de Seve, Suite 409
Montreal, Quebec, Canada H2L 2W5
Association of physicians and researchers involved in infertility medicine.

DES Action Canada
5890 Monkland Avenue, Suite 104
Montreal, Quebec, Canada H4A 1G2
514-482-3204

DES Action USA
National Office
Long Island Jewish Medical Center
New Hyde Park, NY, U.S.A. 11040
516-775-3450

Endometriosis Association
PO Box 92187
Milwaukee, WI, U.S.A. 53202
414-962-9031

Infertility Outreach
P.O. Box 814
Leduc, Alberta, Canada T9E 2Y4

Infertility Facts and Feelings
639 Petrolia Rd.
Downsview, Ontario, Canada M3J 2X8

Infertility Counselling and Support
Joan Shaw
Family Life Centre
5871 Highway #7, Suite 304
Markham, Ontario, Canada L3P 1A3
416-294-2371 or 416-475-0433

The New Reproductive Alternatives
c/o Vancouver Women's Health Collective
1720 Grant St.
Vancouver, B.C., Canada V5L 2Y7
Association to promote legislation and support for donor insemination.

Planned Parenthood Federation of Canada
323 Chapel St., 3rd Floor
Ottawa, Ontario, Canada K1N 7Z2
There are many Planned Parenthood chapters across Canada and the United States that provide information on infertility and safe methods of contraception. Look in the phone book for your area.

Resolve, Inc.
National Office
5 Water St.
Arlington, MA, U.S.A. 02174
617-643-2424
Will provide information and referrals to local chapters in the United States along with lists of specialists in your region and adoption resources.

Vancouver Infertility Peer Support Group
4522-199 St.
Langley, B.C., Canada V3A 6A1
604-530-8291

Fertility Charting

Serena Canada
151 Holland Ave.
Ottawa, Ontario, Canada K1Y 0Y2
There are many Serena chapters across Canada. Check the phone book for local organizations.

World Organization of the Ovulation Method (Billings) Canada (WOOMB)
1262 Hillcrest Ave.
London, Ontario, Canada N5Y 4N4

Adoption

Association of Children's Aid Societies
1027 McNicoll Ave. East, 2nd Floor
Scarborough, Ontario, Canada M1W 3W6
416-491-1664
Provides information and addresses for the 54 different Children's Aid Societies in Ontario that coordinate adoptions.

Canadian Child Welfare Association
2211 Riverside Dr.
Ottawa, Ontario, Canada K1H 7X5
613-738-0697
Provides information on adoption agencies and government services for adoption across Canada.

Contact your provincial ministry responsible for child welfare for more information on local or international adoptions.

B.C. Adoptive Parents Association
P.O. Box 393
Maple Ridge, B.C., Canada V2X 8K9
or
205-15463 104th Ave.
Surrey, B.C., Canada V3R 1N9
604-588-7300

Adoptive Parents Association of Alberta
Box 3674, Station 8
Calgary, Alberta, Canada T2M 4M4
403-255-0566

Families and Adoption
Pat Fenton
134 Clifton Rd.
Toronto, Ontario, Canada M4T 2G6
416-487-9938

Parents Concerned with Adoption
c/o Mitchell Kamiel
14 Kittredge Court
Richmond Hill, Ontario, Canada L4C 7X3
416-737-2211

Foster Parenting

Alberta Foster Parent Association
Bank of B.C. Building
1250-10055 106th Street
Edmonton, Alberta, Canada T5J 2Y2

B.C. Federation of Foster Parents Association
24-800 Cassiar St.
Vancouver, B.C., Canada V5K 4N6

Sex Therapy

Canadian Association of Sex Educators and Sex Therapists
339 Bloor St. West, Suite 213
Toronto, Ontario, Canada M5S 1W7

Women's Health

Saskatoon Women's Health Collective
124-109th St.
Saskatoon, Saskatchewan, Canada S7N 1R2

Toronto Women's Health Collective
24 Lonsdale Rd.
Toronto, Ontario, Canada M5S 1W7

Vancouver Women's Health Collective
1720 Grant St.
Vancouver, B.C. V5L 2V7